From
BOOK *TO*
SCREEN

From
BOOK TO
SCREEN

Modern Japanese Literature in Film

Keiko I. McDonald

An East Gate Book

M.E. Sharpe
Armonk, New York
London, England

An East Gate Book

Library of Congress Cataloging-in-Publication Data

McDonald, Keiko I.
    From book to screen : modern Japanese literature in films / by
Keiko I. McDonald.
        p. cm.
    Includes bibliographical references and index.
    ISBN 0-7656-0387-X (hc. : alk. paper).
    ISBN 0-7656-388-8 (pbk.: alk. paper)
        1. Japanese fiction—1868——Film and video adaptations.
    2. Motion pictures and literature—Japan. I. Title.
    PL747.55.M36 1999   99-10679
    791.43´6—dc21   CIP

Printed in the United States of America

The paper used in this publication meets the minimum requirements of
American National Standard for Information Sciences
Permanence of Paper for Printed Library Materials,
ANSI Z 39.48-1984.

BM (c)   10   9   8   7   6   5   4   3   2   1
BM (p)   10   9   8   7   6   5   4   3   2   1

Contents

Acknowledgments

This study was made possible by the generous assistance of so many people. I am deeply indebted to them all. I would like to express my sincerest gratitude to Donald Richie, my mentor of two decades and the foremost Western authority on Japanese cinema, who offered me as much professional assistance and warm encouragement as possible.

I offer special thanks to Thomas Rimer, chair of my department at the University of Pittsburgh, who provided much constructive criticism. And I am very grateful to Jan-Paul Malocsay, who read the entire manuscript and made useful comments from the viewpoint of a Western audience. I also owe a great debt of gratitude to David Desser, who offered me valuable suggestions.

Kyoko Sato and Kanako Hayashi from the Kawakita Memorial Film Institute, Masatoshi Oba from the Film Center of the Tokyo National Museum of Art, and Kiyotaka Moriwaki from the Kyoto Cultural Museum were wonderfully accommodating by arranging private screenings of a great number of films.

I would also like to thank the Kawakita Memorial Film Institute, the Shochiku Company, and the Toho Company for permitting me to reprint stills.

Research work for this book, which involved a number of trips to Japan, was supported by generous research grants from the Japan–U.S. Education Commission, the Japan Iron and Steel Federation, the Toshiba International Foundation, and the Asian Studies Program of the University of Pittsburgh. To all these organizations, I am truly grateful.

Finally, my special thanks go to the Richard D. and Mary Jane Edwards Endowed Publication Fund.

Introduction

Japanese film, from the outset, tried to enhance its artistic quality, resorting to literature, as if the new rich were anxious to wed aristocracy. Under the name of "Film Version of Great Literary Work," it drew sources from works by master writers—old and new—such as Akinari Ueda, Roka Tokutomi and Soseki Natsume. They were used to attract film-goers just like "decoys."[1]

The anonymous critic's view seems slightly disparaging, yet it does describe the essential character of Japanese cinema's relationship to literature. Setting aside the notion of decoying, one could speak of an entirely new art form having to flourish in the shade of a very old one. It could well be that of all the world's cinemas, the Japanese is unique in its closeness, early and late, to the nation's literature.

This receptivity to literature ranged back and forth in time, making use of sources from the very old to the brand new. One could say there was a range up and down as well. Highbrow, lowbrow, even "no-brow"—all could apply in the climate of superabundant energy that quickly came to be characteristic of this new art form. It is not surprising, therefore, to find that the first word used for a film derived from an "authored" work was respectable enough: *bungei-eiga*, literally "film from literature."

Cinema, however, quickly set about defining and redefining its ways and means—as literature always has, though not so much on the doublequick. By the mid-1930s, *bungei-eiga* was used more narrowly to indicate a connection with a "literary" work—a work whose status in the West would identify it as belonging to belles lettres.

Even so (and long before the age of television), Japanese cinema remained notably inclusive. Many works of popular entertainment found their way into films. A study of that relationship would be a book in itself, rather than the book at hand.

My study concentrates on films related to texts that are self-consciously literary and modern as well. The Japanese word for them is *junbungaku-sakuhin* (literally, "works of pure literature"). *Modern* in this context refers to works written after the Meiji era, that is, after 1868. That year is widely used as a convenient watershed for many aspects of Japanese history and culture, whose ordeal of Westernization is seen as beginning around that time.

I have tried to put my subject in perspective and treat it comprehensively, even as considerations of time and space forced me to limit the number of works discussed. My hope is that the format of this book will serve those aims and, as well, equip readers to study more such works on their own.

The first part is an overview, offering historical and cultural background for understanding some distinctive features of the alliance between *junbungaku-sakuhin* and film. A vast amount of relevant material was generated in the first eight decades of cinema, so again, I have been rigorously selective. I have dealt with those decades piecemeal, looking for intervals in which filmmakers relied most heavily on literary works for enriching and developing cinematic art.

The first such interval is 1907–20, a time of special affinity with *shimpa*, the drama or, often, melodrama, of middle-class domestic life in a contemporary setting. Here we see that prototypical kinship between stage and screen take shape and then gradually yield to a different collaboration between textual material and its cinematic transformation.

That difference established, we jump ahead to the first of two so-called Golden Ages of Japanese cinema: the prewar years 1935–41. (The other such Golden Age came after the war, in the 1950s. Significantly, both these wonderfully rich intervals coincide with high points in the growth of *bungei-eiga*.)

Thus Chapter 2 studies the *junbungaku-undo*, or pure literature movement, and its consequences for cinema. Here I use the work of a few major directors such as Tomu Uchida, Shiro Toyoda, and Hiroshi Shimizu. They were chosen because their work shows how screen adaptations of literature became the mainstream creative force in this first Golden Age.

Chapter 3 moves ahead to the 1950s. Here I focus on the economic aspects of film and literature working together. The film industry was not left out of the Japanese "economic miracle" of the 1950s. Audiences grew at a record pace, thanks in part to the growing sense of national pride and independence that came with success in the marketplace. The return of creative freedom played an important part as well. Wartime and then Occupation censorship had forbidden a number of national themes and subjects important to cinema before the war. Now those themes and subjects returned, and with them a floodtide of creativity.

The major studios were similarly inspired by increasing revenues. They may be said to have cranked out films at an alarming rate. Still, their enterprising spirit gave many a director many a chance to make use of literary sources. Thus, leading nineteenth- and twentieth-century novelists guided directors to themes and issues relevant to life in postwar Japan. Among them were experiences of war and Occupation and changes in family life, especially relative to the roles of women.

Again, given such an embarrassment of riches, I have had to be rigorously selective. Even so, I have been able to focus on directors whose approaches to the transfer of literary work to the screen differ significantly.

Some readers may be disappointed not to find certain famous writer/director collaborations treated here in depth. One example would be the Akutagawa/Kurosawa transformation of short stories into *Rashomon*. Another would be Mizoguchi's use of Tanizaki or Ogai.

I do not labor on such instances because they are abundantly well documented and discussed elsewhere. It seemed more desirable to expand the discussion by directing attention to other directors whose literary interests yielded fascinating films, especially those inspired by women writers. Examples here include Tadashi Imai, Keisuke Kinoshita, and Mikio Naruse.

The latter part of Chapter 3 seemed the place to touch (just briefly) on the status of writer/director relations at the time I wrote this book.

Part Two gets down to the analytical nitty-gritty. Here, the comparison of literary work with the film version (sometimes more than one) labors under an East/West disadvantage. Many of these writers are not known, or not known well, to non-Japanese, and so at some risk of tedium I have had to offer detailed descriptions of their contents. I do apologize, even as I hope that, in the end, the reader will find my analyses worth the details. My best hope, naturally, is that the reader will feel inspired to seek out book and film together!

My analyses themselves are based on the premise that "every adaptation is inevitably an interpretation of its source."[2] Working on that premise, I ask certain basic questions of each pair of works. Given a theme they share, for example, I ask which differences and similarities of approach take shape. Considering how a director has transformed a particular work, I ask if, or to what extent, he modifies its writer's view of social, philosophical, and ideological issues.

This study is intergeneric, but it is not committed to theorizing about the often troubled but important relationship between cinema and literature so much in the forefront of Western scholarship in recent years. My critical method is by comparison simple and straightforward, and I think suitably inclusive. Here the crucial working question is the obvious one: *what* exactly does one compare when comparing works of literature and works on screen?

I begin by treating each film or literary work as a finished product rather than a work "in process." I consider each work a self-contained entity with its own structure. That makes it possible to compare the structure of one with the other.

I also view works from two perspectives: internal and external. A view to the inside studies structure and function: the makeup of parts and how they work together. This is a complex business requiring many a shift of critical insight.

For example, both film and literary work marshal various effects in order to clarify a central problem. A protagonist's role is to give meaning to that problem by relating it to his or her world. Issues have a natural tendency to become problems. Very often, the protagonist makes choices in response to a problem that the given work features front and center, making it truly central. Some choices that are available may seem mutually exclusive; others uneasily compatible; still others apparently "free," a matter of roads taken or not taken. In any event, the protagonist's behavior offers us important clues to the worldview at work, whether it is to be taken as tragic or comic, say, or romantic or ironic. (Readers/spectators must face their choices, too!)

A number of basic constituents in any given work contribute to its structural unity. Characters may operate as individuals or as types. These types may represent some larger entity, such as a system of values or larger-than-life heroes who speak for our fantasies of self and identity.

Events, whether presented chronologically or not, are another important element. Similarly, a historical setting and spatial differentiation (geographic settings for action) function internally.[3]

Symbols may serve internal functions as important as those served by the characters themselves. The meaning of *symbol* has become rather ambiguous in recent film scholarship influenced by new theories. I like James Monaco's definition of symbol as "something that represents something else by resemblance, association, or convention."[4]

The other perspective referred to above—the external one—refers us to the structure a literary work/film exhibits in relation to its audience. Seen from this perspective, the work invites us to relate to it in many ways. We are invited to have feelings about it; to become involved; to make judgments about the good and the bad in characters, actions, and values. As critics, we must decide whether we are being asked to take up an attitude of simple identification with the aspect of the work at hand or perhaps to reject it or maybe to react, to some extent, both ways at once. Can we accept the outcome of the protagonist's action as a logical consequence of his or the work's worldview? We ask that, too. And we ask questions on a widely inclusive level more peculiar to critics than to most audiences: probing into the work's generic mode or modes. Doing that, we address issues of, for example, melodramatic or lyrical or novelistic practice. All this, again, is considered in the light of external structure as it relates to the point of view imposed on the audience.

Needless to say, all the devices (and even deviances) of internal/external structure are brought together by the third basic of literary/cinematic art: technique or stylistics. This is discussed separately in each chapter. First I try to clarify aspects of a given novelist/director's stylistic devices. Then I try to show how their use offers important clues to the thematic progression of the work at hand, or to its manipulation of the audience's point of view.

In the process of comparing any two works, we look first at the structure of each. Then we locate the point (or points) of departure as the film differentiates itself from its "original." Again and again we find ourselves considering the workings of a familiar principle of deletion, alteration, and addition.

Given the necessarily modest scope of this book, I have had to confine intensive analysis to just twelve films. They were chosen from a vast array of *bungei-eiga*, many of them equally deserving.

The first three films have generic change in common. Heinosuke Gosho's

Izu no odoriko (The Izu dancer, 1933) is the first and the best of seven screen adaptations of Yasunari Kawabata's novel of the same title. Its strength comes from the director's transformation of an essentially lyrical work into one that combines two film genres: melodrama and slapstick. This *shomin-geki* dramatizes lower-middle-class life.

Both Shohei Ooka's *Musashino* (Lady Musashino, 1951) and Kenji Mizoguchi's film version with the same title study the issue of adultery, a topic very much to the fore in postwar Japan, when time-honored manners and mores were being called into question on every hand. Yet the novel and the film differ greatly in their modes of presentation. Ooka's work is painstakingly psychological, a novel whose deeply ingrained realism unfolds a tale of characters confronting a changing society. Mizoguchi's film is a study of manners, a story in service of the theme this director pursued relentlessly throughout his career: the plight of women.

Kei Kumai's *Umi to dokuyaku* (The sea and poison, 1986) takes its title and story from Shusaku Endo's novel. Both works examine a highly sensitive topic: horrifying clinical experiments conducted on American POWs by doctors supervised by the Japanese military. Novelist and director handle the story in entirely different ways. As a Catholic, Endo is eager to examine the conscience of the Japanese. His is a religious novel whose chief concern is with his countrymen's sense of sin. Kumai is a leftist. He has it in for "the system," which he holds responsible for the atrocity he studies in chilling detail. In his hands, Endo's religious novel becomes a highly charged political film.

Japanese film history is rich in explorations of social problems, yet very few films have studied the plight of the *burakumin*, the segregated class that used to exist in ancient/feudal Japan. The issue is obviously a sensitive one. We look at it through the work of two directors: Kon Ichikawa in *Hakai* (The broken commandment, 1962) and Yoichi Higashi in *Hashi no nai kawa* (A river with no bridge, 1992). These films stand out as representative of the filmmaker's exploration and interpretation of this difficult and tragic social issue.

Ichikawa's title and story are taken from a novel by the Meiji writer Toson Shimazaki. The director updates Shimazaki's version, giving the protagonist's moral conflict a 1960s resolution. He also endows his female characters with up-to-date manners and attitudes.

Higashi's film takes its title and story from a six-volume novel by another modern writer, Sue Sumii. This director's approach is notable for the cuts it makes in narrative. At the same time, Higashi's characteristic concern with the status of women leads him to introduce a subplot of his own. As a result, his heroine is doubly oppressed: as a female and as a *burakumin*.

Our next two films show directors working from novels with the complex external structure. Junichiro Tanizaki's *Shunkin-sho* (The story of Shunkin) makes use of a double framework as one narrator assesses accounts provided by others and makes deductions accordingly. This is done by a novelist famous for knowing how to engage and disarm his reader.

Yasujiro Shimazu was the first director to attempt *The Story of Shunkin*. He drops Tanizaki's narrative devices altogether. As a result, his *Okoto to Sasuke* (Okoto and Sasuke, 1935) is reduced to a kind of melodrama that makes the best use of the Japanese studio star system. The film tells the life story of its hero and heroine in a straightforward linear order. The camera's ominipresent eye spares the viewer the intellectual guesswork the novelist imposes on his reader, who is asked to reassess the narrator's "reliability" from time to time.

In *Bokuto kidan* (A strange tale from east of the river), the novelist Kafu Nagai employs a convoluted narrative scheme involving a novel-in-progress embedded in the first-person novel of the tale being told. Here, too, the director shies away from the novel's characteristic complexity. Shiro Toyoda's 1960 screen version disposes of the embedded novel and makes Kafu himself the narrator. Having, as it were, hijacked the novelist, Toyoda uses him as witness and commentator on the story, which concerns a romance between a prostitute and a client. Toyoda also gives the novelist a character role connecting the couple.

Another pair of films are derived from short stories whose thematic appeal is universal. Both show a director making effective use of the principles of addition and alternation discussed in the text.

Mori Ogai's short story "Maihime" (The dancing girl) concerns the age-old conflict between the individual and society. It is set in Japan's first period of unsettling swift modernization in the later nineteenth century. Ogai's theme goes hand in glove with director Masahiro Shinoda's lifelong commitment to films depicting the relationship between the individual and society as that of victim and victimizer. Shinoda adds to the story line accordingly, fortifying his hero with more stress and conflict. Ogai was content to leave some aspects of his story in doubt at the end. Not Shinoda. He studies conflict with resolution in mind. His film *Maihime* (*Die Tänzerin* or The dancing girl, 1989) insists on a sense of closure.

Saisei Muro's story "Ani Imoto" (Older brother, younger sister) is set in the turbulent years before World War II. It tells of a violent feud among siblings in a lower-class family. All through the 1950s, director Mikio Naruse pursued issues related to women's struggle with the forces of oppression. Consistent with that bent, he updates Muro's story in *Older Brother, Younger Sister* (1953), setting it in the postwar period. This gives his depiction of two sisters' lives the greater range of choice offered by that period of rapid change in Japanese society. Like Muro, he uses a family feud to focus on the stress created by social upheaval.

Our last three films were chosen for their refreshingly experimental stylistic manipulations. They show what a filmmaker can do with the intrinsic qualities of cinema, especially the expressive power of the camera.

Tanin no kao (The face of another, 1966) is Hiroshi Teshigahara's interpretation of Kobo Abe's psychological portrait of a man's search for a new identity. Novel and film share the contemporary setting and story line. They differ in their approaches to the existential theme. The novel carries a heavy burden of abstraction and philosophy that Teshigahara lightens with a rich array of "filmic qualities," especially avant-garde stylistic conventions.

Sorekara (Sorekara, 1985) is a film adaptation of Soseki Natsume's novel of 1907. As happens so often, here film and novel have the same title. Soseki was a Meiji era writer with a gift for depicting his own milieu and his own kind of man. He tells the story of an intellectual forced to come to terms with a time of momentous change in Japan.

Director Yoshimitsu Morita was born in 1950, in a Japan that was all about change. By 1985, he was known as a versatile postmodern filmmaker. His approach to Soseki's book involves a refreshing transfer from linguistic to visual methods. Calling on the convenient "visual" properties of cinema, and taking full advantage of acoustics and carefully composed settings, Morita allows us to see and feel what looks like and feels like a genuine capture of Meiji era ambience.

Kinkakuji (The temple of the golden pavilion, 1976) is Yoichi Takabayashi's bold rendering of Yukio Mishima's studiously psychological novel. Here the director follows the novelist's lead in thematic orientation even as he adds some fascinating innovations, among them a symbolic method all his own. This results in a new venue of approach to the ending. This film is especially strong in the area of stylistic experiments with fluid spatial and temporal shifts. It shows us how the director goes about transferring an essentially confessional narrative mode from novel to screen.

I hope my book transfers to its readers a heightened awareness of the pleasures and insights that Japanese literature has brought to a cinematic tradition known around the world for its unique character and masterful achievements.

Notes

1. Nihon Eiga Television Producer Kyokai, ed., *Eiga de miru Nihon bungakushi* (The history of Japanese literature seen through film) (Tokyo: Iwanami Hall, 1979), p. 1.

2. Stuart Y. McDougal, *Made into Movies: From Literature to Film* (New York: Holt, Rinehart and Winston, 1985), p. 6.

3. Seymour Chatman considers characters, events, and settings important constituents in the narrative of both fiction and film. See Seymour Chatman, *Story and Discourse: Narrative Structure in Fiction and Film* (Ithaca, N.Y.: Cornell University Press, 1988), pp. 45–48, 107–45.

4. James Monaco, *How To Read a Film* (New York: Oxford University Press, 1977), p. 431.

PART I

Shifts in Creative Emphasis

1

The Camera Looks at Melodrama: 1908–1920

The first attempt to make a Japanese film with the so-called *cinematographé*, took place in the summer of 1897. It offered glimpses of noted sites in Tokyo, among them the famous Nihonbashi bridge. That series of postcard views may be said to have launched Japanese cinema, which soon learned to look for livelier kinds of spectacles. For that, the cinema went indoors, to "views" conveniently framed on stage, in theatrical traditions rich in human interest. In retrospect, it seems only natural that Japanese cinema should have spent its first decade stealing from classical Kabuki and Bunraku theater.

Many cinema scholars have discussed the importance of those early thefts. After all, classical Japanese theater gave the new art of cinema far more than just the plots of plays. The theatrical traditions of Kabuki and Bunraku offered stylistic conventions that were familiar and persuasive. No wonder Japan's first filmmakers took them up. They were still busy wielding the unfamiliar camera. One might say that camera and filmmaker both were too busy learning for them to have stylistic notions of their own.[1]

But of course cameras and filmmakers do just look around. Early filmmakers soon discovered another source of style and subject matter in *shimpa*, an old stage tradition.

Shimpa, or New School Drama, was itself born out of a reaction against Kabuki stage conventions. Its point of revolt was the use of plays with contemporary settings. *Shimpa* was a challenge offstage as well as on, given the climate of political ferment in the late Meiji period. *Shimpa*'s founder, Sadanori Sudo, was a political activist in the *jiyu minken undo*, the Freedom and People's Rights Movement. Acting on behalf of the Liberal Party in 1888, Sudo formed a small troupe whose repertoire was chiefly political, favoring plays about student idealists. They performed works in two genres: *Soshi-geki*, literally "plays about agitators," and *shosei-shibai*, "dramas about students." Both terms gave way to *shimpa* when that "new school" was founded in 1899.

Sudo's successor was Otojiro Kawakami. He did much to improve *shimpa*'s repertoire. He, too, had sought to advance the cause of the Liberal Party, by forming a troupe in 1891. In 1893 he traveled to France, where he had his first experience of Western dramaturgy. It was a revelation he wasted no time sharing with Japanese audiences. The following year, his troupe earned critical acclaim with a detective drama, *Igai* (Unexpected). That success led to two equally successful sequels. Then, when the Sino-Japanese War broke out in 1894, Kawakami returned to what amounted to patriotic potboilers.

Still, *shimpa* continued to develop, achieving what critics consider its high point between 1906 and 1908. Troupe leaders such as Yoho Ii and Minoru Takada eagerly sought out new acting styles and techniques far removed from Kabuki conventions.

Even so, no amount of revolutionary fervor could break the spell of certain Kabuki traditions. *Shimpa*'s drive to be thoroughly modern continued to be compromised by some use of female impersonators and formalized acting styles far removed from realism.

Nevertheless, *shimpa* troupes continued to explore contemporary settings. That led to a more reliable parting of the ways with classical theatrical convention as *shimpa* playwrights learned to take their cues from a wealth of literary sources.

They were most interested in the works of Meiji writers, whose strong suit was melodrama. Among the novels adapted for *shimpa* were Roka Tokutomi's *Hototogisu* (The cuckoo, 1904); Koyo Ozaki's *Konjiki yasha* (The golden demon, 1897–1902); and Yuho Kikuchi's *Ono ga tsumi* (My sin, 1899–1900). Kyoka Izumi was a great favorite. Four of his novels were made into *shimpa* plays: *Koya hiziri* (Priest from Mt. Koya, 1904); *Tsuya monogatari* (Wake, 1904); *Giketsu kyoketsu* (Blood of honor); and *Onna keizu* (A woman's pedigree, 1907).

These plays in effect guaranteed that tragedy would be the mainstay of the *shimpa* repertoire. It was, to be sure, tragedy under the aspect of melodrama, with what today would be called a definite gender bias. One critic describes it this way: "The *shimpa* tragedy makes a grand display of the ego or will of a woman who endures her fate in tears."[2]

The emerging film industry was quick to see the cinematic potential in those *shimpa* adaptations. After all, they were based on best sellers by major Meiji writers. In 1908, Yoshizawa Shokai, one of the earliest film companies, built Japan's first studio under glass in Tokyo. Their second production was the *shimpa* version of Kikuchi's *My Sin*.

Yuho's novel *My Sin* first appeared in serial form in the *Osaka Asahi* newspaper in 1899. Its sequel was published the same way. The *shimpa* adaptation by Yoshizawa Shokai was first staged in October 1900. As we later see, the playwright's *My Sin* would foster a natural and fruitful kinship between cinema and modern literature. It was, in fact, the first known example of a film that would come to be known as *bungei-sakuhin-eiga* (or *bungei-eiga*), literally "film from a literary work."

Yuho's novel belongs to a class of novels popular with Meiji readers. Many were serialized in newspapers and were correspondingly accessible to a general readership. Their protagonists lived in the reader's world, in everyday circumstances heightened by twists and turns of plot that led, eventually, to a sense that the issue at hand had been somehow resolved.

Needless to say, these novels are not self-consciously literary. Like their readers, the novelists are not at leisure to indulge any great strain of richly associative, ambivalent modes of thought. The novels' sense of irony is largely satisfied by the kinds of surprises that make good plot. Their sense of drama tends to be schematic, which is to say melodramatic.

What these novels *do* often share with works of more permanent "value" is a quality of vivid reportage. These novels show us writers examining life in Meiji society. Their readers, like cinema goers from the start, are invited to look at the world around them.

It is easy to see why *shimpa* took these novels up so readily. What remains to be seen is how the new practitioners of Japanese cinema came to "take it from there," as it were.

Let us begin with Yuho's novel *My Sin*. Its structure is based on a familiar narrative pattern of everyday life put in turmoil by events whose working out entails considerable suffering before matters are resolved by an ending enough like "happy" to satisfy readers. The readers of *My Sin*, like the *shimpa* playgoers, would expect to have a good cry at various points along the way. Yuho's melodramatic plot is guaranteed not to disappoint.

Tamaki is the daughter of a respectable country family. She is happy as a student in Tokyo. All that changes, thanks to a motif familiar to Meiji readers in a rapidly changing Japan: big-city manners and mores are apt to corrupt the young and inexperienced. Especially a young woman. Especially one from the country.

Tamaki is seduced by a medical student, Kenzo. She is pregnant. Kenzo is engaged to another girl, Oshima. Even so, he does the right thing and marries Tamaki. But Oshima will not let go. She pressures Kenzo to divorce Tamaki. Abandoned, Tamaki attempts suicide but fails. Her family takes her in, but her child is given away in adoption. (Separation of mother and child is a familiar motif.)

All may yet be well. The whole affair is successfully hushed up. Tamaki's suffering is eased by marriage to a count who knows nothing of her past indiscretion. Tamaki bears another child. Her marriage, however, turns out to be a comfortless one. Her husband is increasingly cold and remote. They go to a fishing village where her husband's family has a summer house. Their little boy drowns. A fisherman's boy drowns trying to rescue him.

Here the plot takes on the sort of complex twist favored by the serial novel and *shimpa*. The two boys turn out to be half-brothers, both Tamaki's children. And the doctor called in is? Kenzo. He comes face to face with Tamaki, the girl he seduced, the wife he abandoned. He is here to certify the death of a boy who is not the fisherman's son but his and Tamaki's.

The rest of the novel works out the theme of repentance with yet more dramatic twists to guarantee the heroine's suffering. Tamaki owns up to her past, which ends her marriage. Kenzo does attempt to atone for his sin by marrying her; but her own idea of atonement takes the form of good works. Tamaki leaves for Taiwan to work for the Red Cross.

In the end, a woman's self-sacrifice heals all. Tamaki learns that the count is dying in Vietnam. She hurries to his side and nurses him back to life. Now it is his turn to repent. He does, so all ends happily after all.

In spite of its predictably melodramatic character, Yuho's novel is a serious attempt to portray a modern heroine whose values are deeply rooted in Confucianism. And since, like *shimpa* in general, *My Sin* is very much a novel of its time, this story shows how a woman living in the early modern age could still be held captive by feudal values. The melodramatic potential of that tension became very much a part of the *shimpa* adaptation, which passed on to cinema.

There were sound practical reasons behind early cinema's interest in melodrama. The first films were limited to effects that could be realized, on the average, in less than a thousand feet of film. The novelty of the medium brought certain limitations with it as well. Moviegoers with few expectations were correspondingly easy to please. It was enough to see the moving "real-life" image; enough to see actors on screen performing pretty much anything.[3] The stage frame/film frame connection was in fact so powerful that many early films took the form of *engeki jissha eiga*, literally "films of ongoing performance" on the Kabuki or *shimpa* stage.

Interestingly enough, that early use of cinema anticipates our own experience of the virtuoso, multimedia "event." The difference is that today's media mix exhibits a range of hi-tech accomplishments, whereas its analogue in early Japanese cinema was created by the technical limitations of cinema in its infancy. Because early film footages were short and subject to technical quirks, they found a place in a hybrid screening-cum-performance practice called *rensageki*, or "chain drama." In such instances, the spectator witnessed a live stage performance interspersed with scenes performed on screen. Movie-house programs from 1910 to 1917 mostly featured this eclectic offering, along with a newsreel, some footage of street scenes, a foreign film, and a domestic "dramatic" picture.

One Japanese historian offers this account of Meiji writers' work transferred to screen by way of *shimpa*:

> Beginning around 1908, *engeki jissha eiga* footage of *shimpa* and Kabuki ongoing stage performance appeared more frequently. Cinema's ability to put a performance "on record" was an important market asset. Stage plays attracted audiences mainly with scripts and performers. By putting plays on screen, the film industry brought theater-goers into the movie house. . . . This period of theater/film overlap lasted about ten years. Even though the drama was shot off stage, acting style and directing followed stage conventions.
>
> Such silent films of on-going stage action were presented along with *kowairo* (dialogue narrators), *benshi* (commentator) and *narimono* (musical accompaniment). . . .[4]

No print of the first film version of *My Sin* exists, but written accounts describe it fairly well. We know, for example, that the number of scenes had to be drastically reduced. The *shimpa* adaptation, like the novel, takes the spectator to some half a dozen locales, one of them overseas. Cameraman/director Kichizo Chiba's *My Sin* featured just two climactic scenes on the beach, one shot on location at Katase, the other at Enoshima. The "stars" were actors from Nobuchika Nakano's *Shimpa* Troupe. Years later, Nakano had this to say about the shooting of his film:

> It was October of 1908. Yoshizawa Shokai suggested that I film an on-going *shimpa* drama. At that time the longest footage available was a thousand feet, so I decided to shoot two scenes to fit in a five to six hundred foot format. One scene showed the beach episode; the other, the two boys drowning. I got a local firefighting crew to erect poles on the beach. A stage curtain was strung between them. That way, the curtain could be raised to show the beach with the drama taking place. . . .
>
> Once we were costumed and ready to go, we took our places behind the curtain. There we could hear the sound of applause. It was coming from a crowd of onlookers waiting patiently for the curtain to go up.
>
> We could also hear cameraman Chiba complaining. He didn't see how we were going to photograph "moving people." . . .
>
> The scene of the two boys drowning was shot at Enoshima. The two kids were so scared they didn't want to get in. They bawled and clung to the rocks. We had to force them to act their part. But finally we got our film.[5]

That film was of a very elemental kind. Chiba tried to create the impression of a drama on stage because the screen space was defined by the curtain fixed to the poles. It never occurred to him to think that a film could be made by cutting through a number of shots. Each of Chiba's scenes was composed of a long shot in a long take. His cinematography, to a great extent, showed the direction early Japanese cinema would take. It would capture stage action as a picture, rather than as a moving image.[6]

Technical constraints being what they were, the film version of *My Sin* released in December 1908 contained only the scene set on Katase Beach. It was of course highlighted by *kowairo* and *narimono*. The other beach scene of the two boys drowning was released a year later as *My Sin, Part 2.*

Another of Yuho's novels was serialized in *The Osaka Mainichi* in 1903. *Chikyodai* (Foster sisters) was even more popular than *My Sin*. It was inspired by an English novel *Dora Thorn* by the now-forgotten Bertha Clay. *Foster Sisters* used a kind of Cinderella story to argue for the superiority of Christian morality over Confucianism as it applied to family matters in Meiji Japan.

Again, the novel was adapted for *shimpa* before Yoshizawa Shokai made it into a film in 1909. Even then, the cast was drawn from the Nakano Shimpa Troupe with Nakano himself as one of the heroines.

That same year, Nakano and Chiba collaborated again on another adaptation of the popular *shimpa* drama *The Cuckoo*. The novel by Roka Tokutomi was published in 1900 and was first staged as a *shimpa* drama two years later.

The Cuckoo explores a familiar theme of a marriage coming to grief. For once, both husband and wife belong to the privileged class. Namiko is the daughter of a general. Takeo is a naval officer, son of a baron now deceased. At first they are happily married. Then three sources of unhappiness ruin it all. The first is Taneo, Takeo's cousin and Namiko's rejected suitor. Then there is the wicked mother-in-law. Finally, Namiko contracts tuberculosis.

Along with those sources of woe, Roka deals in conflicting values, traditional and modern. Takeo is torn between the absolutism of "ie" (the family) and individual moral authenticity. His mother urges him to divorce Namiko, whose illness prevents her from having children. Even though it means the end of his lineage, he refuses to take a course of action he considers inhumane and unethical.

Takeo's choice is dramatically enhanced by the outbreak of war. He is called up for active duty, leaving Namiko unprotected. His mother, encouraged by the vengeful Taneo, takes matters into her own hands. She in effect dissolves her son's marriage by sending his wife back to her family. Namiko soon dies in despair.

Given the ending, the tragic outcome is softened by a sort of high moral tone. Two men in uniform meet and form a bond based on their love of Namiko. One is her father, the other, her husband. They meet at Namiko's tomb. The general assures his son-in-law that her death does not affect his feelings for the husband, who would have protected her if he could.[7]

Even though the novel is old-fashioned melodrama, the novelist does adopt some values and attitudes recognizably "modern." Roka's characters show signs of life above and beyond the requirements of stereotype. Takeo is obviously a man with some complexity of character. His sense of conscience shows us that. More significantly, perhaps, his mother also transcends her stock role as the wicked mother-in-law. She wonders, for example, if there is in fact some internal law that might transcend the "societal" one. The issue of religion and modern society is broached as Namiko lies dying. An old woman brings her a copy of the Christian Bible, which they discuss.

Even so, *shimpa* being the kind of theater it was, its adaptation of the novel spent far less time on such high moral ground. *The Cuckoo* on stage just naturally played up the element of melodrama throughout. Each stereotype played its part. The hapless heroine was left in the clutches of a wicked mother-in-law pitiless in defense of family pride. Even Namiko's beauty is true to type. Her fragile loveliness is marked for death. Her death itself is a slow, wasting disease made all the more poignant by her lovelorn despair. The fact that Namiko was played on stage by one of *shimpa*'s female impersonators only added to the effect. Those actors knew how to endow such a fate with just the kind of poetry that left an audience awash in tears. After all, one of *shimpa*'s chief pleasures (especially for the ladies) was the chance to have a good cry.

The Golden Demon was another *shimpa* play adapted for the screen. The novel by Koyo Ozaki was serialized in *The Yomiuri* from 1887 to 1893 and staged in 1890.

Here the theme is revenge for unrequited love. The beautiful heroine, Otomi, is a shameless fortune hunter. She jilts her fiancé, Kanichi, in order to marry a man who has wealth and social position. Kanichi's revenge goes beyond Otomi to strike out at what he sees as a money-hungry society. His weapon is success—as a usurer. It is a profession despised and of course quite rightly feared by all who worship money.

Koyo's heroine is a new type of woman. She is no submissive victim of the old-style, self-sacrificing morality reserved for women. She is a strong-willed woman determined to make her way in a male-dominated society.

Still, it turns out that she values matters of the heart even more than money. Having married the wealthy Tomiyama, she discovers that her true love really was Kanichi. She refuses to sleep with her husband. She begs her jilted lover's forgiveness. Kanichi is not in a forgiving mood. When he ignores her flood of letters, she gate-crashes a party at his house.

The novel is set in the period that saw the rise of Japanese capitalism. The *shimpa* adaptation shares the novel's focus on the common man's ambivalence toward the new class of prosperous citizen coming into being. Should one aspire to join the ranks of this affluent middle class? Or should one greet this phenomenon with principled disdain or commonplace indifference? Judging by the immense popularity of *shimpa's* melodramatic revenges, audiences enjoyed a richly ambivalent attitude.

Koyo died before he finished his novel, so more than one *shimpa* playwright imagined a suitable outcome. One of them brought the revenge theme to a climax by borrowing two climactic scenes from the novel. In one, Otomi is driven mad by Kanichi's refusal of forgiveness. In the other, fire destroys the house of the greedy man who was Kanichi's master.

Yoshizawa Shokai's rival, Fukuodo, made the first film version of *The Golden Demon* in 1911. It consisted of eleven scenes, all clearly substituting for a live stage performance. The film itself was presented in a way that resembled an ongoing *shimpa* performance. *Benshi* narrator-commentators explained the action on screen, much as they would do in the theater, where they interpreted the action onstage. This use of *benshi* helped set an important precedent. The commercial success of early Japanese cinema owed much to these virtuoso interpreter-performers, whose skills were much admired. Very often, *they* were the box-office draw, not the film!

Mere words on paper cannot convey any real idea of the dramatic and interpretive skills displayed by the *benshi* and their specialist collaborators, the *kowairo*, who in effect dubbed in live dialogue. The best we can do is to study such transcripts as the following, used for the climactic beach scene in *The Golden Demon*. In this instance, the performer was the great virtuoso Shoju Tsuchiya, who was known for his ability to speak in a number of voices, taking all the roles:

Narrator. This is Japan's famous sentimental drama, *The Golden Demon.* The scene is set on Atami Beach.

Kowairo (for the hero): Miya, tonight I speak to you for the last time. Remember the date: January 17th. I will remember this night for the rest of my life. How could I ever forget. A year from now, two years from now I will cloud the moon with my tears. When you see that cloudy moon think of me weeping, hating you.

Kowairo (for the heroine): Don't say sad things like that. . . . I won't forget you.

Kowairo (for the hero): I don't want to listen to you. . . . This is a dream, a bad dream I have dreamed.

Benshi: Kanichi walked silently along the beach, hanging his head. Omiya could not help herself. She followed him.

Kowairo (for the hero): Why shouldn't I weep?

Kowairo (for the heroine): If I marry Tomiya, what will you say?

Kowairo (for the hero): Then you're all set to marry him. What a fickle flirt you are!

Benshi: Kanichi, overcome with rage, kicks the fragile Omiya. . . .[8]

Another melodrama based on class distinctions was staged by a *shimpa* playwright famous in his day, though largely forgotten now. He was Momoo Okura. His play of 1905 was titled *Biwaka* (Lute song). It dealt with a topic bound to engage audiences: the Russo-Japanese War of 1904. In it, the protagonist compensates for his feelings of social inferiority by trying to be a hero on the battlefield. As might be expected, various women pay dearly for his challenge to privilege. The M. Pathé Company made a film of this play five years after its stage debut. A year later, the Yoshizawa Company released another version, as a comedy!

Kyoka Izumi is another novelist renowned for his close association with *shimpa*. Though his subjects ran the gamut from tales of the supernatural, mystery, and adventure to high romance, his dramas of female sacrifice were the most sought after for the stage.

Izumi's *A Woman's Pedigree* was published serially in 1907 and staged the following year as a tragedy of unrequited love. It explores the classical conflict between *giri* (social obligation) and *ninjo* (personal feelings). The hero, Chikara Hayase, undergoes his crisis in Meiji society. The geisha Otsuta is the great love of his life, yet he obeys his teacher's command and breaks with her. The climax of the drama takes place in a famous scene set in Yushima Shrine. There the *giri*-bound Chikara announces his decision to his lover.

We do not really know just when *A Woman's Pedigree* appeared as a film. Even so, a number of critics consider it a seminal work in early adaptations of *shimpa* drama.

In 1894 Kyoka published a novel titled *Giketsu kyoketsu* (Blood of honor). Its heroine is a far more redoubtable figure than the hero. He is a student, she, a showgirl who falls in love with him. She goes into debt to put him through law school. When she cannot repay the balance due, the usurer demands that she become his mistress. There is an argument and a struggle, in the course of which she accidentally kills the man. The climax is ironic: the two lovers have their day in court. Their final meeting is as prosecutor and defendant.

Kunitake Akizuki (l) and Teijiro Tachibana (r) in *The Cuckoo* (1915/17?), directed by Tadashi Koguchi. Courtesy of the Kawakita Memorial Film Institute.

Retitled *Taki no shiraito* (White threads of the cascade), Kyoka's novel was an instant stage hit in 1896. The first film version was made in 1912. Remakes of it appeared for many years thereafter.

This pattern of transfer—works of Meiji literature presented as *shimpa* and then as cinema—led to two important practices that become hallmarks of the Japanese cinema industry. One was *kyosaku*, or "competing literary works." Two, or possibly more, film companies vied with one another by adapting the same best-selling novel. The works could be released simultaneously or at different times. Studios also vied with one another, and sometimes with themselves, on *saieiga* (remakes).

Yuho's *My Sin* offers a striking case in point. It was remade twenty-five times between 1908 and 1956. Yuho's *Foster Sisters* was remade sixteen times before World War II. Twenty-two versions of *The Cuckoo* have been made, the last in 1958. Of the nineteen remakes of *The Golden Demon*, two were made after the war, in 1948 and 1954. *Lute Song* was remade fifteen times in the pre-war period.

None of these figures approach the eighty-three remakes of the *Chushingura* epic that cinema took over from Kabuki/Bunraku. But the motives and methods

Denmei Suzuki (l) and Kumeko Urabe in *The Golden Demon* (1924) directed by Minoru Murata. Courtesy of the Kawakita Memorial Film Institute.

of studio rivalry were the same. Each new remake aimed to be a box-office hit. Naturally, rival remakes weighed in with as many superstars as possible.

No prints of those films survive from the 1910s and 1920s, so it is impossible to know exactly how the art of adaptation fared in the early years. My own research does show that many directors challenged the competition with innovations both technical and contextual.

One good instance is Shisetsu Iwafuji's *Shin hotogogisu* (The cuckoo, new version) of 1909. This version marks the first known use of flashback in Japanese cinema.[9] Nine remakes of *The Cuckoo* were released between 1909 and 1920. One critic notes that some, but not all, reinforced the motif of separation by creating new scenes.[10] Both the drama and the film make much of a scene set in Yamashina station after the couple's divorce. Namiko and her father take the eastbound train. Takeo is traveling west. The two trains pass, giving Namiko just enough time to flutter her handkerchief out the window, letting it fly in an instant of melodramatic poignancy guaranteed to bring hankies to the eyes of audiences of the day. But of course melodrama tends to look for more and more poignant effects, so many remakes of *The Cuckoo* put Namiko on shore as Takeo's ship sails away, taking him off to war.

The critic Junichiro Tanaka has found evidence of development in Chiba's camera technique in his collaboration with Nakano on *The Golden Demon* in

1912. Apparently, Chiba's original intention was to shoot only the beach. Then he noticed the beautiful mountain ranges beyond and decided to include them in the shot. The result was what came to be known as a *pan*, in this case from the mountains to the actors on the beach.[11]

The Yokota Company's 1912 remake of its own *The Golden Demon* expanded the film to thirty-two scenes. Five months later, not to be outdone, the rival M. Pathé Studio released *The Female Golden Demon* featuring Kasen Kinoshita, star of a showgirl troupe enjoying wide popularity just then.

In the second decade of the century two important factors contributed to the popularity of Meiji novels coming to cinema by way of *shimpa* tragedy. One was the founding of the Nikkatsu Company in 1912. It absorbed four other studios: Yoshizawa Shokai, Yokota Shokai, M. Pathé, and Fukuodo. Nikkatsu opened a fully equipped studio at Mukojima in 1913, creating a virtual monopoly of resources favorable to the development of two kinds of films at once. *Kyugeki*, or "old drama," specialized in tales of swashbuckling adventure. The other was *shimpa*, with its "new drama" emphasis on adaptations from Meiji literature.

Nikkatsu was soon challenged by a powerful new rival, the Tenkatsu Company, founded in 1914. Nikkatsu fought back with increased production. Along with its swashbuckling commitments (the historical costume drama *jidaigeki*), the studio scheduled four "contemporary" films a month. Most of those scripts were inspired by *shimpa*.

From the time it went into business in 1912 to the Kanto Earthquake of 1923, the Nikkatsu Mukojima Studio set the standard for cinema derived from *shimpa*-inspired films. That part of its achievement made cinema history in the sense that Nikkatsu did so much to foster an important characteristic of Japanese cinema, namely, the deep and abiding interest in adapting the nation's literature for use on the screen. Nikkatsu's competitive verve also helped foster this tendency. The battle of the remakes was on, and as time went on, competing studios made steady creative as well as financial gains.

My Sin is a case in point. Nikkatsu's version of 1916 was one of twenty-five made of that novel. How does one account for the apparently insatiable fascination with this *shimpa*-inspired work, especially in the early years of Japanese cinema? Critic Tadao Sato offers this explanation:

In *My Sin*, the heroine feels that the children's death is Heaven's punishment for her own sins. Even though the boys themselves don't know that they are brothers, the audience in those days considered their death as the epitome of innocent, genuine brotherhood. They also felt that it was only natural for a mother to be punished for giving birth to an illegitimate child which she then abandoned. . . .

Nowadays the audience might consider it unnatural that children should fulfill their destiny by dying in order to atone for their mother's sins. But the situation was different then. Moviegoers wept over such tragedies and flocked to the theater to see the many remakes of them, expecting each time to clutch their hankies and weep. For them, the mother-child relationship was invincible; the child was all that mattered to the mother and the ideal child was the one who valued the mother above everything else. Thus, for these viewers the utmost tragedy was a mother's separation from her most beloved.[12]

This is not to say that the sons of mothers early in the century took *shimpa* on screen very much to heart. The viewers and weepers were predominantly female. Men tended to mock these films, putting them down as "boring *shimpa* drama versions" and "tearjerkers."[13] Sneers of the menfolk notwithstanding, these films remained in some way essential to the ladies of the day. They furnished the studios with a vast and profitably faithful audience in decades when Japanese cinema was learning important lessons about making films that paid their way.

Two versions of *My Sin* appeared in 1912. One was made by Yoshizawa Shokai shortly before it was absorbed by Nikkatsu. Nikkatsu wasted no time marketing its remake under the unmistakable title *My Sin: New Version*. The following year, Nikkatsu competed with Komatsu Shokai with yet another version, this time titled *My Sin: Sequel*, drawing the matter out to twenty-five scenes.

In the decade that followed, a new version of this film appeared almost every year. *My Sin* became something like an entity separate and apart from *rensageki* (chain drama). The director of Nikkatsu's 1917 version remains unknown, but that version was one of the most famous of the decade, not least because it managed to dramatize most of Yuho's novel, with the usual degree of creative license.

These films being, as they were, a product of the times, the heroines were played by female impersonators. One especially famous *onnagata* was Teijiro Tachibana, noted for convincing portrayals of physical fragility. The actors of early cinema were products of the theater, as camera technique itself was. It was common practice to adopt the one-scene, one-shot method reminiscent of the stage. The tempo of gestures was slow, again in accordance with theatrical convention.

This is not to say that early directors were invariably content to be convention bound. Eizo Tanaka was one who advanced progressive ideas. His 1919 version of *My Sin* broke with precedent in a number of ways. He replaced *kowairo* roles with subtitles and invested each scene with more shots. His innovations were met with furious protest by studio *benshi*, who staged a mass demonstration.

A high point of *kyosaku* was reached in 1917 when Nikkatsu, Tenkatsu, and the Kobayashi Company all took on the same Yuho Kikuchi novel. This time, *shimpa* was bypassed. The novel *Dokuso* (Poison grass) inspired these films directly. It had been a newspaper serial in 1915–16, so the adaptations had the benefit of that advance publicity. The plot concerns the ever-popular wicked mother-in-law and the misery she brings to her son's orphan bride. All three film versions were cast with female impersonators.

Kobayashi Shokai was a small production company, a splinter group that broke with Nikkatsu because of creative differences. Koboyashi's version of *Poison Grass*, directed by Masao Inoue, was a David and Goliath triumph, being rated best of the three by critics impressed with its technical innovations.

Eiji Takagi (l) and Komako Sunada (c) in *My Sin, New Version* (1926) directed by Kenji Mizoguchi. Courtesy of the Kawakita Memorial Film Institute.

Inoue used an actual actress for one of the major roles. He also used close-ups to good effect at a time when many Japanese filmmakers considered them a foreign innovation. Subtitles took over *kowairo* roles. Some subtitles were accompanied by drawings from newspaper stories.

A critic of the day speaks for those who found these changes all to the good:

> What impressed me most in Kobayashi Studio's *Poison Grass* is the successful use of close-ups. . . . When Oshino first meets Kichizo, they are shown in head and shoulders view. This close-up not only helps set the story in motion, but firmly establishes their roles as hero and heroine. Interior scenes set room partitions and alcoves diagonally in relation to the camera. This alignment shows a director taking the trouble to give his settings more depth and reality and pictorial interest. However, close-ups simply failed when they were applied to female impersonators.[14]

The praise of another critic, Yutaka Hara, was differently qualified:

> I am not particularly fond of the way actors perform in Japanese cinema, but this film *Poison Grass* gives me the kind of refreshing experience I have come to expect from films made in the West. It may have been a more refreshing experience, thanks to the superior use made of essentially filmic qualities. The rich and varied plot was advanced by thirty subtitles, an innovation that failed completely. There were forty close-ups, and as many as fifteen outsize ones. . . .[15]

Scant as surviving evidence is, we know that the art of cinema in those early years was, quite literally, feeling its way in the dark. Its first and obvious guide was, quite naturally, the stage. Yet cinema was reaching out to touch a kind of artful unreality whose rules would turn out to be somewhat different. Like any art, cinema needed to be similar to some other arts on its way to becoming art in its own right. It may be that we ourselves are just beginning to appreciate the contribution made there by the Meiji writers behind the scenes. I mean, of course, the literary figures whose works crossed the *shimpa* footlights on their way to the silver screen.[16]

Notes

1. For a study of the relationship between the Japanese classical theater and early cinema, see Joseph Anderson and Donald Richie, *The Japanese Film: Art and Industry*, expanded ed. (Princeton: Princeton University Press, 1982), pp. 21–34. Also see Keiko McDonald, *Japanese Classical Theater in Films* (Rutherford, N.J., London, and Toronto: Associated University Presses, 1994), pp. 23–37.
2. Tadao Sato, *Mizoguchi Kenji no sekai* (The world of Kenji Mizoguchi) (Tokyo: Tsukuma Shobo, 1982), p. 62.
3. Nobuo Chiba et al., *Sekai no eiga sakka: Nihon eigashi* (Film directors of the world: history of Japanese cinema), vol. 31 (Tokyo: Kinema Jumpo, 1976), p. 11.
4. Ibid., p. 12.
5. Junichiro Tanaka, *Nihon eiga hattatsushi* (History of the development of Japanese cinema), vol. 1 (Tokyo: Chuo Koron, 1975), pp. 136.
6. Ibid., pp. 137–38.
7. For the original story, see Roka Tokutomi, *Hototogisu* (The cuckoo), in *Gendai bungaku taikei* (A collection of modern literary works), vol. 5 (Tokyo: Chikuma Shobo, 1966), pp. 1–119.
8. Tanaka, *Nihon eiga hattatsushi*, p. 182–83.
9. Anderson and Richie, *The Japanese Film*, p. 29.
10. Chiba et al., *Sekai no eiga sakka*, p. 12.
11. Tanaka, *Nihon eiga hattatsushi*, pp. 138–39.
12. Tadao Sato, *Nihon eigashi* (History of Japanese cinema), vol. 1 (Tokyo: Iwanami Shoten, 1995), p. 143.
13. Chiba et al., *Sekai no eiga sakka*, p. 14.
14. Tanaka, *Nihon eiga hattatsushi*, pp. 273–74.
15. Quoted by Kikuo Yamamoto in *Nihon eiga ni okeru gaikoku eiga no eikyo: hikaku eigashi kenkyu* (The influence of foreign films on Japanese cinema: film history: a comparative study) (Tokyo: Waseda Daigaku, 1983), pp. 64–65.
16. For example, Mizoguchi's major adaptations of Kyoka's works in *shimpa* mold include *Shin ono ga tsumi* (My sin, new version), *Nihonbashi* (1929), *The White Threads of the Cascade* (1933), and *Orizuru Osen* (The downfall of Osen, 1935). For a further study, see Keiko McDonald, *Mizoguchi* (Boston: Twayne, 1984), pp. 27–32.

2

Literature More "Pure" Than "Popular": 1935–1941

By the mid-1930s, Japanese cinema had grown by leaps and bounds. By then, pictures could "talk," so naturally studios and directors began to think more ambitiously about their scripts. This change was to have momentous consequences for films based on works of literature, the *bungei-eiga*.

Japanese literature offered a wealth of choices that could easily be classified "popular" or "serious." Directors drawn to the latter set a trend that became known as *junbungaku*, or the pure literature movement. Those persuaded to be pure in this sense thought of popular works as emphasizing action and adventure and the less deliberate or complex varieties of romance.[1]

One critic has described the phenomenon this way:

> *Bungei-eiga* originated in the filmmakers' attempt to rely on literature in order to overcome an obstacle met by Japanese cinema in this time of transition: the narrow scope of the scenario format associated with silent film. . . . Given a work of literature as a starting point, they could get closer to ordinary people whose lives they could portray realistically . . . borrowing from literature paved the way to realism.[2]

Studio rivalry played a key role in this development. In 1935 Shochiku moved its base of operations from Kamata to Ofuna. There it became immensely powerful, with widespread ownership of theaters. Nikkatsu also moved in 1935. Its new studio space at Oizumi was part of a vigorous restructuring aimed at correcting a downward trend blamed on recent poor management. Daito Eiga at this date was a much smaller competitor, still struggling to survive.

A fourth major company joined the industry in 1936. This conglomerate was made up of the Takarazuka Theater, the J.O. Studio, and Photo Chemical Laboratories. It became known as the Toho Company. Thanks to its huge capital investment, Toho began with an impressive roster of directors put in place by an effective management strategy that replaced the so-called director system with one laying emphasis on a producer.

Toho and Shochiku quickly became bitter rivals. In 1938, Shochiku succeeded in blocking a Toho-Nikkatsu merger. Yet rivalry yielded a shift in strategy that was to have important consequences for Japanese cinema. Studios moved away from attempts to cut into one another's markets. Instead, each company cultivated its own choice, as it were, of audience. Toho targeted all viewers in their twenties—the greatest percentage of the moviegoing public at the time. Nikkatsu specialized in films about men, aiming to interest both sexes. Other market specialties were shared by the other minor studios.

Film genres adapted accordingly. Shochiku continued to specialize in melodrama. As we later see, the pure literature movement, for all its highbrow aims, brought plenty of new material to that perennially popular form.

Toho made use of *bungei-eiga* to vary and enrich its stock in trade: *jidaigeki* (period films) and comedy. Nikkatsu continued to profit from its popular *jidaigeki* and *chambara* (swashbuckling films), responding to the pure literature movement ideals with scripts dealing with contemporary life.

This climate of varied but intense competition started *bungei-eiga* on its way. Earlier in 1935, Photo Chemical Laboratories used its improved distribution system to float what was apparently a precursor of the pure literature tendency. No print survives of *Horoki* (A vagabond's song), but we know something about the film from the book of the same title. It was autobiographical fiction published in 1930 by Fumiko Hayashi. In it, she details the privations and sufferings of a narrator who dreams of becoming a writer in depression-era Japan.

Photo Chemical Laboratories commissioned Sotoji Kimura to adapt the book for the screen. A critic of the day made note of its picturesque scenes, expressive of the pathos of human existence. He was most struck by one scene depicting the narrator as a girl walking along a beach at dusk with her peddler mother.[3]

In 1935, Yasujiro Shimazu adapted Tanizaki's *Shunkinsho* (The Story of Shunkin). He leaned heavily on the talents of two of Shochiku's top stars, Kinuyo Tanaka and Kokichi Takada. Even so, Shimazu was forced into an uneasy compromise between melodrama and comedy, having to deal with elements of downright slapstick, which were a looked-for ingredient of the *shomingeki* genre Shochiku was famous for. (This film is discussed in Chapter 9).

That same year, Kenji Mizoguchi attempted a film version of the 1907 novel *Gubijinso* (Poppy) by the Meiji writer Soseki Natsume. Mizoguchi had already begun to explore the theme that would characterize his work lifelong: woman's confrontation with a male-dominated, money-oriented society.

In this film, he studied woman in the context of the Meiji literary tradition. Yet his own melodramatic bent got in the way of a genuine rapprochement with Soseki, whose world was alien to him, complicated as it was by a vigorous intellect skeptical about the moral issues of good and evil. Nonetheless, *Poppy* shows two interesting developments in Mizoguchi's filmmaking: a growing interest in contrasting pairs of female characters, and a willingness to experiment with elements of style.[4]

Mizoguchi's 1936 film *Gion no shimai* (Sisters of the Gion) would offer a more vigorous opposition of two female types, the modern and the traditional.

But *Poppy* is already rich in Western modes of representation such as close-ups, reverse-field shots, montage, and point-of-reference shots.

Mizoguchi brings all these to bear on the downfall of a woman who has tried her best to manipulate two suitors. The climactic final scene takes place aboard ship. There one of her suitors shows that he understands her true motives. He tosses a gold watch, a token of her willingness to marry him after all, overboard. The watch is shown in close-up, followed by a montage of the ocean swallowing it up.

The critic Motohiko Fujita sees all these films as tending to be films of manners because "the veteran directors strong in their portrayal of manners and mores of the period sought a new venue in literary works."[5] If one were to choose a landmark work of these early days of *bungei-eiga*, it would be Tomu Uchida's *Jinsei gekijo* (The theater of life, 1936). It would be the landmark work of the pure literature movement, leading to the culmination of *bungei-eiga* in the prewar period. Nikkatsu produced this adaptation of Shiro Ozaki's novel.

The story encompasses the tumultuous period of Japanese history from the First World War to Japan's war with China in 1931. This saga of the Aonari family focuses on the youth and manhood of the son, Hyokichi. He leaves the university without earning his degree and plunges into the life of pleasure open to a young man with his background. He is in effect searching for identity. As the title of the book and film indicates, his search puts him in contact with people of every kind, among them those of the gangster Yakuza class his family belongs to.

Ozaki's novel was written in opposition to the so-called "conceptual" proletarian literature so prevalent then. Instead of setting out to idealize the working class, *The Theater of Life* uses real-life detail in service of Ozaki's chosen theme couched as a question (and a challenge), namely, "How does one live life to the fullest?"

Here that question is applied to a story involving the classical Japanese conflict between *giri* (social obligations) and *ninjo* (personal inclination). It is seen at work, not just in the lives of "respectable" people, but in the Yakuza underworld as well.

Ozaki's family saga was first published in several sets of newspaper serial installments. The first volume *Seishun-hen* (Youth) appeared in 1933. Its sequel the next year was titled *Aiyoku-hen* (Love). When the two were published as a book, the novelist Kawabata gave it a rave review. He said that Ozaki's work succeeded in capturing "life in its flow" not as "a concept."

Kawabata's praise helped make the book such a resounding success that Ozaki felt called upon to follow it up with *Zankyo* (Yakuza survivors) in serial form. He did not stop there. Five more serials appeared over the years, the last in 1960. As so often happens, Ozaki's first effort is considered the best, so it may be for the best that Uchida's film was based chiefly on the part of the saga serialized as *Youth*.

Uchida is generally faithful to Ozaki's story line, though he is clearly most concerned to portray Hyokichi's student life and love for Osode, the daughter of a restaurateur. His treatment prompted one critic to hail it as an "independently invincible film" or "the rare instance wherein the reality depicted in the original is successfully transferred onto the screen."[6]

Certainly the film gains strength from Uchida's concern for the oppressed. He shows a convincing sensitivity to the cares and concerns of people who may be described as struggling to hang onto a just-under-middle-class standard of living in the face of social and economic forces running amok worldwide. Uchida's refreshingly candid approach owes much to his deft use of sharply defined visual images.

He is particularly successful in depicting changes in the character of the young Hyokichi's father, Hyotaro. The actor Isamu Kosugi was cast in both these roles. Critic Tatsuhiko Shigeno sees this cinematic device as helping "project a straightforward image of the father's character passed on to the son and emulated by him."[7]

Shigeno is referring to the fact that Hyotaro tries his best to live up to his motto, "Try to be strong and better every day." But the old man's luck runs out. He goes from being a Yakuza boss to just another morphine addict. He struggles and fails and finally shoots himself.

In the film, Isamu Kosugi must play that failed man and the son who is much like him. The father-son bond must serve a cause of sharing that fate—but not entirely, not to the same bitter end.

The son's emulation of the old man's energy is most vividly depicted in a sequence at Waseda University. Hyokichi objects to the construction of a statue of the president's wife. He leads fellow students in a protest. This is no idealized picture of youthful idealism. Hyokichi and his fellow protesters are shown drunk and rowdy in what looks like Uchida's celebration of carefree youthful energy of the kind that commonly goes awry, degenerating into grown-up posturing and violence, the very stuff of politics. He shows that happening too, and soon enough, as students bicker and split into factions over questions of university reform.

Even Hyokichi's love for Osode is seen as turning from youthful exaltation to depressing burden. A telling detail speaks for that change as we see her pressing against him; the camera singles out her *geta* (clogs) falling off and rolling down into the river.

That scene is intercut with one showing a woebegone Yakuza, Kiratsune, entering the dilapidated house of his former boss, Hyotaro. The critic Fujita has observed that these vividly defined images say a lot about Uchida's studious gaze at the frustration and disillusionment of individuals who have reason to feel left out in the period of momentous and fateful change that was Japan in the 1920s and 1930s.[8]

This film is richly endowed with images that speak for a sense of historical malaise. A huge old oak tree stands in the Aonari family's yard. Clearly, Uchida means to suggest that this ancient living thing transcends the human turmoil played out in this house. We see Hyotari fire a bullet into the tree, telling his son to grow stronger. Gesture and message make obvious sense.

Isamu Kosugi (l) and Chieko Murata (r) in *The Theater of Life* (1936) directed by Tomu Uchida. Courtesy of the Kawakita Memorial Film Institute.

Uchida's version of *The Theater of Life* turned out to be a seminal work for the convention of remakes. A number of directors rose to Ozaki's challenge to locate "the theater of life" in any number of times and places close at hand in everyday life. Each of the novelist's first three volumes were adapted individually. Sometimes they were collapsed into one filmscript. Some thirteen film versions have been made to date.

Uchida himself returned to Ozaki years later, in 1968. This time, he took just one part of the Aonari family saga, making it fit the Yakuza genre format for which Toei Studio had become famous. Released with the title *Jinsei gekijo: Hishakaku to Kiratsune* (The theater of life: Hishakaku and Kiratsune), this film studies the friendship of three Yakuza forced to deal with the basic Japanese conflict between *giri* and *ninjo*. Even on that high moral ground there had to be a showdown scene, whose bloody character is clearly reminiscent of the swashbuckling (*chambara*) action films Toei made so profitable in the 1960s.[9]

The immense popularity of Uchida's *The Theater of Life* prompted even some veteran directors to follow in his footsteps. Among them was Sotoji Kimura. He took up the challenge offered by Saisei Muro's short story "Ani Imoto" (Older brother, younger sister). This work won the 1934 Literary Confab Club Award. As we see in Chapter 11, the original story concerns the love-hate relationship between two siblings in a lower-class family. Its poignancy derives from some complex psychological realities hidden underneath the commonplace hard facts of life among the down-and-out.

Kimura successfully transferred the story's psychological dimension onto the screen. The experienced actors he used deserve a good deal of the credit.[10] Among them was Isamu Kosugi. Critics at the time gave him high praise for his double role in *The Theater of Life*. He was particularly convincing in the role of Muro's archetypal down-to-earth patriarch.

Another veteran director inspired by Uchida's success was Mansaku Itami. He was a *jidaigeki* specialist, and so his choice of text was a natural one: Naoya Shiga's "Akanishi Kakita" (Kakita Akanishi). This short story from Shiga's middle period (1917–27) parodies the theme of family feud and intrigue used in so many celebrated Kabuki and Bunraku plays.[11]

The feud in this case involves the Date clan. Shiga's tongue-in-cheek rendering includes such touches as major characters named after various fish and shellfish. His two heroes begin as lowly retainers who turn out to be gentlemen in disguise. They are Date clan spies sent to Edo to infiltrate a plot to destroy their lord's legitimate heir.

Shiga pokes no end of fun at his characters before aiming for a note of true-life heroism at the end. One of the spies is Kakita Akanishi, whose name incorporates *kaki* (oysters) into a general impression quite unlike one's idea of a cunning diplomat. He is a lumpish, naive fellow whose notion of a binge is all about sweets, not sake. He might pass for brainless if he did not dote on chess. The other spy, Masujiro Aoshima, is his opposite in every respect. His given name is a play on *masu* (trout). He is the right stuff for spying, being handsome, sociable, and self-assured, and quick-witted enough to survive a partner like Kakita.

The omniscient narrator's story, like any comedy of errors, pretends to take its absurdities seriously. It begins with a stomachache. Kakita has overindulged and is convinced that he is about to die. The blind masseur Anko is called in (*Anko* means "sea-devil"). Thinking that vital information is dying with him, Kakita tells Anko where he has hidden the intelligence report he and Masujiro have prepared.

Chatty Anko is effective only as a gossip, leaving to spread the word that Kakita cured himself by cutting his belly open and sewing it back up. Something like that did happen in a grotesque parody of ritual suicide. Kakita is happy enough to have survived. But the question remains: will Anko blab? And so the plot lurches forward as mishaps multiply.

Of course there has to be a love affair. It grows out of starkly practical necessity. The two spies need an excuse to leave the service of the enemy lord who has taken them on as lowly retainers. How can they leave without arousing suspicion? Ugly Kakita sends a love letter to the beautiful maid Sazae (named for a kind of seashell). All the court will know when she recoils in horror. What can Kakita do but leave in order to die of shame somewhere? But lo, Sazae sends a favorable reply. Nothing to do but send her a second, more passionate letter. It, however, goes astray, so Kakita gets his wish after all. Now he has to leave town, and his pal with him. They accomplish their mission and all ends well.

The narrative does achieve some demanding effects. The reader understands that the author is up to something better than masterminding stooges. But what is it? An element of suspense carries us forward. We are genuinely surprised when Anko's killer turns out to be Masujiro, forced to act by the danger posed to so many by the old man's gossip. Finally, we find out who Kakita and Masujiro really are and that the apparently bungled spy mission has served a serious purpose.

Like many an author intent on poking fun, Shiga finds it hard to stop smirking. Why else would his omniscient narrator pass on a "rumor" that the bad guys got even with Masujiro later on? Why the parting arch assurance that he would satisfy our curiosity about Kakita and Sazae if he could? Were they really star-crossed lovers? Did they get back together? All the narrator can say is that nobody knows.

Like any parody, Shiga's story can survive only on its own terms. All the more reason for a film director to take full advantage of its brevity. Mansaku Itami did just that, expanding plot and characters to serve his needs in *Akanishi Kakita* (Kakita Akanishi, 1936). His *jidaigeki* is made in a boldly experimental style that parodies its own period film genre and much else besides. Itami begins by standing some basic genre assumptions on their heads. In *jidaigeki* made during this period, we expect a larger-than-life hero and one who is handsome, too. Here the director gives that spot in the limelight to the ungainly Kakita, played by the heartthrob *jidaigeki* star Chiezo Kataoka.

He balances that upset with another, double casting the good guy samurai Kataoka as the bad guy Kai Harada. Shiga's villain was a mere mention of a name, so Itami was free to imagine him. Thanks to Kataoka's skill, the result was a virtuoso display of contrasting acting styles. Kakita was portrayed in a broadly humorous slapstick style. Harada's speech and gestures took cues from stylized Kabuki.

Itami obviously enjoyed taking liberties, but he could be shrewdly economical, too. Shiga spends a fair amount of text on Kakita's first appearance as an unprepossessing, down-at-heel samurai in lowlife surroundings. Itami works quickly to convey the same impression.

His opening sequence begins with two retainers discussing the ridiculous appearance and manners of this new guy, Kakita, who has joined their ranks. It is pouring rain outside. The camera takes note of a stray cat running for cover in a dismal alleyway. The sounds of sloppy weather mix with Chopin's famous "Raindrop" etude. The two retainers peer in through a window at Kakita in his shabby room. He is playing chess by himself in dim lantern light. The camera closes in on a big wart by his nose.

The film, like haiku, makes good use of oblique reference. Most episodes end with a diagonal wipe signaling an ellipsis. The scene between Kakita and Sazae became a model for many period films that followed. The lovers are part of

Mineko Mori (l) and Chiezo Kataoka (r) in *Kakita Akanishi* (1936) directed by Mansaku Itami. Courtesy of the Kawakita Memorial Film Institute.

a lady's entourage. Kakita is asked to give Sazae a new name. The camera cuts to a pond ringed with ripples. "Sazanami!" Kakita says. Let her be called Little Ripples. Who can doubt that Kurosawa had this scene in mind when his hero gives himself a new name in *Yojimbo* (1961) and *Sanjuro* (1962)?

Itami is notably restrained when it comes to swordplay in this film. Only at the end does the villain put on a display in the best traditions of Kabuki. The camera zooms in and out to catch Harada's stylized appearances and disappearances in a hallway whose point of reference is the *byobu* (folding screen) that adorns the room.

The film, unlike the story, leaves no loose ends of plot lying around. Masujiro is captured by the villains and killed. And yes, true love finally does find a way. Itami charges this scene with stylistic devices old and new in a touching show of comedy.

Sazae/Sazanami has left the court and returned to her parents. Kakita comes to call. He is seated facing her. Her parents sit nearby. After the usual polite introductions, a camera trick causes the father to disappear after he says, "Please stay as long as you want." The mother vanishes likewise, saying the same. Then Sazanami says it, too.

The Japanese audience sees the obvious bow to Kabuki modes of representation. The camera plays along with this more stylized approach. It stops moving freely and frames the scene as if taking a seat in the Kabuki theater. Mendelssohn's "Wedding March" speaks for the guaranteed happy ending of the comedy.

Itami's good-humored parody was a rarity. Most directors at the time took their pure literature commitments rather more seriously. Shiro Toyoda became a mainstay of the *junbungaku* movement, taking up writers who explored many of the issues troubling Japanese society in the 1930s. His range of interests included novels of agrarian life and feminist revolt.

Critics and viewers both were moved by Toyoda's first significant *junbungaku* film, an adaptation of Yojiro Ishizaka's novel *Wakai hito* (Young people, 1937). Ishizaka's work was serialized in the prestigious literary journal *Mita bungaku* at intervals from 1933 to 1937. Its appeal was based on a vivid depiction of the exuberant passions of youth and the sufferings of an intelligentsia faced with a dilemma posed by exalted notions of freedom at odds with the rigid social discipline imposed by an increasingly militaristic government.

The novel is set in a missionary school for girls. The curriculum emphasizes Western values based on the development of individual character. Ishizaka's heroine, Keiko Enami, is not the kind of Japanese girl one met in novels of the time. She is no paragon of long-suffering submission. She is a rebel and worse yet, she is bright. Having started life as an illegitimate child, she makes claims on life that society considers illegitimate, too. She falls in love with her teacher and lets everyone know it.

The teacher, Mazaki, has also charmed a colleague, Hashimoto. As a committed Marxist, she is theoretically opposed to his liberal views. As a woman, she finds him hard to resist.

Mazaki, too, is torn in the sense of having to ask himself, *Which woman will it be?* Two crises help clarify the terms of his choice. First he discovers that Hashimoto is a Marxist. Can he love a Marxist, no matter how female? Then he is badly beaten by a group of sailors unwisely exposed to his political views. Keiko nurses him back to health. He is a liberal, not a libertine, so gratitude heightens his conflict. He feels called upon to choose between being a teacher and being a man.

The second crisis forces the issue. Hashimoto is arrested. Mazaki is inclined to join her in principled exile somewhere, but what about Keiko? The rebellious youth makes a noble sacrifice. Her teachers are free to consider themselves failures in society's eyes; yet they look forward to starting anew, with love as their source of moral strength.

Toyoda's film version of this story is remarkable chiefly for what it says about the tendency of censorship to brew weak beer. Hashimoto's Marxism simply vanishes. She becomes an intellectual perceived as "radical," though nothing she says or does gives the label any meaning. So much for the very real dilemma facing intellectuals in Japan at the time, and in Ishizaka's novel.

Film critic Tadao Sato blames this impoverishment for the lackluster impression left on the viewer by Toyoda's Y*oung People.* Even the timeless tension of

Haruyo Ichikawa (l) and Den Ohinata (r) in *Young People* directed by Shiro Toyoda. Courtesy of the Kawakita Memorial Film Institute.

male/female relations cannot survive the loss of the novel's ideological point of conflict.[12]

The ending itself suggests that Toyoda was responding to censorship, either actual or anticipated. His script resolves none of the real human issues. We have no idea what happens to Mazaki and Hashimoto. We learn nothing about Keiko's final relationship with Mazaki.

In the final sequence we see Keiko wandering in a storm after an argument with her mother. She meets Hashimoto. They are reconciled after the manner of rivals satisfied to embrace a common set of principles. A long shot shows them standing face to face on this stormy night. Hashimoto delivers a long discourse on society's unfair treatment of illegitimate children. As she advises Keiko to rise above her circumstances by leading a life beyond reproach, the camera closes in. A close-up guarantees that Keiko is receiving this advice in the proper spirit of sincere determination to live up to it. The final shot leaves Hashimoto watching in the foreground as Keiko vanishes in the distance.

Toyoda, like so many Japanese directors of the day, was a studio workhorse, so he did two more adaptations in 1938. The plot of the screenplay for *Nakimushi kozo* (A cry baby apprentice) follows Fumiko Hayashi's short story rather closely. Keikichi is a fatherless boy whose mother sends him away when her new man does not want him around. He is passed from one aunt to another, then sent back to his mother. Her common-law husband has lost his job and they have to move, so the boy is uprooted again.

Hayashi's story is a sensitive psychological portrait of an unwanted child. Her point of view is inside the boy. She looks at the world through his sense of loss and alienation. Any child might feel lost in a world new to him; the unwanted child is doubly lost. But this story is not just an exercise in larmoyant futility. Hayashi shows Keikichi drifting into adolescence, into that stronger, more definite sense of self, however troubled. In one brilliant passage she conveys his growing sense of relationship through the excitement he feels watching a male cricket courting a mate.

Toyoda is satisfied to let the camera speak for the life of this boy. The story is the same, but without Hayashi's psychological focus, it becomes a series of loosely connected episodes devoid of ideological themes or symbolism. Its perspective is correspondingly large, taking in the manners and mores of Tokyoites during the period of unrest and uncertainty of the 1930s.

The film is more interesting for its portrayal of women coping in different ways with their roles as the weaker sex. Keikichi's mother sacrifices her son to save her own pitiful portion of security as a common-law wife. Two of her sisters live in legitimate married misery. One has married a good-for-nothing. The other

Fumio Hayashi (l) and Tsumugu Fujii (r) in *A Cry Baby Apprentice* (1938) directed by Shiro Toyoda. Courtesy of the Kawakita Memorial Film Institute.

has married for love, but to an unsuccessful painter. Both are trapped in poverty. The one reasonably happy woman in the family is the sister determined to make it on her own as a professional woman.

Novel and film both leave the boy's future an open question at the end. They differ in the feelings they impart. Hayashi makes no commitment to hoping for the best. Keikichi has been hit by a truck. He wakes to find himself in a hospital bed, lapsing back into sleep. The world of dreams seems like the only place that is really safe. For him it is somewhere outdoors, in nature teeming with life. But where will he go when he wakes? He has to go somewhere. But where? Hayashi does not guess for us.

Toyoda does. In his version Keikichi comes home to find the family gone. The camera stares at the empty house. The boy comes back out and walks toward it. He pauses to reach up and pick a pair of white socks hanging from a tree, overlooked in the hurry to leave. He holds them in a way that suggests a cherished memento, a sign of his yearning even for a mother who has deserted him. A violin plays a classic melody expressing loss and longing, Grieg's sweetly melancholy "Sonveig's Song."

A long shot follows Keiichi walking along a path near the house. A deep-focus study in shrinking-shot size ends as he vanishes in the distance, where a mountain looms in the background. He is singing the "Mount Hakone" song. He learned it from a kindly stranger, the flute player who took him in and advised him to grow up strong, no matter what. Here at the end, Toyoda appears to be relying on a symbol to convey his guess about this boy: he will survive to struggle up the mountain of his fate soaring skywards on ahead.

A Cry Baby Apprentice anticipates a genre of films about children that blossomed briefly in these last years before World War II. These films emphasize the child's perspective on the world. At the same time, they convey a message that adults in the 1930s had reason to hope would be true: despite socioeconomic forces making victims of so many families, children would survive and grow, even without the help of adults.

Toyoda's second film, *Uguisu* (The nightingale), drew on the story of the same title published that year by Einosuke Ito. Here the frame of reference is a subgenre that called itself agrarian literature. Ito's tale is an episodic account of peasants responding to poverty and deprivation with cunning, simplicity, and often woeful ignorance.

Toyoda gave Ito's episodic structure the benefit of methods Edmund Goulding used so beautifully in his 1932 classic, *Grand Hotel.* The Goulding-Garbo magic spell was woven within the confines of a single hotel, with events spanning just two days. The various episodes focused on the comings and goings of people whose victories and defeats created a microcosm of the world at large.[13]

The setting of *The Nightingale* is worlds away from any grand hotel. This story plays out in a rural police station in northern Honshu. Poor peasants come and go, a class of petty criminal created by the need to survive times of cruel deprivation.

Haruko Sugimura (c) in *The Nightingale* (1938) directed by Shiro Toyoda. Courtesy of the Kawakita Memorial Film Institute.

Toyoda's scenario expands to include a country railway station, giving the narrative more causal continuity. Among the crowd of peasants is a seasonal worker on his way to Hokkaido. We witness his pitiful poor man's parody of a man of means insisting on the discount fare. A farmer's daughter, sold to a house of prostitution in Tokyo, is waiting for the train with the broker who arranged the deal. The girl's elementary school teacher happens along and calls the police.

The scene shifts to the police station as the parties involved negotiate. (The girl was being sold to pay a debt so small it could be settled with the teacher's pocket money and some help from the police.)

The parade of life continues through one episode after another. Some are grim reminders of terrible hardship, as when a man is arrested for stealing chickens to pay his wife's hospital bill. Some episodes are marked by ironic humor. The police are giving an unlicensed midwife a very hard time when a pregnant woman is brought in. She cannot be left to give birth in the street. There's nothing these men can do but stand aside while the "criminal" midwife exercises her professional skill.

This film was shot at record speed, in eleven days. Toyoda had no Garbo or Barrymore to work with, only a supporting cast borrowed from the *shingeki* (New Drama) stage. Haste and casting together give this film the look of a sketchy stage drama. Even so, it offers a fascinating glimpse of rural hardship as seen by writer, director, and actors themselves caught up in the toils of that difficult time.

Toyoda's next film adaptation used the work of another writer whose work reflects on issues of contemporary social malaise. Tomoji Abe's novel *Fuyu no yado* (The inn in winter) traces the decline of Kamon, a formerly prosperous landholder. This head of an old, distinguished family is reduced to the status of a laborer. Poor and ashamed, he takes to drink, and drink takes all. Having sold all his property, he moves to live in a shantytown.

The silent film survived in Japan through the 1930s, so one of its finest stars was available to give the drunken Kamon an impressively dark and menacing presence on screen. Yet even Yasutaro Katsumi could not carry the script alone. Abe's novel belonged to the "conceptual" genre of intensely inner, psychological, and intellectual treatments of contemporary issues. Toyoda just did not have that turn of mind. His camera eye takes in the scene of Kamon's catastrophe and its consequences for those who depend on him; but nothing in this view gives meaning to Kamon's loss of humanity as he yields to despair.

Toyoda, like most Japanese directors of the day, was a studio workhorse under pressure to keep up with production schedules that seem insane today. He probably did not have time to lose much sleep over the failure of *The Inn in Winter*. More worrisome, no doubt, was studio pressure in relation to the vigorous competition for literary scripts.

We have seen how *kyosaku*, or film rivalry, had become a feature of the Japanese cinema industry very early on. In the 1930s, one of the most vigorous rivalries centered on Kan Kikuchi's novel *Utsukushiki taka* (A beautiful hawk). It was wildly popular as a newspaper serial in 1937.

The heroine, Yumiko, is the woman every woman wanted to be: beautiful, intelligent, aristocratic—and determined to make her own choices in life. She is an orphan and the ward of her uncle, a count. Her spirited personality and astonishing beauty attract the attention of her cousin's fiancé. Worse yet, she is something of a seductive loose cannon because she stubbornly refuses to accept the fiancé her uncle has picked for her.

As a punishment, Yumiko is given to the care of a notorious educational martinet. The woman's son soon falls in love with Yumiko.

Clearly, this was a story made in cinema heaven. The studios did not wait for the public to see how it all came out. The novel was still being serialized when three of them—Shochiku, Toho, and Shinko—made *A Beautiful Hawk* a classic instance of *kyosaku* by announcing the same release date for their screen adaptations: 1 October 1937. Of course, competing studios had to do more than trot out their most marketable stars. Each screenplay had to give the novel a different "take." The result was three Yumikos to the novel's one. Each screen heroine was given a somewhat different character and outcome.

Nikkatsu gave the lead to a new recruit from the Takarazuka Theater, Yukiko Todoroki. Her distinctively "modern" beauty was matched with an unmistakably modern Japanese woman. This Yumiko is a test case of progressive ideas boldly espoused, a free spirit bravely rebelling against the hidebound small-mindedness of those around her.

Toho's screenplay was written by a master of the art, Shinbi Yubi. His version modernized the story as a whole, giving all the characters parts that emphasized new trends in manners and mores. Audiences must have sat up straight on seeing this strong-willed Yumiko confidently taking her place in a world of women and men so different from the world outside the theater doors.

Shinko was the holdout. True to its commitment to *shimpa* melodrama, this studio wrung hankies with a Yumiko foredoomed by her gifts to enjoy lasting unhappiness.[14]

Each of these versions of *A Beautiful Hawk* played its bit part in the history of *kyosaku* and then vanished, forgotten and forgettable. Even so, the brief moment in the limelight for these three films marks a fascinating point of change in the competitive spirit of the time.

The change came abruptly, after the outbreak of war between China and Japan in July 1937. The Home Ministry issued stringent regulations affecting studio production and distribution. No sound film could be longer than 5,000 meters. Scripts were not to promote frivolous behavior or Western notions of individual freedom, especially not with respect to women. A Motion Pictures Law was drafted in 1938, to take effect in 1939. It subjected every script to careful scrutiny by a board of censors.

Clearly, the search for marketable forms of innocence was on. It does not take much juggling of cause/effect and dates to credit the censors with a little golden age of films about children. Critics see it lasting from 1937 to 1941. Films made then show *bungei-eiga* adding children's literature to its stock in trade.

Hiroshi Shimizu is a director largely forgotten now, but his name is inseparable from *jido-eiga* (films about children), and his work is well worth looking into. His lifelong career of devotion to children—on screen and off—began with two films in this difficult time before the war.

Kaze no naka no kodomotachi (Children in the wind) ranked fourth among the ten best pictures of 1937 chosen by the prestigious film journal *Kinema jumpo*. The screenplay follows the plot of Joji Tsubota's children's book about two brothers, Zenta and Sanpei. Their childhood world of loving parents and carefree pleasures turns into a sad nightmare when the police arrive to arrest their father. He is jailed, charged with embezzlement. Hard times quickly follow. Their mother is forced to get a job. The brothers are separated, the younger, Sanpei, being sent to live with an uncle. The rest of the story focuses on the boy's determination to return home. In the end, he and his brother prove their father's innocence.

Here at the outset Shimizu made inspired use of a rubric that would become his trademark. He had a gift for getting children to act naturally, especially in the outdoor settings that figure in most people's notion of idyllic childhood. This is not to say that Shimizu stages fuzzy, cute scenarios. His effects are balanced between realistic views of the regrettable forces at work in the lives of children and those moments of redeeming joy we all remember—and that this director locates mostly in nature.

Masao Hayama (l) and Bakudan Kozo (r) in *Children in the Wind* (1937) directed by Hiroshi Shimizu. Courtesy of the Kawakita Memorial Film Institute.

Children in the Wind begins in an alleyway outside the brothers' house. Sanpei comes out and heads down the alley to the back of the screen. He is the leader of his gang of small boys. His rival, Kintaro, is shown hanging back alone, then tagging along.

A series of dollying shots, all taken from a distance, show the children at their innocent play, as if caught unaware by the camera's watchful eye. They run across a field and swim in the river. Their restless motions are caught—now here, now there—by the camera's panning. We get a sense of children in perfect harmony with nature, their joie de vivre as yet unspoiled by knowledge of the growing world.

Though the scene is perfectly ordinary, its details prepare us for what is to come. Kintaro's exclusion from the happy group anticipates the crisis even then developing. His father is a stockholder of the factory managed by Sanpei's father. Kintaro's father takes over by falsely accusing Sanpei's father of embezzlement.

The alleyway returns as the scene of a bitter loss of innocence, thanks to a gain in experience. After Sanpei's father is taken away by the police, we see him standing alone in the lower front of the screen. Now he, not Kintaro, is the one left behind. In the distance, where the alley joins the street, he sees his rival playing with the gang.

A final scene uses the same real-world "set" to show a reversal of power now that the crisis is resolved. Kintaro's father has been arrested. Kintaro is seen alone once again.

The alley localizes our sense of Sanpei's growth through experience, child though he is. The last several shots ironically reinforce a sense of clear division between the worlds of children and adults. Sanpei invites Kintaro to join their gang. Shimizu affirms that this reconciliation, so unlikely in the grown-up world, is in fact a premonition of inevitable change as these small ones grow up to become knowledgeable and tragically fallible adults.

In 1939, Shimizu used another children's book by Joji Tsubota for *Kodomo no shiki* (Four seasons of childhood). Again the novel and the two-part film share the plot concerning two young brothers in the familiar narrative scheme of stability, upset, struggle, and resolution. This time, however, the action encompasses not just one summer but a full year. Each narrative element is charged with more variation than in *Children in the Wind*.

The causal chain is expanded by a sudden disclosure of withheld information. The same two small brothers, Zenta and Sanpei, are living happily in their village. They make friends with Ono, a kindly old man in a neighboring village. His benevolent wisdom suggests an idyllic link between the worlds of children and grown-ups. Another stage of enrichment comes with the revelation that Ono is in fact their grandfather. By getting to know him, they have healed an old family rift: their father's disinheritance caused by his marrying without his father's approval.

What might have been a happy ending turns into a crisis when the boys' father dies suddenly. Even so, Part 2 begins on a happier note. Ono has managed to take his grandsons in. Yet another crisis arises when the greedy villain, Rokai, takes control of the family's factory. He seizes it as collateral for a debt the boys' late father owed.

The film, like the novel, shows these innocent children effecting a reconciliation out of the reach of warring adults. Unlike the gang in *Children in the Wind*, who merely reflect the adult power struggle in their play, this film's children behave with a generosity that contrasts sharply with the malice of the grown-up world. Despite the misery Rokai has caused them and their family, Zenta and Sanpei continue to play with the villain's son. Moreover, the son upbraids his father for taking possession of his two friends' toys. In the end, harmony is restored once more.

Again Shimizu's cinematic rubric takes charge in his portrayal of the children, especially in distant dollying shots creating a vision of their happy play together. The camera follows them outdoors, gliding along to capture views of their joyous games in the open air of the countryside.

Children in the Wind and *Four Seasons of Childhood* established Shimizu as a master of the children's film genre to which he would devote his life. Having discovered his talent for using children as main characters, he sought out amateurs, sometimes recruiting street urchins.

Koji Shima was another notable director in this genre. His *Kaze no Matasaburo* (Matasaburo the wind god, 1940) was adapted from a Kenji Miyazawa story published in 1931 in the periodical *Jido bungaku* (Children's literature).

Shima was attracted to the author's use of local color in a style that mixes realism and symbolism.

The story itself is simple. A new boy joins the class in a little country school. Matasaburo is a stranger from the north and has red hair. At first, the children do not know what to think. Then they become friends and share escapades, mostly outdoors. Then Matasaburo has to leave.

Miyazawa sets his story in his own hometown in Iwate Prefecture. His children are children of nature, very much at home in their rural landscape. Matasaburo's red hair earns him a place in their world of childhood fantasy. He becomes the personification of the wind in this windy part of Japan.

Miyazawa's stylistic élan comes to the fore in a dream one of the children has. Wandering alone in a field of tall grass billowing and gleaming in the wind, he snuggles down and falls asleep. In the child's dream, Matasaburo flies in a transparent cape, wearing shoes of shining glass. He wakes to find a horse standing over him.

That sudden switch from fantasy to reality would trigger no end of special effects in a film today. Shima's mix of the two owes much to his gift for telling detail and picturesque scenario. Like Shimizu, he also knows how to make the most of country life. The critic Tadao Sato has observed that Shima was success-

Kazumasa Hoshino (l) and Akihiko Katayama (r) in *Matasaburo The Wind God* (1940) directed by Koji Shima. Courtesy of the Kawakita Memorial Film Institute.

ful in "a leisurely description of the children's curiosity about and admiration for the unknown in a simple yet poetic environment."[15]

Shima also adds deft acoustical touches to his use of the visual properties of cinema.[16] As Matasaburo flies, he is accompanied by soaring music, which halts the instant the dreamer awakens. Mist that had gathered over the sleeping child vanishes in that instant, too.

Shima's *Jiro monogatari* (The story of Jiro, 1941) was adapted from a novel by Kojin Shimamura. It was published in five parts beginning in 1936. A sixth part was left unfinished at Shimamura's death after the war.

Shima's screenplay is based on the first two parts published in 1936 and 1937. These best-known parts of the work depict Shimamura's own sadly unhappy childhood. Born into a wealthy family, Jiro is raised by three different mothers. Soon after his birth, he is sent to foster parents because his mother is ill. He returns home at the age of four, but his invalid mother dies when he is ten. When he is twelve, his father remarries.

Shimamura's theme of a child unhappily adrift changes somewhat in Shima's film. The director concentrates on the child's attachment to his foster mother and his gradual awakening to his real mother's affection. The strength of this approach lies in its transfer to the screen of Shimamura's sensitive portrayal of a lonely child's emotions.

Like Hiroshi Shimizu, Shima had a knack for casting amateurs in his films. He, too, had a gift for eliciting unself-conscious performances. Both directors knew how to limit dialogue and stage-managed speech and facial expressions. It was clearly better working to arrange a situation in which a child could just "act naturally."[17]

Here we follow a lonely child around in a rural landscape. We watch Jiro take his place outdoors, a child of nature, whatever his family ties. Long shots show him climbing a tree, playing with a goat, picking his nose with rapt attention. Sadao Sato notes that Jiro's ambivalent attitude toward his birth mother is suggested simply but powerfully in a scene drawn from perfectly ordinary family life.[18]

In this case, Shima dramatizes the mother/child relationship by calling on a basic given of Japanese life in the country. It is a summer night, time to go to bed. The room partitions have been removed so that air can circulate—a common practice, especially in the country. Jiro's room is next to his invalid mother's. She is in bed, as she usually is. He wants to be close to her, but he does not know how to ask. Finally, he lies down and rolls slowly from his room into hers. A close-up of her face seen from his perspective shows tears rolling down her cheeks. This simple scene enlists our sense of sharing the child's feeling of closeness, his new awareness of his mother's emotion. Not a word is spoken. Yet Shima clearly communicates the child's sense of having bridged the emotional gap opened up by long separation from his mother.

One of the film's most memorable moments depicts Jiro's strong attachment to his foster mother, Ohama, played by Haruko Sugimura. After an interval of

Yukihiko Sugi (l) and Chieko Murata (r) in *The Story of Jiro* (1941) directed by Koji Shima. Courtesy of the Kawakita Memorial Film Institute.

separation, they are reunited in a scene that resolves the drama in this work. It is a local shrine festival, a nighttime celebration complete with festive music, fire-crackers, and stalls of vendors selling all manner of treats and toys. It is one of those occasions of delirious childhood joy—and Jiro is enjoying it with the "mother" he loves best.

The scene is shot in one long take. The camera pauses while Ohama buys Jiro a fox mask. Then it follows their progress through the crowd. It stops when Jiro drops his mask in a puddle and Ohama retrieves it for him. The camera pans to take in the lion dance attracting their attention. It is performed on a makeshift stage. Ohama and Jiro take their places in the closed scene captured by the camera's long gaze. No close-up of the woman and child is necessary. The scene itself speaks for Jiro's childlike joy in this unforgettable feast of delights.

His waking next morning also speaks for the keenness of his suffering, his sense of deception, of betrayal. Because Ohama is nowhere to be found. Here the camera cuts from room to room to follow his increasingly troubled search. A lateral pan speaks for his sense of a world so suddenly empty.

Overhearing his mother and grandmother talking, he learns the truth. Ohama has left for a new life far away. The camera follows the boy's desperate search outside. The scene ends on a country bridge. The camera shows the fox mask floating downstream, then over a waterfall. As the music on the sound track swells, we understand the boy's final gesture.

Bungei-eiga of excellent quality continued to appear despite the pressures of censorship and the general turmoil tightening its grip on Japan and the world at large. Viewed in retrospect, two works stand out as representative of the best that was achieved in "pure literature" cinema: Kozaburo Yoshimura's *Danryu* (Warm currents, 1939), and Tomu Uchida's *Tsuchi* (The earth, 1939).

Warm Currents was possibly the last adaptation from literature that celebrated an intellectual woman's struggle to define her own mode of life in a society opposed to that freedom. The film script was based on the playwright Kunio Kishida's 1938 novel serialized in *The Asahi*. Deeply imbued with the principles of French avant-garde theater, Kishida was very active in modernizing the Japanese theater. He translated Jules Renard's plays and wrote many himself, becoming an established figure in Japanese romanticism. As a novelist, he was affiliated with *Shinkankakuha* (New Sense School), a literary group whose members included Yasunari Kawabata and Riichi Yokomitsu.

Kishida described his *Warm Currents* this way:

> The theme of this novel has to do with the beauty and the ugliness in our lives, caught up as we are in a conflict between the real and the ideal. I am not promoting any "new ethic." I want to answer this question: How can feelings rooted in tradition manifest themselves in this turbulent modern age?[19]

Kishida's central characters have internalized that conflict. The hero, Hibiki, a self-made businessman, is called back from Taiwan by his former boss, whose poor management has brought a hospital to the brink of ruin. Hibiki comes to the rescue out of a traditional sense of obligation to the man he once worked for.

Having done his duty by coming to the rescue, Hibiki finds himself embroiled in a rather modern romantic conflict involving two women. Keiko is his former boss's daughter. She is a decidedly modern woman with a decidedly modern view of marriage. She rejects the traditional arranged marriage that women of her age and social class had been brought up to expect. She follows her heart, dissolving an engagement when she finds herself less than passionately inclined to her fiancé.

Still, the novelist Kishida is also a romantic playwright. He attributes Keiko's steadfast individualism in part to her samurai forebears. Furthermore, her disinclination to wed her fiancé, Hibiki, is not that absolute. She does love him in some sense, but she sacrifices him out of a sense of obligation to her friend Gin.

Gin is a nurse, and in some respects she is a modern woman, too. She claims her due as a professional, and protests to the hospital management when a colleague is reprimanded for dating one of the patients. But deep down, and in spite of herself, Gin is Keiko's opposite. Gin wants to be guided by love, by personal inclination, not submission to duty. But, as Kishida is at pains to make clear, this quest for love is different from the Western woman's pursuit of emancipated ego. This love via personal inclination (this is a novel, remember) is part and parcel of the traditional Japanese woman's blind devotion to the man she loves.

Hibiki is stung by Keiko's refusal of his offer of marriage, but he is not entirely unwilling to transfer his affections to Gin, which Keiko urges him to do.

The melodramatic strain in the plot is redeemed by Kishida's psychological insight into his characters and a vivid portrayal of the manners and mores of Japanese society in the 1930s. His novel is also rich in period detail related to actual historical events

The young scriptwriter Kozaburo Yoshimura was commissioned to adapt Kishida's novel after the veteran Yasujiro Shimazu opted out. Yoshimura, like Kishida, has to dramatize "the essentially Western manner of love" as practiced by a new generation seeking to "accommodate it in the Japanese cultural ambiance."[20]

Given the nature of Japanese society at the time, Kishida offered his reader a reassuringly contemporary background for character drama played out in unfamiliar psychological territory. That done, the novelist working in words could enlist the reader's interest in an in-depth analysis of characters whose motives and actions looked strangely eclectic.

Yoshimura, working on screen, set the psychological complications aside in favor of the clearly delineated action-reaction of romance-melodrama. After all, that was Shochiku Studio's mainstream stock in trade. Yoshimura relied on the expressive power of the camera, and on the experienced scriptwriter Tadao Ikedo, whose love scenes are charged with a refreshingly vivid exchange of dialogue.

Fashion also has its say in this film. We see how businessmen, professional women, and upper-class ladies dress in support of their real-life roles. A number of scenes contrast a woman in traditional kimono with Keiko's clear preference for fashionable Western clothes. The camera is studiously attentive to every detail of her expensive tailored suits and boldly assertive hats. One can well imagine the largely female audience of 1939 holding its breath, not knowing quite what to make of this brave new world of Japanese femininity.

As if that were not enough, Yoshimura also has a way of posing Keiko against a background with some unmistakable sign of the Western world in it. She drinks coffee in a modern coffee shop. Through the plate-glass window behind her, we catch a glimpse of a cathedral.

The sound track is also given to touches of Western innuendo. Strains of a Chopin etude steal in as Keiko decides not to marry Hibiki after all. Altogether, Yoshimura is exposing his audience to just the sort of thing the censors would shortly be condemning as "too overtly exotic."

Worse is to come. When Keiko breaks her engagement, she does it in a manner quite unlike the traditional scene depicting tender feminine regrets in domestic surroundings. She walks into her fiancé's office and breaks with him quite frankly.

That same coffee shop is home to another confrontation one might expect to take place in more intimate surroundings. This time a traditional Japanese woman versus a Japanese woman of the future is portrayed. Keiko and Gin meet and confront the fact that they both love the same man. It does not matter to Gin that Hibiki treats her like any boss treats an underling. She loves him and wants to serve him accordingly. Even though Keiko has decided to give him up, and Gin is her friend, she is painfully aware of being still a rival for his love.

Yoshimura underscores this element of paradox with a series of insistent close-ups. At one point he fills the screen with each woman's face in blow-up. The contrast is unmistakable. Gin's love is traditional, humble and sincere. Keiko's is defiantly proud, even in defeat.

Here, too, clothing underscores the theme. Gin wears a kimono; Keiko has on a high-fashion Western outfit, this time with a chic beret. Again, the camera flashes to the image of a cathedral. Again, Chopin returns. The camera settles into a medium-long take of the women facing one another across the table. Gin says that she will be content just to continue working for Hibiki in the hospital. He may be distant, even hard, but never mind. Her happiness lies in just being near him.

The viewer today may be tempted to enjoy an ironic touch not present to audiences in 1939. Yoshimura is just balancing the equation required by his theme. We see this later when Keiko returns to the office to break with Hibiki, thereby setting him free to respond to the passive advances of her friend.

Tadao Sato has noted that Japanese romantic cinema is apt to fall silent when the time comes for a male to declare his love. He suggests that the traditional code of male conduct does not allow much direct verbal thrust.[21]

Warm Currents offers an interesting break with tradition in this respect. After Keiko breaks off their engagement, Hibiki leaves his office and returns home. He finds Gin there and offers to escort her home. As they draw near, she suggests that they walk on a bit farther. Hibiki says that he will walk anywhere as long as he is with "his wife." Gin, overjoyed, asks him to repeat what he has said. She asks politely, calling him "Sir." Hibiki chides her for that, then says, "I said, 'my wife.'" He also confesses that Keiko has rejected him.

The element of spontaneity in Hibiki's declaration does not survive in English translation. Neither does the touch of discretion that prevents it from seeming condescending. One might say that sincerity meets sincerity here in a manner distinctly Japanese. Certainly this little exchange is one of the most memorably refreshing love scenes in Japanese cinema. Another that comes to mind is in Tadashi Imai's *Mata au hi made* (Until the day we meet, 1950). There, the lovers kiss good-bye with a windowpane between them.

In *Warm Currents*, novel and film have very different endings. Kishida's concern to reconcile the opposing forces at work in his story leads him to conclude with an image of an old woman's courage. She is, in fact, Keiko's mother. Born to privilege, she has seen the family fortune vanish, her husband die, herself reduced to poverty. She is living out her days with Keiko in a small town far away from Tokyo.

Hibiki has come to visit, bringing his fiancé, Gin. She will stay a while in order to learn the housewifely arts required by her new social status. The novel ends as Hibiki, Gin, and Keiko watch the old lady walk across a bridge, carrying a heavy shopping bag. This woman who lived all her life waited on by servants and driven by a chauffeur is now reduced to this. And yet she faces the future with confidence and dignity.

Yoshimura's closes with an image of much younger courage—with Keiko, Japan's new woman, played by the stylish and beautiful Mieko Takamine. She is determined to face the world on her own terms, even as she concedes defeat in love. How to express her feelings on screen without a novelist's flow of words?

Yoshimura shows her meeting Hibiki on the beach to say good-bye. She congratulates him on his engagement to Gin, then turns to the ocean. The camera studies her closely. It takes note of her shapely legs, snug in a skirt. Then her face, bathed in tears. The camera cuts to waves coming ashore. Keiko dips her hands and wets her face and then turns to smile beautifully, bravely, at Hibiki, waiting on the sand. Another shot shows her joining him briefly, then walking on alone. The Chopin etude returns, this time to swell in full symphonic version. The camera follows in a diagonal shot as Keiko wanders on, a solitary figure on the edge of the ocean's immensity.

Yoshimura's film created something of a sensation among younger viewers, who thought of him as helping to create their "new generation." College students debated this question: "Which woman do you prefer, Keiko or Gin?"

Equally thought-provoking was another question addressed by a critic at the time of the film's release:

> Very few films to date have dealt with the aspect of competition in the male world of business. This is a kind of standing block in the growth of Japanese cinema. However, *Warm Currents*, adapted from Kunio Kishida's novel, touches on the subject when it shows Yuzo Hibiki struggling to manage a hospital.[22]

Tomu Uchida's *The Earth* offers an especially telling example of literature and cinema coming together in a notable film despite all the pressures created by studio bosses anxious to please an increasingly officious censorship. The script was based on Takashi Nagatsuka's novel *Tsuchi* (The earth) which first appeared as a serial in the *Tokyo Asahi* in 1911–12. This monumental novel in the *nomin bungaku*, or agricultural genre, is still considered a masterpiece of modern Japanese literature.

Like "naturalistic" French novels of the nineteenth century, *The Earth* offers a "slice of life" view of its subject. Like many of those novels, it details a progress of grinding poverty among peasants considered virtually indistinguishable from the earth and its seasons. Only Nature herself (personified thus) has the power to rise above a human condition reduced to basics this grim. What small consolation there is derives from the idea that decay and death in Nature are part of a cycle that includes rebirth and renewal. Meantime, the brighter side of that cycle is seen in human nature, too, if only piecemeal, in glimpses quickly lost sight of as the way of the world continues darkly chaotic.

Nagatsuka's story is set in the early twentieth century, at a time of severe agricultural depression in Japan. Hardship follows hardship as Kanji's little family sinks deeper into poverty for reasons beyond their control.

The story is set in motion when Kanji's wife, Oshina, dies. She has supported the family at home by peddling tofu while he worked elsewhere as a seasonal

Mieko Takamine (l) and Shin Saburi (r) in *Warm Currents* (1939) directed by Kozaburo Yoshimura. Courtesy of the Kawakita Memorial Film Institute.

laborer. Now he is stuck where there is little work. The mother's burden falls on their sixteen-year-old daughter, Otsuji. There is a younger brother to tend and work on their little plot of land. Soon Kanji is caught stealing vegetables and firewood to make ends meet.

The seasons come and go in a rhythm of scant harvest and hungry waiting. Still, they work hard and things look up briefly. Then Oshina's father, Uhei, comes to them. He is no longer able to work. All it takes is one old man to tip the scale again.

Uhei and Kanji are not on speaking terms. Then a fire destroys the family's shabby house and the old man's shack nearby. Uhei feels responsible and attempts to hang himself. This act of compunction brings the family together again. And so they struggle on.

The narrative events unfold chronologically, with numbers of detours into past memory. Piece by piece the picture completes itself. Only after the funeral do we learn that Oshina died of tetanus caused by a self-induced abortion. Almost every family memory is a tale of human misery.

Nagatsuka takes great pains to present Otsuji as a paragon of goodness, purity, and perseverance. It is she who holds the family together. Compassion is her strong point. After the fire, she gently caresses her brother's burned head, her grandfather's burned cheek. She never asks how the fire broke out.

This seems dark, unpromising stuff for cinema, but Uchida had a history of success with *bungei-eiga* based on complex works of literature. In 1936, he had adapted Shiro Ozaki's *The Theater of Life*. The next year, he did Yutaka Mafune's *Hadaka no machi* (Naked town). Then he took on *Kagirinaki zenshin* (Unending advance), based on a magazine serial written by the director Yasujiro Ozu and then turned into a screenplay by the renowned scriptwriter Yasutaro Yagi. This film was praised for being a *"bungei-eiga* liberated from the original novel."[23] All these films got good reviews. *Kinema jumpo* put *Naked Town* in fifth place on its list of the best films of 1937. *Unending Advance* was chosen number one.

Characters were drawn from a variety of social and professional backgrounds in these films, but Uchida's focus was the same throughout. He was consistently concerned to present the lives of individuals "left behind in the progress of the times and fraught with the feelings of defeat and frustration."[24]

In *The Earth,* Uchida extended that concern to those least likely to catch up with progress in an age of industrialization: poor peasants in bondage to the land. Uchida had planned to adapt Nagatsuka's novel in 1936, after he finished *The Theater of Life*. He wanted to work on a theme of "the life of rice."

While he was still formulating his plans, the novel was adapted for two other venues. In October 1937 a stage version of *The Earth* was presented by the Shin-Tsukiji Troupe. In May of that year director Kenji Mizoguchi collaborated with scriptwriter Yoshikata Yoda on a radio drama. Mizoguchi wanted to make a film as well, but the project fell through.[25]

Uchida himself had a hard time getting support for his project. The Nikkatsu Tamagawa Studio had been doing *bungei-eiga* since 1935, thanks to the enthusiasm of its head, Kanichi Negishi. He supported Uchida now, too, but the film ran into serious trouble after shooting had begun. Some of the studio's top brass felt certain that government censors would come down hard on a film depicting landlords in conflict with tenants. They also thought the public would never pay to see helpless peasants living miserable lives.

The balance was tipped in Uchida's favor by a broad base of support from studio staff, including the other directors. Shooting resumed on a set built in a rice paddy not far from the studio grounds. The film took a year and a half to complete, partly because the changing seasons played the same important role they did in the novel.

The print that has been preserved has been cut somewhat. Some footage is missing at the very end. Still, it shows that Uchida followed Nagatsuka's narrative fairly consistently. Most of the major events in the life of Kanji's family are presented in relation to the cooperative ventures of a farming community: rice planting, harvests, and festivals.

Uchida's script adds an important scene showing peasant girls who work as laborers in a silk mill. This was a direct reference to a form of servitude clearly related to the dismal effect on the poor of Japan's push to become a capital-driven industrial economy. The scene was shot on location at Nagatsuka's birthplace.

The approach throughout could be called quasi documentary. The camera is clearly attempting to record the life of Kanji's family in convincing detail. We witness the hardships they endure from man and nature, too.

We see father and daughter exhaust themselves with buckets of water in a futile attempt to save their rice crop in time of drought. Varying shot sizes appear anxious to capture every detail of their struggle. We see muscles knotting in their legs as they trudge over difficult terrain. A long shot of Otsuji bending under the weight of a basket offers a glimpse of this young girl's weary strength. Deep focus on her motion from screen top to bottom measures the distance she has to walk in the blazing sun.

A medium shot follows Kanji yoked to buckets swaying from the bamboo pole laid across his shoulders. The most citybound viewer can see the cost to muscle and bone of this primitive method of irrigation, the only method available to peasants as poor as these.

A series of close-ups of the ground itself shows buckets of water vanishing in earth whose thirst is clearly unquenchable by any such means. An extreme long shot suggests that these two human figures are as natural as clods in this hard fought battle to win a living from difficult soil. Even so, there are grateful moments, too. The sight and sound of water in a paddy doing well, at least for now, shows dogged persistence paying off—at least a little.

Isamu Kosugi (l) and Akiko Kazami (r) in *The Earth* (1939) directed by Tomu Uchida. Courtesy of the Kawakita Memorial Film Institute.

We know from contemporary accounts that the missing end of the film did offer a ray of hope—more than Nagatsuka could think to offer. Apparently, Kanji's family is seen clearing a field in a forest. Even Uhei is doing his part, tending the cooking pot. A lark nearby is singing.

Uchida's many collaborators in the studio reaped the rewards of their long-sustained effort. Despite its unglamorous subject, *The Earth* was a box-office hit. It ran three weeks. (Hits finished faster in the 1930s.) *Kinema jumpo* voted it the best picture of the year. It received the Ministry of Education award. Film critic Taihei Imamura appeared to be speaking for many in the audience at the time when he wrote:

> *The Earth* lets you know what it feels like to be a dirt-poor peasant struggling to be what he is and nothing else. I have never seen the sweaty, sun-burned face of a peasant up close. . . . The number of films made about poor farmers is dismally small—all out of proportion to their numbers everywhere in the world. These people are not real for many of us. Film-goers in every country should thank Tomu Uchida for showing us the real thing.[26]

Bungei-eiga flourished for such a short time before cinema was swallowed up by a world at war. Yet, looking back, one cannot help but be impressed by the breadth and depth of this genre, thanks to the numbers of fine writers and directors it brought together. Brief as its flourishing was, this show of literature transformed on screen made a major contribution to cinema history. Any comparison of these films with those made earlier clearly shows how important *bungei-eiga* were in developing greater maturity and sophistication in many of their directors.

As we see in Chapter 3, the *junbungaku* movement paved the way for another Golden Age of cinema after the war, in a very different social and cultural climate in Japan.

Notes

1. Joseph Anderson and Donald Richie, *The Japanese Film: Art and Industry*, expanded ed. (Princeton: Princeton University Press, 1983), p. 122.
2. Motohiko Fujita, *Nihon eiga gendaishi: Showa junendai* (The modern history of Japanese cinema: 1935–45) (Tokyo: Kashinsha, 1977), p. 34.
3. Tadao Sato, "*Horoki*" (On a Vagabond's song), in *Nihon eiga sakuhin zenshu* (A complete collection of Japanese films) (Tokyo: Kinema Jumpo, 1974), p. 234. For an English translation of excerpts from the original story, see Elizabeth Hanson, trans. "A Vagabond's Song," in *To Live and to Write: Selections by Japanese Women Writers 1913–1938*, ed. Yukiko Tanaka (Seattle: Seal Press, 1987), pp. 104–25.
4. For a more intensive study of *Poppy*, see Keiko McDonald, *Mizoguchi* (Boston: Twayne, 1984), pp. 34–36.
5. Motohiko Fujita, *Nihon eigashi no soshutsu: Jidai o utsusu kagami* (A history of Japanese cinema in the making: The mirror that reflects the era) (Tokyo: Goryu Shoin, 1983), p. 51.
6. Sachio Togata, quoted in ibid., p. 52.
7. Quoted in ibid., p. 53.

8. Fujita, *Nihon eiga gendaishi*, pp. 34–35.
9. For a study of Uchida's 1968 adaptation of this Ozaki novel, see Keiko McDonald, "The Yakuza Film: An Introduction," in *Reframing Japanese Cinema: Authorship, Genre and History*, ed. Arthur Nolletti Jr. and David Desser (Bloomington: Indiana University Press, 1988), pp. 165–92.
10. Toshimi Aoyama, "*Ani imoto*" (Older brother, and younger sister) in *Nihon eiga sakuhin zenshu*, p. 31.
11. For an English translation of this work, see "Akanishi Kakita," in *The Paper Doll and Other Stories*, trans. Lane Dunlop (San Francisco: North Point Press, 1987, pp. 65–81.
12. Tadao Sato, *Nihon eiga no kyoshotachi* (The master directors of Japanese cinema) (Tokyo: Gakuyo Shobo, 1979), p. 409.
13. For a study of the influence of *Grand Hotel* on Japanese cinema, see Kikuo Yamamoto, *Nihon eiga ni okeru gaikoku eiga no eikyo: hikaku eigashi kenkyu* (The influence of foreign films on Japanese cinema: film history: a comparative study) (Tokyo: Waseda Daigaku, 1983), pp. 522–27.
14. Akira Shimizu, "*Utsukushiki Taka*" (A beautiful hawk), in *Nihon eiga sakuhin zenshu*, p. 37.
15. For a study of wartime government censorship, see Anderson and Richie, *The Japanese Film*, pp. 128–30; Junichiro Tanaka, *Nihon eiga hattatsushi* (History of the development of Japanese cinema), vol. 3 (Tokyo: Chuo Koron, 1976), pp. 11–26; and Kyoko Hirano, *Mr. Smith Goes to Tokyo: Japanese Cinema under the American Occupation, 1945–1952* (Washington, D.C., and London: Smithsonian Institute, 1992), pp. 13–17.
16. For a study of his use of acoustics in his *Yamasanzo* (Mountain shrine path, 1942), see Taihei Imamura, *Nihon eiga no honshitsu* (The essence of Japanese cinema), reprinted ed., vol. 3 of *Imamura Taihei eiga hyoron* (A collection of Taihei Imamura's critical essays on film). (Tokyo: Yumani Shobo, 1991), pp. 95–97. The original volume was published in 1943.
17. Sato, *Nihon eiga no kyoshotachi*, p. 94.
18. Ibid., pp. 93–94.
19. Quoted by Tadasumi Imamura in "Koki" (Appendix) of vol. 13 of *Kishida Kunio zenshu* (A complete collection of Kunio Kishida's works) (Tokyo: Iwanami, 1991), p. 293.
20. Tadao Sato, *Nihon eigashi* (The history of Japanese cinema) vol. 2 (Tokyo: Iwanami, 1995), p. 17.
21. Ibid., pp. 16–17.
22. Takamaro Shimaji, ed. *Sekai no eiga sakka: Nihon eigashi* (Film directors of the world: the history of Japanese cinema), vol. 31 (Tokyo: Kinema Jumpo, 1976). p. 105.
23. Fujita Makoto, *Nihon eigashi no soshutsu*, p. 57,
24. Ibid.
25. For more information, see "*Tsuchi*" (The earth), in *Uchida Tomu kantoku tokushu* (Retrospective on Uchida Tomu), vol. 90 (Tokyo: Film Center, 1992), p. 37.
26. Imamura Taihei, *Eiga to bunka* (Cinema and culture), Reprinted Edition, vol. 3 of *Imamura Taihei eizo hyoron*, pp. 150–51. The original volume was published in 1940.

3

More Freedoms, More Troubles: 1951–1959

Economic, political, and cultural factors all joined forces to effect a remarkable growth in Japanese cinema in the early 1950s. The film industry was not left out of the decade's economic miracle, which was especially favored by the flow of procurements during the Korean War (1950–53). New construction soon restored the number of theaters to the prewar figure of 2,641. By 1959, that number had nearly tripled to 7,401.

The return to national independence with the San Francisco Peace Treaty of 1951 had a direct effect on the development of both artistic and popular cinema. For example, *jidaigeki*, especially the swashbuckling *chambara* variety, returned to captivate an audience hungry for a genre forbidden during the Occupation, when feudal subjects were banned.

In *gendaigeki* (contemporary drama), release from Supreme Commander for the Allied Powers' (SCAP) strict censorship and guidelines also offered film-makers new flexibility in their choice of subject matter. Many directors turned to contemporary themes, some playing to antiwar sentiments, others to the conflict between individualism and pressure for social conformity,

The four major existing firms (Toho, shin-Toho, Daiei, and Shochiku) were joined at this critical juncture by another, the Tokyo Eiga Company, commonly called Toei. Toei was to make valuable contributions to popular cinema, putting into effect a demanding new market strategy of double features of medium-length films.

Bungei-eiga prospered side by side with popular cinema. Modern literary works provided a wealth of sources for filmmakers anxious to explore themes consonant with the rapid social and cultural transformation under way in Japan.

The experience of war on the battlefront and at home had been sensitive topics during the Occupation; now, filmmakers old and new were anxious to address it as a major theme. Another and equally significant range of themes dealt with questions related to coming to terms with a changing postwar society. Women's issues became especially relevant to a female audience expected to benefit greatly from a new constitution that altered women's roles in fundamental ways, at least on paper.[1]

Kurosawa's *Rashomon* marked the beginning of a Golden Age in the sense that it awakened the international audience to the rich heritage of the Japanese cinematic tradition. A great deal has been written about Kurosawa's adaptation of two short stories: Ryunosuke Akutagawa's "Yabu no Naka" (In the grove) and "Rashomon."[2] Still, one can hardly mention his achievement without pausing to consider the sure touch he brings to adapting these two works.

In "In the Grove," Akutagawa invests the Rashomon gate with multiple meanings. A dismissed servant leaves by way of the gate of his master's house—a fit symbol for the life of a law-abiding citizen. In contrast, the Rashomon gate, once a glorious southern entrance to the capital, is shown degraded, serving as a hideout for thieves and petty criminals. Unclaimed corpses are also abandoned there. The gate has become a world in itself, a microcosm representing the religious, moral, and political chaos prevailing in twelfth-century Japan.

The gate also symbolizes the boundary between two worlds: an entrance from one level of existence to another. The servant, waiting for a break in the rain, must decide what he will do with his life. Does he emerge from the gate morally intact or corrupted? This is the central question posed by the author. Akutagawa shows the man passing through a series of moral conflicts. By the time he vanishes into the depths of night, his descent into the bestial is complete.

Kurosawa's film retains the original symbolic function of the gate. But he enriches it with a contemporary comparison—with the chaos of postwar Japan. Akutagawa's ruined gate, like the servant's flawed complexion, speaks for a world deformed beyond redemption. Kurosawa insists on a ray of hope, though signifying it ironically by means of a gargoyle and a signboard still intact in blinding rain.

Kurosawa is a moralist whose premise of a tortured, fragmented world leads to a question demanding a committed inquiry: 'Where is the basis for hope of renewal to be found?' The second version of the woodcutter's story and the final sequence, both added by the director, serve as possible answers. The woodcutter's decision to adopt the abandoned baby is clearly altruistic, clearly a means to save a fallen society. Moreover, this redeeming instance of a compassionate individual obviously takes the place of institutional responses, as evidenced by the priest in this tale.

The 1950s also saw new and important work by another veteran director, Mizoguchi. This was a case of a filmmaker returning to a theme he had pursued throughout his career: the plight of women. All the more reason to adapt contemporary Japanese fiction to his purposes. He began with *Yuki Fujin ezu* (A picture of Madame Yuki, 1950), based on the then current bestseller by Seiichi Funahashi.[3]

The story is set in a postwar Japan seething with social and moral change. All distinctions of class have been abolished, especially those reflecting aristocratic privilege. Both the novel and the film follow the declining fortunes of the beautiful heiress Yuki, daughter of a count, whose title, like all titles, now means nothing. Further conflict derives from women's new freedom from traditional constraints. Yuki is torn, body and soul, as she feels constrained to choose between her sexually captivating husband and a classical platonic relationship with a novelist.

Funahashi's success was based on a category of fiction called *kanno shosetsu* (erotic novels or novels about sexuality). His account of Yuki's conflict focuses on the subtly erotic overtones of an affair described in terms of manners and mores of an aristocracy clearly in the last stages of refining itself out of existence.

Mizoguchi and his screenwriter Yoda were more interested in adapting this tale to a *Zeitgeist* with a future in postwar Japan. Accordingly, they shifted their emphasis from Yuki to the decidedly less tentative soul searching of the male protagonist, a middle-class novelist—changed to a *koto* teacher in the film. (He was played by Ken Uehara, the best-looking actor then playing roles in the soft-touch tradition.)

A more vigorous source of conflict in the film derives from another unmistakably postwar touch. Yuki and her husband turn out to be too incorrigibly high class not to be swindled out of their property by two up-and-coming vulgarians, the singer Ayako (mistress of Yuki's husband) and her manager, Tateoka.

It follows that Yuki's loss of faith in husband and lover should lead to her suicide. She can find no other way to resolve her conflict; there is no other escape from the vulgar materialism of this new postwar world in which people like Tateoka and Ayako will prevail.

Mizugochi's turned next to Tanizaki's novella *Ashikari* (The reaper of rushes). It became *Oyusama* (Miss Oyu, 1951). Novella and film both treat the heroine, Oyu, as a modern-day prototype of a Heian lady: a woman of the higher class, beautiful, elegant, and accomplished.

But, film and fiction part company when it comes to mode of narration. Tanizaki's views of Oyu are oblique, as if he means to ask us to see her through an ancient gauze curtain. He makes use of layer upon layer of narrative types. A narrator-traveler watches at a distance, while a *koto* recital is held at a mansion in the country. Another equally distant observer, also on a journey, tells the narrator the story of Oyu. This second teller's account contains yet another version of Oyu's story, since he also offers his father's testimony related to him when he was a child.

Mizoguchi discards this complex evidence in favor of a straightforward account of Shinnosuke's infatuation with Oyu. Our access to the "mystery" of this woman is largely confined to the witness of a single character. Mizoguchi also creates his characteristically masterful atmosphere, enriching our vision of Miss Oyu through carefully selected props and exquisite sets designed by Hiroshi Mizutani. All this is seen through the fluid, sensitive camera work of Kazuo Miyagawa.[4]

The plight of women in a changing society returns as the theme of Mizoguchi's next film, *Musashino Fujin* (Lady Musashino, 1951). Here the issue is adultery. It was no longer a crime in postwar Japan, whose constitution abolished a number of such feudal constraints and punishments, especially as they pertained to women.

This filmscript drew on the work of the best-selling novelist Shohei Ooka. As we see in Chapter 5, Mizoguchi and Ooka approached this timely topic in radically different ways. The novelist made use of a detached, Stendhalian observer of human nature. Mizoguchi preferred direct involvement in the facts of any case involving a fallen woman and the sensual world in which her calamities were rooted.

Mizoguchi's next adaptation of modern literature was *Sansho Dayu* (Sansho the bailiff, 1954), based on a short story by Ogai Mori. This vision of society looks back to twelfth-century Japan, that "dark age when people did not fully know what it meant to be human."[5] Like Mizoguchi's classic *Ugetsu* (1953), this film depicts an individual's coming to terms with an oppressive feudal structure. The principles of addition and alteration are clearly at work in the process of transference. The short story and the film share the basic narrative pattern of separation, self-sacrifice, and reunion. Nevertheless, Mizoguchi gives a distinctly different flavor to dramatic high points such as the ordeal of brother and sister struggling to survive in Sansho's slave camp and the reunion between mother and son. He does this in order to accommodate the theme he labored on for so long: women sacrificed in a world understood as belonging to men.

In Ogai's story, a religious talisman in the shape of a small Buddhist statue works a kind of magic in service of Zushio and Anju, a brother and sister forced into slavery. As slaves, they are branded, but the talisman erases their scars. Mizoguchi omits that strain in the narrative, wanting to use Zushio's slavery as the medium for the boy's painfully slow and uncertain maturing and redemption. At first, long years of slavery change him for the worse. He obeys the ruthless master Sansho's order to brand an old slave who has failed to escape. Zushio is saved from becoming a monster by his sister in yet another classic Mizoguchi instance of man redeemed through woman's noble sacrifice.

Most importantly, Ogai's work ends on a positive note. Zushio, appointed provincial governor, announces the abolition of slavery and is reunited with his mother. Mizoguchi adds a tragic dimension. Ignoring Imperial opposition, Zushio frees the slaves and then resigns his position and sails to Sado, a remote island to which exiles are banished. In a final climactic scene, Mizoguchi's cinematic rubric, especially the tracking pan, resolves the film's thematic conflict. Zushio's mother, Tamaki, is shown as the pitiful thing she has become, blind, attempting to chase a bird with a stick near her tumbledown shack. She is calling out to her children. The camera tracks up to Zushio approaching his mother. A medium shot shows Tamaki touching the talisman Zushio carries (the Buddhist deity). A close-up studies their embrace. This happy/sad reunion is suddenly lifted to a plane of contemplative detachment as the camera moves left in order to show an old seaweed gatherer at work.

The film ends with a stasis: the beach with heaps of seaweed in windrows swept by the waves. This image finally consummates the various water images used earlier: the pond that engulfed Anju; the desolate ocean where the mother's cry for her children died away. This final shot returning to the sea invokes a rhythmic sense of life, of a natural order restored. While suggestive of the beginning of a new life for mother and son built on the wreckage of their experience, this final stasis invites a larger synthesis familiar to Japanese audiences: the universal principle of *mujo*, the passingness of all things human. This universal law transcends all human sense of loss, offering a way to balance the claims both of hope and despair.

Kurosawa and Mizoguchi may be considered the giants among directors who rose to the challenge of modern Japanese literature after the war. But another five directors were notable in this field as well: Keisuke Kinoshita, Seiji Hisamatsu, Mikio Naruse, Shiro Toyoda, and Kon Ichikawa.

Kinoshita, who had returned from France after long years of study, took a serious look at Japanese culture, especially its feudal remnants. *Onnna no sono* (Women's garden, 1954), was based on a Tomoji Abe novel titled *Jinko teien* (Man-made garden). Set in a women's college noted for a curriculum strong on fostering traditional virtues, the film concerns a student's suicide and the resultant turmoil on campus. The superintendent of a dormitory, a paragon of strict adherence to venerable rules and regulations, is pitted against students who represent postwar democratic values.

Yoshiko Kuga (l), Mieko Takamine (cl), Hideko Takamine (cr) and Keiko Kishi (r) in *Women's Garden* (1954) directed by Keisuke Kinoshita. Courtesy of the Kawakita Memorial Film Institute.

Hideko Takamine (c) in *Twenty-four Eyes* (1954) directed by Keisuke Kinoshita. Courtesy of the Kawakita Memorial Film Institute.

Kinoshita's next film, *Nijushi no hitomi* (Twenty-four eyes, 1954), was voted best picture of the year by *Kinema jumpo*. The script was adapted from a novel by Tsuboi Sakae.[6] Here the director took a much harsher line with traditional values. His film is, in effect, an indictment of Japanese imperialism, with its die-hard emphasis on the importance of self-sacrifice for women in their role as the weaker sex. Kinoshita uses melodrama to soften what otherwise might have become a work too politically charged.

The best-selling novel chronicled the life of an elementary school teacher, Oishi. Set on Shodo Island, the novelist's birthplace, the story takes place between 1929 and 1949. It concerns Oishi's assignment to a school with just twelve pupils. Her relationship with these children spans the tumultuous period of Japan's imperialist expansion marked by the China incident of 1937, the Tripartite Pact of 1940, and finally World War II. The ending brings the narrative pattern of solidarity-dissolution-solidarity full circle. Oishi returns to teaching after losing her husband and youngest child. She is reunited with the surviving members of the original twelve.

Twenty-four Eyes is perhaps the best of Tsuboi's melodramatic novels. It makes effective use of mood shifts signaled by children's songs and their guileless perspectives on adult life and social forces generally. Tsuboi is a master of sentimental indulgence kept in bounds by careful narrative control. She takes pains to set a scene whose clues seem genuinely relevant to the sociopolitical milieu her children inhabit. She also balances points of view, taking us in and out of complex interactions between children and adults whose sense of the world and human relationships are so different.

Kinoshita's film is faithful to the original narrative. He is, if anything, more determined to capture the feeling of a chronicle enriched with genuine elements of contemporary witness. Therefore, he counts heavily on the power of film to combine music with the expressive power of the camera. In scenes of emotional intensity, Kinishita lets us hear popular children's songs associated with certain sentiments as a background. He uses close-ups freely, giving us easy clues to the feelings of individual characters. He interweaves variations on contrasting moods— joy and sorrow, for example, or tension and release—as they correspond to the events in the lives of the teacher and her students. He may well be the first director to make full use of music as a leitmotif to identify variations on this theme.

A particularly apt example is found in the sequence showing the children walking along a country road to visit their sick teacher. As they set out, "Oborozukiyo" (Night with a misty moon) is heard on the sound track. This song describes the afterglow of sunset shining across a field of mustard in bloom. It clearly corresponds to the peaceful mood of a village as yet untouched by the threat of war. Oishi's house turns out to be too far a walk for children their age. They grow weary and begin to cry. A series of extreme long shots shows them straggling along the road as they near their goal. These shots evoke their sense of being lost and helpless in an unfamiliar place. Here the song leitmotif, "Nanatsu no Ko" (Seven baby crows), describes the bond between the bird and her young ones—an obvious reference to these children's attachment to their teacher. The song merges with the children's weary weeping to create a lyrical effect typical of Kinoshita, making our entry into these pupils' minds natural and irresistible.

The shot size suddenly changes. It singles out one boy in a close-up as a token of the twelve children in hunger and distress. The shift in mood is provided by a passing bus with Oishi in it. The children's despair vanishes. Now they weep for joy to see Oishi getting out of the bus. A dissolve takes us to her house, where the children are enjoying a home-cooked meal with their teacher.

The novelist Tsuboi approaches the issue of Imperialism and its toll on human life from a more objective perspective than Kinoshita. Oishi's response as mother/teacher/widow contrasts sharply with the worldview of her son, Daikichi. Tsuboi delves into the boy's mind as he, inspired by the rising militaristic spirit, grows ashamed of his own mother. Kinoshita's approach is more straightforward, if one-sided. Disregarding the son's inner reality, he makes the heroine his mouthpiece for an indictment of Japan's Imperialism.

For example, the conversation between Oishi and her eldest son, which is lifted almost word for word from the novel, expresses the director's strong antiwar sentiments. Having lost her husband in war, Oishi declares that one honorable death in the family is enough. She does not think highly at all of her pupil

Yasukini's mother—the approved paragon of courageous motherhood glad to send her son into battle, telling him to fight bravely for the motherland. Oishi says all she herself wants is to be an ordinary human being, a mother who values the life of her son.

The film, like the novel, ends with a reunion of Oishi and her surviving pupils after the war. Film and novel both cannot resist the sentimental appeal of this occasion, with its heart-rending account of the consequences of war on individual lives.

The most notable example is Sonkichi, who was blinded and now works as a masseur. He of course can only see in his mind's eye the photographs passed round—pictures of Oishi surrounded by the twenty-four bright eyes of the children she taught so lovingly.

Kinoshita makes the most of a scene that by its nature is tearful to overflowing. Close-ups shine wet with tears, and in Japan, where a good cry is considered a legitimate pleasure of cinema, few eyes in the audience were likely to be dry as the sound track replays the song about the mother crow and her young ones. The critic's more distant, severer "take" on this finale suggests that its stress on fatalistic circularity presses down too hard.

Kinoshita's next lyrical experiment is rather more sophisticated. *Nogiku no gotoki kimi nariki* (You are like a wild chrysanthemum, 1955) is based on the poet Sachio Ito's short story, "Nogiku no Haka" (The tomb of chrysanthemums, 1906).

The narrator of Ito's simple tale remembers his experience of early love and sorrow. As innocent teenagers, he and his cousin Tamiko pass from friendship into love. A cynically practical adult world intervenes. The narrator is sent away to school. Tamiko is forced into a loveless marriage and soon pines away and dies.

When asked what prompted him to adapt a story from half a century before, Kinoshita had this to say: "Nowadays love among young people has become frivolous. I want to portray pure love between teenagers—in a lyrical style opposed to today's modern trends."[7]

Kinoshita's script in the main is faithful to the original, though he makes significant additions at the beginning and the end in order to underscore his lyrical (*read:* sentimental) purposes.

Ito's narrator begins by explaining why he is writing about events that took place ten years before. He takes us immediately back to the past, describing his home in the country and the circumstances that brought Tamiko to live with his family.

Kinoshita's opening is much more elaborate. It begins with the narrator, now an old man, visiting his home. He is seen on a boat slowly drifting down the river. Superimposed is one of Ito's *tanka* poems about the autumn wind eliciting reminiscence. Brief as it is, this moment in the film achieves an exquisite balance between poetry and prose. The conversation between passenger and boatman is interspersed with lines from Ito's poem. This fluidity of text runs through the film, all the poems being taken directly from Ito's own collection.

From the outset, visual images, dialogue and poems all point to the merciless progression of time passing beyond human control—the idea of *mujo* deeply rooted in Buddhism. The old boatman talks about the narrator's family, members of the landlord class bankrupted by postwar land reform. Tears shine in the passenger's eyes as he lapses into a soliloquy describing the past.

In the flashback sequences that follow, most of the shots are placed in an oval frame that speaks for the careful rounding reminiscence may bring to everyday events in the past. This thoughtful innovation is Kinoshita's own.

He also makes use of a powerful cinematic rubric to enrich the lyrical evocation found in Ito's text. Most importantly, scenes depicting emotional highpoints are presented through a typically Japanese cinematic convention: a combination of long takes and long shots. When, finally, Tamiko and Masao part, the entire scene is captured in a take lasting a minute and a half. It is broken only by two brief close-ups in close succession. The camera's studied look records the young couple's every movement. Masao boards a boat, while Tamiko and her aunt Omasa stand onshore. The camera abruptly switches to a close-up of Tamiko's face in tears, followed by Masao's equally sorrowful expression. The rest of the take—finishing the long shot—is given to the departing boat. A guitar and mandolin play softly on the soundtrack.

The critic Masaaki Tsuzuki has this to say about Kinoshita's sparing use of close-ups in scenes of heightened emotion:

> The most important tearful scenes are marked by Kinoshita's persistent use of long shots. He does not limit the camera's eye only to human emotions, but lets it express and impress upon us the tragic aspect of the background: nature and old houses and the like.[8]

Another strongly charged moment is captured in a long take lasting roughly three minutes. Here, Masao learns of Tamiko's marriage from Omasa. For close to two minutes, the camera's distant, steady gaze rests on them as they stand under a tree in the schoolyard. Masao says good-bye and walks away. Omasa follows. Suddenly the camera, still in long shot, pans along with them until Masao disappears into the school building. The pan lasts a little over one minute. Just as Mizoguchi did, Kinoshita lets Masao's body do the talking. His slow walk and fidgeting motions convey his distracted sorrow.

Kinoshita's determination to be convincingly lyrical extends to shifting the setting to a new locale. Ito's tale takes place in Chiba, on the Tone River, the largest in Japan. Kinoshita films farther inland, in Nagano (Shinshu), his own favorite landscape, which is blessed with great natural beauty. This change of venue also speaks to another issue explored in greater depth in novels such as Toson Shimazaki's *Hakai* (The broken commandment). It is a clear case of a locale being known to deserve its reputation for clinging to values inherited from Japan's feudal past.

Kinoshita cast two new talents as his young lovers: Shinji Tanaka and Noriko Arita. Arita, in fact, was still a student at Gakushuin High School (Peer's High

Shinji Tanaka (l) and Noriko Arita (r) in *You Are Like a Wild Chrysanthemum* (1955) directed by Keisuke Kinoshita. Courtesy of the Kawakita Memorial Film Institute.

School). Kinoshita makes the most of a refreshing ambiance derived both from these genuine ingenue players and the idyllic outdoor setting they perform in.

Ito ends his story with the narrator's brief description of his present status: unhappily married, still lamenting his lost young love. Again, Kinoshita works hard to sustain what seems too strong a melodramatic mood at the end. The next-to-last sequence shows Masao weeping aloud as his grandmother explains how Tamiko died, pining for him. His anguished cries continue, merging even with the musical swell as the camera cuts to a field of wild chrysanthemums in bloom. The scene then switches to the cemetery. The old narrator stands reciting another Ito poem at Tamiko's tomb: "Autumn deepens./The field lies bare./No visitor comes to your tomb,/only the chirping cricket."

Still, the phenomenal success of Kinoshita's *Twenty-four Eyes* created a "Tsuboi boom" in the publishing and cinema industries. One after another of her books became best sellers, so the major studios acted quickly as each came out.

Two of her children's tales appeared on screen in 1955 and 1956, first *Kaki no ki no aru ie* (The house with a persimmon), then *Zakkyo kazaku* (Multiple families living together). The latter was adapted by Seiji Hisamatsu, who had discovered Tsuboi's cinematic potential on his own. His *Onna no koyomi* (Women's calendar, 1954) was in fact the first film adaptation of the writer's work, whose mark on the industry would continue to be her depiction of women's issues.

Tsuboi's novel *Koyomi* (Calendar) is set on her native Shodo Island, a place blessed with warm weather and beautiful natural surroundings. She received the prestigious Shinchosha Literary Award when this book appeared in 1940.[9] It is a saga that depicts three generations of women who form a powerful and resourceful matriarchy in the absence of male domination. The mainspring of this autobiographical novella is the image of womankind generally; women are shown capable of challenging their environment through personal moral strength and maternal affection.

Calendar, in fact, studies the dissolution of such a matriarchy. The story begins at the end, with the family reduced to the two youngest daughters still living together at home. The younger, Mie, plays housewife, while her sister, Kuniko, teaches school. These two sisters represent different attitudes to the position of women. Kuniko is for independence. Mie is engaged. The following chapters, all but the last, unfold the twenty-year history of their family's disintegration.

The theme of female sacrifice begins with the mother, Ine. Her own mother spares Ine the horrors of marriage among the patriarchal gentry by allowing her daughter to marry a man farther down on the social scale. Unfortunately, this turns out to be trading the oppression of patriarchy for the unforeseen horrors of poverty. Significantly, Ine derives strength from her afflictions, among them frequent pregnancy and illness. She nonetheless takes the initiative in restoring the family fortunes.

All but the two of Ine's daughters choose dependence over independence. They enter into the bondage of the patriarchal family. Now the youngest, Mie, prepares to follow in the footsteps of the silent sufferers who have gone before. Even so, Tsuboi invests Mie with a shade of independence. It takes the form of a rebellious little experiment with life in Osaka. Once there, however, she is overwhelmed with inexplicable loneliness and realizes that she cannot survive on her own.

Kuniko is the only one who steadfastly refuses to sell herself into the slavery of marriage. Her security must come from her profession as a teacher. Once the sole male heir is gone, she is courageous enough to assume responsibility for the family name. In Kuniko the familiar theme of matriarchy returns.

The ending of the novel focuses on a family reunion that brings the five surviving sisters together. Thematically, it serves as a revelatory moment for Kuniko. The three who are married soon hurry back to their lives of quiet desperation. Mie is ready to follow suit. Their plight confirms Kuniko in her determination to be independent. She seems ready to take that risk at the end of this powerful saga of Japanese women's lives in the 1920s, in a society that was still very much male-dominated.

Anxious to accommodate the audience in the 1950s, director Hisamatsu makes a number of changes in his film script. Most important, he updates the setting in order to address contemporary issues such as women's status and decision making in a postwar Japanese society. Scraps of dialogue and commodities in daily life offer a vivid glimpse of the sociocultural climate of this period. Mie is seen riding a brand new bicycle. Nylon stockings are luxuries. One sister, Takako, mentions that her husband has been arrested on suspicion of having thrown bottle grenades, a common manifestation of communist protest in the early 1950s. Then, too, Mie's fiancé is updated and upgraded. He is a veterinarian whose profession places him at the center of the effort to modernize this little agrarian community.

Hisamatsu also limits the action to the present generation represented by the five sisters. The spotlight is shared by the two who remain on Shodo Island: Mie (played by Kyoko Kagawa) and Kuniko (played by Yoko Sugi). They are shown to be close despite their very different attitudes toward a male-dominated society. This is evident from the outset when we see Kuniko busily tending her morning glories as a smiling Mie comes out from the house to join her. The camera's generous notice of the ocean stretching behind them shows how much they are a part of this peaceful island.

The film's climax expands on the sisters' reunion at a memorial service. In the novel it serves to link past and present generations. Here, Hisamatsu brings the five sisters together in order to present a picture of woman's plight in a democratized postwar society. All except Kuniko accept passive submission as their fate.

The eldest, Michi (played by Kinuyo Tanaka), is worn out from childbearing and poverty, yet she still values family above all else. She saves her share of the delicacies served to take back to her children.

Ranko Hanai, Kinuyo Tanaka, Yukiko Todoroki, Yoko Sugi and Kyoko Kagawa (from left to right) in *Women's Calendar* (1954) directed by Seiji Hisamatsu. Courtesy of the Kawakita Memorial Film Institute.

Takako (played by Yukiko Todoroki) is married to a man imprisoned for his political views. She willingly returns to her role of dutiful wife awaiting his release, supporting herself by working long hours as a drudge.

Kayano (played by Ranko Hanai) has in fact arrived grimly determined not to return to a tight-fisted, abusive husband who sees in her nothing but a source of cheap labor. Yet her rebellion is short lived. When her husband shows up, she leaves with him, apparently content with bondage after all.

Mie is seen ready to follow in her sisters' footsteps, though a touch of modern spirit leads her to choose a better sort of man.

The final sequence reconciles the motifs of confrontation and reconciliation. In the novel, Mie's trial rebellion takes her to Osaka. In the film, she does something more practical. Her fiancé has been posted to northern Japan, so she decides to visit him. She gets as far as Osaka. Her sense of duty to Kuniko (*giri*) proves stronger than her inclination to personal happiness (*ninjo*), and so she hurries back home.

But the next scene shows the sisters in conflict as their value systems clash. Kuniko refuses to be enslaved by a man. Mie is willing to accept the bondage that goes with that bond. Nevertheless, the sisters have a bond of their own, as we see when Kuniko embraces Mie, congratulating her on her engagement. This parting shot is convincing, partly thanks to the camera's quiet lateral pan which seems to locate this peaceful little island in the calm embrace of the sea.

Hisamatsu took advantage of the Tsuboi "boom" in 1955 by adapting her short story "Tsukiyo no Kasa." (Umbrella on a moonlit night). Here again, Tsuboi addresses her favorite problem: the difficult lives of ordinary women in the changing world of postwar recovery. The narrator is a housewife mother of three married to a self-centered husband. The story begins with her description of herself and her friends: "We were housewives who for some twenty years had relied solely on our husband's pocketbooks."

The hectic pace of modernization in postwar Japan offers these women two alternatives: rigid adherence to traditional roles or a breakaway transformation. The narrator and her friends choose the latter, though they are painfully aware of a basic difficulty: they are all a little old to be setting out to recapture the precious little rebelliousness they remember having had as girls. Now they form a club. Progress in the club's affairs depicts a gradual transformation in these women as they move from mere chitchat to discussion of popular books and even political issues.

Tsuboi does not oversimplify the psychological consequences of this bid for freedom. She follows the progress of the narrator's ambivalence, which makes her feel guilty about leaving the house and tempts her to resign from the club. The novelist ends her story, nevertheless, on a note of quiet celebration in honor of the virtues of patience, flexibility, and caring. Even in a society so rapidly democratizing itself, the narrator reaffirms her point about balance in marriage and family as she reflects on the joy these have brought her and her husband. Since the husband is the unyielding one, any move toward reconciliation must come from her.

She goes to meet his train. Without even noticing her, he opens an umbrella under a cloudless sky and heads home. The narrator follows quietly "behind this strange figure holding an umbrella in the moonlight."

Any film script based on such a simple, unassuming tale had to expand on its few events. Hisamatsu starts by dispensing with the first-person narration. The narrator becomes one of the major characters, Ritsuko (played by Kinuyo Tanaka). This woman's relationship with her husband remains the central issue, but to it are added three subplots detailing the married lives of Ritsuko's friends. This gives the film a more complete set of conflicts and is bound to interest an audience caught up in the stresses and strains of traditional values in the process of being replaced by self-consciously new "modern" ones.

Oddly enough, the women's club is replaced by a truly ancient talking place for women: an old well, a place for washing clothes and gossiping. Each of the women who meet there experiences life in a way that turns her sense of accepted values on its head.

Haruko has been quite content with her role as traditional housewife. Her husband is a happy-go-lucky fellow. It never occurs to her not to trust him. Then she discovers the "other" woman. Another character, Kanako, is a widow with a child. She tries to survive on her own but fails. Her moment of clarity is all about compromise. She agrees to marry a widower. Mie, a newlywed, is already feeling like a widow. She resents her husband's frequent business trips. She has to learn some difficult lessons about the value of perseverance and endurance. Finally, she realizes that her marriage is worth the price.

The end of the film, like the end of the novel, affirms the bond that unites Ritsuko and her unforthcoming husband.

Like Hisamatsu, Mikio Naruse distinguished himself by working closely with women writers. He was especially interested in the work of Fumiko Hayashi. She used autobiographical methods to explore the sorrow and pathos of women trapped in wretched situations that bring out their sense of moral integrity.

Naruse's first Hayashi script was *Meshi* (Repast, 1951). It was based on an extended serial cut short by the author's sudden death.

Hayashi's story studies the values governing the behavior of a harried housewife trying to decide how much independence she is entitled to. The romance has gone out of Michiyo's marriage to Hatsunosuke. The daily effort to make ends meet has worn them down. Hayashi seeks to show how financial hardship can destroy a marriage.

Satoko, Hatsunosuke's niece, comes from Tokyo to visit her uncle and aunt in Osaka. Satoko is young, fun-loving, and flirtatious. Michiyo finds her shockingly modern. They clash over issues of propriety and respectability, especially in connection with men. Michiyo becomes jealous of her niece. She thinks her husband is spoiling this girl, whose attractions he obviously appreciates.

The novel follows a well-patterned causality as Michiyo's conflict leads to separation. When Satoko leaves Osaka, Michiyo goes too. She moves in with a

Setsuko Hara (l) and Ken Uehera (r) in *Repast* (1951) directed by Mikio Naruse. Courtesy of the Kawakita Memorial Film Institute.

married younger sister in Tokyo. Just as the novel expands on the theme of husband and wife living apart, the author's sudden death leaves it unfinished, with no clue about its outcome.

Hayashi's death left Naruse free to expand on the original. He adds a happy ending that celebrates the value of marriage even as new postwar freedoms are working against it. He makes especially good use of locale and atmosphere in downtown Tokyo where, finally, Michiyo and Hatsunosuke end their separation in a touching drama of love revived.

Michiyo has, in fact, already written a letter to Hatsunosuke, telling him that she thinks their separation might as well be permanent. Now, suddenly, she learns that he is coming to visit her. She leaves the house in a panic, only to run into him on the street.

The camera follows the chase from afar. Michiyo hurries on ahead, but Hatsunosuke catches up with her. Just as he does, a parade comes down the street, a joyful procession following a portable shrine. The pair are trapped in the crowd and carried along by the festive music. A cut shows them taking refuge in a cheap restaurant. Hatsunosuke says in an offhand way that he has been offered a better position but has put off accepting it until he can talk with her. He adds that he knows how hard it has been for her to keep house on a small budget. Her face plainly shows that his concern has taken her by surprise. Their eyes meet. We have not seen this intimacy between them before. In a close-up, she smiles, offering him the rest of her beer. He savors it with obvious relish.

Naruse provides full closure to the couple's reconciliation. On the train back to Osaka, Hatsunoske falls asleep beside his wife. She looks at him contentedly, tearing her letter into small pieces. Her voice-over soliloquy puts Naruse's obvious intentions into words. She has decided that a married woman's best chance of happiness lies with marriage itself—with doing all she can to help her husband in his struggle to build a life for his family in a difficult world. Naruse is not suggesting, however, that Michiyo's life will be easy.

His final shot offers a general truth about the fate of such women. The camera cuts to a familiar locale: the downtown alley where they live. A housewife does her washing in a tub in front of her door. Other wives crowd around a huckster selling vegetables, all hoping for a bargain.

In 1952, Naruse turned to another Hayashi novel, *Inazuma* (Lightning). This time he applies his theme to a middle-class family. Here Hayashi offers a tale of discord in the household of a single mother. The family consists of a mother notably unlucky in her choice of men. Each of her four grown-up children has a different father.

Naruse's slice-of-life approach depicts the pathos of their lives as the weak-willed, desperately impoverished mother is reduced to dependency on her good-for-nothing children. The son is a dispirited loafer unwilling to serve as a responsible head of the family. The eldest daughter is a cynical opportunist. She schemes to marry her youngest sister to her own lover for money. The second daughter, a widow, returns home to do nothing but bemoan her misfortunes.

The exception is the youngest, a "modern" type who rebels against the lifestyle of her siblings. She is the only one responsibly employed; she is a bus conductor. It is a humble job, but she makes it serve to move her out of the house and live on her own.

Naruse invests this tale of everyday simple misery with drama in a style to match. His script makes no attempt to sophisticate the story. Dialogue is as brief and monotonous as real life. Feelings run high but there is no attempt at verbal display. Like Ozu, Naruse uses just three standard shots: close-up, medium, and long, medium being his mainstay. As Tadao Sato and Kyoichiro Nanbu observe, this film has the typical Naruse flavor, the one that "leads you to think that life is worth living no matter how dull and uneventful it is." [10]

The following year, Naruse's interest in the novelist Hayashi yielded another adaptation, *Tsuma* (Wife). The script is based on *Chairo no me* (Brown eyes), another exploration of Hayashi's favorite theme: crisis in the marriage of an ordinary lower-middle-class couple in postwar Japan. Here novelist and director take very different approaches to the subject.

Hayashi examines this cooling marital relationship by balancing the couple's different points of view. She makes remarkably good (and good-humored) use of the wife's brown eyes as a central metaphor. The couple's marriage was an arranged one. At their first meeting, Juichi was taken with Mineko's nose, not her eyes. Only after they are wed, does he begin to notice her eyes. They become an indicator of the couple's shifting relations. When she accuses him of something, they take on a golden sheen. When she quizzes him, they seem needle sharp.

Matters are brought to a climax by adultery. Juichi beds a widowed colleague, Sagara. They go to Atami for a lovers' tryst. Mineko first confronts her husband, then his paramour. Making up for this showdown, she finds her eyes shining gold like an animal's. Her husband sees the same effect. It terrifies him. He feels like "a defendant in the presence of a judge."

Yet Mineko's full fury is reserved for the other woman. She feels like a predator preparing to pounce. She hates Sagara, not Juichi. And yet the novel ends, not with her defiant defense of her marriage, but with Juichi's decision to divorce his wife.

Here, too, Naruse plays turnabout with the original. He dispenses with the brown eyes of the title—after all, the film was shot in black and white—in order to focus on Mineko's moral conflict.

As with most of his films, Naruse is meticulous when it comes to establishing the givens of his story. Here he offers a detailed visual description of a marital discord obviously destined to become far worse. Mineko is seen clearing the table as her husband gets ready to leave for work. Nothing is said. Each is oblivious to the other. Even the little gestures of loving care are missing. She does not even offer to help him with his coat. What we have is interior monologue from each. The sound track relays their complaints about the stagnation of a marriage now ten years old.

The film makes us witnesses to the widening rift between the couple and to Juichi's growing intimacy with Sagara and Mineko's reaction to it. Naruse takes a different view of this liaison. In his script it is not really adulterous, or not so in a fleshly sense. It is more a matter of seeking mutual, almost platonic, sympathy.

The outcome, too, is different, though in its way equally grim. Mineko heads for a coffee shop, intending to confront the lovers there. Juichi is in fact waiting for Sagara. They plan to slip away to a spa together. Sagara never comes. She sends a letter announcing her decision to break off with him. And so the marriage is saved by this rival's unintentionally cruel "right" decision. The story comes full circle. Mineko and Juichi continue their marriage, incompatible as before. After such stress, has nothing changed?

The closing scene repeats the opening, unfolding the same monotonous workaday routine. Preoccupied husband leaving for work. Sullen housewife taking up her round of chores. And again no conversation, only interior monologue. As he walks to the station, Juichi ponders divorce. Is it the only way? His thoughts trail off into the tentative, to hang on a single word: "But . . ." The camera cuts back to the house. As she cleans, Mineko considers her options. How can she make a living on her own? Music on the soundtrack swells as she poses the film's final question: "What does it mean to be a woman and a wife?"

Naruse continued in this vein. In his script for *Bangiku* (Late chrysanthemum, 1954) he combined three short stories by Hayashi: the one that serves as his

Mieko Takamine (1) and Ken Uehara (r) in *Wife* (1953) directed by Mikio Naruse. Courtesy of the Kawakita Memorial Film Institute.

title, plus *"Shirasagi"* (White Heron) and *"Suisen"* (Narcissus).[11] Each tells the story of a middle-aged woman facing what looks to be a grim outcome in life.

Kin rose from underclass to lower middle class by working as a geisha. Hayashi charts the course of a life shaped by grim determination to put money between herself and the misery of her origins. Now retired, she pursues her business interests with single-minded ferocity. Money is the be-all and end-all for her. And so at fifty she lives alone, a grasping, unpleasant hag waited on by a maid who is mercifully deaf.

The other two women have suffered drastic decline. Tamae in "Narcissus" was reckless in her youth. A thoughtless marriage led to dire poverty. She is now a maid at a love hotel. Her insecure future is made worse by the escapades of a good-for-nothing son.

In "White Heron" Tome began life as a great beauty. Her father essentially sold her. Various men essentially bought her. She gave herself to drink. Now, at thirty-eight, she cleans toilets in a company. Her young adopted daughter is following in her footsteps, beginning life as some man's mistress.

Naruse might have taken an omnibus approach, using one grim case history after another, each with its different background details, motivations, and values. Instead, he wrote a script that puts these three women on common ground. All are middle-aged geisha who once served the same establishment. They are still close, long after retirement.

Tamae and Tome live together and take care of one other. Each is the other's only guarantee against the worst that poverty can do to women with nothing left to sell. Kin is the enterprising one. She has become a loan shark. Among her clients are her former co-workers, who pay the going rate.

Naruse adds another retired geisha to this forbidding mix. This one, Nobu, is happily married. She and her husband run a small eatery. It serves as a meeting place for all four women. The eatery is a convenient point of comparison as various women stop in. Kin's visits with Nobu have nothing to do with friendship. She comes to collect on a loan. Tamae comes looking for a good listener, someone to condole with on her hard life. Tomi comes to drink with her old friend Nobu. Once, after Kin refuses her a loan, she gets completely drunk.

Naruse does retain the main causal line of each original: Kin's reunion with her former paramour; Tamae's relationship with her prodigal son, who finally settles down and gets work; and Tome's relationship with her daughter, Satoko.

The only radical change comes in his treatment of Satoko. Naruse invests her with all the values consonant with postwar Japanese society. She becomes Tome's illegitimate, not adopted, daughter. Satoko accepts this social handicap as a challenge to be met with courage and determination to make a life on her own. A waitress in a modern coffee shop, she marries a man of her own choice, unlike Hayashi's character, who settles for mistress status.

Naruse's main narrative focus throughout is on money-hungry Kin. Unlike Hayashi's fifty-seven-year-old heroine, who clings to youth by having affairs with younger men, this Kin uses men merely as a means of making money. Her tight-fistedness is evident from the beginning. Her maid, being deaf, comes at a discount. She herself lives like a miser. She is shown driving a hard bargain in business deals.

Naruse does retain the dramatic highlight featuring Kin's reunion with her former lover, Tabe, after a lapse of many years. As in Hayashi's story, this incident serves to show how time has taken its toll. When they were young, these two were consumed with passion. Now, each merely tries to cheat the other out of some money. These lovers, who consumed their passion in their youth, are now two strangers who try to take advantage of each other for money. Hayashi alternates between Kin's inner thoughts and Tabe's. Naruse lets Kin's behavior and interior monologue convey her sense of this man. Before he arrives, we see Kin use ice to firm her face. She orders her maid to prepare a proper meal, something that Kin never does for herself.

Tabe arrives and wastes no time telling Kin that he is on the verge of bankruptcy. Clearly he only came to touch her for a loan. The scene climaxes on a sadly ironic flare-up. Kin has treasured a picture of him all these years. She throws it on the charcoal brazier. He is drunk. She throws him out. The sequence ends with a shot of him leaving the house in the pouring rain, vanishing from her life.

Haruko Sugimura (l) and Ken Uehara (r) in *Late Chrysanthemum* (1954) directed by Mikio Naruse. Courtesy of the Kawakita Memorial Film Institute.

The film itself ends by bringing the four former geisha full circle. They have not really changed. Friendless and haggard, finished with men, Kin hurries off to inspect some property she means to invest in. Nobu still runs the eatery with her husband, partners faithful to their bond in a world so rich in harsh realities. Tamae's son has deserted her for a new job in Hokkaido. Tomi's daughter, always independent, has married for love. Tamae and Tomi will share a dingy little house for the rest of their days.

The final scene reinforces the changing world these three hapless women must live in as they age. Tomi and Tamae stand on a bridge. A young girl in fashionable Western dress passes by, walking like Marilyn Monroe. (The "Monroe" style of walking was a bold new fad in Japan in 1954.) Tomi is sternly disapproving. Naruse injects a bit of good-humored irony here, as the middle-aged, homely Tomi swings her hips in pathetic imitation of the girl. Pathos and humor meet as Tamae and Tomi laugh and walk away together, having at least their bond in a world so cruelly faithless.

In 1955, Naruse turned to yet another Hayashi novel, *Ukigumo* (Floating clouds, 1949–51).[12] This time, his affinity with Hayashi really paid off. His film, *Floating Clouds*, was voted best picture of the year by *Kinema jumpo*. The story covers the tumultuous years from 1943 to 1947. Like the novel, the film script follows the career of a young woman victimized by men and war.

The novel actually begins after World War II, when the heroine, Yukiko, a repatriate from overseas, is released from a refugee camp in war-torn Japan. Hayashi uses a large scar on Yukiko's arm as the flashback device leading her to reminiscence about her life as a typist in French Indochina between 1943 and 1945. Against that exotic setting endowed with great natural beauty, Hayashi recounts a tale of a young woman's struggle to survive, and especially her inclination to capitalize on her physical charms.

Yukiko's first flashback focuses on her dead-end affair with Tomioka, a married man, and on the rivalry between him and his colleague Kono. In a scuffle with Tomioka, Kono accidentally hurts Yukiko. Her scar is a souvenir of that triangular relationship.

The rest of the novel describes Yukiko's confrontation with adverse conditions. Her relationship with the philanderer Tomioka continues, even as she beds first one man and then another. Her body becomes a kind of weapon. In the end, the scene shifts from Tokyo to Yakushima, a remote island far removed from civilization. Yukiko has followed Tomioka there, and there she dies of illness.

Hayashi invests this melodramatic tale with considerable psychological depth through some superbly insightful descriptions of Tomioka and Yukiko. Naruse's narrative focus is radically different. He concentrates on portraying Yukiko as a

Hideko Takamine (l) and Masayuki Mori (r) in *Floating Clouds* (1955), directed by Mikio Naruse. Courtesy of the Kawakita Memorial Film Institute.

woman betrayed by her lover, yet continuing to survive what appear to be insurmountable obstacles.

A brief comparison of key events shows how differently novelist and director approach this story. The reunion between Tomioka and Yukiko takes place in a shabby love hotel in war-torn Tokyo. Hayashi labors on their sense of disillusionment. In the image of the tired lover, Tomioka sees "a fragment of his fate." Though overwhelmed by a sense of guilt, he finds himself unconsciously dragged into a dangerous liaison. His mind wanders back to Indochina, to scenes of passionate love he now dismisses as simply figments of his imagination. Yukiko also feels frustrated as she finds her ex-lover completely drained of passion and spirit. Only loneliness holds them together; they are unable to rekindle "the passion of the past."

Naruse dispenses with this psychological scrutiny. Instead, he focuses on the lovers' chilling relationship in war-torn Japan. Thus, in the love-hotel sequence, Tomioka and Yukiko kiss while the hustle and bustle of a nearby market and a popular song on a radio outside invade the room. The scene dissolves away just once, and briefly, to show the lovers together in a Southeast Asian jungle; there they kiss, fiercely oblivious to nature's abundance.

Perhaps the most obvious difference between the original and the film comes at the end. Still anxious to underscore the note of disillusion, Hayashi attempts a sense of closure. Tomioka is off in the mountains working when Yukiko dies. Hayashi offers this sad assessment of Yukiko's feelings; dying, she experiences the "hollowness of a woman who has not been loved by anyone." Now, at the end, Yukiko finds herself too weary to recall those events in Indochina that have been the source of her strength.

What follows is a rather lengthy description of Tomioka's reaction to Yukiko's death. He cries in remorse like a child. He asks himself what it means to be a human being. Nevertheless, Hayashi does not forget to expose the egoism and selfishness of the man who has exploited Yukiko. It turns out that the nurse who has been nursing Yukiko is pregnant by Tomioka.

A month after Yukiko's death, Tomioka visits Kagoshima, where Yukiko became ill earlier on their route to Yakushima. He drinks and buys a woman, using the money Yukiko left for him. He does not want to return to Yakushima or to Tokyo. The novel ends with its title image: with Tomioka comparing his life to the drifting clouds.

Naruse eschews such a psychological approach, preferring to concentrate on portraying a heroine victimized by men and societal forces having no relation to traditional family ties. Yukiko dies all alone. Naruse is notably restrained, letting the camera comment as she lies dying. A cut to the window shows the shutter flapping in the stormy wind. This seems to herald something sinister. Another cut shows Yukiko in a medium shot attempting to crawl out of bed to shut the window. Another shot shows her desperation, then her collapse. A cut to trees swaying in the storm outside says everything we need to know about an uncaring world.

Naruse spares his hero the various embarrassments of manly egotism that Hayashi details so carefully. The maid is not pregnant by him. He does not go on a drunken binge. The film ends with a candid portrayal of Tomioka's remorse. A close-up shows him weeping, begging forgiveness. The camera tracks back to offer a medium shot of him alone in the room. It takes note of the dismal surroundings in which Yukiko died and where he now must live. Rain beats against the window. The final epitaph is a quote from Hayashi's *Horoki* (A vagabond's song): "The life of the flower is short and it is full of suffering."

Naruse's interest in modern novelists was largely confined to Hayashi in the early 1950s. In 1954, however, he took up Kawabata's *Yama no oto* (The sound of the mountain). Faithful to the original, his film of the same title charted the growing affection between a man and his daughter-in-law, a victim of her husband's philandering. Through shifting points of view, Kawabata studies the psychology of the individual characters as they experience emotional turmoil.

Naruse prefers to view events chiefly as they are perceived by the father. He does, however, pay meticulous attention to the ambience suggested in the novel. The main set was designed to resemble Kawabata's own house, and shooting was done in its vicinity.[13]

In 1956, Naruse found his subject in another female writer, Aya Koda. Her short story "Nagareru" (Flowing), studies a geisha house on the decline as seen through the eyes of a housemaid. Traditional and modern values clash as a mother, herself a geisha, tries and fails to influence her daughter.

Naruse's film, *Flowing*, was a failure in many aspects. For a start, unlike Mizoguchi, he was not at home in the world of geisha. Naruse's instincts served him best with the urban underclass. Critic Kohei Sugiyama put it this way:

> Naruse does not consider this [the geisha house] a special place. . . . He does not present it as a world apart, a place associated with pleasure. To him it is no different than an alleyway where children go to play. . . .
>
> The film does not evoke any vivid or surprising impressions of geisha life. It displays none of the vivid character Naruse brings to his films about ordinary townspeople.[14]

Three years later, Naruse adapted Saisei Muro's best seller, *Anzukko*. This was his second film version of Muro's work, the first being *Older Brother, Younger Sister* (discussed in Chapter 11). *Anzukko* puts the director back on familiar ground: a marriage on the rocks. Anzukko, daughter of a prominent novelist, marries Kyokichi. Dissatisfied with a salaried job, he wants to be a novelist, too. This ambition runs counter to Anzukko's wish for a more economically stable life. In this film, Naruse's focus shifts from the wife to the husband. Instead of dwelling on Anzukko's reaction to a spouse she comes to consider a good-for-nothing, the film explores the psychology of a man who marries into a distinguished family only to find himself struggling to be on a par with an accomplished father-in-law.

While Naruse was being so notably author-faithful, Shiro Toyoda was reaching out to a number of modern novelists. *Gan* (Wild geese, 1954, released in the United States as *The Mistress*) was adapted from the novel by Ogai Mori. Takeo Arishima wrote the novel adapted for *Aru onna* (A certain woman, 1955). *Mugibue* (Wheat whistle, 1955) was adapted from Saisei Muro's *Sei ni mezameru koro* (The time of sexual awakening).

Toyoda took up other leading modern writers, too. *Neko to Shozo to futari no onna* (A cat, Shozo, and two women, 1956) used Junichiro Tanizaki's novella. *Yukiguni* (The snow country, 1958) was adapted from Yasunari Kawabata's lyrical novel. *Anya koro* (Dark night passing, 1959) was based on the psychological novel by Naoya Shiga.

These adaptations could easily fill a lengthy chapter. Failing that, let me offer a quick survey of Toyoda's characteristic strengths and weaknesses, especially as they relate to works of literature adapted for the screen.

The Mistress was ranked eighth in the lineup of best films chosen by *Kinema jumpo* in 1954. Toyoda's script makes radical changes in the Meiji-era novel.[15] Set in 1880, twelve years after the Meiji Restoration, novel and film share a central problem: how a beautiful woman confronts traditionally oppressive values espoused by a self-consciously "new" society. This new Japan has accepted the

Hideko Takamine (l) and Hiroshi Akutagawa (r) in *The Mistress* (1954) directed by Shiro Toyoda. Courtesy of the Kawakita Memorial Film Institute.

capitalist ethos of the West, and much of its style and know-how, even as it clings to values inherited from its own feudal past.

In this story Suezo, a loan shark, makes Otama his concubine—a marriage of convenience between aggressive materialism associated with the West and the East's own compliance with male sexual drive. A woman like Otama serves the ancient double standard. If anything, it is made worse by the new capitalist mentality. A mistress is yet another status symbol money can buy. Even chastity gains in value by virtue (pun intended) of the fact that it can be had for ready money.

The medical student Okada represents a new class of Japanese intellectual anxious to move in the mainstream of modernization. In the end, he leaves Japan to study medicine in Germany. He becomes a peculiarly suitable focus for the socioeconomic yearnings of a woman who suffers the age-old fate of being bought and sold.

Toyoda's script is a radical departure from the novel in two ways. First, he simplifies the narrative ploy. Ogai's narrator just happens to be a friend of Okada's. We sense that his second-hand view of events limits his grasp somewhat. Yet he persists in reporting on Otama's inner state. He breaks in on his own story, behaving like the omniscient narrator in a book. We do not quite understand how he knows what he claims to know, or we do not understand until the end, when we learn what Ogai has kept from us on purpose all this time. The narrator, it turns out, befriended Otama after his friend Okada left the country. The two halves of his hearsay do "fit."

Toyoda's second radical departure from the original concerns Otama's reaction to the facts of her life. Ogai's Otama is the traditional silent sufferer: dutiful daughter, dutiful concubine. She is a woman of convenience, outwardly at least. She does have a dream, however. She even thinks she has found a way to act on it. She has become obsessively curious about the young medical student who passes her house around the same time every day. She daydreams about him, even in the presence of her master. Having been, as it were, unfaithful in a dream, she decides to be unfaithful in reality, too. She plans it carefully. Her master is out of town. She will invite Okada in to dine, then. . . . But fate plays an ironic trick. That day, for the first time ever, Okada passes her house accompanied by someone else. It turns out to be the narrator, who later will become her friend. She does not know that and neither do we. What is obvious is that the would-be rebellious mistress has missed her one and only opportunity.

Toyoda's heroine plots the same rendezvous, but she has aroused Suezo's suspicions. She has given signs of being discontented. Suezo comes home unexpectedly on purpose on the fatal day. He finds a feast laid out, obviously not for him. In the ensuing scene Otama rebels. She comes right out and says she can no longer abide the kind of life she is leading.

Toyoda has prepared her for this climactic moment. Unlike Ogai, he shows how a woman acts on her dream of love. We see her following Okada all the way to the university. There she spies on him. He sells his dictionary to a secondhand bookstore. Otama buys it and takes it home. We have seen a fishwife expressing contempt for Otama as a kept woman, refusing to sell to her maid. Otama goes to the fishwife's place of business herself to buy something special for Okada. Having paid for her purchase, she gets even for the fishwife's earlier slight. She gives her address and says, in effect, "Deliver it to me—the concubine!"

Fate is no kinder to Otama in Toyoda's script. After the blow-up with Suezo, she storms out of the house. It is her luck to see Okada get into the carriage with his German mentor. She knows he is leaving, going far away. Otama wanders on the shore of a pond. A wild goose flies. What better symbol of a tender farewell denied her? What better bird to express her yearning to be free, to fly far away herself?

Suddenly the camera shows her face in outsize close-up. Her expression is pitilessly blank. The closing long shot shows her standing in the rain, umbrella unfurled, a lonely woman blending in with a dreary day. Will she return to Suezo? Can she possibly survive on her own, burdened with an aged father? We are given no clue. This is not a film with a comfortable, conformable conclusion.

Toyoda's heroines tend to exhibit Otama's flair for challenge and confrontation. They also tend to get nowhere really, ending up morally improved only in the sense of living difficult lives with courage.

The heroes these women are paired with (or against) tend to be consistently feckless. This thematic constant can be seen in *The Snow Country*, Toyoda's adaptation of the Nobel Laureate Yasunari Kawabata's novel, written between 1934 and 1947. Here the director's commitment to the communicativeness and contemporaneity of his medium seemed to give him even more creative freedom to modify and transform Kawabata's work. The result was a film whose different thematic orientation explores the camera's expressive power to the fullest.

Kawabata's novel concerns the protagonist Shimamura's search for a holistic vision for his life. His quest leads to the snow country, to unpolluted nature and two "clean women" there. A complex configuration of images of nature, woman, and fire is designated "The Milky Way" by Shimamura toward the end. After an epiphanal experience with it, he feels redeemed and returns to civilization, to Tokyo.

Toyoda's film shifts the focus from hero to heroine, to one of the two women, the geisha Komako. She is searching for an identity she can live with. Her conflict has to do with issues of social constraint and individual freedom. Toyoda dramatizes her conflict through shifting relations with Shimamura and the other woman, the beautiful young Yoko.

Toyoda also clarifies his narrative pattern by freely modifying and eliminating images and events invested with symbolic overtones in the novel. Thus the Milky Way configuration vanishes. Even the novelist's insistent use of mirror images is not given the same depth of symbolic meaning. For Kawabata, Yoko's reflection suggests beauty too ethereal to possess in human terms. For Toyoda, it become a medium for both aesthetic effects and narrative tensions.

Ryo Ikebe (l) and Keiko Kishi (r) in *The Snow Country* (1958) directed by Shiro Toyoda. Courtesy of the Kawakita Memorial Film Institute.

A critical comparison between the two works would take us far beyond the scope of this chapter.[16] One example speaks well enough for a poignant difference between these two versions of Shimamura's quest. The final section of the film shows Komako's obligation to Yoko fixed once and for all by an incident that is entirely Toyoda's creation: Yoko is disfigured in a fire. (In the original, she dies in it.) This catastrophe serves to submit Komako to life as a geisha in a society whose money/male ascendancy lays such intolerable burdens on women. Yet Komako faces her maternal responsibilities with a heightened awareness of the plight of her sex.

The novel ends with a remarkably concise description of Shimamura's epiphany: "The Milky Way ran through him." The film achieves its final insight through an ugly confrontation between Komako and the disfigured Yoko. The spiteful Yoko says that she is determined to be a burden on Komako. A close-up of Komako's face offers cues to her complex inner struggle. Thus far, the film's thematic progression has suggested bondage: it seems that she has given up her dream of freedom of her own free will. Instead of asserting her claim to personal happiness and becoming Shimamura's lover, she will remain in the snow country, taking care of Yoko. Thus this unfortunate woman's complex emotions of determination, courage and resignation are crystallized in close-up.

They are also confirmed by the two long shots that follow. They follow Komako walking through the streets of the town and on toward the mountain. She becomes a tiny figure vanishing in the distance. The fusion of her figure with the surrounding snowy landscape is not expressive of final desolation or alienation. Rather, she may be seen as being in her element after all, in harmony with nature, with the snowy landscape for which her town is famous. To be sure, these final shots do suggest a resigned acceptance of a limited role in life; but this is resignation enriched with awareness gained through suffering.

The Snow Country is not among Toyoda's best film adaptations of "pure literature." In many instances, the director's pictorial rendition of the given landscape outweighs the thematic substance. External constraints—studio pressures for a good box-office lead—seemed to be responsible for areas of undoubted banality.

Toyoda's 1959 film, *Dark Night Passing,* is a more apt example of a veteran filmmaker doing poorly by a literary masterpiece. Naoya Shiga's psychological novel uses a narrator to chart the stages of an intellectual's struggle to find an identity. Two obstacles stand in Kensaku's way: his illegitimate birth and his wife's infidelity. The novel itself was written in stages, and slowly, appearing as a serial in a literary magazine between 1921 and 1937.[17]

Toyoda replaces the narrator with the camera. The silent objectivity of the lens fails to endow Kensaku's inner torment with the convincing immediacy Shiga labored so hard to create. The dialogue in the script is similarly weak. So is the actor Ryo Ikebe's performance.

The film's banality is especially painful in the final climactic sequence. Faithful to the original, Toyoda shows Kensaku climbing the mountain and going behind a bush to suffer an attack of diarrhea. The rising sun, seen from his perspective, suggests the purging of all the agony he has experienced. In visual terms, a strange imbalance between the natural and the artificial robs this moment of any heightened sense of being. The vast stretch of the landscape around him—nature's bounty—is magnificently captured by the camera. On the other hand, the bush— the economically built set—does not fail to escape our attention. Critic Tadao Sato cites the frequent cutbacks between the two as one of the most damaging effects on the aesthetics of the film.[18]

Versatile is the only word for Kon Ichikawa's pursuit of modern Japanese literature in the 1950s. He was a prolific filmmaker who ranged far and wide in search of scripts. He was also exceedingly lucky, married as he was to the brilliant scriptwriter Natto Wada.

Wakai hito (Young people, 1952) was adapted from a novel written by Yojiro Ishikawa before World War II. As we have seen (in Chapter 2), Toyoda got there first. His 1937 version captivated audiences with its presentation of Ishikawa's refreshing new type of woman: the young girl, born out of wedlock, who challenges convention by daring to listen to her heart and live accordingly.

That kind of young woman was hardly news in the boldly democratic, re-form-crazy world of postwar Japan. That might be why Ichikawa's version failed to attract much attention.

After his 1955 adaptation of Soseki Natsume's novel *Kokoro*, Ichikawa turned to works with guaranteed contemporary interest. Among them was Michio Takeyama's *Biruma no tategoto* (The harp of Burma). Published in 1946, this novel's mission was frankly didactic: to inspire youth with hope for the future of a nation struggling to survive defeat in war. Takeyama sought to do this by em-phasizing the traditional value system, the Buddhist ideal of altruism, as embod-ied in his soldier hero, Mizushima.

The novel had been around for a decade by the time Ichikawa took it up. The author's didactic purpose might look like old news in 1956. For that reason, Ichikawa's film concentrates on an aspect characteristic of his mastery: his study of "the most intimate of psychological revelations."[19]

In this case, the hero's "most intimate" revelations come piecemeal, in stages, as slowly his life makes sense in a classical awakening. His experience of war becomes a transcendental "proof" that goodness exists and is at work in the world.

No wonder Ichikawa found this complex novel difficult to adapt. He com-pletely transformed the narrative and made virtuoso use of the visual properties of cinema, cross-cutting especially.[20]

Shoji Yasui in *The Harp of Burma* (1956) directed by Kon Ichikawa. Courtesy of the Kawakita Memo-rial Film Institute.

One of Takeyama's most important narrative devices is withheld information. His story is told by a member of the singing company, whose perspective is obviously narrow. Still, the plot's guiding purpose, as the title suggests, is a desire by this "singing" company of soldiers to find their comrade Mizushima.

Do they succeed? Takeyama keeps his reader in suspense until the end. Only then, on the ship headed back to Japan, do we know that the captain has a letter from Mizushima. Only when he reads it to the men do we learn of Mizushima's decision to remain in Burma and bury their fallen comrades. Unfortunately, a reader is apt to find this revelation anticlimactic.

Ichikawa wisely avoids that pitfall. Right from the start he shows two different responses to defeat in the war. The singing company represents a new kind of soldier, one motivated by the individualism that will characterize postwar Japanese society. Accepting defeat as part of the human condition, they hope to survive confinement in a POW camp and work for the reconstruction of their country, each in his own way.

Another company is made up of old-style Japanese soldiers. Their values are traditional, collective. They feel a moral imperative to fight on to the bitter end, preferring a dutiful death to the shame of surviving defeat.

Mizushima's role is to bridge the two. His mission is to persuade the diehard traditional soldiers to adopt his company's strategy of accepting defeat and surviving it.

Ichikawa's narrative proceeds by way of intercutting between the singing company in the POW camp and Mizushima on his journey. Thanks to our access to both parties in this debate, we the viewers enjoy an omniscient point of view. It is as if we become one with the camera eye.

One sequence stands out as pivotal in all these cross-cut scenes. It takes place on a bridge. As the singing company marches across, they pass a priest who resembles Mizushima. The men themselves are left merely puzzled by this resemblance. We are given a wider perspective on events taking place. Ichikawa gives us a quick review of the stages of Mizushima's spiritual quest. At the heart of it is a scene that resolves his sense of conflict. He sees a group of British nurses holding a memorial service for the unknown soldiers.

Up to this point, Mizushima has suffered his own Japanese variety of the national narcissism that all parties to the war were guilty of. He has seen the enemy as being not really quite human. Now he realizes that he was wrong about that; moreover, that these strange Brits have altruistic feelings like his own. Suddenly he realizes that all the races fighting in this war are capable of his elevated notions about the value of human life.

A close-up shows Mizushima covering his face with his hands. It is succeeded by a rapid sweep of flashbacks to the previous three stages of his confrontation with death. Mizushima's determination is now clear: he will not go back to Japan.

Another bridge scene follows. It repeats the shot of Mizushima, or a priest resembling him, passing his comrades. This time, however, an unnamed member of the singing company speaks in voice-over. He casts his war experience in a new light, saying "That priest was Mizushima."

The film ends like the novel, aboard ship, with the reading of the letter. In the film, the camera singles out the man who spoke on the bridge. Here, as in the novel, we sense the anticlimax. But Ichikawa has transferred Mizushima's high sense of mission to this man's face. This has the effect of drawing us closer to the point of the film. We see how Mizushima's high-minded self-sacrifice connects the old Japan with the new; how his comrades, "new" individualists though they be, will carry that spirit back to a country so badly in need of uplift in every way.

Ichikawa adapted three more ambitious literary works before the end of the decade. *Enjo* (Conflagration, 1958) was based on Yukio Mishima's highly acclaimed psychological novel *Kinkakuji* (The temple of the golden pavilion). Ichikawa negotiated rights with the temple authorities for a solid year; he was that determined to make this film. Unfortunately, he was not allowed to use Mishima's title because the authorities feared that might damage the image of this venerable temple.

A detailed study of Mishima's novel is be given in Chapter 15 as it relates to Takabayashi's screen version. Here, it is enough to say that the novel is intent on psychological scrutiny, while Ichikawa prefers to explore the social and cultural forces at work in the protagonist's life. Mishima's golden pavilion lies at the center of a complex metaphorical structure the hero elaborates in his tortured mind.

Ichikawa sets all that aside in favor of a straightforward presentation of the temple as a customary icon of eternal beauty. For him, it elicits no ambivalent reaction, only powerful associations with a rich cultural inheritance the Japanese are proud to call their own. The enemy he studies is not the madness within but vulgarity and corruption without. Ichikawa insists on the contemporary relevance of this story. His script suggests that the state of the nation itself could be provocation enough; that the troubled young acolyte sets fire to the most transcendent symbol of Japan he knows on purpose in order to protect its sempiternal purity from the contagion of a debased, materialistic, secular new society.

Ichikawa shows how this betrayal of the divine is served by commonplace human weakness and vulgarity. A GI and his girl visit the temple. To them, it is just another tourist attraction. It, as well as another, can serve as a trysting place, and for an affair that is sadly sordid. Another clear index of so much that is amiss in this new secular Japan is seen in the behavior of the head priest. He falls very far short of his vaunted saintliness. As a child, the protagonist had witnessed his own mother's adultery. That memory is especially cruel now that he serves as an acolyte in precincts that should be hallowed and holy but really are not. Mishima dealt in these matters, too; but Ichikawa binds them together in his own strong way in order to show how they contribute to the destruction of a handicapped but sensitive young man.

The opening sequence is Ichikawa's creation. He begins where Mishima left off: with the fate of the protagonist after the fire he set. The novel ends abruptly, going up in flames as Mizoguchi torches the temple, even in the act feeling great relief. In the film he is next seen aboard a train, escorted by several policemen. He leaps out. The camera follows, cutting to a field where the police catch up with him. This flashback begins the version on screen. Mishima had been content with a simple confession that begins the young man's account.

Nobi (Fires on the plain, 1959) is Ichikawa's adaptation of Shohei Ooka's novel about wartime atrocities and survival. The book was highly acclaimed for the philosophical and religious questions the author asked about human nature. Ooka places his characters in conditions so extreme that they face a test of survival rarely faced. These men must eat a fellow human being if they are to live. Ooka asks a terrible question: can a man's humanity survive this test, or does it revert to beast?

The narrative deals with this controversial subject by shifting back and forth in time. It is a confession, the tale of a soldier sent to the battlefield on Leyte where starvation turns out to be the enemy he must overcome or die.

Looking back, this young man describes an ordeal that leads to a climactic moment of agony. There comes a time when the only way he can survive is to eat the flesh of his fallen comrade.

Ooka was a devout Christian, so he sees the hand of God working directly to prevent his young hero's descent into bestiality. The novel's ending gives a sense of closure as it tells us what happened to him after the war. Ooka takes us to the mental hospital where the protagonist has committed himself. He is seen as maladjusted, not insane. He cannot return to normal life as a husband and member of society. His confession ends with an affirmation of his Christian faith. He has thought long and hard about "the unknown assailant" whose blow prevented him from giving in to hunger in such a horrible way. He concludes that he was saved by a "transfiguration of Christ Himself."[21]

Ichikawa and his scriptwriter wife, Natto Wada, simplified Ooka's convoluted narrative structure. They discarded its twofold spatial and temporal dimensions, taking us right into the battle.

Ichikawa even manages to invest the dramatic highlight of the soldier's moral crisis with a touch of black humor. Here the starving soldier actually gives in and tries to eat a piece of his comrade's flesh, only to find himself unable to bite with teeth loosened by malnutrition.

The film also offers its own sense of closure to the soldier's experience. In place of the transcendent religious experience Ooka worked so hard to explain, Ichikawa returns us firmly to the plane of realizable human experience. A last long shot suggests the young man's return to the embrace of civilization by showing him staggering across a field in the direction of smoke rising up from what must be a fire in some village.

Ichikawa took on another difficult adaptation in 1959: Tanizaki's *Kagi* (The key). This novel's frank treatment of sex had made it a *succèss de scandale*. That aspect alone might suggest a detailed study of the difference between book as read and script as seen, between a confessional diary on the page and the same account clearly visualized on screen.

Here, let me just point to a few of Ichikawa's radical departures from cinema as usual. Tanizaki's shocking novel enters a realm of Eros inhabited by a middle-aged college professor and his wife. They are facing, first, the daunting prospect of growing old. If they lived according to accepted norms, passion would fade, leaving them content to be more rational and reasonable—companions at peace unto the last. Not so fast, says this professor. He thinks he has it all worked out. He will awaken his wife's latent sensuality, and with it, his own faltering prowess that is so troublesome to him now. She does catch fire. They do, as it were, burn together as before, even better than before. But success turns out to be fatal. The professor's health is under threat, but he can no longer help himself, and so he dies.

Even before that climactic moment, the wife has passed beyond the bounds of married passion. She seduces her daughter's fiancé. In him, she sees the sexual athlete that she wants her husband to be, and that he wanted himself to seem.

The daughter herself is caught up in this game. She has her father's deviousness, if not her mother's passionate abandon. So it transpires that this worldly cynical young woman and young man marry and live as a *ménage à trois* with a libidinous mother/mother-in-law!

What might have been mere epic soap opera, American style, some decades before its time is actually a wonderfully skillful novel. Tanizaki's builds tension in his plot by carefully manipulating the reader's point of view. Up until the husband's death, the narrative makes use of diaries kept by man and wife. The reader sees first one and then the other describe the same event. Their different interpretations create a definite sense that both witnesses are in some way unreliable.

We are thrown off balance by the notion that each diary is a secret record, furtively made, of the progress of this most peculiar infidelity between man and wife. Each describes sensations they have shared, but deceitfully, since the professor's aim is to arouse her without discussing his purpose or need.

Then this surprise. We learn the reason for our unease. The deception is worse than we think. Each of these diarists is pretending to write for himself or herself alone, but each is counting on the other to be reading his/her account on the sly! This duplicitous relationship between characters and diaries has the effect of distancing the reader. We do not identify with either character. We study only the outcome, weighing deception against deception.

After her husband's death, the wife is free to read her own mind. She discards "the mask of deception." She candidly describes "a number of things" she has so far "hesitated to put in writing while he was alive." Now we see her making a few necessary corrections to her previous reports. We ourselves must re-evaluate the inferences we have made so far.

By the end of the novel we feel that we have passed through a labyrinth that Tanizaki has built on purpose to guide our powers of inference along a torturous course. The two individuals' motives have been revealed; the result of their mind-reading game stands before us.

Here, too, is the crowning irony: the wife, well and truly aroused, now lives under one roof with her daughter and her daughter's husband. The husband is young and strong, a serviceable male made in the powerful erotic image her aging husband had in mind to create.

Again, Ichikawa simplifies his author's elaborate means to the given end. The film, *Kagi* (Odd obsession), depicts the same intriguing game, but offers a very different outcome. More important, Ichikawa's progress along the way is far less devious, though equally dramatic in its way. He relies heavily on the camera's expressive devices, especially wide-angle shots and cross-cutting. He uses camera placement to position his subject with great insight and suggestive power. Altogether, he achieves a number of effects whose purpose is to distance the viewer and register shock. The viewer identifies with the camera, which functions like an omniscient narrator.

The first four scenes clearly illustrate Ichikawa's modus operandi. He begins by stating the premise of this tale in beautifully ironic, clinical fashion. The young intern, Kimura, describes the various stages of aging in a subtle, mockingly ironic tone. He is lecturing us! At one point he points a finger directly at the audience and says, "No one one can escape growing old. Not even you, who are going to watch this film."

Next, a variety of points of view quickly put us in a properly detached, clinical frame of mind as we study a series of characters and values in conflict.

The camera cuts to the doctor's office. We see the protagonist Kenmotsu insisting on a hormone injection despite young Doctor Kimura's warnings. We see him leave the hospital and board a trolley. The squeaking of the trolley bears a clear resemblance to an irregular heartbeat. Kenmotsu gets off, and freezes on the film. This is a jolt. Have we guessed right? Is this heart failure or only a teasing visual clue making us want to see what follows?

The freeze frame leads to a cross-cut. We see Kenmotsu's wife Ikuko in Doctor Kimura's office. Ichikawa's moment of transition has confused us momentarily for a reason. He wants to promote a sense of caution in the face of the events unfolding.

The alert viewer is now firmly aware of being positioned for detachment. Ikuko's behavior seems perfectly normal, modest, and wifely, when she says in all apparent innocence that she does not want to talk about her sexual relationship with the husband.

Then her eyes meet Kimura's as she goes to leave. There is something pointed about the display of indifference in her eyes, something in the way Ichikawa has depicted her actions and her motives. Given these clues, we suspect that this respectable married woman is wearing a mask. She is hiding something. Ikuko goes home in a taxi. When she gets out, she freezes too. This time we feel sure that detachment and caution are going to pay off.

Another cross-cut takes us back to Doctor Kimura's office. Now he is with the couple's daughter, Toshiko. She does not come in, but she stands in the doorway upbraiding Kimura for having stood her up on a date. There is something snide in her tone, a hint of something hidden and sly. We feel slightly repelled— just enough to detach us from her.

We have met the four main characters. All is in readiness. We ourselves are now, as it were, in place. The next scene brings them all together. They are seated around a table in the living room of Kenmotsu's house. Kimura has come for a visit. In place of close-ups and other point-of-view shots, Ichikawa gives us a number of wide-angle frames, as if to avoid establishing any definite point of view on this scene. He has made his position clear. He is urging us to study these people, their actions and interactions, and to guess what's going on, what motivates them. The director wants to make each one of us an omniscient observer, someone whose perspective is more inclusive than that of any of these characters.

The plot proceeds pretty much as it does in the novel. But Ichikawa has added a character, the maidservant Hana. She is not well treated. We see Ikuko taunting the poor old woman, whose vision is very poor. Yet she sees what is going on. That much is clear.

Hana, in fact, is something like a seer. The judgment on the events in this tale is left to her. Kenmotsu has died, a victim of the hormone injections he insisted on. Now, at the end, with Tanizaki's ironic *ménage* in place, Hana poisons Kimura, Ikuko, and Toshiko. Vengeance is an elderly housemaid. And we know why.

But lo, there is a final irony. Ichikawa springs it on us now. Hana confesses to premeditated murder. Her eyesight is not to blame, she says. She knew very well that the red container was dish soap, the green container rat poison. She knew. She tells the police she did. They refuse to believe her. The poor old thing must be suffering from senile dementia. The police have their own explanation. It is stolidly conventional. Professor Kenmotsu's death left his wife and daughter too poor to live decently, and so they committed suicide. Young Doctor Kimura joined them in sympathy. Case closed.

Clearly, much more could be said about writers and directors working together in Japan in the 1950s. It stands to reason that a nation caught up in such a moil and toil of reconstruction should want to study the work in progress in books and on the screen.

It follows that directors would have their work cut out for them when they looked for ways to combine books and cinema. Their efforts continued unabated as the war and the Occupation receded into history, to be succeeded by changes coming to be seen as equally momentous.

Directors continued to work with writers male and female, old and new, mainstream and experimental. Among the writers most sought after by directors were Kobo Abe and Sawako Ariyoshi. Abe's novels about identity crises in contemporary Japan elicited four adaptations by Hiroshi Teshigahara in the 1960s.

Ariyoshi's *Koge* (Fragrant flowers) and *Ki no kawa* (The River Ki) offered other directors more opportunities to explore the saga of women's progress, one of the major thematic constants in postwar Japanese cinema.

Notes

1. For an overview of the changing status of Japanese women, see Yoriko Meguro "Women in Japan," in *Teaching Guide for Women in Japan* (New York: Japan Society, 1993), pp. 1–19.
2. For a most comprehensive study of *Rashomon*, see Donald Richie, ed., *Rashomon* (New Brunswick, N.J.: Rutgers University Press, 1990).
3. For a further analysis of this film, see Keiko McDonald, *Mizoguchi* (Boston: Twayne, 1984), pp. 89–93.
4. For a more comprehensive study of this film, see ibid., pp. 93–99.
5. Hajime Takizawa, "*Sansho Dayū*" (On Sansho the bailiff), *Eiga Hyoron* 11 (May 1954): 69. For an extensive comparison of Ogai's original and Mizoguchi's film version, and the folklore that inspired Ogai's work, see Tadao Sato, *Mizoguchi Kenji no sekai* (The world of Kenji Mizoguchi) (Tokyo: Tsukuma Shobo, 1982), pp. 204–15.
6. For a more comprehensive study of this film, see David Desser, "*Twenty-four Eyes,*" in David Desser and Merry White, *Childhood and Education in Japan* (New York: Japan Society, 1991), pp. 30–34.
7. Quoted by Masaaki Tsuzuki in *Nihon eiga no ogon jidai* (The golden age of Japanese cinema) (Tokyo: Shogakkan, 1995), p. 213.
8. Ibid., p. 225.
9. For a more detailed analysis of this novel, see Keiko McDonald, "Tsuboi Sakae," in *Japanese Women Writers*, ed. Chieko I. Mulhern (Westport, Conn.: Greenwood Press, 1994), pp. 418–19.
10. Kyoichiro Nanbu and Tadao Sato, *Nihon eiga hyakusen* (One hundred selections of Japanese cinema) (Tokyo: Tabata Shoten, 1973), p. 123.
11. For an English translation of "Suisen," see "Narcissus," in *Japanese Women Writers: Twentieth Century Short Fiction*, trans. Noriko Mizuta Lippet and Kyoko Iriye Selden (Armonk, N.Y.: M.E. Sharpe, 1991), pp. 46–57.
12. For an English translation of the novel, see Yoshiyuki Koitabashi and Martin C. Colcott, trans., *The Floating Clouds* (Tokyo: Hara Shobo, 1965)
13. Audie Bock, *Japanese Film Directors* (San Francisco and Tokyo: Kodansha International, 1978), p. 132.
14. Heiichi Sugiyama, *Eizo gengo to eiga sakka* (Film language and film directors) (Tokyo: Kuge Shuppan, 1978), pp. 177–79.
15. For a comparative analysis of Toyoda's *The Mistress* and Joseph von Sternberg's *Blonde Venus*, see David Desser, "*The Mistress*: The Economy of Sexuality," *Post Script* 2011, no. 1 (Fall 1991): 20–17.
16. For an intensive analysis of the film, see Keiko McDonald, "*The Snow Country*," in Thomas Rimer and Keiko McDonald, *Teaching Guide for Japanese Literature on Film* (New York: Japan Society, 1989), pp. 51–58.
17. For an English translation of this novel, see William Shibley, *Dark Night Passing* (Chicago: University of Chicago Press, 1979).
18. Tadao Sato, *Nihon eiga no kyoshotachi* (Master directors of Japanese cinema) (Tokyo: Gakuyo Shobo, 1979), p. 221.
19. Donald Richie, *Japanese Cinema: Film Style and National Character* (Garden City, N.Y.: Anchor, 1971), p. 196.

20. For a more intensive analysis of this film, see Keiko McDonald, *Cinema East: A Critical Study of Major Japanese Films* (Rutherford, N.J.: Fairleigh Dickinson University Press, 1983), pp. 88–100.
21. For an English translation, see Ivan Morris trans., *Fires on the Plain* (New York: Knopf, 1957).

PART II
Writing as Directed:
A Re-creative Experience

4

A Lyrical Novella Revamped:
Gosho's *Izu Dancer* (1933)

Yasunari Kawabata's novella *Izu no odoriko* (The Izu dancer) has been adapted for the screen six times since it was published in 1926. That number seems small, considering the nature of the story. After all, it offers the time-honored romantic theme of young lovers separated by social barriers.

The most recent adaptation is Mitsuo Wakasugi's 1976 vehicle for teen pop idols Tomokazu Miura and Momoe Yamaguchi and is hardly a version to single out for praise. Of course, social barriers are not what they used to be, and a film of the 1970s may be expected to reflect that fact. In any event, the first film version of *The Izu Dancer* is the best: Heinosuke Gosho's work for the silent screen in 1933. Any director could mine the melodramatic vein in Kawabata's tale, but Gosho's pioneering work surpasses the others by accommodating the novella's lyrical aspects to the *shomingeki* genre in which he was himself most comfortable.

Critic Masaru Kobayashi's comments on this film offer a good starting point for analysis:

> Kawabata's original brings an element of pathos to its celebration of the feelings and experiences of a young man on his travels. His journey takes on an aura of touching loneliness so characteristic of the author. Doubtless this is why various directors have adapted this novella for the screen. The first such attempt yielded an excellent adaptation by the youthful team of Noboru Fushimi and Heinosuke Gosho. Even though sound pictures were becoming popular at the time, silent films were still going strong—films like *Umarete wa mita keredo* (I was born but, . . .) and *Dekigokoro* (Passing fancy). As its scenario shows, [Gosho's] film is rich in musical motifs, theme songs and dialogue. I don't know why it wasn't made as a talkie. What intrigues me more is why so many sound versions of *The Izu Dancer* have failed to compete with this pioneer film. Perhaps it only goes to show how talented Fushimi and Gosho were as collaborators.[1]

Anecdotal evidence suggests that Gosho had labored long and hard on a dramatization of Kawabata's novella some years before sound came to the screen.[2] By 1932 he had been given due credit for the first successful sound picture in Japanese cinema, *Madamu to Nyobo* (A neighbor's wife and mine, 1931). One would assume that his return to the silent screen represents a kind of fidelity to a concept so long in process. (Then, too, it must be said that all the *shomingeki* films Ozu made around this time were silent films.)

At any rate, once that decision was made, Gosho did a beautiful job of adapting a relatively short novella to the rather expansive format of the Shochiku Company's trademark *shomingeki* picture. How did he do it?

To begin with, Gosho makes good use of the principle of addition/alternation. While retaining the main thrust of Kawabata's plot—the student/dancer romance—Gosho complicates the outcome by adding another dimension. The story of young romance is supported and complicated by a second plot line dealing with relations between travelers and townsfolk. The film offers a melodramatic romance played out in a richly plotted context of life in a small-town spa. In that rural setting we see the drama unfold with various complications of love, greed, treachery, and some human kindness, too.

In order to see how Gosho transferred the original on to the screen, we need to look at Kawabata's novella. The central problem of *The Izu Dancer* concerns the narrator-protagonist's search for a self-image he can live with. The story is told from his point of view, in first-person confessional mode.

The narrator introduces himself as a twenty-year-old high school student (today's college undergraduate) embarking on a journey. He does not confine himself to strict chronological order; instead, he offers us various recollections, flashbacks that Kawabata cleverly manipulates as part of the narrative device of withheld information, using the narrator's motives and actions to create suspense.

The film's central problem is not offered to the reader until the sixth chapter, well on the way to the end of the story. There the narrator offers this striking clarification: "At the age of twenty, I reflected long and hard before realizing that my sense of being an orphan had warped my character. I had taken this journey to escape a well-nigh suffocating melancholia which I dared not reveal to others."[3]

We see how his journey offers two ways out of his emotional quandary: he can retreat, or he can reach out. His journey shows him taking the latter alternative. He meets and takes up with a troupe of traveling performers. Gradually, thanks to them, he frees himself from his orphan's anomie.

The various stages of his awakening are rendered through his responses to members of the troupe. They are, of course, not the kind of people with whom he would ordinarily come into contact. As we later see, that dimension of social difference lends a definitive poignancy to his love affair with the dancer, Kaoru. As so often with stories of this kind, love leads to self-awareness, even as it makes for a final sad awakening.

Since the narrator's story is not told day by day, the first encounter he describes takes place on his fourth day on the road. He describes his third encounter with the traveling players, then his previous two encounters with them. That done, he reverts to strict chronological order for the rest of his account. The one break in that true-life ordering of events comes in Chapter 6. There he finally discloses his motive for the journey, a motive he has concealed from us long enough.

Right at the outset, Kawabata establishes the motif of journey to "the other side," where his hero's life will be purified before he returns to his "real" life in the city.[4] The Amagi Pass, with its views of deep ravines and primordial forest, suggests the nearness of boundaries as mysterious and forbidding as those the young man faces in himself. Rain falls in torrents, as if to anticipate the violence of emotions that will purify this seeker.[5] The opening chapter clinches this motif with a familiar Kawabata image: a tunnel the train must pass through, carrying the narrator and his newfound companions.

The story is set in motion when the narrator meets the troupe again. It is clearly a case of three times being the charm. The young man's "silence" and "gazing" alert us to his feelings when he comes across the players at a teahouse. He has eyes only for the dancing girl, but he does not declare himself: "I sat down face to face with the dancing girl, and hurriedly took a pack of cigarettes from my kimono sleeve . . . I still remained silent."[6] The girl is in fact a great beauty. Kawabata's young man thinks of her as a figure "from a historical picture." She looks to be about seventeen. Yet her glorious mass of lovely black hair is done up in the old way, and it frames the delicate oval face of a classic Japanese beauty.

We understand the young man's infatuation immediately. What he must do now is take us back with him in memory to the beginnings of his joy and pain.

He lost his heart the first time he saw her, a dancing girl with a drum, traveling with her companions. From that moment, he himself became "a traveler at heart." That brief remark is a clue to the novel's motif of quest for release from orphan consciousness. The second time he meets the troupe, he is lost in wonder all over again, gazing at the girl: "On the second night of my journey, the troupe came to perform at my inn. Sitting on the stairs half-way up, I gazed intently at the girl dancing down below."[7]

The element of unblemished youth in her beauty soon provides a major source of tension in the plot. The young man must face the paradox of his desire: he yearns to "contaminate" the purity whose loss he fears with equal force.

He spends four days with the troupe before he and the girl are separated. In that time, he learns that her name is Kaoru, but he consistently refers to her as "the dancing girl." Does he want to shield her behind a certain anonymity? The narrator's consciousness does endow her with a certain abstract quality. To him, she represents a beauty "untouchable" and "unattainable." His own experience of her in the flesh is notably distant—a purely visual contact such as any member of an audience might have of her on the stage, or a connoisseur have of a beautiful woman in a painting.

The narrator's conflict between desire and fear is first presented during his expected third meeting with the troupe. His feelings of revulsion for a sick old man at the teahouse is in stark contrast to his attraction to the dancing girl's purity. The old man is propped up near the hearth, looking like "a person drowned, his swollen body a hideous blue." He looks at the narrator with eyes that appear already rotting in his head. The narrator stands transfixed, gazing in horror at this "mountain monster" buried in a rubbish heap of old letters and bags.

The old man's wife turns the narrator's attention to the dancing girl by referring to her change from child to beautiful maiden. As if the present contrast were not horrid enough, the old lady goes on to set the dancer's virgin beauty in a repulsive context. She speaks contemptuously of the low-life character of roving entertainers. She adds that the sleeping arrangements of such people are just desperately casual. She insinuates that everything depends on the nature of the given "client."

The narrator's ambivalent feelings are fully engaged. He is at once desirous of being Kaoru's protector and her ravisher: "The old woman's spiteful remarks inflamed me so much I thought I would let the dancing girl stay in my room this night."[8]

He thinks back to an incident that marred the first day he met the dancing girl. Serving him timidly, she had spilled tea. One of her companions exclaimed: "How disgusting! This girl has become male conscious!" The narrator remembers that moment. Then, he had experienced a peculiar desolate feeling caused by the thought that a creature so lovely and so pure would some day be sullied. Now, having heard the old woman's contemptuous remarks, he experiences quite another sensation. He wonders if the dancing girl is in fact a *virgo intacta*. Worse yet, he finds his earlier desire to protect her unsullied purity suddenly gone.

Even so, his doubts revert to a kind of fear that night. There are sounds of merriment in the inn. Then silence. Not so much as a footstep anywhere. The narrator describes his feelings: "I lay there wanting to sharpen my eyes. I wanted to look into the heart of this darkness, to see what its silence meant. In my anguish I was thinking: this may be the night the dancing girl loses her innocence."[9]

An incident the next morning shows his fears to be unfounded. The narrator uses many images drawn from childhood to convey his relief and celebrate a purity still unsullied. Even his fixation on the girl's abundant hair returns with an ironic twist:

> Suddenly I saw a naked woman run out of the bathhouse gloom. Standing at the end of the dressing room, she shouted something, holding out her arms, like someone ready to leap into the water. She was completely naked. Then I realized: it was the dancing girl. Looking at her white body, her long legs like young pagonia trees, I felt "pure water" welling up in my heart. . . . She was still a child—a child happy to catch sight of me, leaping naked into sunlight, standing on tiptoe. I laughed and laughed, overwhelmed with joy. My head was clear as if my doubts have been all swept away. . . .
>
> Thanks to her wonderful head of hair I had taken her for seventeen or eighteen years old. And she was dressed for that age too. No wonder I was mistaken.[10]

The child image, with all its "movement" associations, is in stark contrast to the static, abstract quality of the earlier image of the figure in a historical painting. The plot turns on the narrator's appreciation of this difference. He decides to tag along with the troupe on its travels, becoming a part of their small society. His transformation is literally encoded in a change of hat. He tucks his school cap away in his bag, buying and wearing a hunter's hat instead.

Again, his strange vacillation between desire for conquest and fear of the consequences is expressed through his perception of the dancing girl's physical charms. The same day he changes hats, he sees her sharing a bed with another girl. She still wears traces of stage makeup. Her lips are still a provocative red. Kawabata plays with the color image, giving the young man these words to describe his reaction: "That erotic sleeping posture tinged my heart." But then, as if to suppress all carnal thoughts, he goes on to say that the dancing girl jumps out of the bed to offer him "a chaste little curtsey."

The narrator's transformation from student to man of the world is eased by a day's layover. He and the troupe have been staying at separate hotels. The difference in their lodgings expresses their differing social status. Now that he is, in a sense, one of them, he can invite the players to his room. That done, his own visits to their shabby inn can be spontaneous and "free." This easygoing camaraderie forges a bond, smoothing the way for the journey that will end in the narrator's "purification" or "liberation." Needless to say, the lowly entertainers serve as catalysts in this process:

> They could see that my kindness to them was free of vulgar curiosity and prejudice. They took me to their hearts, because I didn't treat them like vagabonds, people of a certain kind. Soon it was agreed that I would visit their place in Oshima.[11]

Even before they continue on the final leg of their journey, the narrator and the dancing girl become more aware of each other. This is expressed through physical images carefully balanced in color and movement. While they are engaged in a game of *go* in his room, her "unnaturally beautiful black hair" almost touches the narrator's chest. Her face suddenly "flushing," she rushes away. Later, at her inn, the narrator reads her a *kodan* tale. He notes her shining "black" eyes are "fixed" on his face. When she laughs, it is "like a flower."

The final stage of preparation for the narrator's transformation takes place on the fourth day of the journey. Again, images and events serve as prelude to his epiphany. The travelers must cross a mountain, as if in search of a new world. The morning sun shining over the ocean warms the mountainside. The dancing girl walks behind him, always maintaining "a distance." It is as if their relationship were free from the emotional involvement that closeness might have incited. The narrator drinks at a mountain spring, like a pilgrim or a participant in ritual purification. The women of the troupe made him drink ahead of them, saying that the water, touched first by a woman, would not be "clean." On a less exalted note, the narrator expresses disapproval when he sees the dancing girl brushing a dog with her comb.

He drinks from the spring in dazzling sunlight. He feels pure of heart, innocently accepting the women's whispered praise of him as "a very good person."

He looks at the sunlit mountain, feeling "refreshed in spirit." He will need that refreshment.

The rest of his story turns again and again to the motif of separation. Immediately after the narrator's exalted experience, the party encounters a signboard: "No Beggars or Traveling Performers Allowed in This Village."

The narrator and his friends descend from the mountaintop to the sea-level port of Shimoda. What better place to encounter the difference between high ideals and the everyday concerns of unredeemed humanity?

That difference soon works to separate the narrator from his friends, especially the dancing girl. Soon after they met, he and she had hefted one another's baggage. Her drum was far heavier than his school bag. What better index of differing status? What clearer indication that the only fate they share is being what they are, each in such a different sphere?

The narrator stays with the troupe at their kind of inn. It is frequented by entertainers and merchants of shoddy goods. Various members of the troupe encounter old friends. The narrator's sense of being out of place is complicated by money worries. In fact, the money question forces him to leave for Tokyo the following morning.

The dancing girl's mother refuses to let her go to the movies alone with him the night before. Obviously, he is already seen as an outsider whose motives are in question. The dancing girl's image in his mind now shifts to associations with a lifeless child. After she has begged for permission to go to the movies with him and has been denied, he watches her playing with the innkeeper's children. He looks for some clue to her state of mind, but sees none. Her face no longer radiates youthful exuberance. She seems absentminded, indifferent. There is nothing left to say, or so it seems. As the narrator leaves the inn, she seems to be entirely absorbed in petting a dog. Does she care at all? He hesitates to speak. This view of her is cruelly unlike so many in which she figured as the child of unblemished purity, the very picture of innocent liveliness on their journey through the mountains.

Kawabata labors on the image of fixity in the narrator and the dancing girl's final parting. It begins with the narrator's symbolic gesture of donning his school cap once again. He sees the dancing girl squatting on the beach. She does not move to meet his approach. Her farewell is all a silent bow. After he boards the ship, he notices the dancing girl pressing her lips together, gazing into the distance. Her silent response is broken only when the ship sails away: only then does he see her in the distance, waving something white. As one critic notes, this figure gives the impression of the dancing girl being reduced to a "puppet" on the Bunraku stage.[12] Then, too, the theatrical image echoes the narrator's first impression of her as "a figure in a historical painting." Together, they reinforce the unattainable virgin beauty of the dancing girl that Kawabata has taken pains to express throughout this novella.

The end of the narrator's journey works on the motif of rejuvenation. He cannot act out his epiphany through his communion with other passengers. He does, however, communicate his feelings to a boy who wonders about his tears:

". . . I have just said good-bye to someone." It came out very naturally. I did not mind his seeing me cry. I was not thinking of anything. I felt as if I were quietly sleeping in pure satisfaction.[13]

The narrator's liberation from his orphan's complex is once more reinforced through his gesture of sharing and kindness. Needless to say, such diction returns to adorn the narrator's description of his feelings.

He eats the sushi rolls offered by the boy, as if he forgot "they belonged to the other." He sleeps, sharing the boy's cape. With "a beautifully absorbent" mind, he accepts the other's kindness with a new spontaneity. Helping an old woman purchase a train ticket in Tokyo is now a natural act for him. The narrator feels that he has achieved a sense of oneness. Kawabata concludes the narrator's journey of quest with the sentimental lyricism for which he is noted:

In utter darkness, feeling the boy's warm body next to me, I could not stop the flow of tears. I felt sweet comfort as if pure water had filled my mind and now was emptying as tears.[14]

Gosho's film gives Kawabata's tale a very different orientation. The film is more like richly human drama firmly set in a rural community hit by a "gold rush." Newcomers and locals interact, becoming players in roles ranging from romance to comedy. Values clash and motives intertwine as the plot works out its tensions.

While the novel focuses on the youth's journey of quest offered in a confessional mode, the film develops two major plot lines involving relationships: one male and female, the other vengeful and scheming. Following the major events in the novel, the first entails the student Mizuhara's growing intimacy with the dancing girl Kaoru and their inevitable separation. The second plot pits two newcomers against an honest local inhabitant. Kaoru's elder brother, Eikichi, joins forces with the cunning prospector Kubota to squeeze money out of Zenbei, an innkeeper in the little spa.

The student Mizuhara links the two causal lines. As he becomes intimate with Kaoru, he volunteers to be a mediator/negotiator between Eikichi and Zenbei. The resulting plot is complicated and expanded by means of the familiar narrative devices—withheld information, misunderstanding and miscommunication, as we later see.

The opening sequence emphasizes the materialist outlook that prevails in this little rural community. It is shown through the interaction between a policeman, construction crew, and Kubota. The prospector has just come back to town. He finds this quiet backwater besieged with prospectors now that gold has been struck. The policeman is looking for a geisha who has run away from an inn, leaving her bill unpaid. We also learn that the innkeeper has struck it rich, too, both in the mine and at the inn where business is booming. Things are so good that he has his own geisha under contract.

When the scene cuts to the inn, our sense of the innkeeper changes radically. We expected him to be greedy and grasping. Not so. As his name suggests (Zenbei translates to "Goodheart"), he is not at all spoiled by wealth. Take, for example, the geisha who left without paying her bill. Zenbei wants her found because he is genuinely concerned about her; he fears that she has eloped with an unsavory character.

The subsequent sequence expands its counterpart in the original, counting heavily on comic interaction between newcomers and villagers. In the original, the young student and the troupe pass by a placard warning beggars and entertainers to stay out of town. That image has ironic implications here, since the narrator must overcome just that kind of social discrimination in order to free himself from his orphan complex.

In Gosho's film, the placard itself sets things in motion and helps establish intimacy between the student Mizuhara and the dancing girl's troupe. A village child sees a vagabond priest knock the placard down. The priest frightens the child away. The troupe, not seeing the sign, enter the village. A fight ensues as a villager accuses Kaoru's brother Eikici of knocking the placard down. Mizuhara acts as mediator. A touch of humor is provided by the child, who returns as a witness. The village man is forced to apologize to Eikichi. In his frustration he hits the child on the head. The child bawls out: "What's wrong with telling the truth like I was taught at school?" This kind of slapstick is deeply ingrained in the *shomingeki* genre; here it sets the tone for the comedy running throughout the film.

The rest of the film's action is structured around withheld information and revelation of truth as Gosho advances the two plot lines. It is gradually revealed that all these major characters who meet by chance on the road are more than casual acquaintances. In the original, Kaoru and Eisaku are from a humble family. Here they turn out to be children of a prospector who died before he knew that he had struck it rich. Zenbei's son, Ryuichi, who is a Gosho addition along with his father, happens to be Mizuhara's senior at the same university.

While retaining Mizuhara's journey with the troupe as the basic story line, Gosho develops the vengeance and romance plots side by side. The first plot line begins at the hot spring. It shows Kubota attempting to blackmail Zenbei's family. He claims to have helped Zenbei discover the gold mine. He is chased out of the inn. Several scenes later, he is in cahoots with Eikichi in another dishonest scheme. Kubota plans to pit Eikichi against Zenbei, claiming that the inn proprietor bought the mine from Eikichi's father for nothing, even though he knew about its mother lode.

The resulting confrontation is rich in withheld information and misunderstanding. Zenbei reproaches Eikichi's greedy materialism. He tells him to bring Kaoru to the inn if he wants money so badly. Eikichi accuses the innkeeper of wanting to buy "his sister" to make her a geisha. That accusation turns out to be richly ironic, since Eikichi is completely blind to Zenbei's real intention, which is revealed later. For the present, Eikichi storms out of the inn.

The romance plot line advanced in parallel with the other until this moment offers us a glimpse of Kaoru and Mizuhara's mutual fondness. The initial shot

Kinuyo Tanaka (l) and Den Ohinata (r) in *Izu Dancer* (1933) directed by Heinosuke Gosho. Courtesy of the Kawakita Memorial Film Institute.

captures the smiling Mizuhara watching Kaoru give candy to the child struck by the irate villager. Then, as Mizuhara proposes to travel with the troupe, Kaoru's shy manner yields to the song subtitle expressive of her feelings: "I am a floating leaf/Guided by waves. /The prime of youth is spent/On an endless journey. /Awake or sleep wherever I am/My love will bloom." Later, in the bathhouse scene, Kaoru speaks shyly of her fondness for Mizuhara. She is especially fond of his unaffected good nature.

Information on Kaoru and her brother's past is partially disclosed to Mizuhara in the barbershop scene that follows. The loquacious barber tells him that Eikichi is a good-for-nothing wastrel who ran through his inheritance. It seems that Kaoru had to become an entertainer to rescue them from abject poverty. He also warns the young man against becoming their traveling companion.

An embarrassed smile on his face is our only clue to Mizuhara's reaction. But he goes directly from the barber's chair to the change of hats, which signals his intention to go with the players after all. Here, however, the hunter's hat carries a somewhat different implication related to Gosho's changes in the story. In place of Kawabata's emphasis on the narrator's "orphan complex," we have a more straightforward motive: Mizuhara dons the hunting hat because he wants to fit in with his newfound friends. This gesture confirms Kaoru's earlier remark in praise of his unaffected good nature.

The same scene also discloses another link between the major characters. Zenkichi's son, Ryuichi, runs into Mizuhara, introducing himself as a fellow college student. Mizuhara barely has time to stash his hunting hat out of sight in his kimono before this potentially embarrassing encounter.

The subsequent scene of Mizuhara's night stroll brings the two major plot lines together as the young man volunteers to mediate a quarrel between Kaoru and her brother. The scene opens with a shot of Mizuhara walking through the deserted street and stopping to gaze in the direction of Kaoru's inn. Her room on the second floor is still lit. Talking to himself, he wonders aloud what Kaoru might be doing at this hour. He soon finds out that she is arguing with Eisaku. Mizuhara's encounter with them is structured around the devices of misunderstanding and withheld information. Greed and revenge motifs also merge. Eisaku tries to persuade his sister to become a geisha at Zenbei's inn. He needs money to prospect for gold, the better to get even with Zenbei. Kaoru refuses. Mizuhara tries to reconcile the two, telling Eisaku he should reconsider his vengeance scheme.

The romance/vengeance plots are once more fortified in the subsequent scene of Kaoru and Mizuhara's stroll. It opens with the melodramatic subtitle song: "The cloudy sky over Amagi Mountain brings rain like tears. /An autumn wind blows through mist from a hot spring. /Into the distant roar of tides it disappears /like our memories of the past."

The panning camera follows them from the bridge down to the bank of a stream. Here Mizuhara offers his spiritual support of Kaoru, saying that whenever she is in trouble, he will help her in any way he can. The subtitle, along with her smiling face, expresses her response repeatedly, loud and clear: "I am glad. . . . I am glad!"

The promise to help Kaoru is soon tested by a confrontation between Mizuhara and Zenbei. Having the wrong idea of Zenbei's real intentions, Mizuhara vows to see that justice is done to Kaoru and Eisaku. An initial long shot shows the young man and the innkeeper facing each other in front of a window. Conventional crosscutting between the two in close-up follows Mizuhara's progress as mediator.

Lengthy subtitles render Mizuhara's naive speech denouncing Zenbei's opportunistic greed. The innkeeper listens to the young man's accusations and moralizing. Then he speaks. The truth behind all his previous behavior is revealed: he has set up a savings account in Kaoru's name, depositing her share of the gold-mine claim. He has been hard on Eikichi, hoping that the young man's easygoing attitude about money would change. Last but not least, he asked Eikichi to bring Kaoru to the inn so that she could be under his protection.

Our view of the two men's reconciliation is given in another long shot of the two facing each other. This time, ease of tension is the theme. Every nuance of movement speaks for it, continuing through a variety of shots. A maid steps in and steps out. Then tension mounts once more as Zenbei offers another important piece of information. This one touches Mizuhara directly. Zenbei speaks of his intention to marry Kaoru to Ryuichi. A close-up of Mizuhara's face registers only surprise, as does the subtitle: "Kaoru for your son?"

Except for hinted eloquence, we are given no direct visual clues to the unhappy youth's feelings. The innkeeper begins to eat a bean cake. A long shot shows Ryuichi outside the window. He enters and invites Mizuhara to his own room. They leave together. All this time, the camera is drawn back, taking in Mizuhara's gestures of feigned cheerfulness, speechless as he is.

The rest of the film moves toward the lovers' final separation at the expense of the vengeance/scheming plot. As may be expected, Gosho's melodramatic overtones propel the action forward.

Again, information that is unavailable to Kaoru—Zenbei's intention—causes a rift between the lovers. The journey sequence that immediately follows the truth-revelation scene at the inn shows Kaoru trying to catch up with Mizuhara, who is walking very quickly. Here Kaoru is much more outspoken about her feelings than her counterpart in the novella. The subtitle renders her confession: "My sister scolded me when I told her that I really like you. . . . But I can not help liking you."

Gosho takes pains to let the actress Kinuyo Tanaka emulate the innocent dancing girl still unspoiled by contact with the grown-up world. Thus, her confession coupled with her innocent gaze into Mizuhara's face augurs well as a spontaneous expression of true feeling. When they stop for water, however, Mizuhara gives the girl's candor a rude check. Kaoru expresses a desire to go to Tokyo. He replies that people are better off living where they were born.

After the party arrives at Shimoda, Mizuhara is shown lying in his room at the inn, dreaming about Kaoru. The subtitle song lends its sentimental overtones to a definite prelude to Mizuhara's departure from Kaoru's life: "When can we meet again?/Though many a spring may pass/Will we ever speak to one other/Under blooming cherry trees?"

This element of tearful sentimentality takes charge of the remaining scenes of the film. Mizuhara's sudden decision to leave for Tokyo puts Kaoru and Eikichi in emotional turmoil. Together with subtitles, a series of cross-cuts, all in close-up, among the three clearly registers their different responses. The brother is worried that members of the troupe might have offended Mizuhara, being as they are from a different social class. Mizuhara tries to hide his real emotion, claiming that he must return to school. Kaoru begins to weep, as does her brother; neither suspects the real reason for Mizuhara's departure. Kaoru runs out of the room. Eikichi runs after her. A point-of-view shot from Mizuhara shows them still in tears, brother consoling sister. The dissolve, which provides an elegiac tone for the scene, yields to the boat Mizuhara is scheduled to board.

Gosho pursues the same melodramatic vein in the following scenes depicting the lovers' parting. A shot of the boat yields to the subtitle song: "Our dreams are not gone; I am a migrant bird; Crying does not help; Tears don't bring back bygone days." As in the novel, Mizuhara dons his student cap again, signaling the end of youthful freedom and a return to his allotted, and confining, place in life. He gives the hunting cap to Eikichi, who leaves the lovers alone.

Another melodramatic convention is provided by Mizuhara's request for Kaoru's comb. This hair ornament is deeply rooted in the Japanese cultural context as the object the woman would give to a departing husband or lover. Unlike her counterpart in the novel, Kaoru continues to tell Mizuhara how fond she is of him. She asks him to return to Oshima in the summer and asks if she can write to him.

The ensuing scene is built around revelations again charged with melodramatic overtones. For the first time, Mizuhara discloses Zenbei's intention. Kaoru's reaction is directly presented in both visual and verbal terms. Her tearful face is shown in close-up. She falls to the ground, while the subtitle speaks for her: "All my hope is gone. . . ." Mizuhara helps her to her feet. She clings to him, still in tears. The couple is also rendered in close-up. Mizuhara says: "Going to the Yukawa inn is not only best for you but for your brother too. . . . Please keep what I have said in your mind, and help your brother find a purpose in his life. . . ." Gosho lets the camera speak for Kaoru's suffering.

The melodrama here is rescued from cloying excess by a series of intercuts away from the lovers. Eikichi is shown in a medium shot as a bystander; then a boatman is shown announcing the departure of the ferry.

A long shot of Kaoru alone on the beach suggests that the lovers have parted. But this is not the case. Once more, Gosho adds a melodramatic moment not in the original. Kaoru and Mizuhara have one more brief moment together so that Mizuhara, finally, can speak for himself: "Kaoru, I . . . I'm fond of you. I really love you."

The two are shown facing each other in close-up. Mizuhara's serious face then yields to Kaoru's face in tears through the reverse field set up. Then a pen, a memento for Kaoru, is registered in close-up. This finalizes their inevitable separation.

As we have seen, Kawabata's young hero responds warmly to his fellow passengers on the journey home. Thus the novelist's conclusion is given over to an exquisite evocation of the youngster's growth and purification. Gosho's last farewell is all for those whom Mizuhara has left behind. Kaoru's unrequited love is rather overplayed in a series of close-ups of her tearful face and her brother's. Just when it seems the film must end in a surfeit of weeping, the camera cuts to Kaoru's mother and some others arriving. They have come too late to see Mizuhara off. Their fondness for him is expressed in a parting gift of persimmons; they are good for seasickness, they say.

The rest of the coda details various stages of Kaoru's emotional plight, letting her face and body and movement speak for them. A vast stretch of water yields to a close-up of her face, still in tears, with the pen in her hands. A high angle shot of the ship yields to a long shot of Kaoru running along the beach. Another close-up shows us still more tears. A dissolve lends an elegiac texture to the screen. A long shot of Kaoru prostrate alone on the beach reinforces the sense

Kinuyo Tanaka in *Izu Dancer* (1933) directed by Heinosuke Gosho. Courtesy of the Kawakita Memorial Film Institute.

of desertion. The panning camera suddenly moves to record her fruitless effort to catch one last glimpse of the lover disappearing from her life. We see her running along the beach until a cut to the ocean leads to a panning shot of Kaoru still running. Though Mizuhara's subsequent response to the leave-taking is not accessible to her, Gosho provides narrative legibility to the audience by inserting just one shot of the young man aboard the ship, his face bathed in tears. A subtitle underscores the mother's understanding of the situation as she says, "My child really liked that student!"

Shots of Kaoru waving her handkerchief and weeping crowd the screen. Still in tears, she takes out the pen, which the camera faithfully observes in close-up. The film ends with a long shot of Kaoru clutching the memento. Sentimentally overcharged as this final shot is, it does pose an important question about Kaoru's fate. It is up to us to ask it because Gosho has deliberately left us this narrative gap. The question is, of course, will Kaoru be adopted by Zenbei's family?

Despite the cloying sentimentality of Gosho's ending, his version of *The Izu Dancer* achieves a deft combination of two genres: *shomingeki* and melodrama. His skill made an important difference to the Shochiku Studio's development along those lines.

Notes

I am grateful to *Asian Cinema* for permitting me to reprint my article, which appeared in vol. 9, no. 1 (Fall 1997).

1. Masaru Kobayashi, "*Izu no odoriko* ni tsuite" (On *The Izu Dancer*), in *Nihon eiga shinario koten zenshu* (A collection of scenarios of Japanese classical films), vol. 2 (Tokyo: Kinema Jumpo, 1966), p. 156.
2. Gosho Heinosuke, "Jisaku o kataru" (Gosho on Gosho's films), *Kinema Jumpo*, no. 101 (October 1994): 38.
3. Yasunari Kawabata, *Izu no odoriko* (The Izu dancer) (Tokyo: Shincho, 1950), p. 34. The translation is the author's. For the English translation of this novella, see Edward Seidensticker, trans. *The Izu Dancer* (Tokyo: Hara Shobo, 1961).
4. The critic Tsuruta points out the basic narrative pattern of the journey to "the other side" shared by Kawabata's *Yukiguni* (The snow country) and many other Japanese writers' works. See Kinya Tsuruta, *Kindai bungaku ni okeru mukogawa* (The other side in modern Japanese literature) (Tokyo: Meijishoin, 1986).
5. The novelist Yukio Mishima also claims that Kawabata's constant thematic concern with virginity is already evident in this work. See "*Iu no odoriko ni tsuite*" (On *The Izu Dancer*) in Kawabata, *Izu no odoriko*, pp. 167–68.
6. Ibid., p. 8.
7. Ibid., p. 9.
8. Ibid., p. 11.
9. Ibid., p. 17.
10. Ibid., p. 19.
11. Ibid., p. 28.
12. Masanori Tachibana, "Iiki kara no tabibito" (A traveler from a different world), in Hideo Takubo et al., *Nihon no sakka: Kawabata Yasunari* (Japanese writers: Yasunari Kawabata), vol. 13 (Tokyo: Shogakkan, 1991), p. 123.
13. Kawabata, *Izu no odoriko*, p. 40. Italics are mine.
14. Ibid.

5

Freedom to Stray from the Straight and Narrow: Mizoguchi's *Lady Musashino* (1951)

Both Shohei Ooka's *Musashino Fujin* (Lady Musashino, 1950) and Kenji Mizoguchi's film version (1951) are set in the heady democratic climate of postwar Japan, a time that saw an evolution of the civil code. Adultery as a crime had ceased to exist. It vanished from the statute books as the 1947 civil code evolved along more "democratic" lines in postwar Japan. But of course the human fact of adultery persisted, taking on new meaning, even new urgency, as Japanese society looked for ways to renegotiate the moral terms of this tricky and sometimes tragic phenomenon.

One literary critic had this to say about such an issue as a topic in these changing times:

> Postwar Japanese literature, in alliance with the socialization of "I" and the search for the total novel—the general trend advocated by various critics—absorbed in itself new subject matter and points of view. This development found itself, both centripetally and centrifugally, in an interpretation of various political and social phenomena from an ideologically oriented view, and also an investigation of the inner reality of individual characters.[1]

What, then, might a novelist and filmmaker make of this social incertitude as it applied to a tale of adultery in contemporary Japan? We have a chance to see the answer in Shohei Ooka's novel of 1950, *Musashino Fujin* (Lady Musashino), and Kenji Mizoguchi's 1951 film of the same title.

The novel and the film share the central problem of the individual characters' coming to terms with a changing society. Yet the novelist and the filmmaker are wide apart in their approach to this problem because they have very different ideas of the overall effect they desire in a work of art. Ooka is very much the detached Stendhalian observer of human psychology. He wants to show how the values of individual characters clash when they confront a changing society. In contrast, Mizoguchi labors to celebrate the platonic love between the two major characters, Michiko and Tsutomu, but fails to give their relationship any psychological depth. As a result, his work is reduced to a kind of melodrama combined with a film of manners reflective of the sociocultural milieu of the 1950s. This generic difference between the two works is very strongly demonstrated in their respective endings, as we later see.

"Is the psychological movement of a person like *d'Orge* outdated?"[2] Ooka's *Lady Musashino* starts with this epitaph from Raymond Radiguet's *The Ball at d'Orge*. An excellent critic of his own work, Ooka claims that he wrote this book with the intention of "restoring the Romanesque in the modern period and at the same time letting the Romanesque face its difficulty."[3] What he implies is that he tried to break new ground by making the novel a romantic narrative charged with psychological realism.

The novel focuses on the various stages of Michiko and Tsutomu's conflict as they try to come to terms with a postwar society. Their relationship is complicated by Michiko's husband, Akiyama, who tries to seduce another man's wife, Tomiko, who in return makes advances to Tsutomu. This quadrangular relationship is further complicated by the fact that Tomiko is married to another cousin of Michiko's, Ono.

What fortifies the central problem is the social and psychological dimensions of the novel. Through the dynamic interplay of their relationships, Ooka not only offers various venues for adapting to a society in the throes of transformation but probes the psychology of those affected by its myriad changing mores.

The novel is structured around a well-patterned causality. The first three introductory chapters describe the social conditions and establish relationships between the characters. Ooka saw fit to explain a rather noticeable methodology: "The novel must be based upon the given social conditions with respect to adultery. Otherwise, it will be read as the I-novel."[4] The middle part (Chapters 4 to 9) develops two plot lines defined by two relationships: Michiko-Tsutomu and Tomiko-Akiyama. Tomiko's seduction of Tsutomu and Akiyama's suspicion of Michiko's affection for Tsutomu, along with Ono's financial decline, complicate these two lines. The last three chapters focus on the theme of betrayal, as the two plot lines are brought to resolution. Michiko, abandoned both by her lover and her husband, resolves her crisis through suicide.

Ooka employs two major narrative devices to give his novel psychological depth. One involves authorial intervention. Though his presence interrupts the narrative flow, the omniscient author serves both as a moralist and an objective commentator. As a result, we are forced into the point of view of the author-narrator, who considers himself to be the center of consciousness. Ooka's other device makes use of eye and nature imagery. Nature's functions are seen as twofold. Nature reflects the social changes that are happening to the Akiyama and Ono families, but it objectifies individual psychology. Counterpointed with nature are human eyes. The main characters' shifting awareness is powerfully conveyed through their responses to one another's eyes. These two devices interact closely as the author steps in to interpret for the reader the main characters' very act of seeing or being seen or their perception of nature.

In the first three chapters used to establish the conditions for adultery, Ooka posits a state of internal decay both in nature and the people at Hake. He sees both forms of decay as caused by social changes. Hake is a part of the Musashino Plain, which is noted for its bountiful nature. Before the war, Michiko's father improved the landscape in his retirement. The most striking aspect of Hake is its abundant underground water and green trees—convenient fertility symbols of which Ooka makes good use. But the aesthetic appeal of these natural resources has been sacrificed to economic necessity. Michiko's father, in order to survive postwar inflation, has sold his trees. The chestnuts are no longer seen as objects of visual pleasure, but as a source of income. He also disregards the productive use of the well water as a nuisance. Nature is therefore perceived as a source of difficulty, not of solace. The increasing deterioration of the landscape already foreshadows the destiny of the Akiyama family: its coming dissolution, culminating in Michiko's death.

This state of nature also prefigures Hake's deterioration from within and without. Postwar moral laxity is represented by two "outsiders" who return to Hake after the war. Kenji, a childhood acquaintance of Michiko, is casually promiscuous. Tsutomu, a repatriate, has lost any trust in human nature. He surrenders himself to the *carpe diem* attitude increasingly prevalent among the young in the aftermath of war.

Ooka uses a tightly schematic set of characters to act within this changing system of values. As he himself says, Michiko stands for the conventional morality, for submission to the demands of paternal authority and devotion to a husband. Her opposite, Tomiko, is coquettish. Tomiko was a notable flirt even in school, and has a lover after her marriage. She stands for sexual liberation, for the new morality.

Ono represents the feudal values of male domination. He never doubts the double standard. Taking his own extramarital relationships for granted, he considers his wife to be his possession. Akiyama offers a contrast of sorts. He is a professor of French literature and claims to be a Stendhalian. He cultivates a self-consciously intellectual form of male ego. He sees adultery for what it is, and follows his inclination that way with a certain analytical relish and more than a touch of cynicism.

Significantly, the "new morality" is represented by those who married into the families of Hake from outside. The seemingly peaceful relationship between each married couple is disturbed by Tsutomu. When he was young, he left Hake and later went to war, serving in Burma. Returning, he plays a dramatic role in Hake, bringing out an element of discord hidden just beneath the surface. One might say that Tsutomu helps create, and exacerbate, an inevitable postwar conflict between old and new moralities.

Thus the middle part of the novel expands on two romantic fronts, as mentioned earlier. Michiko's relationship with Tsutomu develops in three main stages: gradual attraction to each other, inability to commit to passion, then separation.

The Tomiko-Akiyama relationship goes from worldly wise adultery to a cynical parting of the ways. These two plot lines are fortified by the novelist's exploration of characters' psychological responses to one another and to the socio-cultural conditions affecting their relationships.

Two important narrative events are central to the development of the Tsutomu-Michiko affair. Both entail a rendezvous away from Hake. The first occurs when Tsutomu asks Michiko to go for a walk on the Musashino Plain. The second, their moral crisis, happens on a visit to a reservoir. In both instances Ooka's narrative devices—authorial intervention and nature/eye imagery—propel themselves forcibly.

Chapter 4, titled "Koigabuchi" (The deep lake of love) describes the first instance. For Tsutomu, who has suffered the trauma of war, nature seems the all in all. It contains both beauty and decay. The abundant water consoles him. At the same time the ruined airfield and abandoned flower gardens remind him of the impact of the war even on this remote area.

Toward the middle of this chapter, nature is shown in parallel with the love taking shape between Michiko and Tsutomu. The rhythm of the running water corresponds to their shifting attitudes toward each other. When Tsutomu asks her out to see the reservoir, Ooka first presents nature as a mixture of sound and silence:

> The hill is thickly covered with tall zelkovas and oaks. The road under them is quiet. The silence is broken only by the sound of the running water. It comes from somewhere up in the hill, tumbling noisily down to wind along, crossing the road before it runs to meet the river in the field. The first time it runs across a low place in the road, the water moves like a living thing.[5]

The relationship between Michiko and Tsutomu becomes more intimate as they go into the forest and come into closer contact with nature: "The two of them moved as one with nature. Their footsteps took some rhythm from the sound the running water made."[6] Nature reflects their psychology more pervasively as Tsutomu's attentiveness to the running water awakens the same response in Michiko. The splash of the water becomes louder, as if to match their beating hearts.

Michiko's view of the world is also seen in terms of response to nature. The lovers meet a farmer who tells them that the source of the watershed is called Koigabuchi. According to legend, a woman drowned herself there, yearning for the man who left her to fight a war. The sense of Michiko's imprisonment in love is complete when her vision is blocked by the riverbanks with a railway running along one shore. Ooka adds only: "She felt captured." The squeaking wheels of the passing train make her shiver, as if in revulsion for feelings she must consider morally reprehensible.

The powerful eye image now returns to reinforce the couple's mutual attraction to each other. When she looks at "her lover," their eyes do not meet. Until they gaze into each other's eyes to confirm their love after this trip, Tsutomu must keep guessing at her eyes' intent.

When he first returned from Burma, Tsutomu saw Michiko's eyes filled with tears. This happened when he announced that he would be living somewhere else, rather than staying with her and her husband. But now he realizes that her eyes are different in color. He also wishes that she loved him, even as he wonders if he is mistaken about the look of love in her eyes.

Here, Ooka interrupts in true Stendhalian fashion:

> Michiko considers the fact that being cousins is an obstacle to any real consummation of love between man and woman. Tsutomu is content to think that the strength of their affection is itself proof of love. Readers may find the difference between man and woman in their own responses to love. A woman instinctively distinguishes love from other feelings while a man arbitrarily labels all kinds of affection as love. If we interpret affection his way, then all kinds of feelings associated with it claim to be akin to love.[7]

In the second tryst between Tsutomu and Michiko, nature again serves to describe their subtle psychological state. As they set out on their journey, Michiko hears cicadas in the trees near a station. Unlike Akiyama and Tomiko, who find nature disturbing their tryst, she responds appreciatively. The insects' music conjures up the vast Musashino Plain filled with their chorus. Her peaceful involvement in nature is then taken over by a sense of release—release from the agony of love that she has thus far experienced.

But the author alerts us to elements of discord in this seemingly harmonious landscape, as if to comment on Michiko's subconscious uneasiness about this tryst. The rich fields of wheat and vegetables look very symmetrical and appealing, but in the farthest distance a tank is seen soaring up intruding on the idyllic view. Moreover, the wheels of the train squeal as it clings uphill. A series of water images follows. First, Michiko and Tsutomu see water behind a dam. Its stillness corresponds to the quietude the lovers are experiencing. When they decide to walk close to a man-made lake, however, the omniscient author's voice offers a wry comment. "Lovers are just naturally drawn to bodies of water."[8]

Their attempt to reach the lake is frustrated by a No Trespassing sign. Once more the author interrupts the narrative flow with a brief comment: "The lovers who longed for the water were betrayed."[9] Brief as it is, this statement looks forward to the inevitable tragic ending. Then, too, this seemingly harmless inclination tips the balance toward a more dynamic psychological probing of the lovers' felt reality. While Tsutomu is filled with happiness, Michiko shifts to a mood of self-reflection. She wonders whether the feelings she has had for Tsutomu are genuine or not.

In the middle of this chapter, the idyllic scene suddenly changes. Ominous cumulonimbus clouds announce a storm as a sudden wind sweeps over the couple. Again, changing nature moves in parallel to their shifting feelings. Their love, under control up to now, yields a passionate embrace. Only momentarily, however, rather than objectify the lovers' psychology, nature is seen running counter to it. Even as nature becomes more and more threatening and violent, their love begins to seem more peaceful. Tsutomu feels a maternal affection on Michiko's lips, while she experiences a kind of innocent relief and sweetness.

From this point, nature is not just there but is personified as if to convey the immediacy of the lovers' felt reality in a more dramatic way. The mountain covered with clouds presides over the lake "like a disheveled woman." The pouring rain attacks the lovers. The storm sets the stage for their climactic conflict between personal needs and social conventions. Tsutomu cannot control his passion, which Michiko resists at first. But at the final moment, she is ready to surrender. Then it is Tsutomu who curbs his passion. He hears something breaking outside the building. But the sound strikes him as "being like a cry wrung from Michiko's very soul as she moves to yield to him."[10] Her soul seems to plead with him not to "proceed any further." At this moment, the eye image is effectively introduced to express the lovers' responses to this moral crisis: Tsutomu watches Michiko's closed eyes, which look like "a sharp cut wound on her agonized face."

With this climax as a turning point, their relationship becomes less passionate. Michiko now finds herself pulled back toward traditional morality. Through suffering, she realizes that Tsutomu will sacrifice his life once he commits himself to an illicit relationship with her.

As mentioned earlier, various narrative events focusing on the triangular or quadrangular relationship reinforce the Michiko-Tsutomu plot line. One of the prime examples occurs in Chapter 5, immediately after their walk on the Musashino Plain. Here, through his deft use of nature interacting with eye imagery, the author already hints at the familial discord that will later become paramount. He first calls the reader's attention to a natural setting fit for a tense encounter:

> Only the chirping of cicadas sounded in the trees above. The sound of running water grew louder, the closer they came to the place where the fountain in Hake fed into the pond which spilled into a quiet stream whose banks were a mass of daffodils.[11]

The author's psychological study focuses on a matter of butterflies, Michiko and Tsutomu responding to them while Akiyama looks on. One butterfly is big and black, the other smaller and brown. Akiyama is overwhelmed with jealousy, seeing his wife and her cousin gazing at them admiringly. Both Tsutomu and Michiko find the butterflies analogous to themselves. She imagines the brown butterfly to be female when she sees it struggling to escape the aggressive male. She also feels trapped in a relationship with Tsutomu. He, meantime, imagines the black butterfly to be the male. He sees the female as cruel, rejecting the male's advances the minute he touches her. Thus, their movements appear to corroborate the thought that he will strive for Michiko's love in vain. Akiyama suddenly appears, awaking both lovers from their reverie. Obviously, Akiyama stands for the intrusive reality of social mores running counter to individual freedom.

Ooka concludes this chapter by affirming the love of these two cousins, returning to his use of eye imagery: "Their eyes met. It was no longer possible to doubt the meaning of the light in one another's eyes."[12]

As mentioned earlier, the novel advances two plot lines: the Michiko-Tsutomu's attraction and the Tomiko-Akiyama liaison. This allows Ooka to offer a contrast of trysts. While Tomiko's husband is away on a business trip, Akiyama asks her out for a few days' leisure trip. Their responses to nature speak for the abortive aspect of this union. They board a crowded train to a hot-springs resort. Akiyama is first excited over the trip, but the train, packed with peddlers, soon makes him miserable. This shift in mood is externalized through the scenery passing outside the window: the volcanic range of Mt. Fuji looks so solemn and lofty, filling the entire window frame, yet Akiyama feels suffocated and tense. Tomiko also becomes despondent, regretting this hasty action triggered by Tsutomu's rejection of her advances.

More nature images continue to function as objective correlatives to feelings arising out of this tryst. Mt. Fuji, covered with clouds and a rather dull light shining through them, reflects a sense of their unfulfillment. Ooka comments: "They feel lonely like lovers walking along outside some boundary of love."[13] Ironically, when they take a boat on the lake, they pass by the area famous for its legend of two despairing lovers.

The novel takes a different turn when Tsutomu leaves Hake in order to resolve his and Michiko's moral dilemma, temporarily at best. This is where Ooka introduces another dimension of social conditions as he develops his fictional characters. We see his four main characters caught in money matters. Akiyama's opportunism is the only thing that ties him to Michiko long after he has lost interest in her. She is the sole heir of the Miyaji family. He has already taken possession of half of her inheritance. When he discovers that the other half has been left to Ono to rescue him from bankruptcy, he begins to consider divorcing Michiko. In this situation, Akiyama continues his affair with Tomiko.

Monetary interest keeps the two lovers together. Tomiko becomes emotionally desperate when Ono cuts off her allowance. She tells herself that she will continue to see Akiyama as long as he is able to provide her with money. Her rebellion against the traditional values comes to the fore as well. Far from feeling guilty about her affair with Akiyama, she assumes that matrimony is only a facade and does not prevent her from doing what she wants.

Seen in contrast to Tomiko's freedom, Michiko's traditional outlook is given its due weight. Akiyama not only accuses her of being an inadequate wife but condemns her for offering financial assistance to Ono without her husband's consent. Showing no resistance to this accusation, Michiko lets Akiyama be a tyrannical husband. Worse yet, she suffers his infidelity in silence.

Once Michiko's suffering is established, the novel's pattern swiftly moves to another stage of her moral dilemma in relation to Tsutomu. The lovers are brought together once more when Tsutomu visits Hake. This happens in Chapter 11, titled "Kamera no Shinjitsu" (The truth caught by the camera). Social convention and individual freedom—the chief sources of tension thus far—are brought into more dynamic conflict. Michiko now takes a strongly traditional moral stance. She cannot allow herself to be with Tsutomu. He criticizes her conservative views.

Even so, their conflict this time is resolved with a lovers' pledge: they will love one another platonically. According to Michiko, this pledge alone can transcend "the morality" created by society.

The rest of the novel develops this causal line, showing how the ideal of platonic love is threatened as much by external forces as it is by human weaknesses. Instead of keeping his reader in suspense about the outcome, the moralist Ooka follows the lovers' pledge with some cynical hard questions: "To whom did he plight his truth? Michiko was mistaken. Vows of this kind are only exchanged in the presence of God."[14]

As the author predicts, Tsutomu's breach of promise takes place sooner than the reader might expect. On his way to Tomiko's place, he reasons that it is futile to wait for social conventions to change. He reckons that by that time he and Michiko will be too old to consummate their love. This psychological shift also corresponds to a change of scenery. When Tsutomu leaves Michiko's old house and approaches Tomiko's Western-style one, he feels that he has come to a different world. Needless to say, Michiko's wooden palings offer an obvious conservative contrast to Tomiko's liberal expanse of turf. By the time Tsutomu reaches her place, we see him already thinking of an excuse for accepting Tomiko's earlier proposition.

No wonder we expect an easy victory of commonplace human frailty over a high-minded lovers' pledge. But Ooka puts an irony of circumstance in the way. Tsutomu finds Tomiko in a refusing mood, seconded by Akiyama's sudden arrival.

The ensuing picture taking at the end of Chapter 11 is a vital cog in the narrative progression as it contributes to the final resolution of Michiko's moral conflict through her death. Tsutomu suggests that the three of them take pictures. The camera's eye offers another configuration of that imagery used to describe the tense triangular relationship in terms of seeing and being seen. As Akiyama takes a picture of Tomiko and Tsutomu, he notices that, at the last moment, the young man puts his hand on her shoulder. Tsutomu in turn takes a picture of the other two, sensing abortive love between them.

These pictures also serve the novel play with irony. What the two men think of the pictures is very different from Michiko's interpretation. The omniscient author explains. Yet he also delays Michiko's response to the photography, letting that serve the tragic outcome of her emotional quandary.

The last three chapters show how Michiko's trust in human beings is betrayed not only by the people around her but by social conditions as well. The dramatic tension is sustained as she is pitted against the other four major characters: Tsutomu, Akiyama, Tomiko, and Ono. The first external circumstance leading to her tragedy is Akiyama's demand for a divorce.

That strain is followed by the shock of seeing the picture of Tsutomu and Tomiko. Akiyama deliberately leaves it for Michiko to find. Her belief in human innocence is completely shattered. The minute description of her shifting emotions is made possible again through Ooka's deft use of eye imagery. Concupiscence is what she sees in Tsutomu's eyes as shown in the picture. This leads her to reflect on what she has done to him. Her self-control was partly motivated by a desire to serve the best interests of her community in Hake. Only now, overwhelmed by pain, doe she realize that Tsutomu has interpreted her behavior as a sign of her lack of interest in him.

Money, as it relates to the values of Akiyama's opportunism, precipitates Michiko's tragedy. Tomiko is pressuring him to marry her. Ironically, he needs Michiko's inheritance to do so. His own work of translating Stendhal has not been going well. Again, Ooka lets eye imagery convey Michiko's growing self-realization. In the eyes of her husband, who claims that he would never depend on her property for financial support, she sees for the first time "beastly lust" and begins to wonder why she has been married to him for ten years.

Ooka says simply, "Michiko thought that everything was over for her."[15] Nature seems to echo her decision to kill herself. Destructive elements of the rain "which beat the earth around the old house and ran down from the drains" sound like a strange kind of chorus. Rain also encloses the old house at Hake, as if to suggest a sense of entrapment in a complex web of circumstance.

Michiko's suicide is spiced with irony. Again, eye imagery dominates. Tsutomu's determination to be faithful to Michiko prevents him from confronting her in person. Instead, during his visit to Hake, he watches her from a distance in secret. She is about to perform her last ritual. What he sees as a dose of medicine is in fact a fatal dose of sleeping pills. Ironically, in order to avoid succumbing to her eyes and thus facing her in person, he leaves his place of hiding. Again the omniscient author offers a moral on this ironic twist of the lover's plight: "Fate does not stop weaving the human drama, sensitive to each person's necessity."[16]

The last chapter brings the four survivors together for what the moralist Ooka emphasizes is a difficult reconciliation between social conditions and the individual life. Michiko's approach of death puts Akiyama at the mercy of a very rigid ethical social structure. He sees himself in the position of the husband whose illicit love affair has caused his wife to kill herself. Yet this egotistical husband refuses to accept responsibility. He hates Michiko and is determined to claim that Michiko died for Tsutomu, no matter what people may say.

Ono and Tomiko must also bear some brunt of the burden of social norms. Yet they use those very norms as a way out. After her tryst with Akiyama and causal love affair with Tsutomu, Tomiko copes with her life by returning to Ono. Ono, in turn, takes his unfaithful wife back without a fuss.

As Michiko predicted, Tsutomu finds himself unable to keep his vow to Michiko and succumbs to Tomiko's blandishments. They spend a night together. The following morning, Ono comes looking for his wife. Watching them leave, Tsutomu sees the weight of social convention bearing down on Ono. He realizes that his own challenge to society by such means as adultery is simply meaningless.

Is it simply her desire to escape from the role of estranged wife that tempts Michiko to suicide, or is it her realization that Tsutomu is unable to keep his pledge of love? Her motive, though seemingly clear, is kept ambiguous. In this last chapter, too, the omniscient author again steps in to detect the importance of Michiko's solemn act: "It was purely accidental that Michiko's attempt did not fail. Tragedy does not happen in the twentieth century except by accident."[17]

After the publication of this best seller of Ooka's, the feudal view of adultery was studied in other notable films. One might mention two examples reviving classic plays of Chikamatsu. One was Mizoguchi's *Chikamatsu monogatari* (The crucified lovers, 1954) based on *Daikyoji mukashigoyomi* (The almanac maker, 1715) and Tadashi Imai's *Yoru no tsuzumi* (The night drum, 1954), adapted from *Horikawa nami no tsuzumi* (The drum of waves at Horikawa, 1706).

Lady Musashino was Mizoguchi's earlier attempt to explore such a new thematic potential, but this film is recognizably a typical Mizoguchi work in its venue: the fate of a woman held captive by an unsupportive environment. This time, he focuses on the fate of an upper-class heroine in the throes of postwar social changes as her innocence is betrayed and destroyed by those closest to her. Mizoguchi faithfully follows most of the major events of the novel, whose story tells of a relationship between Michiko and her unmarried cousin, Tsutomu. The two meet

Masayuki Mori, So Yamamura, Yukiko Todoroki and Kinuyo Tanaka (clockwise) in *Lady Musashino* (1951) directed by Kenji Mizoguchi. Courtesy of the Kawakita Memorial Film Institute.

Kinuyo Tanaka (l) and Akihiko Katayama (r) in *Lady Musashino* (1951) directed by Kenji Mizoguchi. Courtesy of the Kawakita Memorial Film Institute.

social obstacles that lead inevitably to a tragic ending. Ooka's major characters are also retained on screen, as they offer different ways of coping with postwar society. But the film's greatest departure from the original in characterization is Mizoguchi's treatment of Michiko and Tsutomu.

The novel's heroine vacillates between individualism and conformity in a more dynamic manner than her counterpart in the film. In the climax of her moral crisis, which happens when the lovers/cousins visit a hotel, Michiko is ready to surrender to her inner urge. It is Tsutomu who listens to the voice of reason and halts their progress on to passion.

For Mizoguchi, whose ideal heroine always was the nobly self-sacrificing woman of high moral integrity, such deviation from social norms on Michiko's part is not acceptable. He presents her as a paragon of the traditional morality in her efforts to cling to her identity of chaste wife. The film thus studies the tragedy of such a woman, betrayed by love, and an unsupportive environment, even as she continues to be enslaved by social pressures. Then, too, Tsutomu's character in the film is given a much more melodramatic touch: he undergoes a kind of moral transformation on Michiko's deathbed, while such a display of virtue is not available to Ooka's hero, as he is cast in a more realistic mold. In this respect, Tsutomu's character is consonant with the typical Mizoguchi male; he is the one who is redeemed through a female sacrifice.

In fact, *Lady Musashino* is a good example of a film whose screenplay is impoverished by a rigid moralistic scheme. The characters come to represent moral choices more than actual human beings. The film starts out with a lack of vital information—details of each character's social background and lineage, which contribute to the clash of value systems and make the novel's treatment more dynamic and, for that matter, more plausible than that of the film. Ooka does his background work in the first chapter. He renders a detailed account of the Miyaji family, whose samurai status, old lineage, and prestige have molded Michiko's traditional upbringing. He also explains how Akiyama's impoverished background as a farmer's son contributed to his opportunism and to the resentful rebelliousness against the Miyaji family as his betters. Tomiko's liberalism—her elopement and loss of virginity before her marriage to Ono—becomes a plausible explanation of her continuous display of moral relativism. Tsutomu's ties with his cousin Michiko derive from a sad family history. His father committed suicide after Japan's defeat in the war. Then Tsutomu's stepmother proved unkind to him after his own repatriation.

Mizoguchi dispenses with all that history and in general sacrifices psychological depth to easy melodrama. He even neglects Ooka's deft imagery and banishes Ooka's omniscient narrator. The difference between the two works has a lot to do with what is essentially novelistic or cinematic. Mizoguchi counts very heavily on the camera's expressive power, leading the spectator to work out various visual clues to the inner state of the characters.

As we have seen, Ooka shows Michiko and Tsutomu watching butterflies at a climactic moment in their relationship. Mizoguchi simply dispenses with their little insect drama with its obvious counterpart on the human scale. Instead, he lets the camera do the talking in order to convince us of the doomed relationship between Akiyama and Michiko caused by Tsutomu's presence. The initial shot shows us Akiyama confronting Michiko and accusing her of undue attentiveness to her cousin. Michiko argues that she is a faithful wife. Then another shot includes Tsutomu in the foreground. We understand that the previous shot represents Tsutomu's view of the scene between Akiyama and Michiko. Through this simple transition in point of view, a potentially powerful connection is made between those shots of the couple arguing and their lodger spying on them. Nevertheless, we are still denied access to any greater psychological depth in this unhappy triangular relationship.

Mizoguchi does gain some expressive power from a cinematic focus he is famous for: the attention paid to a woman's gait. Time and again in his best films he uses gait as a powerful index of a woman's inner state. Exquisite examples of this occur in *Gion no shimai* (Sisters of the Gion, 1936) and *Saikaku ichidai onna* (The life of Oharu, 1952). In *Lady Musashino*, this expressive tool is coupled with occasional close-ups of the heroine's face in order to give the audience clues. This works well for such dramatic highlights as the walk Michiko and Tsutomu take across the Musashino Plain. Their enjoyment of the scene is conveyed through

Kinuyo Tanaka (l) and Akihiko Katayama (r) in *Lady Musashino* (1951) directed by Kenji Mizoguchi. Courtesy of the Katakita Memorial Film Institute.

a series of long shots mixed with occasional medium ones. Michiko's white parasol suggests an image of her as a tiny flower blooming in a wilderness.

In order to indicate the approaching moral crisis created by their growing affection for one another, Mizoguchi subtly interrupts the flow of movement: the couple stand and squat, as if to break with the smooth transition of scenery all around. Michiko approaches the bank of the stream and squats. Finally, she stands and folds the parasol, ready to confront the standing Tsutomu, whose back is shown to us. Shot continuity is also broken by a sudden close-up registering Michiko's emotional turmoil. Then, a long shot shows the lovers moving in ways that suggest a fear of meeting their mounting emotions face to face. Tsutomu squats, while Michiko tends to move away from him.

Though in general Mizoguchi neglects Ooka's use of nature to convey emotional states, there are significant exceptions. One is this walk the cousins take. Mizoguchi makes use of water imagery to suggest a break in the continuity of the couple's movement. First we are shown a close-up of the shallows. This is a point-of-view shot from their perspective, but at the same time its "shallowness" says something about the beginning of their mutual attraction. A later close-up interrupts the rhythmical flow of the couple's movement caught in a panning camera: it shows the river source in the so-called Koigabuchi (The deep lake of love) as seen along the couple's line of sight. The point in this transition in the depth of water is obvious as we see Michiko and Tsutomu become more aware of their love during this rendezvous.

A similar pattern is used at the moment of moral crisis. Michiko and Tsutomu stay overnight at a hotel, taking shelter from a thunderstorm. The scene consists of several shots, a few of them long takes. At first, the cousins are seen in relation to Western furniture. Tsutomu, pushing Michiko onto the bed, begs her to give in. Michiko resists, insisting that the platonic bond is stronger and purer than any physical one would be. She stands up and moves away. Tsutomu follows, insisting that he loves her. He goes to the window and sits on the desk. Michiko then moves to stand by him. One shot—almost a long take—records a series of movements in a way reminiscent of *shimpa* performance. They move away to squat on the floor. Michiko stands and Tsutomu kneels. Then he stands up and she sits down. Typically Japanese, they are afraid to look into each other's eyes again. Thus, their upward and downward movements together and alone suggests subtle emotions of conflict: Michiko's determination to uphold her morality despite her love for Tsutomu, and his unwilling surrender to her plea.

Like *Yuki fujin ezu* (A picture of Madame Yuki, 1950), Mizoguchi's adaptation of Seiji Funahashi's novel with the same title, *Lady Musashino* ends with the inevitable sense of entrapment clearly demonstrated by the heroine's suicide. The degree of difference in the generic molds of the Ooka novel and Mizoghichi's film is evident in the way each treats Michiko's death at the end.

As mentioned earlier, Ooka makes use of shifting narrative voices and irony to give psychological depth to characters. Akiyama, eager to defend his respectability, denies that his philandering has caused his wife's death. This college professor and Stendhal scholar has no other perspective to offer on this sad human outcome. Ooka must step in and supply it. Thus the omniscient author says, "Even at the time of her death Akiyama was convinced that Michiko died because she was betrayed by Tsutomu. He did not realize that she had died because he himself had abandoned her. This school teacher always placed himself outside the real situation, living in the world of literature, the subject he taught."[18]

In contrast to the selfish Akiyama, who did not take responsibility for his wife's death, Ono is presented as the husband who sees things as they are. He is also generous enough to forgive his wife's infidelity.

In the end, Tsutomu comes to accept the traditional social conventions still molding individual life in postwar Japanese society. He sees "society" in the huge back of Ono, who accompanies Tomiko home. He realizes that adultery itself is not a good instrument of social change. The way in which he can challenge a force larger than himself is rendered in rather ambiguous terms: "Tsutomu knew how to resist social pressure. He was free to risk his life—a life considered lost already in Burma during the war."[19]

Tsutomu feels only despair when he thinks about how his challenge to society can be executed only through death, and that with death his pledge to Michiko will end. This is the point of irony that Ooka's novel works toward in the end.

Tsutomu is kept uninformed about the suicide of Michiko, his true love, as Ooka steps in to say:

> Strange are the ways of the human mind. . . . Ono was tense at the moment when he allowed his adulterous wife to come home, no questions asked. He was not sensitive enough to perceive the nature of Tsutomu and Michiko's love, but he felt that breaking the news of Michiko's suicide would make Tsutomu a kind of monster. That he was afraid to do.[20]

In contrast to the novel's intense psychological drive to the finish, Mizoguchi ends his tale on a note of innocence betrayed, casting it in the melodramatic mold. He also focuses on a transformation of the characters. First, all are brought to Michiko's deathbed. Tsutomu, Tomiko, Ono, and Aikyama, along with a doctor and a nurse, are shown seated around the dying woman's *futon*. Unlike the selfish Akiyama of the novel, who blames his wife's death on somebody else, Mizoguchi's husband accepts responsibility. Tomiko also repents. She clings to Michiko and cries out for her forgiveness, her gesture reminiscent of the *shimpa* tearjerker.

Mizoguchi counts on the camera's expressive power, even on its legibility. He resorts to a series of close-ups that scrutinizes each character's emotional status. When Tomiko weeps, her face is an open book of repentance. The camera rests in close-up on Michiko for all of her lengthy dying speech to the effect that she must die in order to make Tsutomu happy.

Tsutomu himself emerges as a much purer character in this final sequence. He rebels against the values of materialism represented by Akiyama and Ono, declaring that he will refuse all rights of inheritance given to him in Michiko's will. That done, he stands and leaves the house.

Unlike the novel's open ending about Tsutomu's future, the film's conclusion suggests a determination to lead a new life in a Japan then undergoing the throes of modernization. Mizoguchi does this by letting various formal tools of filmic narration give important clues on Tsutomu's course of action: indexing, panning, and shifts in point of view.

The final scene begins with a long shot of Tsutomu walking along a path on the Musashino Plain. We see his expression of earnest intent as he approaches the camera. How do we account for this? We need to combine various elements given earlier with some presented now. Thus we see a long shot of Tsutomu continuing to walk across the plain, which commands a view of scenery lower down. Then the panning camera, following his line of sight, directs our attention to what lies below it: ugly downtown Tokyo, destined to reach out and spoil this unblemished landscape. Here, the scene given such visual clarity echoes Michiko's dying worlds to Tsutomu: "The Musashino you love so much is an illusion. It's gone. Factories, schools and the city of Tokyo are what the real Musashino Plain is all about."

The subjective shot yields to an objective long shot of Tsutomu facing the scenery below and walking in the direction of Tokyo. Though we are barred from insight into his inner thought as he turns his back on us, his forcible, vigorous step speaks for his determination to build a new life in Tokyo. Then, too, the school uniform he wears attests to his conversion. Earlier, he had been scolded for wearing his old repatriate uniform to school, and he protested that he was more comfortable that way. He was also seen leading a decadent student life, spending more time in cafes than in classrooms. Mizoguchi should have us see how the plain has been the proving ground for Tsutomu's sense of himself and the world.

Tsutomu has learned the importance of human trust, but also its frailty. His enthusiastic step suggests a determination to honor Michiko's dying wish: "You must get a new start in life. Build on a new foundation. The new plain shows that it can be done. Please show to the world that the promises we have made one another were not in vain. I will watch over you always. . . ."

This melodramatic final touch is hardly surprising, given Mizoguchi's life-long devotion to the theme: man redeemed by woman's noble sacrifice, or strengthened by female spiritual support. As Tsutomu disappears from sight, the craned camera views the streets of Tokyo, a clear index of Japan's hectic pace of modernization in the aftermath of war.

That final view inevitably harkens back to Mizoguchi's opening, inviting us to reflect on it anew. Using the constantly moving camera and various shot sizes and angles, he earlier introduced us to the individual components of the plain: tall trees, streams, narrow paths, and finally the old hedge of Michiko's house. The plain looks very much alive. Even so, from the outset we are reminded that unwelcome forces lie ready to invade from within and without. We see Michiko and Akiyama walking along a country path, having been evacuated from their bombed-out house in Tokyo. They see an American airplane flying overhead. It is a clear sign of confusion toward the end of the war.

Despite its melodramatic weakness, especially in character portrayal, *Lady Musashino* contains some outstanding instances of Mizoguchi's expressive devices. Counting what the camera can do in terms of selectivity and depth, he quickly sketches in scenes that the novelist takes some pages to describe. For example, in the opening chapter, Ooka labors over a description of the Miyaji family's traditional house, referring to its vast grounds and good view. The variety of trees that adorn the house is depicted as follows:

> He never tires of his view of Mt. Fuji, changing as it does with the weather and the seasons. He [Miyaji] who loved trees planted many rare kinds to enhance the scenic beauty of a place so richly forested before. The trees around the house were planted very close to it, so there leaves would not interfere with views of the mountain. . . .[21]

In the film, the rich interplay between the crane shot and deep space takes care of the same effect in just three shots. In the opening sequence described above, Michiko and Akiyama follow a path running alongside an imposing wall. Continuing to frame the couple screen right, the panning camera literally emphasizes the extent of the wall's length, itself an index of the occupant's social status.

Within the same shot, the panning stops as the camera cranes to show them entering a gate to the house that turns out to be the Miyaji property. We get an overview shot of the compound: the large courtyard in the foreground and the house in the background, surrounded by trees. Then, another shot follows the couple to show them entering a main room.

In the subsequent shot, a view from the crane returns once more to register the couple and the father in the foreground. Deep focus draws our attention to a corridor in the middle ground, and the courtyard in the back, with the imposing wall against which a manservant is busily raking fallen leaves. In a very economic manner, this single, inclusive shot impresses on us the social prestige associated with the Miyaji family.

Such deployment of the film's technical potentials (visual potentials) is strongly demonstrated in Tsutomu and Michiko's walk through the Musashino Plain. Again, Ooka devotes lengthy pages to a description of the places they pass and the natural phenomena that draw the couple's attention. Ooka describes a running stream they see: "The natural path which passes through a slope adorned by tall sycamores and oaks is all quiet. Silence is occasionally broken by the water . . ." [22]

All Mizoguchi does is let the camera do the talking by showing a series of long panning shots of the couple walking through the field. Michiko asks what that sound is. A close-up follows to show the stream, its murmuring sounds on the sound track.

Another salient example of Mizoguchi's cinematic rubric is found in a number of scenes depicting the decadent life of postwar youth in Tokyo. An apt example is the scene of the cafe frequented by coeducational college students. Attired in fashionable Western clothes, girls in sleeveless blouses cross their legs and smoke—shocking social behavior at the time. Western music plays on a phonograph. Tsutomu comes and kisses a girl. The camera moves to the left, following his movement to show another group of girls and boys seated around a table. He joins them and tries to kiss another girl. Almost unrestricted lateral panning is expressive of a mixture of freedom and restlessness experienced by these students, who for the first time are thrust into the coeducational system favored by postwar democratization.

The contrast with Michiko could scarcely be greater. She is shown in a traditional kimono, most often properly seated on the *tatami* mat. Mizoguchi's expressive camera also studies other contrasts. More immediate to Michiko's experience is Tomiko's affirmation of the new morality in her clothing. She is frequently shown in a tight, low-cut dress with a fashionable wide-brim hat. Unlike the novel, the film places her assignations with Akiyama in Tokyo. At one point in the film, she is shown dancing tipsily with different men in a bar, much to Akiyama's displeasure.

As shown earlier, despite an avowed similarity in narrative, Ooka's *Lady Musashino* and Mizoguchi's film version vary widely in their thematic focus and mode of representation. The novelist relies heavily on the metaphoric dimension of imagery and controlled shift in points of view to forge his strong bent toward psychological realism. The film director, oriented toward melodrama about the fate of women, makes the best use of his own stylistic hallmarks: fluid camera movement combined with deep space.

Notes

1. Koji Nakano, *Zettai reido no bungaku: Ooka Shohei-ron* (Literature of absolute zero: *on Shohei Ooka*) (Tokyo: Shueisha, 1976), pp. 132–33.
2. Quoted in *Musashino fujin* (Lady Musashino), in *Ooka Shohei zenshu* (The complete works of Shohei Ooka), vol. 2 (Tokyo: Chuo Koron, 1976), p. 31 .
3. "*Musashino fujin* Noto" (Notes on *Lady Musashino*), in *Ooka Shohei zenshu*, vol. 11 p. 213.
4. Ibid.
5. Ooka, *Musashino fujin*, p. 36.
6. Ibid., p. 37.
7. Ibid., p. 42.
8. Ibid., p. 64.
9. Ibid., p. 65.
10. Ibid., p. 69.
11. Ibid., p. 46.
12. Ibid., p. 47.
13. Ibid., p. 62
14. Ibid., p. 89.
15. Ibid., p. 105.
16. Ibid., p. 115.
17. Ibid., p. 126.
18. Ibid., p. 127.
19. Ibid.
20. Ibid.
21. Ibid., p. 4
22. Ibid., p. 36.

6

Religion and Politics:
Kumai's *The Sea and Poison* (1986)

In 1945, in the final months of the war, eight captured American fliers were used as subjects for medical experiments in vivisection. The perpetrators of this atrocity were connected with the Medical Faculty of Kyushu University and the Western Division of the Japanese Army. After the war, Fukujiro Ishiyama was arrested and charged with being directly responsible for these clinical murders. Before his case could be brought to trial, however, he committed suicide in prison.

Shusaku Endo studied this gruesome episode in *Umi to dokuyaku* (The sea and poison), a novel whose publication in 1957 brought the author a number of literary awards. In 1986, Kei Kumai adapted Endo's work for the screen. Taken together, these two works offer an interesting example of novelist and director approaching a subject in very different ways.

Endo's focus may be called religious. He uses his lifelong concern with Christianity to explore an atrocity committed at a time of crisis in Japan. His novel is an examination of national conscience, a study of the Japanese perception of crime and punishment.

Kumai's film version of the novel is unabashedly political. His leftist views lend themselves to investigation and indictment of what he sees as "the system" at work in this terrible train of events. He anatomizes that system on both sides of the Pacific, faulting both the wartime Japanese government and military oligarchy and the victorious powers of the United States.

Kumai's international approach is less surprising when we consider the date of his film. By the 1980s, a widening rift between America and Japan was again becoming a matter of concern on both sides of the Pacific. Then too, because of this radical difference in generic orientation between novel and film, changes in point of view and characterization are bound to take place.

Let us begin with the novel, to see what Kumai had in hand as a director thinking in terms of film.

Endo uses his terrible story to study the problem central to every question of conscience: how does an individual take responsibility for his or her own actions? Where does one draw the line when circumstances invite, or even force, a person to take part in criminal acts? What does it mean to be truly human and truly individual? Where is the source of moral clarity to be found? Does a person placed in such a morally precarious state retain a sense of humanity? Or does any such distinctively "human" quality sink down out of sight as the individual joins the little groups of people and whole societies struggling to survive the physical destruction and moral disorder of war?

Endo asks these difficult and complex questions in *The Sea and Poison*. Since he himself is a Christian, his view of morality puts a Christian emphasis on free will and personal accountability. But he is Japanese, too, and correspondingly sensitive to the historic difference imposed by his non-Christian nation's different approach to questions of conscience.

This is particularly true where a "sense of sin" is concerned. One critic poses Endo's basic question this way: "The Japanese don't fear specific sins, but are nonetheless afraid of being sinners. Where does this national trait of ambivalence come from?"[1]

Endo takes his time preparing the reader for the complex issues that give his question its tragic focus. Then, too, the equally complex points of view he uses throughout the novel are a powerful narrative tool for exploring its central thematic event. [2]

Though all his major characters are in the medical profession, they offer a range of individual responses to the crisis enveloping war-torn Japan in the last phase of the War in the Pacific. The opening part, titled "The Sea and Poison," introduces a first-person narrator. But he soon yields to an objective narration of events that implies the presence of the omniscient author. The second part, "Those on Trial," consists of three sections. Two are transcripts of confessions by the nurse Ueda and the intern Toda. The third confession uses the omniscient author's objective narration to view the experience of another young intern, Suguro, from the inside out, so to speak. Those same three characters are brought together in a final part, "Until Dawn." There the author scrutinizes the inner life of each after they have taken part in the clinical murders of the American servicemen.

Another of Endo's strengths lies in his deft and imaginative rearrangement of major narrative events. He dispenses with linear progression, weaving past and present together. Shuttling back and forth, he shows how intimately related past and present are in the mind of a person contemplating acts and their consequences. As we have seen, Endo is particularly interested in the individual whose views partake of some sense of sin.

The opening chapter of *The Sea and Poison* is set firmly in the postwar period. It describes the narrator's contact with his doctor, Suguro. We see how this patient, quite by accident, acquires a special interest in his physician.

It all begins with gossip, chance remarks let drop when Suguro's name comes up. At a wedding in F City, a guest mentions that Dr. Suguro was involved in "that incident." The narrator's curiosity is piqued. He changes from passive listener to active researcher. Making deft use of images and shifts in time, Endo shifts his focus from the narrator's outside investigation into Dr. Suguro's subjective experience.

As its title suggests, the sea is the novel's controlling metaphor. The narrator invokes it first: "Beyond the city I could see the ocean. The sea was a piercingly vivid blue. . . ."[3]

Similar symbolic implications accumulate. At this stage, we have only a vague feeling that the sea is counterpointed with some notion of poison. By and by, we catch Endo's drift.

Later on, that metaphor recurs as we witness young Dr. Suguro's developing moral crisis. He sees and hears in terms of that comparison. Though many critics (and Endo himself) offer their own interpretations of this complex image, its meaning can be inferred only through our synthesis of the major characters' shifting perception of the sea. Only at the end of the novel do we come to realize that the sea symbolizes the all-inclusive love of a Christian God, as we later see.

The narrator's discovery of his doctor's past and his subsequent visit to the scene of the crime enables him to reconstruct "that incident" in his own way. After his return from F City, the patient-turned-investigator gradually becomes a kind of inquisitor as well. He manipulates Dr. Suguro like a policeman seeking a confession, working his criminal into a corner.

After his treatment, the narrator hears the doctor muttering to himself: "Because nothing could be done. At that time nothing could be done. . . . If I were caught in the same way, I might, I might just do the same thing again."[4]

The doctor's soliloquy is immediately followed by another important image: the mannequin in the menswear shop. It gazes out at the world with something like a smile around the mouth. One critic considers the mannequin's face reminiscent of the mysterious passive expression shared by Buddhist statues and the Japanese themselves.[5] He sees it in marked contrast to the expressions worn by statues of Christian saints. The image is thus suggestive of a Japanese national character—a certain complacent peacefulness associated with the self-centered life the Japanese live, free from the restless, questing conscience of the Western Christian worldview with its troubling sense of sin. (According to Endo, Shintoism has become a way of ritual, fostering the spirit of ancestor/nature worship and the like, rather than any active, outgoing religious spirit among the Japanese.)

The mannequin's silent gaze and Suguro's soliloquy together effect a smooth transition, taking us into the doctor's world of inner experience. The next four sections deal with events from the omniscient narrator's perspective, even as they allow Suguro to clarify his view of "the same thing" for us. At the same time, Endo keeps expanding his central metaphor of the sea.

We quickly realize that the question the novelist poses is this: how does the individual face an ordeal that forces him to choose between moral authenticity and loss of conscience?

Adopting Suguro's perspective on "that incident," Endo introduces us to its *mise en scène*: a hospital clinic where war has brought about an unholy alliance between medical and military establishments. We see how the head of Suguro's department, Dr. Hashimoto, is pitted against his rival, Dr. Gondo, in a contest to see who will chair the department of surgery. The values of the young interns

Suguro and Toda are contrasted, too. Suguro exhibits a certain degree of genuine human feeling, which puts him at odds with the rest of the medical staff. We see this in his sympathy for a poor old woman who has been given less than a year to live.

Toda advises Suguro to shake off his attachment to this dying patient. He claims that in time of war such sentiments are worse than meaningless for a doctor, being downright harmful.

Endo uses a series of operations to advance the novel's causal line. The ways major characters react to them tell us much about their inner lives as well.

Dr. Hashimoto's patient is Mrs. Tabe, an upper-class woman whose tuberculosis is in an advanced stage. The operation performed to save her fails. He falsifies his records in order to save face by avoiding responsibility. He declares the operation a success—claiming that the patient died only later. Even so, Hashimoto and his allies need desperately to save face, so they push through a plan guaranteed to curry favor with the Japanese military. This is the series of experiments "for social advancement" leading to the use of American POW's as vivisection subjects.

Now Suguro must face and fail the most crucial test of his moral fiber. He is forced to pledge his cooperation with superiors bent on evil. Later in the same chapter he ponders his decision.

Throughout Part 1, Endo searches for evidence of humanity even in a young man who has allowed himself to be led in such a bad direction. Suguro's moral promise (call it) is found in the area of compassion for the nameless old lady who was his first patient. Despite the acute shortages of wartime, he slips the old woman a lump of sugar whenever he can. Part of his anguish on seeing her corpse is the memory of her simple delight in secretly nibbling his gift of sugar.

Then, too, the old woman has been an exception in her own right in the godless world of the hospital. It was she who kept faith with the traditional Saint Shinran, asking another patient to read his sermons and chant his songs for her. Thus, in her way, and paradoxically, this anonymous, despised old creature served as a kind of saving spiritual presence for Suguro, helping him cling to some semblance at least of moral sanity in this dehumanized society.

There is more to her function in Suguro's life. Only at the end of Part 1, after he has consented to the clinical experiment, does Suguro realize it. Here Endo lets the two interns ponder the question of divine presence, the question he has deliberately postponed until this moment:

"If you think you should have refused, you still have time to do it."

"Uh."

"Will you refuse?"

"I suppose not."

"Do you think there's a God?"

"A God ?" . . .

"Look, a man has all sorts of things pushing him. He tries by all means to get away from fate. Now the one who gives him the freedom to do that, you can call God.'

Suguro sighed. "I don't know what you're talking about."

The glowing tip had gone out, and Suguro laid the cigarette down on the desk top. "For myself, I can't see how whether there's not a God makes any difference."

"Yes, that's right. But for you maybe the old lady was a kind of God."

"Yes, maybe."[6]

The second part of the novel, titled "Those on Trial," continues to pursue this thematic constant of the Japanese consciousness/nonconsciousness of guilt in a Christian sense.

It begins with the nurse Ueda's confession. Here Endo goes into a detailed account of her earlier days to explain how her moral character was conditioned by environment. She portrays herself as a spinster led into marriage with one of her patients because she wanted to have a child.

The couple's brief stay in Manchuria, while seemingly happy in a material sense, taught her to exploit the conquered. She becomes "accustomed to beating" her Manchurian maid relentlessly. Yet her child was stillborn, she had to have a hysterectomy, and her husband proved to be a philanderer. All these aspects of unhappiness led to what an outsider might call deformation of character. She herself sees it this way: "My womanhood was torn from me, and there was nothing else for it but to go through life a crippled woman."[7]

The rest of her confession concentrates on her subsequent experience at the hospital where she found reemployment after repatriation. This is where her thwarted moral character consoles itself with variations on a theme of revenge.

This deformation motif is explored through a deft contrast between the two female characters: Ueda and Hilda. As her name suggests, Hilda is German, a former nurse now married to Dr. Hashimoto. She does not know it, but he is involved in the vivisection experiments.

Hilda is introduced as a devoted volunteer at the hospital. She brings homemade biscuits to poor patients packed into a neglected common ward. Her character is invested with many qualities of saintliness, among them a hard-working cleanliness. She washes the patients' filthy underwear and rinses their urine bottles clean.

Ueda's confrontation with Hilda begins on a personal note. The German wife, obsessed with sanitation, stops this nurse from touching her little boy for fear that he might contact tuberculosis. The women glare at each other as if "gambling for his affection."

A more serious incident elevates their conflict to a kind of allegorical battle, a convenient enough device for an author setting out to explore issues of the divine presence in human life. Advised by the medical assistant Asai, Ueda attempts to administer a fatal dose of anesthesia to a patient gasping for breath in her last hours. Hilda interferes, calling the procedure attempted murder. Her accusation explains the theological connection here: "Even though a person is going to die, no one has the right to murder him. You're not afraid of God? You don't believe in the punishment of God?"[8]

Ueda's reaction to Hilda is rendered in directly physical terms. She hates Hilda's smell of soap; it is the same soap she uses to wash the patients' clothes and underwear. She finds this Caucasian woman's hands—dry and chapped, again, from caring for patients—more dirty-looking than evidence of saintly self-sacrifice. Then, too, Ueda is disgusted by the sprinkling of blonde hairs on the Western woman's hands.

These repulsive sense impressions take on an element of fixation in nurse Ueda's fight against the good as embodied in Hilda. We first see her fall prey to this revulsion when Ueda submits to Asai's advances. They return when she accepts his offer to be an attending nurse for Professor Hashimoto's clinical experiment on the American POWs. They return again to reinforce Ueda's crippled conscience as she listens to the sound of the sea, taking malicious pleasure in the idea that Hilda has no idea of her husband's part in the vivisections: "That night in Dr. Asai's arms, I opened my eyes, and I could hear a gloomy, deep drumming noise—the roaring of the sea again. And the scent of Mrs. Hilda's soap came back to me again. Her right hand—A Western woman's skin with the downy hair growing on it. I thought: soon a scalpel is going to cut into white skin just like that."[9]

Entitled "A Medical Student," the second section of this part unfolds the intern Toda's confession. It traces his life from early childhood, focusing on the life of hypocrisy he led.

Endo makes a great deal of eye imagery throughout. The first instance occurs in the classroom when Toda is an elementary school pupil. His composition is a clever fabrication purposely charged with scenes of "boyhood innocence and childlike feelings." Ironically, the teacher calls his composition "conscientious." Toda notices a fellow pupil, Wakabayashi; his penetrating gaze and wry smile say that he cannot be fooled.

Wakabayashi's eyes became a haunting presence in Toda's life. His presence inspires a mixture of guilt and humiliation. It is as if he were undergoing internal combat between good and bad:

> When I think now of the expression in his eyes, I know that they were by no means the eyes of an accusing judge; nor were they the eyes of conscience threatening punishment. It was no more than a matter of two boys sharing the same secret, in whom the same seed of evil was implanted.[10]

Nevertheless, Toda's interpretation runs counter to that of readers with a surer grasp of analytical judgment. Endo seems to suggest an existence of a God (in a Christian sense), the notion of divine power that the Japanese lost touch with even in their earliest days.

At another point in his recollection, Toda watches his classmates bullying Wakabayashi. He hopes that they will give the helpless boy a sound drubbing. Yet when he sees the teacher approaching, Toda tries to stop them in order to look good. But lo, Wakabayashi's glasses are knocked off in the scuffle, and for the first time ever, Toda looks directly into the other's eyes in the light of a setting sun. He senses something omnipotent in them and is overwhelmed by the feeling that they are "looking into the fathom" of his heart.

The two boys meet for the last time just before Wakabayashi is transferred to another school. Toda says good-bye, but he can no longer gaze into those eyes because they are downcast. Wakabayashi takes with him any fear of God Toda might have known. In high school Toda steals the precious specimen of a butterfly collected by his biology teacher, pinning the blame on somebody else. At that instant, Toda feels all guilt and fear of punishment vanish. He has become an advanced case of amoral self-interest. Already in senior high, he commits adultery.

Now, as an adult, Toda pauses to wonder what made him turn away from God: "Despite what I've written, I didn't think of myself as a person whose conscience had long been paralyzed. For me the pangs of conscience, as I've said before, were from childhood equivalent to the fear of disapproval in the eyes of others—fear of the punishment which society could bring to bear. . ."[11]

Paradoxically, the greatest challenge to amoral self-interest comes in the shockingly amoral climate of the wartime clinic, when he is asked to serve as an intern in "that incident." The conscience he thinks long since dead now springs to life, forcing him to face some unpleasant questions: "Having done this most fearful of deeds, will I suffer my whole life through?"[12] His sense of moral dilemma is short-lived, however, because all that really counts for Toda is fear of social censure.

A short chapter titled "Three O'Clock in the Afternoon" closes Part 2. It offers an objective account of the preparation for "that act," this time from Suguro's perspective. Eye imagery returns in a poignant contrast. When two POWs are brought in for examination, Suguro notices that one of them has gentle blue eyes and an easygoing, amiable smile. On the other hand, the nurse Ueda impresses him as a woman "of dark mood, always fixing her gaze into the distance." Chief Nurse Oba's face is like a Noh mask as usual. With fearful eyes, Suguro himself looks at Toda, "whose expression shows pain for an instant, but taken over by a mocking, challenging smile."

All his peers represent the godless world devoid of human compassion and conscience. But Endo still keeps reinforcing Suguro's tormented conscience. Thus, this intern finds himself unable to assist Toda in administering ether to the POW on the operating table.

If Suguro exhibits an awareness, though feeble, of God that still prevails in the Japanese race in spite of dehumanizing war, Mitsu, a patient, offers another instance. She is found again reading Buddha's sermon to a dying patient. Importantly, the sermon points to the doctrine of Karma in Buddhism: what is done in a previous existence affects the present and the future. Mistu thus represents those old folks who believe in powers divine.

The final part, entitled "Until Dawn," brings the main characters together as it exposes their world of inner experience during and after the vivisection. The most salient feature of Endo's narration is the shifting point of view. It starts with Toda's perspective, then switches to Suguro's. The second section offers a more complex web, as their point of view alternate, interrupted once by nurse Ueda's. The novel concludes with Suguro's inner reflection. Importantly, as each individual character's introspective mood increases, so does the length of his or her interior monologue.

These multiple viewpoints thus focus on each intern's attempt to define his own conscience. When the medical staff begin to experiment on the POW, "the word of killing and being killed" simply means an abstract concept for Toda. He does not feel "any sensation about killing."

That cruel nonchalance is contrasted with Suguro's more humane response. When the first incision is made, he starts talking to himself: "He won't make it! He won't . . ." When he recalls his boss's earlier operation on Mrs. Tabe, which the others faked as a success, he is overwhelmed by a sense of powerlessness and humiliation.

Again an eye image returns in a different context. This time it is an index of society's seeming desire to know why Suguro is unable to ally himself with the values of wartime government. One of the officers stares at him with angry eyes, as if to ask how a young Japanese like him could be such a weakling.

Endo continues to emphasize Suguro's growing remorse through eye imagery. After the operation, Suguro sees the fulfillment of a carnal passion in the officers' glaring, bloodshot, "ugly" eyes. At the same time, his own inner voice returns to accuse him of having "murdered" the innocent patient. He is forced to make the inevitable decision that he will leave the hospital.

One more time eye imagery returns as a manifestation of divine judgment. After the clinical experiment, Suguro steps into the common ward with its crowded patients. There he feels as if all eyes were focused on him, the guilty one.

Among the three staff collaborators, only the nurse Ueda is shown as being beyond-redemption evil. Again the controlling metaphor of skin is used to describe her moral paralysis. She relishes the parallel between the POW's white skin slit with a surgical knife and Hilda's downy hand, which she hates so much.

Ueda's interior monologue allegorically expresses her sense of victory over her enemy, especially in Hilda's resemblance to such compassionate Christian icons as the Blessed Virgin Mary: "No matter how much of a blessed saint Mrs. Hilda is, she has no idea of what her own husband did today. But I know all about it."[13]

The final part of the novel brings Suguro and Toda together, as their experience is rendered from the latter's perspective. Once more, the two characters' inner worlds are pitted against each other.

Here the central metaphor of the sea returns with poignant significance. Toda sees Suguro gazing out to sea, a sea that is then shining brightly. He himself looks upward, seeing only black sky. The sins he has committed since his childhood come to mind, but to him everything remains the same.

The novel ends with Suguro's inner reflection conveyed through a deft juxtaposition of visual and mental images. Left alone, he gazes out into "the sea shining amid the darkness." Suguro tries to "seek something there." The light becomes consonant with the whiteness of "clouds" in the poem he recalls. But he cannot recite it verbally: "When the clouds like sheep pass. . . . In the sea over which moist clouds sail. . . . Sky, your scattering is white, white/White like streams of cotton . . . ."[14]

The "sea" at the very end thus recapitulates all the earlier instances of its appearance. It has been most closely associated with Suguro and has appeared during his moral crisis. His perception of the sea is rendered in both visual and auditory terms. As mentioned earlier, the sea is initially introduced from the narrator/patient's perspective, when he finds the sea piercingly blue. From that point on, however, Suguro comes to be most closely associated with it. Suguro sees the "darkened sea" after he is told by Toda that the patients are simply rungs in a ladder to professional advancement. He also hears the sea after he is forced to accept Professor Shibata's order to cooperate with the vivisection: "When Suguro opened his eyes in the blackness, he heard the distant roar of the sea, the dark mass of the sea surging up over the shore, then the same dark mass falling back again."[15] Then, at the end of the novel, the sea, caught from Suguro's perspective in the final section, is dazzlingly white.

In Ueda's case, her contact with the sea remains only auditory. The sounds of waves heard in the darkness bring her inexplicable loneliness. She stretches out her hand as if to search for something. Then, "the road of the nocturnal sea" assails her heart like "dark drum beats," when Hilda accuses her of the premeditated murder of a patient. The fact that Ueda does not see the sea indicates moral consciousness.

The same is true of Toda. While he tries in vain to define his own conscience, he hears a roar whose source he cannot determine. He equates it with the wailing cry of sorrowing people, with sounds of grief cursing itself. But that night he hears the long, empty sound one more time and thinks that it is the roar of the sea. But then he realizes that the roar of the sea would have to come from a different direction.

A number of critics (including the novelist himself) offer multiple interpretations of this metaphor.[16] They all agree that the sea is contrasted with an image of poison. In my view, that poison must speak for whatever aspect of Japanese culture has numbed the sense of conscience that Endo is at pains to study in his novel. The all-embracing sea, which traditionally is seen as cleansing and purifying all that flows into it, stands for the realm of the Christian God. For Endo, it is the realm of conscience not within reach of the Japanese, though they may be subliminally aware of it. That is why the sea remains distant to all the characters. For those whose conscience is paralyzed, even the physical sea is an abstract entity. They cannot see it; they can only hear its roar.

Like Endo's novel, Kei Kumai's film *The Sea and Poison* studies Japanese perceptions of social crime and punishment. Kumai puts it this way:

> The film was never intended as a means of denouncing the medical profession. Man has long been noted for loss of conscience when placed in extreme situations. I wanted to define, examine and describe this horror through the medium of film.[17]

Nevertheless, the film does tend to analyze, rather than attack, the given horror. One might say that the film is strong on indictment and weak on the world of inner experience and characterization that Endo brought to his subject.

While the novel's central problem concerns the individual's confrontation with a godless world, the film works at some remove from actual religious references. It tends rather to recast questions of individual conscience in terms of dehumanizing war.

Kumai dispenses altogether with the complex web of points of view Endo uses so deftly in his psychological study of the various characters. The director is not content to show events from the points of view of the three individuals involved in the vivisection (i.e. Suguro, Toda, and Ueda). For him, those three have limited experience and exposure to offer.

Kumai wants more, and so he experiments with character by creating the U.S. military intelligence officer who is given a crucial dramatic role in the film. This character, Hattori (played by the Eurasian Masumi Okada), is in charge of the postwar interrogation that forces the three protagonists to confess. In that role, he serves as a powerful link between past and present. He also functions as Kumai's most powerful tool in a fierce indictment of "the system" serving the interests of the United States.

Kumai also takes advantage of film's intrinsic quality of freedom in space and time. He cross-cuts between the interrogation and the narrative events as recollected by the three being questioned. Some of the psychological depth in character delineation lost in the film is made up for by a variety of acoustic effects Kumai puts in place.

Sometimes he renders a character's inner life through interior monologue in voice-over narration. He uses a great variety of diegetic and nondiegetic sounds to set appropriate moods for scenes: eerie electronic and lyrical piano music, the metallic sounds of surgical tools, and the roar of the sea.

The film consists of the three versions of confessional testimony provided by Suguro, Ueda, and Toda. Each version shares the interrogator's focus on the question of motive: what led this individual to take part in this atrocity?

The interrogator is by turns threatening and ingratiating as he brings each suspect closer to full confession. We share his gradual initiation into the world of each suspect's inner experience. This device is not quite as effective as Endo's. It is partly a matter of Kumai's interrogator being so anxious to get his man. He is all about pinning the suspect down and getting a confession. He does not develop the novelist's interest in that subject's remote past. That is a pity because, as we have seen, Endo's novel is itself a telling investigation into the motives of these three suspects. He shows how in each case the crime committed is deeply rooted in the past experience of each as an individual—and as a Japanese in a socio-cultural climate that has numbed their moral conscience.

The film opens with a series of shots of the sea, the central metaphor shared with Endo's novel. As in the original, the sea is presented in poignant contrast to the element of poison in human life. Each suspect's confession partakes of this central metaphor, though the film fails to raise it to a religious level in a Christian sense, as we later see. Kumai's metaphor comprehends only the suggestion that even in a dehumanizing time of war a "poisoned" human such as Suguro has his place in dissolving and resolving a sea of shared humanity.

Kumai's film begins with credits superimposed on views of various aspects of the sea. The effect is one of a rhythmically flowing montage: the sea with waves, waves lapping the beach, beach sand stretching away to meet the distant horizon. A background of lyrical piano music confirms an impression of Mother Nature seen as peaceful and serene. The same is true of the setting sun as the credits end.

Then a shocking sudden transition turns setting sun to searchlight. In a flash we have gone from reassuring reverie to the grim reality of war. The camera pans down and away from the dazzling searchlight, going through the motions of searching for a fugitive. It comes to a halt on iron bars. What we take to be a prison turns out to be an interrogation room. An American intelligence officer is seen threatening the intern Suguro. He wants a full confession. He wants to know every detail of Suguro's "daily routine" at the university hospital.

A close-up of Suguro's terrified and agonizing face yields to a bird's-eye view of F City, as he describes his daily routine for us and the interrogator. No dissolve—that normal cinematic punctuation—is used for this transition in order to forge a sense of interaction between past and present in the suspect's consciousness. That temporal shift is signaled only by Suguro's initial voice-over narrative.

The "daily routine" of his confession is nothing like what we expect. Everything he has to say underscores the horrifying truth behind the atrocity. Here was a medical profession abandoning its ethical standards under pressure from the opportunism and greed of certain individuals in positions of authority.

As in the novel, Japanese doctors see their Japanese patients as subjects for callously self-serving experiments. We can readily believe that these individuals are capable of progress on into the horrors they inflict on the prisoners of war. Unfortunately, Kumai's approach is rather heavy-handed. He is too anxious to expose and castigate the hypocrisy that prevails among these medical professionals.

Unlike their counterparts in the novel, Kumai's interns are much less interesting. They are mere stereotypes, underlings incapable of independent, individual moral crisis, even as the power struggle between their superiors involves them in horrifying ethical consequences. Professor Hashimoto is portrayed as the very epitome of "authority." Making the rounds of the wards, he is followed by his entourage. Patients and employees make way, bowing obsequiously.

Kumai is at his best when presenting the clinical horrors that reveal the depths of hypocrisy these medical professionals are capable of. During the operation on Mrs. Tabe, he makes especially good use of the camera's versatility of movement/angle and shot size. He brings an almost newsreel-like immediacy to the surgery in progress. A series of long shots of those involved interacts with close-ups of an individual face covered with a surgeon's mask. The camera also cuts to the patient's lung in close-up as it is dissected.

The medical staff's responses to the patient's death are again rendered in close-up, as the camera cuts from one face to another. Their eyes loom above faces still in operating-theater masks. The camera's omniscience becomes our own as Kumai invites us to scrutinize these eyes.

A cut to the outside of the building offers a glimpse of Dr. Hashimoto's enemy in this factional war. A long shot surveys Professor Gondo's body language. Restless and nervous, he paces back and forth, obviously anxious to be the first to hear the results of the operation going on inside.

The way Hashimoto's party fake the operation is presented very simply. Mrs. Tabe's corpse is wheeled out of the operation room past her mother and sister. They are presented as hapless victims of physician worship. The camera registers their joy over the "success" of the operation as assistant Asai lends his powers of blandishment to that cynical lie.

In contrast to those schemers, Suguro is endowed with a much more humane and vulnerable character than his counterpart in the novel. This is obvious from his relationship with the "old woman." Kumai makes the most of his habit of slipping this poor soul lumps of medical glucose. A medium shot shows Suguro sitting very close as he puts one of these treats in her mouth. A close-up shows her happy smile, something rarely seen in the atmosphere of grim reality that prevails in this hospital.

Kumai reinforces that bond with an episode of his own invention. In a sequence showing the effects of an air raid on the clinic we see the old woman sitting alone in an empty room. She is abandoned, too weak to flee. A close-up shows Suguro desperately searching for her. Another close-up shows him holding her tightly under a bed while shells explode all around.

Throughout Suguro's confession, Kumai reinforces the horrors of war in two dimensions. The first, as we have seen, is the collapse of medical ethics witnessed by the interns. The other is a more general view of a Japanese population suffering the consequences of a war entering its last phase.

Endo treats the latter dimension as a given of his novel's time and place. Kumai insists on giving it life, letting the camera report a full range of horrors. A montage series of shots shows patients and staff fleeing the clinic when bombs begin to explode. A cut to a curtain blown in by the blast is followed outside, both in close-up. Casualties are presented in newsreel fashion as evacuees cluster in a narrow corridor watching the wounded being carried away.

As in the novel, Suguro's link to his humanity in time of dehumanizing war is presented through his consciousness of the sea. This central metaphor, which opened the film, is reintroduced after Suguro is forced to agree to assist Dr. Shibata in his experiment on "the old woman." Their conversation is viewed mostly in medium or long shots, the camera often focusing on Suguro's back. This denies us access to any expressions that might give clues to the truth of his psychological responses. But the subsequent interior monologue, aided by the sea metaphor, provides ample evidence of his tormented conscience. The voice-over narration runs: "My dream has been to open a small clinic, but now this has been shattered."

Lyrical piano music merges with his voice-over narration of the poem about the sea with white clouds over it. Kumai takes this poem as is from the novel. Here, as there, the poetic stanza Suguro recites twice expresses his desperate effort to search for God. But such deeper implications are lost in the film as the sea image itself suddenly intrudes on this sequence. This has the effect of making the sea into a universal archetype of oblivion and escape as it relates to Suguro's yearning for the world of wish fulfillment—a world in which man lives in harmony with divine presence.

The sea image returns once more during Suguro and Toda's conversation after the unsuccessful operation on Mrs. Tabe. At first, they are posed against the concrete wall atop the hospital building, as Toda argues that faking the time of death was justified by Dr. Hashimoto's need to save face. The sound track echoes with the bang of a heavy metal door. That sound, together with the concrete wall, reinforces our sense of a hard, impersonal world of medicine robbed of all compassion by the war.

Suguro, however, still has conscience enough to ask the basic ethical question: "Is this the way my profession is?" His interior monologue repeats that question when he is left alone. Suddenly, lyrical piano music prevails on the sound track, and the camera pans to the right. Still in monologue, he says that he cannot answer this question. From Suguro's perspective, the ocean comes into view. A cut to his face in close-up yields to a concluding shot of the ocean. Its symbolic implication is now much more straightforward. It is a manifestation of humanity that still remains in Suguro's life, or that realm of humanity he searches for so desperately in a world that seems bereft of everything humane.

For a third time, the sound of the sea is heard in Suguro's confession. He and Toda are discussing death as part of their daily life. The entire scene is rendered in a long take. Electronic music steals in as if to fill some void. Toda associates it with the wailing of the dead. He leaves, leaving the camera's long gaze on Suguro alone. The music changes to evoke the roar of the sea, as if to underscore Suguro's subliminal consciousness of a divine presence.

Eiji Okuda (l) and Ken Watanabe (r) in *The Sea and Poison* (1986) directed by Kei Kumai. Courtesy of the Kawakita Memorial Film Institute.

The camera cuts to a patient's room. The chiming of a bell for Buddhist prayers combines first with electronic music, which then yields to something lyrical on the piano as we see Suguro facing the old woman's death. A close-up of the glucose piece found in the dead woman's hand speaks for the bond of humanity between this hapless doctor and his helpless patient.

Suguro himself may not be aware of the little conscience he still has, but his subsequent interior monologue—taken straight out of the novel's context— tells us of it: "That old woman was what I wanted to keep alive!"

The next sequence deals with Suguro's forced acceptance of his role in the upcoming vivisection experiment. His confession does not explain why he failed to bow out while he had the chance. Instead, a shot of the ocean marks a temporal transition. It returns us to the interrogation room where Hattori reiterates the unanswered question for us, but the wrong way round. He directs it in such a way as to force an admission of guilt from Suguro. He is too eager to make this prisoner confess that hatred for the enemy was his reason for taking part in the atrocity.

Interestingly, the leftist Kumai is bent on a twofold indictment: of the Japanese political system, especially the military, which allowed such atrocious conduct; and of the U.S. military, which he sees as eager to take revenge. Kumai's interrogator, Hattori, becomes less a character and more of an ideological tool, a stereotypical bully on the side of the law. Aware as we are that Suguro was in some respects a victim of circumstance, it is hard not to feel an amount of relish in the way the camera views the violence he is subjected to. Hattori attacks him first with words, then physically, pushing him around, even banging his head against the steel bars of a room so much like a prison cell.

The scene concludes with a bird's-eye view of the room, as if to emphasize that likeness. The cagelike wire surrounds every dimension as interrogator and military police loom over the hapless Suguro. Even so, the bully's victim admits to no more than having been too exhausted and demoralized to have made the right decision. It is as if Kumai is urging the audience to fill in the gap by answering the difficult question posed: what led the young intern to take part in an act so appallingly inhumane?

The American interrogator's character still fails to develop in the second brief confessional interlude, this time with the nurse as the center of attention. The scene opens with a contrasting approach that verges on the ridiculous. Here the bully is a mild-mannered, persuasive male chauvinist. No menacing voice or attitude here. Hattori sits side by side with the suspect. Everything about the scene suggests that confessing, even to such a dreadful crime, can take place in a genial atmosphere. Kumai dispenses with Endo's account of various events that molded Nurse Ueda's moral character: her bad experiences with men, her life in China during the war. Her confession has no real content, no moral center to it.

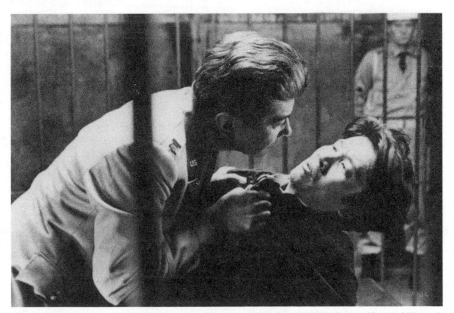

Masumi Okada (l) and Eiji Okuda (r) in *The Sea and Poison* (1986) directed by Kei Kumai. Courtesy of the Kawakita Memorial Film Institute.

Instead, Kumai's version enlarges the motif of revenge and hatred. He magnifies Endo's incident involving Ueda's affection for Hilda's little girl. (In the novel, the child is a boy.) Kumai's nurse obviously suffers the pangs of frustrated motherhood as she tries to embrace the little girl. A cross-cut between them and Hilda in the distance emphasizes the difference between actual mother and frustrated one. A shot of Hilda's astonished expression yields to another showing her separating the two. Hilda simply tells the nurse not to touch her child because she may contract tuberculosis.

A cut to the interrogation room affirms that revenge on Hilda was Ueda's sole motive for participating in the vivisection. The rest of her confession adds to that theme. It was Hilda, for example, who prevented Nurse Ueda from giving a dying patient a fatal injection. Another villain is Ueda's lover, the assistant Asai. He uses her neediness to pressure her into taking part in the medical experiment.

As in the novel, her confession also partakes of ocean imagery. Here it becomes more inclusive. It now suggests that the sea of humanity washes over some poisonous human evil. As Asai and Ueda have sex, the sound of waves merges with wind rustling the bedroom curtains. Their talk in bed is all about ways to finish Dr. Hashimoto professionally—him with his declining career and Caucasian wife "who acts like a saint." These malicious lovers seem completely unaware of the existence of the sea nearby. The sound of their voices overcomes the murmuring of the sea, even as we sense a feeling of void—call it moral—opening up around them.

The motif of hatred and revenge is once more reinforced when the camera cuts briefly to the interrogation room. As the interrogator's military boots stamp on the hard concrete floor, Ueda's mechanical tone of voice adds another touch of impersonality: "I hated Hilda." Suddenly the camera shows us the sea, as if to suggest that with those words Nurse Ueda loses touch with the sea of humanity.

Our last glimpse of the sea occurs with Asai and Ueda in bed again. This time, the curtain of the bedroom window is open, and the camera takes note of the sea outside. A gull's cry merges with the sound of the waves. Again the lovers pay no attention to the beauty nature offers them. Instead, Asai is seen persuading his lover to take part in the upcoming clinical experiment. A reverse-field shot confirms their line of sight: each is gazing into the other's eyes, oblivious to all around them, even when a steamship adds its horn to the sound of the gulls and the sea.

Again, Ueda talks of hating Hilda. She mockingly recalls the German woman's question: "Aren't you afraid of God?" Then she asks Asai if Caucasian skin is difficult to cut. A shot of the two looking at each other yields to a concluding shot of the sea with *rolling waves*; it is an omnipresent shot, not the one expressive of the lovers' aural perception. It hints of the very "divine anger" to which Hilda was referring.

Unfortunately, Nurse Ueda's confession, as presented by Kumai, impoverishes Hilda's character, too. The novelist had enriched the German woman with all manner of associations speaking for the element of divinity in everyday earthly form. As we have seen, Endo uses a commonplace like the smell of soap to lend Hilda that aura.

Here, too, Kumai's character fails to get beyond the stereotype. Hilda is the compulsively clean German *Hausfrau*, a former nurse playing a complacent Florence Nightingale role. The camera observes her volunteer work with a notably unsympathetic eye. We are shown her insistence on proper hygiene creating an amount of panic among patients who fail to understand her aims.

As mentioned earlier, the final part of Endo's novel offers a complex web of points of view as it focuses on the clinical experiment and the effects it has on those who take part. Kumai simplifies the rhetorical stance involved, closing the film with Toda's confession.

Most of the major events are seen from Toda's perspective. Nonetheless, the director does use the omnipresent camera to render some objectivity to the narration. Kumai also makes the best use of an intrinsic quality of cinema —flexibility in spatial and temporal shift—in order to urge the audience to achieve a total vision of Toda's plight. Again, the American interrogator asks the fundamental question: "What made you partake of such inhuman conduct?" Here, Hattori's tool is Toda's own diary, which records his nihilistic attitude, especially his inner indifference to death. Like the novel's counterpart, this intern tries to define his own conscience as he attempts to reconstruct the past. Thus, in a flashback, he speaks of his reaction to Mrs. Tabe's death: "When I stepped out of the operating room, I did not feel any pity for her."

The camera then cuts to the interrogation room for a glimpse of the clash of values. Initially Toda and Hattori are seated face to face across the desk. An MP's boots make a threatening sound as he moves in the background. Ninety-degree pan and reverse-field shot alternate to show how interrogator and suspect relate to one another. Hattori, with all his prejudice against the enemy and limited "intellectual" insight, is blind to Toda's motive for keeping a diary.

Here Kumai extends Toda's role to a political level. The intern, assuming the role of "interrogator," lashes out at Hattori, asking if he was ever insensitive to all the many instances of death on the battlefield. Thus he serves as a mouthpiece for Kumai's indictment of all that the U.S. military represents. The camera starts closing in on Toda when he accuses the United States of bombing Nagasaki and Hiroshima.

The subsequent cross-cuts between Hattori and Toda, all in close-up, record their heated exchange. Hattori asks Toda if he has any conscience as a human being. Strangely, this question, which Endo's intern put to himself so insistently, is taken straight from the novel's context. Then, too, Toda's answer is simply a repetition of what his counterpart in the novel offers: "For me, pangs of conscience had been nothing but my own fear of accusation in others' eyes and also of the punishment that society would inflict on me."[18]

Kumai's interrogator takes the bait and yells: "This time you've gone too far. You'll be dead!" The scene ends with a close-up of Toda silent. It is for us to scrutinize his expressionless face and guess at the emotional quandary within.

What follows is the continuation of Toda's account of his interaction with Suguro before the vivisection. Brief as it is, it concerns the two interns' differing responses to the question of divine presence. Again, a series of intercuts between the two, mostly taken in close-up, provides legibility to their emotional state. Suguro's face is an open book of remorse and despair, when he asks if there is a God. His sense of guilt is also clear in his cry: "Killing a man alive! I will suffer from the consequence for the rest of my life." Toda's face is again a blank mask as he says simply that God is something like fate, which liberates a human being.

A cut to the interrogation room shows Hattori typing the verdict on the accused. His typewriter clatters along with the same lyrical piano music that served as prelude to the medical experiment narrated by Toda.

This final segment is the weakest in the film. Kumai is just too noticeably more eager to indict the system than he is to focus on the psychological dimensions of the characters involved. We are left with the perspectives of two young interns witnessing a clinical atrocity. Kumai's camera gives unsparingly of the details of that horror. Long shots of the medical staff and military officers surrounding the operating table alternate with close-ups of the body laid open. At one point, a monstrous blow-up of the beating heart fills the screen.

Here, too, Kumai lets the stereotypical polarization of characters serve as a means of indictment. Compared to the naive POWs, the Japanese military officers seem too casually evil to be at all convincing. Kumai is so repelled by everything the wartime military stands for that he cannot resist a really grotesque touch. A bottle containing the POW's heart is brought in as if to serve as a delicacy for a senior officer. The effect is more like grim farce than serious indictment of actual evil.

Another puzzling aspect of the vivisection sequence is Kumai's sudden reference to Hilda. A super close-up of the POW's pulsing heart yields to a series of intercuts between Toda and Suguro, equally in close-up. These shots appear to aim for a stark contrast in reactions: Toda's face is immobile, a mask; Suguro's is an open book, the very picture of fear and shock. The heart beats together with, but out of synch with, what appears to be a song sung by a woman. The camera cuts to the exterior to show a long shot of Hilda walking with her little girl. What are we to make of this single shot? Since in the previous sequences Hilda is not well drawn (she is a far remove from Endo's Blessed Mother figure), we are left with a vague approximation of a kind of metaphor for moral conscience. Then, too, Hilda's song continues on the sound track even as the camera returns to the horrors in the operating room.

Nonetheless, stylistically, the final section draws its strength from cinematographic economy. Kumai deftly alternates points of view and omnipresent shots to let us see the individual characters' responses to the operation as a whole.

One notable example involves Suguro. Initially, a long shot of the party around the operating table makes us conscious of the omnipresent camera. On the sound track, the sound of the incision merges with the POW's groan. A close-up shows Suguro closing his eyes. The following shot of Toda's face in close-up, with eye line matching, confirms that he is watching his friend's reaction carefully. The camera cuts to Suguro's face, also in close-up, as seen from Toda's perspective; his eyes are still closed. A cut to the officer watching Suguro is again caught from Toda's perspective. The next shot shows Suguro tugging at the gauze mask covering his nose and mouth.

This shot is ambiguous. Is it seen from the officer's point of view or Toda's? The subsequent shot clarifies the matter as Toda's eye line indicates that he is watching Suguro closely.

The film ends with a recapitulation of two major events taken directly out of Endo's novel: Ueda's challenge to Oba, the head nurse, and Toda and Suguro's interaction.

The first is fairly short, focusing on Ueda's verbal attack on her supervisor. The scene is conveyed mostly in alternating close-ups of each woman. Their dialogue is taken word for word from the novel. Oba orders Ueda not to talk to anyone about the operation. Ueda snaps back with an obviously loaded question about Oba's fanatic loyalty to Dr. Hashimoto. Her supervisor is reduced to silence. The cues to each woman's shifting emotions are all visual. Oba's expression changes from bullying boss to uneasy hypocrite. Ueda's expression changes from glum subservience to open triumph.

Endo works to arrive at a psychological explication of the effect of the operation on Ueda. As we have seen, he uses her interior monologue and recollection of events to show her sense of revenge on Hilda focuses on her enemy's fair skin. She also derives satisfaction from knowing that Nurse Oba is in love with Hilda's husband. Kumai, however, is notably weak in this dimension.

The same may be said of his depiction of the final meeting between the two interns. Endo probes the minds of these young men quite effectively, using metaphor and the characters' own recollections. For the novelist, F City in wartime blackout signifies death, whereas the sea shimmering white offshore suggests the triumphant power of love after all. Toda's moral inertia is deftly explored as he recalls various childhood incidents and, more recently, "the red piece of flesh" he himself removed from his lover's womb. Nothing can penetrate his cynical defenses, not even the horror of a prisoner of war dissected alive. As we have seen, the image of the sea Suguro remembers in a poem brings the novel full circle as, in the end, he searches desperately for some sign of a higher power in charge of this universe of pain.

The problem with the ending lies in Kumai's fidelity to text as text. He transfers all the dialogue to the screen without much probing into the inner reality of the interns. For example, Suguro introduces the motif of punishment, saying that they deserve it. Toda maintains that all he cares about is the possibility of punishment, adding that there is nothing much to worry about. These are his words, taken out of the novel's context: "You and I happened to be in this medical department in this particular period, and were led to participate in a vivisection on a P.O.W. If those who are going to punish us had been in the same slot, couldn't they have done the same thing? That's what societal punishment is about."[19]

As might be expected, the ending of the film departs radically from the novel by extending the issue of societal punishment to the plane of international politics. It is preceded by Suguro's consciousness of guilt expressed through a montage. The sea, seen from Suguro's perspective, triggers his memories of the source of his guilt: it rapidly dissolves into the water running on the floor of the operating room and then to the POW struggling in vain against the medical staff. A shift from Suguro's inner experience to the world of politics yields to a shot of the head nurse and Ueda among those on trial. The voice-over narration ironically clarifies the "societal punishment" to be inflicted:

> After a few years the international situation changed and U.S. and Soviet hostilities led to the Korean War and a redefinition of Japanese international political leanings. Soon after, those still in custody were released from prison.

So much for society's "punishment." This is Kumai's dire indictment of a system that allows the violators of moral order to go unpunished. Images of war also suggest the likely repetition of the dehumanizing circumstances that have provided the context for this film. The final shot continues to reinforce this sentiment by offering an overview of the abandoned interrogation room. Its cagelike, metallic, almost skeletal quality hearkens back to the U.S. interrogator's futile attempt to avenge the murder of his countrymen. The piano leitmotif returns to merge with the sound of the sea.

Kumai may be said to have turned Endo's highly psychological and religious original into a somewhat less complex film too firmly in the grip of political issues, which concern him always. Thus, his adaptation, departing from his initial intention of exploring the horror of loss of conscience, has been reduced to the film's strong indictment of the system, both Japanese and American.

Notes

1. Kenkichi Yamamoto, "Endo Shusaku: Sono Ikkanshita shudai" (Shusaku Endo: his consistent theme), in Jun Eto et al., *Nihon no sakka: Endo Shusaku,* (Writers of Japan: Shusaku Endo), vol. 22 (Tokyo: Shogakkan, 1991), p. 35.
2. For a comprehensive study of the points of view Endo uses in this novel, see Renji Hiroishi, *Endo Shusaku no subete* (All about Shusaku Endo) (Tokyo: Chobunsha, 1991), pp. 62–81.
3. Shusaku Endo, *Umi to dokuyaku* (The sea and poison), trans. Michael Gallagher (New York: New Directions, 1993), p. 29. Originally published by Peter Owen (London, 1972). Copyright © by New Directions.
4. Ibid., p. 30.
5. Hiroishi, *Endo Shusaku no subete*, pp. 69–71.
6. Gallagher, *The Sea and Poison*, pp. 78–79.
7. Ibid., p. 88.
8. Ibid., p. 98.
9. Ibid., pp. 102–3.
10. Ibid., p. 108.
11. Ibid., p. 118.

12. Ibid., p. 126.
13. Ibid., p. 164.
14. Ibid., p. 167.
15. Ibid., p. 75.
16. For example, the critic Yamamoto claims that the sea represents Suguro's "unfathomable fate which cannot be controlled by his will and conscience." See Kenkichi Yamamoto, "Endo Shusaku: Sono ikkanshita shudai," vol. 22, p. 33.

    On the other hand, Hiroishi argues that the sea symbolizes the Japanese spiritual climate—the pantheistic world in which they are contented to reside. See, Hiroishi, *Endo Shusaku no subete*, p. 67.

    Endo himself simply states that the sea, contrasted to poison within a human being, can be the sea of benevolence or love. By so doing, he leaves the interpretative task to the reader. See Shusaku Endo and Yasumasa Sato, *Jinsei no dohansha: Endo Shusaku* (Life's companion: Shusaku Endo) (Tokyo: Shunjusha, 1991), p. 138.
17. *The Sea and Poison*, pamphlet (Tokyo: Herald Enterprise, 1986), p. 1.
18. Gallagher, *The Sea and Poison*, p. 164.
19. Ibid., p. 166.

7

The Modern Outcast State: Ichikawa's
The Broken Commandment (1962)

Kon Ichikawa's *Hakai* (The broken commandment) began in 1961 as a televised dramatization of Toson Shimazaki's novel of the same title first published in 1906. Toson's pioneering work of social realism created a sensation in this version, and so the director collaborated again with his scenarist wife, Natto Wada, on the film the following year. It, too, was a great success. The prestigious film journal *Kinema jumpo* ranked it as the fifth-best film of 1962.

Set in the late Meiji period (1903), both novel and film depict a young teacher's coming to terms with himself and society's lingering feudal prejudice against his class of *burakumin*, then Japan's minority group. But novel and film take strikingly different approaches to a topic still sensitive in the Japan of the 1960s.

To begin with, making the best use of "literary properties," Toson took pains to explore the psychological dimensions of his hero's struggle in great detail. Ichikawa, in contrast, relies on cinematic properties, especially visual legibility. Counting on the camera's expressive power and temporal freedom, Ichikawa dispenses with Toson's lengthy literary discourse. Instead, he lets us see and feel the suffering and pain of the outcast in a more direct way. In fact, one critic says:

> Generally, Ichikawa's method is to accommodate the original source to his own taste and critique it through visual images. Accordingly, his film version of *The Broken Commandment* reflects this mode of representation and is highly acclaimed as *The Broken Commandment* in a sense Ichikawa's own.[1]

In order to see how Ichikawa achieves this desired effect, we need to go back to Toson's novel.

Most critics consider *The Broken Commandment* the crystallization of modern realism.[2] Written during the Russo-Japanese War of 1904–5, it probes the conflict of a young teacher, Ushimatsu, who was born a *burakumin*.[3] The drama spans a relatively short period from 26 October to 12 December 1904, a time in which external and internal factors closely interact to determine the fate of the social outcast hero.

As is often mentioned in the novel, the Meiji government's edict of 1871 freed the *burakumin* of their burden of exclusion from the Edo period's four-class system. Their new status was to be that of *shinheimin*, or "new commoners."

Nevertheless, this legal redefinition had no effect whatsoever on the actual lives led by *burakumin.* They were still subject to the prevailing view of them as, in effect, subhuman. In 1902 a campaign on their behalf was mounted by various members of the upper classes in such places as Okayama and Osaka Prefectures, but little progress was made. The feeling was that discrimination could be fought only with improvements in *burakumin* education, manners, and hygiene. Those concerns delayed actual political measures eight years beyond the publication of Toson's *The Broken Commandment* in 1906. The first nationwide group, the Imperial Organization for Equality, was formed in 1914 with advice and help from some noted politicians.[4]

The central problem of *The Broken Commandment* is how Ushimatsu comes to terms with himself. It maps out the various stages of the young protagonist's identity crisis until he finally comes to accept his difficult social status. Ushimatsu's conflict unfolds on two levels: He must defend himself against an oppressive society with all its prejudice and insularity. This combat with the external world in turn triggers inner conflict, as he is torn between liberated ego and constraints of reason. Should he reveal the social identity he has managed to conceal and thus lead a life faithful to his conscience? Or should he continue to lead a deceitful life as a respected member of society? That question of choice shapes the novel.

Needless to say, events conspire to bring this conflict into the open. Faithful to his father's parting command to conceal his social origins by every means possible, Ushimatsu becomes a master of deceit.

Toson shows the reader what it means to live as an *eta* (a derogatory term used for this minority group) in Iiyama, a small country town in Shinshu. People there consider *burakumin* "defiled." We read about one Ohinata who is dismissed from the hospital because he is rumored to be a *burakumin.* He is also kicked out of his boardinghouse when the other lodgers refuse to live under the same roof with the likes of him.

All Ushimatsu can do is suffer internally: "Taking pity on the unfortunate Ohinata and lamenting the irrational, inhuman treatment meted out to him, he thought about the *eta*'s miserable fate."[5]

This unpleasant incident causes the young man to change his own dwelling. He moves into the temple. What better way to cut himself off from any possibility of contact with *eta*?

But a point of contact develops, willy-nilly, taking charge of Ushimatsu's inner turmoil. It all begins with a book caught sight of in the window of a shop. The author is Rentato Inoko, a teacher who lost his position at a teacher's college when he revealed his *eta* origins. He refuses all shame on that account and has written this book, *Confession.* It begins with a statement of fact: *I am an eta.* He has written this book to explain his commitment to the improvement of the underprivileged.

Ushimatsu's studies the book in the window: ". . . his heart beats with excitement, just seeing the author's name." He spends his last yen to buy the book. Inoko becomes a secret mentor—all the more so, since Ushimatsu is a teacher, too. Toson brings mentor and disciple face to face in a carefully prepared dramatic highlight of the novel.

Ushimatsu receives a telegram announcing his father's death. He is given emergency leave to go home. The journey motif is used to map out his quest for a way to live more truthfully. His immediate sensation is one of relief at leaving the small-minded horrors of Iiyama behind:

> The farther he got from Iiyama, the more he felt light and free. Treading the gray soil of Hokkoku Path, he went climbing a hill, passing through a mulberry field, basking in the bright sunlight. . . . He felt invigorated.[6]

The plain spreads before his eyes, and a wide stretch of the Chikuma River comes into sight. Given this larger view of the world, what better moment to meet Inoko? He, too, is aboard the train. Only now does the novelist tell us that Ushimatsu is not in a sense a complete stranger to the author of *Confession*. He had in fact sent Inoko a get-well note after reading about his recent illness in the newspaper.

Still, their first face-to-face meeting has a profound effect on Ushimatsu's inner conflict. He realizes that his feelings of sympathy and reverence for this mentor figure originate in their shared identity. Yet Ushimatsu cannot bring himself to confess that fact to Inoko, even when he knows that confession is the *sine qua non* of any real communication between them. The best he can do on the train is promise himself to tell Inoko the truth the next time they meet. From a narrative point of view, this initial meeting serves to set in motion a chain of events that will alter Ushimatsu's fortunes for the worse. On the train, he catches a glimpse of Takayanagi, a candidate for the Town Council of Iiyama. Through Inoko, Ushimatsu learns that the mercenary Takayanagi has married a *buraku* girl for her money. The fact of his own uneasy connection with the *burakumin* means that this small-town notable can identify Ushimatsu's destination as one linking the young, respected elementary school teacher to the undesirable class. So it is Takayanagi who will circulate the rumor that Ushimatsu is from the *buraku*, a sufficient cause for the young man to become *persona non grata* in Iiyama.

Ushimatsu's second encounter with Inoko takes place in his hometown. Their growing intimacy is set against a background of expansive rural scenery. Obviously, Toson intends for us to see the wholesome outdoor atmosphere as conducive to frank and open discussion. As they walk toward Inoko's inn, Ushimatsu feels that the moment is right for his confession, even as his defensive reflex forbids it:

> How could he possibly tell his secret—and such a deadly serious secret—to anyone, even to someone who has known this shame? He started to confess, then hesitated—only to blame himself for that. He was too afraid to go on. He had lost the struggle.[7]

The narrator baldly prepares us for his next attempt: "The time had come for Ushimatsu to shed his heavy burden."

After his father's funeral, Ushimatsu accompanies Inoko's party on their way to another town. The night before, the young man had compared himself to "grass growing under frost." Fear and deception were robbing his inner life of its vitality. He thinks that if only he could break through, he could spring to life again, just as melting frost unburdens the grass.

Yet again his determination falters when he is left alone with Inoko. Even as he prepares to confess, he hears his father's voice: "That solemn, commanding voice echoed in his heart: Conceal your origins! . . . He felt some invisible force holding him back, opposing every argument. The voice re-echoed: I command you. Do not forget!"[8] Worse yet, on this same journey his uncle, now the father figure, repeats that self-same warning.

Ushimatsu's father has been gored to death by a bull. After the funeral, he must witness the slaughter of the beast. Toson uses this appalling scene to underscore his young hero's sense of inner conflict. The splattering blood and hacked-up carcass suggest a horrifying parallel between the fates of beast and his outcast community of *burakumin*. Then, too, the butchered animal supplies an especially gruesome and forceful reminder of his moral dilemma:

> "Don't forget!" His father's deathbed warning promised to seep into every part of Ushimatsu's body during his life time. . . . "Will you forsake a parent?" the voice seemed to ask in a reprimanding tone. . . . Ushimatsu could not help thinking how much he had in fact changed. He was no longer the innocent child who obeyed his father without hesitation. . . . And now this chasm had opened up, this difference between a mentor counseling courage, outraged by a merciless world, and a father demanding subjugation. Ushimatsu was at a loss, not knowing which to follow.[9]

Such is the nature of his inner struggle as the bull is reduced to bloody chunks of beef. That horrid change fixes itself in Ushimatsu's mind even as he prepares to obey his father's command: "Nothing to do but go back to Iiyama and lead the life he knew so well."[10]

But the novel turns on that failure of courage. Ushimatsu returns to Iiyama, where things change rapidly. Rumors of Ushimatsu's outcast origins spread among his fellow teachers, changing his principal's attitude drastically.

Ushimatsu's conflict takes on a far more drastic dimension. He is set in directly personal opposition to an entire small society, one characterized by prejudice and insularity: no wonder the young man felt "as if some fierce, invincible force was directed against him."[11]

How, exactly, is the rumor spread among the teachers? What will Ushimatsu do? The novelist spends five chapters portraying Ushimatsu's sufferings before he answers these basic questions. Because he is a novelist, Toson balances his hero's misery between forces good and evil, even as the reader has to wonder if and how the young man will survive his ordeal.

Ushimatsu's colleague Ginnosuke Tsuchiya is the embodiment of goodness. His evil opposite is one Katsuno, son of a government education inspector. Toson endows him with all the prejudice, hypocrisy, arrogance, and sycophancy one could hope to find in an unworthy educator. It is Katsuno who spreads the rumor about Ushimatsu's lowly status and presses the principal to dismiss him.

Toson invests Tsuchiya with qualities of innocence, rectitude, and benevolence. He also uses him for a deft bit of narrative double-take. It begins when Tsuchiya, in all innocence, mistakes Ushimatsu's aloof and melancholy air for love sickness. The principal's inclination to dismiss the young teacher is deflected by this news.

Tsuchiya's goodness runs so deep that his friendship for Ushimatsu is unaffected when he learns the truth about his origins and personal conflict. This is not to say that the good man is blind to the horrors of prejudice and discrimination in Iiyama. In fact, by the end, he is quite ready to leave for a job in enlightened Tokyo.

Ushimatsu, meantime, finds himself increasingly attracted to Oshiho, the girl Tsuchiya mistook for his lady love. The attraction was in fact there. At the outset of the novel, Ushimatsu is seen responding to Oshiho's misfortunes.

Her father, Keinoshin Kazama, was also a colleague. He had been treated unfairly, being fired without a pension. Kazama represents the samurai class adversely affected by the Meiji Restoration. Now that her family has been deprived of social prestige and wealth, Oshiho is sent to the temple for adoption.

Toson's preferred image for this pair of star-crossed lovers is one of darkness. For example, Ushimatsu is shown catching a glimpse of Oshiho leaning against the old wall in a darkened corridor.

Ushimatsu dreams of her fondly on the way to his father's funeral. In his dream, Oshiho's image melds with that of Otsuma, his childhood sweetheart. Otsuma, also from a privileged class, is now married accordingly. In Ushimatsu's dream Otsuma's face changes into that of another lovely woman: Oshiho. His subconscious desire to rise above his origins could scarcely be more plainly seen.

A similar conflation occurs when the bereaved Ushimatsu receives a letter of condolence from Shogo, Oshiho's younger brother. It includes a message of "best regards" from his sister. That, too, calls up memories of childhood yearning— then for Otsuma, now for Oshiho. Both women, of course, were socially beyond his reach:

> If Ushimatsu had not experienced the tragedy of being born an *eta*, he would not have felt such strong nostalgia for the girl. He would not have felt that his youth had been utterly wasted.[12]

After his return to Iiyama, Ushimatsu's fascination with Oshiho takes its cues from the temple where she lives. In his mind, she becomes almost a deity. Alone in the main hall with a Buddhist statue of Kannon, he thinks only of Oshiho. In this quiet, secluded atmosphere, he compares his love to a flower adorning an ancient tomb. He repeats Oshiho's name over and over again.

He also looks forward to attending the abbot's sermon. Oshiho is there with all the others. Ushimatsu's sense of her as "unattainable" is expressed in terms as remote and rarefied as are his hopes of making her his own. The fragrance of her hair drifts his way through the assembled worshipers. He trembles with pleasure, seeing her smile as she caresses her brother. No wonder Ushimatsu's sense of himself turns on a tortured anguish of alienation: "Who could possibly be more miserable on a night like this than a man with a secret like his—the *eta*'s secret misery?"

The only way Ushimatsu can express his fondness for Oshiho is through her younger brother. Ushimatsu decides to help Shogo get through school.

Oshiho's confession of her love for Ushimatsu occurs only after the climactic moment when he reveals his dreadful secret. Until then, Toson limits their contact to nonverbal encounters pointedly rich in images of darkness:

> Ushimatsu saw Oshiho in the corridor leading to the second floor. Even in the gathering dusk Ushimatsu was struck by her deathly pallor and darkly sorrowful eyes. She returned his gaze, as one might look at a person vanishing from view. They bowed to one another in silence.[13]

Since their first encounter, Ushimatsu has gradually learned the details of Oshiho's misfortunes. Keinoshin has told him that he is her father. A visit to Keinoshin's house shows why poverty led this couple to give up their daughter for adoption by the abbot and his wife.

A more dramatic revelation explains Oshiho's tearful sorrow. Ushimatsu has fled the rumor mongers by shutting himself up in the temple. There he learns from the abbot's wife that the holy man himself has committed adultery in his heart—his adoptive daughter Oshiho being the object of his lust. The poor girl has done all she can to defend herself, but the old man's persistent bad behavior is forcing his wife to think of divorcing him.

Ironically, the way this Buddhist priest is breaking one commandment helps Ushimatsu find the strength to break quite a different one. But first the novelist wants to explore other causalities.

Oshiho's situation is remedied by flight. She returns to her impoverished family. The abbot's wife remains with her husband, hoping to reform him.

A grimmer sequence of events concerns Inoko's death. The author has come to Iiyama to campaign for his lawyer friend Ichimura, who is running for a seat on the town council. His opponent is Takayanagi—the man who has married a *burakumin* girl for her money. Inoko exposes Takayanagi's hypocrisy at a campaign rally. Takayanagi gets revenge by having Inoko killed. From this point on, however, the story takes a dramatic new turn. Inoko's death radically alters Ushimatsu's course of action. Revelation on two levels draws him out of his self-centered agony. First, he realizes that his own indifference to Takayanagi's anxiety to conceal his wife's social origins actually prompted the man to distract attention away from himself by spreading the rumor about Ushimatsu. That might have done the trick had Inoko not brought Takayanagi's secret to the attention of the electorate. Now that Inoko has been murdered, Ushimatsu sees what he has lost by not confessing to his mentor in time:

At last he sees through his own deception—the lie he has been living. Trying so hard to hide, he succeeded only in damaging his character. Concealing his shame had left him not a moment's peace. He had kept deceiving himself. . . . It would be better to act like a man and tell the world that he is an *eta*. Rentaro's death taught him this lesson.[14]

The climax of the novel unfolds in Chapter 22. First, the abbot's broken commandment is mended. His wife tells Ushimatsu that her husband has begged forgiveness. From a narrative point of view, that resolution prepares the way for Ushimatsu's ironically positive breaking of a commandment.

In the serene atmosphere created by the wife's prayerful chanting, Ushimatsu writes a letter resigning his position at the school. Toson reiterates the father's commandment yet again:

No matter how you are treated by others, no matter who they are, never tell them where you come from. If you allow yourself to be led astray by emotion, if you forget my commandment, then you will be well and truly made a social outcast.[15]

The reader has seen Ushimatsu thinking again and again of begging his father's forgiveness. We know that he has seen Takayanagi arrested and that he worries about a pupil he knows is a *burakumin*. We are scarcely surprised by his climactic confession. Ushimatsu tells his class what he is and asks his pupils for forgiveness:

"When you go home, please tell your parents about me. Tell them how sorry I am for hiding my lowly birth. . . . I am an *eta* . . . an impure human being. . . ."
      Thinking that he had not done enough, he took two or three steps back, knelt down on the floor, and repeated his plea for forgiveness. . . .[16]

From this point on, the novel quickly moves into the resolution of the causal line of Ushimatsu's fate. The subplot of Oshiho's life after her departure from the temple also merges with this primary line. Toson concentrates on the major characters' responses to Ushimatsu's disclosure of his identity.

Initially, two persons who have been sympathetic toward Ushimatsu are brought together. Their dialogue reveals that Ginnosuke's friendship with Ushimatsu is still unshaken, despite his newly acquired knowledge of the latter's social status. More important, the dialogue serves as the narrative device for a disclosure of withheld information. Oshiho confesses that she has known about Ushimatsu's humble origins all along. Just as Ushimatsu envisioned in his dream earlier, Katsuno told Oshiho his secret.

It is Ginnosuke who acts as a liaison between the unfortunate Ushimatsu and the sympathetic Oshiho. He tells Oshiho that Ushimatsu has loved her all this while, even when he knew that society considered them worlds apart. She replies that she is ready to follow Ushimatsu for the rest of her life: "Her answer surprised Ginnosuke. Love, tears and determination were all there in her positive 'yes.'"[17]

Even so, Toson is forced to rely on a *deus ex machina* to bring the couple together. Inoko's wife sympathizes with Oshiho and volunteers to take custody of her until Ushimatsu is settled enough to marry. More important, Ohigashi, the outcast whom Ushimatsu saw expelled from his inn, returns as Ushimatsu's benefactor. He is about to leave for Texas, where he plans to farm; he needs the help of a young man.

Toson has been accused of taking the easy way out. Just as easily, one might consider the history of discrimination in many a twentieth-century context and conclude, with Toson, that Texas is not too far to go if you are a Japanese outcast seeking release from centuries of prejudice.

The conclusion of the novel does work rather hard to show that prejudice has remarkable staying power, even in a rapidly changing world. This time, we are shown how childhood innocence is betrayed by adult knowledge. The principal is pitted against Ushimatsu's pupils, who are still emotionally attached to him even after they know his secret. As readers, we know that the principal was jealous of Ushimatsu's success in the classroom long before there was any question of a shameful secret.

Now Ushimatsu's pupils want a half day off from school to see him off at the station. The principal responds to their request with a piece of character assassination, drawing a very bad picture of Ushimatsu's motives and behavior. He does not mind giving Ginnosuke's pupils a chance to see their teacher off.

All those who are in tune with the changing times and friendly with Ushimatsu leave this insular community in the end. Ginnosuke has been offered a position at a high school in Tokyo. Oshiho will also join Rentaro's wife in Tokyo. The innocent children's education will be left in the hands of those who resist the currents of times, as the conclusion echoes the principal's earlier remarks:

> The principal considers himself already an educator of an older generation, a far cry from this of Ginnosuke and Ushimatsu. . . . Times have changed, and nothing is more threatening than the new age. He himself has no intention of growing old and feeble.. . . . He will not be pushed aside by these brash newcomers. He will take appropriate action with any who display sympathy with these so-called new ideals.[18]

The novel ends with Ushimatsu's last glimpse of this small-minded provincial town. Its idyllic landscape is powdered with snow, as if to emphasize its faraway character, safe from any touch of turmoil found in the world outside with all its political upheavals and social change:

> The row of houses on the opposite bank was broken first by tall temple buildings, then by the old castle ruins. All were covered in obscuring snow. The white walls of the elementary school, and the bell tower, both clearly visible in fair weather, today seem swallowed up by snowy sky. Ushimatsu looked back at the town two or three times, sighed deeply, then turned away for good with tears running down his face. His sled began its run across the snow.[19]

While remaining faithful to the central problem of Ushimatsu's coming to terms with his life, Ichikawa's film version is, in its own right, an ambitious attempt to deal with the plight of the oppressed. He is also not afraid to give Ushimatsu's moral dilemma a more convincing avenue of escape than Texas. As we have seen, Toson's contemporaries criticized that remove as being just too much like a ready-made solution. Today, of course, we live in an age that prides itself on confrontational directness, so leaving for Texas will never do. In fact, the Wada-Ichikawa reading of *The Broken Commandment* is notably willing to accommodate the present-day audience. Their treatment of Inoko's wife is a good example. As we later see, she is much more fully developed in the film than in the novel and is a woman endowed with a strong personality and beliefs.

Although Ichikawa retains most of the important narrative events that bear directly on Ushimatsu's moral conflict, he radically simplifies most of them. This is welcome relief from Toson's penchant for lengthy and often redundant descriptions of his suffering hero's inner reality.

At the same time, Ichikawa takes full advantage of his medium. He uses the camera to help us see and feel Ushimatsu's misery in ways peculiar to cinematic art. Ichikawa makes the best of cinema's nimble shuffling of events in time. His flashbacks give us direct and insightful access to cause and effect, especially when he combines Ushimatsu's recollections with their immediate psychological consequences.

In the novel, the reader's knowledge of the historical setting is taken for granted. Ichikawa feels obliged to make sure, offering his audience this introductory subtitle: "This is a story from the past when class discrimination still existed." Toward the middle of the film he adds some more concrete signposts, backing up a reference to war with a series of shots of soldiers going off to battle.

Another subtitle concludes the drama by giving the scene of Ushimatsu's outcast sufferings a very specific time and place: "It was in December, 1904, the first year of the Russo-Japanese War, that Ushimatsu left Iiyama."

As we have seen, the novel opens in Iiyama, where it will close. Ushimatsu witnesses the spectacle of an entire small-minded little town shunning a *burakumin* like himself. Things in Iiyama have not changed when, at the end, we see a sadder and wiser Ushimatsu turning his back on the place.

Ichikawa approaches the story in a different way. He opens in Ushimatsu's village, with the bull's attack on his father and the son's return to attend the funeral. This narrative change emphasizes the personal, inescapable circularity of *eta* life. No matter where he goes, no matter how skillfully he conceals his identity, the *burakumin* will never escape the torment and anxiety of having been born—there. His birthplace defines him. One might say that a *burakumin*'s birthplace casts him out, by making him an outcast.

The opening scene speaks for Ichikawa's desire to portray the life of an unfortunate man who must live cut off from the outside world. After surveying the surrounding mountains, the camera offers a long-shot view of a man and a bull as part of this natural setting. Then Ichikawa lets the camera witness the gamekeeper's death. He approaches the bull with some salt. A close-up shows us the bull's fierce eyes. The camera conveys the feel, the rhythm and the momentum of his charge. The gamekeeper's surprised attempt at evasion is shown in crosscut. Shots of various sizes in a reverse-field setup show him being gored by the bull. A close-up shows us the gamekeeper's terror of approaching death. His body rolls. The camera studies his corpse lying among stems of bamboo. Then it ends the scene by following the bull's retreat: shot size decreases as he gallops away and disappears.

The dissolve yields to a shot of a hired hand walking down a mountain path in the evening. Another shot introduces a small *buraku* with a number of houses crouched together at the foot of the mountain. Even this single shot visually confirms our sense of the isolated seclusion in which all outcasts suffer.

The next scene brings these *burakumin* together in the small shack where Ushimatsu's father lived. The camera's survey of its dilapidated interior is a poignant commentary on the life led there. This narrow room does not even have regular *tatami* mats; only rough straw mats are spread on the earthen floor. Later on, we get a clearer sense of the dismal life the *burakumin* lead as Ushimatsu's uncle describes the sorry life the deceased led after his son left home.

The uncle is surprised to see his nephew enter. Only now do we learn that the opening sequence is more than a merely factual depiction of a fatal accident. It turns out that Ushimatsu knows about it only through a premonition. Suddenly that opening sequence may be understood as an extension of the son's imagination. As the camera closes in on him, a flashback shows the young man taking night watch in the yard of the school where he teaches. The serene atmosphere is broken by the sound of a man sobbing. A close-up registers Ushimatsu's consternation as he realizes that the sound he hears is his father's grieving call to him. That voice merges with music at the end of the flashback.

Following that powerful evocation of the father-son tie, we now hear the uncle issuing a stern reminder in his brother's name: "Your father wanted to say 'Hide Ushimatsu, never tell who you are!'" Using the uncle, Ichikawa leans heavily on the burden of self-sacrifice the father had borne in order to give his son a chance to lead a normal life. We learn that the father had been headman of the *buraku*. Then, having managed to send his son off for a decent education, he decided never to see the boy again. That was why he had come to this poor place, to live in the meadow at the foot of the mountain. The father's abiding wish was for his son to be spared the horrors he himself had known, living as an outcast.

The funeral sequence also establishes Ushimatsu's decision to follow his father's commandment, the decision that inevitably meets both internal and external obstacles. Here, too, Ichikawa provides a sequence charged with emotional overtones as he introduces an element absent in the original: another outcast's response to the death of Ushimatsu's father. As if to curse the fate of being born under the unlucky star, or to indict the society that takes discrimination for granted, an old hired hand reminisces:

"When I heard Mr. Segawa calling to the bull, I thought that he was going to kill himself. . . . I don't think he was forced to die, but his cry seemed to be appealing to Heaven. He wanted to tell Him about the sorrow and humiliation of the *burakumin* and the agony of living in such a mountain like a hermit or a dead person."

Again his flashback lets us see and feel the immediacy of the old man's experience. The screen dissolves into the mountain with no human figure at all.

Soft music merges with Mr. Segawa's hoarse voice calling to the bull. Then the figure of the old gamekeeper roams into the picture. Cross-cutting between his sad face and the bull's fierce eyes ends the old hired hand's reconstruction of Mr. Segawa's suicide attempt.

The funeral sequence concludes with another death scene, this one in the slaughterhouse. Toson belabors the appalling details in order to elucidate the plight of *burakumin* and Ushimatsu's witness, which is all the more painfully ironic because butchering was a monopoly of the despised *burakumin*.

Ichikawa simplifies this episode by giving a quick, newsreel view of a cow routinely reduced to hunks of beef. No viewer could miss the horrific irony in this view of the profession a young man like Ushimatsu would have been relegated to if he had not escaped to become a teacher.

After providing ample evidence of *burakumin* suffering on home ground, Ichikawa takes us to Iiyama. There we see the scene that opens Toson's novel as townspeople chase an outcast out of the local inn. It echoes the earlier images of defilement in the slaughterhouse. Some of the outraged guests refer to this *burakumin* as defiled. After he is dragged away, some even sprinkle purifying salt.

The rest of the film includes the major events of the novel, following Toson's central theme of Ushimatsu's coming to terms with his life. Ichikawa does, however, enrich his account with a great many flashbacks, which offer a somewhat different access to Ushimatsu's inner struggle. This method renders legibility to the close interaction or causality between the past and the present as it enlarges our view of Ushimatsu's suffering.

The first example of this occurs after Ushimatsu sees the unfortunate outcast thrown out of the inn. Ichikawa's young man is much more outspoken in his indictment of society's treatment of the *burakumin*. Ginnosuke Tsuchiya has come to visit him at the inn. Still agitated by what he has seen, Ushimatsu says:

"What's the difference between the *burakumin* and the ordinary citizen? We know that historically, the *burakumin* class was created to satisfy the needs of politicians. . . . We live in a new age now. Aren't many *burakumin* going to war as infants of the Emperor?"

After Tsuchiya leaves, the overwrought Ushimatsu gives vent to his feelings by stabbing himself in the arm with a small knife, exclaiming: "Look! This is human blood, no different from any other Japanese. Why do I have to be discriminated against? Why do I hide my identity? Father! Teach me why!"

A dissolve flashback takes us back to his father's funeral. Ushimatsu is seen clinging to the freshly dug burial mound. The young man's show of grief in the isolated mountain spot is a powerful visual statement. Even after death, the *burakumin* are shut out, cut off from full and proper burial ritual.

That flashback yields to a scene depicting Ushimatsu's temporary answer to his own anguished question. He realizes that he has no choice but to continue hiding his social identity. We see him pulling a cart filled with his belongings as he takes the precaution of moving to new lodgings.

As in the novel, Ushimatsu's relationship with Inoko forms the core of the central causal line. But Inoko's influence as a mentor figure on Ushimatsu's decision making is given a different venue of approach. Ichikawa continues to explore his stylistic vein of flashbacks to show how Ushimatsu's past meeting with this man committed to liberation of *burakumin* affects him now. This chronological rearrangement of events maps out Ushimatsu's gradual attraction to the alternative Inoka offers: life as a *burakumin* openly demanding social justice.

As in the novel, we see Ushimatsu making his surreptitious purchase of Inoko's *Confession*. Why would he take this risk in a small-minded small town like Iiyama? What does this young fellow have in common with an author famous for choosing to share the difficult fate of the *burakumin*?

Ichikawa satisfies our curiosity in a flashback that makes the connections we need. Ushimatsu's recollection is preceded by a shot of him completely absorbed in the book he has just purchased. The opening line of *Confession*, "I am from a *buraku*," dissolves into the scene of Ushimatsu's journey home in his recollection.

A shot of a mountain road shrouded in mist opens this sequence. It is peopled with obvious *burakumin*. A mother and daughter walk along singing a melancholy song. A barefoot hoodlum in tattered clothes looks at the world with shining, stray-dog eyes. A strolling beggar-musician plays a vulgar tune on his samisen. The soft orchestral music of the sound track yields to the percussive twang of the samisen; that change confirms our sense of a truly dismal atmosphere. Again, this is Ichikawa's means of letting the contemporary audience know what *burakumin* life was like at the time in which the novel is set.

Another dissolve leads to the mountaintop, where Ushimatsu is shown meeting Inoko for the first time. Here we see how different Ichikawa's outcaste hero is from Toson's.

In the novel, this encounter "locates" Ushimatsu's radical transformation in a moment of insight into his inner conflict. Inspired by his mentor's fidelity to his own soul, Ushimatsu is almost led to follow the same path. Yet, in the company of the others, he misses the opportunity for full confession.

Ichikawa gives us a suffering hero still bound by his father's commandment. It takes Inoko's strong leadership to show Ushimatsu the way to self-awareness. The director underscores Inoko's mission both verbally and visually. We hear him deliver what amounts to a hectoring, unsettling sermon to the young men on the mountaintop:

"My fellow outcasts are content to lead a hand-to-mouth existence in seclusion, even as they envy others who are truly free. . . . They never want to address the social injustice which ruins their lives. . . . The greatest obstacle in the way of my movement for *buraku* liberation lies in the *burakumin* themselves. Don't you think it is our mission to strengthen their resolve?"

Then Inoko's challenges Ushimatsu directly: "Once I was cowardly enough to hide my identity. Do you want to be a coward for the rest of your life?"

A series of reverse-angle shots in close-up examines each character's emotional intensity until Ushimatsu is singled out as he adamantly denies his outcast status. Yet the camera takes note of his drooping shoulders, a fit enough index of his weakening defenses. Then it cuts to Inoko closing his eyes and sighing deeply.

Inoko encourages Ushimatsu to read his *Confession* in that same encounter. He explains that it describes how a rumor about his lowly birth led him to a public confession and subsequent expulsion from a prestigious job at a teacher's college.

As in the novel, Inoko's remarks tell us that Ushimatsu has corresponded with him before this, their first meeting. We also find out why Inoko has seen fit to challenge Ushimatsu's hidden life. Inoko's health is failing. He sees a possible successor in this young man. Clearly, Inoko's book does more than offer Ushimatsu the chance to see the need to escape self-deception; it suggests that he share his mentor's courage, and his fate as well.

Even though Inoko appears to have mapped out the young man's future by fixing on him as a possible successor, their second meeting works in the opposite direction. By this time Ichikawa has shown us Ushimatsu selling a used bookstore his copies of all Inoko's works. Having seen that, we now see Inoko coming to the temple to visit Ushimatsu, who insists that he does not know him!

Thanks to a convenient shadow, a third party witnesses this encounter. It is the abbot, who turns out to be breaking a commandment of his own as he lusts after his adoptive daughter, Oshiho.

Ichikawa manages to lighten this scene with a favorite narrative device: black humor. The abbot's wife joins him after Inoko leaves. Seeing Ushimatsu heading for his room, she says fondly that they ought to have adopted a young boy like Ushimatsu.

The abbot tells her "not to be sarcastic." The conversation he has overheard between Inoko and Ushimatsu leads him to guess the young man's secret. The very idea of being foster-father to a *burakumin* is utterly abhorrent to the good abbot, even as he takes his own incestuous desires in stride.

As we have seen, Inoko's murder prevents Toson's hero from making his confession. Ichikawa's protagonist has shown us a more complex reaction to this charismatic reformer. Having felt himself drawn away from his father's command by Inoko's forceful arguments, Ushimatsu rejects his mentor, only to suffer that much more decisively when news arrives of the murder.

Again, Ichikawa uses a flashback to reconstruct the circumstances of the crime as Ushimatsu knows them through Inoko's wife. A long shot opens our view of Inoko's solitary figure walking along a snowy path. A medium shot registers Inoko's awareness of something unusual. Intercuts between Inoko and the man following him finally yield to a long shot of the two as the distance between them decreases. Their struggle continues in a series of long shots, continuously reframing assailant and victim in the center. Inoko crawls out from under his assailant, who nevertheless manages to strike him in the head with a rock. The sound-track music swells as a deep focus takes notes of people rushing from the background to the foreground.

This sequence begins and ends without any cinematic punctuation cuing us to a past event. For example, the flashback scene directly cuts to a close-up of Inoko's face. Such an abrupt transition, in turn, emphasizes the immediacy of Ushimatsu's feelings about Inoko's death. The next sequence is even more intense in its feeling and is obviously climactic: we see Ushimatsu breaking down in class and asking his pupils to forgive him for deceiving them.

As in the novel, Ichikawa creates a gradually mounting tension. His daily routine of returning their assignments is first introduced. The song "Momotaro" (Peach boy) is heard coming from the next room. Japanese audiences cannot fail to note its reference to childhood innocence, which is here soon to be compromised by exposure to a very ugly feature of grown-up experience. The happy chatter of the classroom is suddenly stilled when Ushimatsu announces that this is his last day.

A low-angle long shot takes in the beginning of this scene as Ushimatsu starts to describe the plight of *burakumin*. The camera looks at him from the back of the room as he stands at his desk. The students' posture shows that they are listening intently. In a subtle way, this long low shot celebrates the teacher's courage as he accepts his fate at last.

Ichikawa retains most of the soliloquy offered in the novel. He and Wada add dialogue, giving Ushimatsu this urgent appeal to his pupils: "I beg you to remember that I am the one who told you this: that *burakumin*, despised as they are, are human like you. They are born innocent babies, and remain human until they die. They are not demons or animals!"

Ichikawa lets the camera do the work of the novelist's many words describing this traumatic moment for teacher and pupils. The opening long shot yields to a medium shot of Ushimatsu when he says that he comes from the *buraku*. We see his trembling hands and legs. His desk keeps him from collapsing completely. The camera cuts to groups of the children in medium shots. Some sit open-mouthed; all clearly show their consternation.

As Ushimatsu reminisces about the happy days he spent with them, teacher and pupils share the same emotions. A close-up singles out Ushimatsu's tear-stained face. The children's sobbing merges with the lyrical music that has stolen in. Then the camera draws back at a 90-degree pan as Ushimatsu begins to act out his repentance. He is shown stepping forward from his desk. Another shot, this time in a medium take, shows him kneeling; we do not see his face, but his bent back speaks for his feelings.

Again, Ichikawa takes a camera shortcut, switching to a room where a teacher is telling Ginnosuke what is going on in Ushimatsu's classroom. We see Ginnosuke's reaction as he rushes out and into Ushimatsu's class. A long shot shows him approaching Ushimatsu, still in the kneeling position, surrounded by pupils and colleagues. It is Ginnosuke who takes him away.

This climactic sequence ends with a cut to the snow-covered forest where Ushimatsu is seen wandering. A long shot clearly registers the young man's sense of dejection and alienation as his solitary figure merges with the uninviting wintry surroundings. The camera closes in as he begins to ask his late father's forgiveness.

Throughout this rather lengthy soliloquy, Ichikawa provides much more narrative legibility to his hero's felt feeling, even as he falls into the verbose sentimentality that was Toson's besetting sin. Ushimatsu summarizes various stages of his suffering: his father's sacrifice to educate him; the sense of spiritual freedom experienced through his education; the internal conflict that, paradoxically, freedom bred in him; his betrayal of his mentor, Inoko; and, ultimately, his betrayal of his father. What can he do but turn to thoughts of self-imposed exile? "I am alone, Father. I am nameless, and my love is unrequited. I am on my way to a journey of repentance for the broken commandment. . . ."

Withheld information does play a crucial part in reversing the course of action to which Ushimatsu has resigned himself. At this stage, he has yet to realize that people free of small-minded prejudice against *burakumin* do exist. Ichikawa makes good use of his hero's blinkered view of the world, arranging a twist of fate for the young man that is far more convincing (not to mention interesting) than a sentence of transportation to Texas. The director does this by combining two causal lines: Ushimatsu's shifting response to his father's command, and his liaison with Oshiho.

In novel and film both, this forbidden love reinforces the primary theme of Ushimatsu's coming to terms with his own life. This love, like any love, adds its share to the existing conflict. Unlike Toson, who concentrates on the various stages of Ushimatsu's psychological responses to Oshiho, Ichikawa gives his young hero romantic anguish centered on causes outside himself: gradually, he discovers the details of Oshiho's unfortunate life. The narrative device of withheld information becomes especially important here.

Ushimatsu meets Oshiho at the temple just after he arrives in Iiyama. Earlier, his friend Keinoshin Kazama had accompanied him as far as the temple gate, but would not explain his reluctance to enter. Ushimatsu, alone, sees Oshiho for the first time, her face bathed in tears. He is astonished when she begs him, a complete stranger, not to leave the temple, but to stay a few hours. Several sequences later, we find out why. Ushimatsu learns from the abbot's wife that Keinoshin is Oshiho's father and that the girl was put up for adoption after her mother's death.

Ichikawa uses the novel's pattern of information withheld and revealed to apply a different sort of pressure to Ushimatsu. He brings father, daughter, and Ushimatsu as prospective bridegroom together as Keinoshin urges a marriage

Eiji Funakoshi (l) and Raizo Ichikawa (r) in *The Broken Commandment* (1962) directed
by Kon Ichikawa. Courtesy of the Kawakita Memorial Film Institute.

between the two youngsters. Of course, Ushimatsu has not revealed his secret,
so his friend has no idea that he is proposing what prejudice would consider a
monstrous misalliance between a girl of the samurai class and an outcast. (The
novelist had left this possibility in the realm of chance and Oshiho's individual
courage.)

The music on the sound track suddenly stops, leaving only the sound of a
restless wind. The scene ends with a shot of each of the three in a pensive mood.
A medium shot shows father and daughter facing the camera, while Ushimatsu's
back is toward us. The wind persists. We are not really given any visual or verbal
clue to the reason for each character's sudden lapse into such a mood. We can
only guess, putting together some rather tentative clues Ichikawa gives us. The
wind suggests that the father's proposal adds another dimension of anxiety
to Ushimatsu's already anxious state of mind. The camera's sly glance earlier
caught Oshiho's blushing face at the time of her father's proposal. Now she
seems to wonder what has caused Ushimatsu's lukewarm response to his father's
suggestion.

The truth is disclosed at multiple levels in one of the dramatic highlights
used to bring Oshiho and Ushimatsu together. This happens after the climactic
moment of Ushimatsu's confession to his students. Though the narrative here
follows the novel, Oshiho is endowed with a much stronger, more sensitive personality. Ichikawa lets us see this visually and verbally. As Oshiho and Ginnosuke

Raizo Ichikawa (1) and Shiho Fujimura (r) in *The Broken Commandment* (1962) directed by Kon Ichikawa. Courtesy of the Kawakita Memorial Film Institute.

search for Ushimatsu, a branch brushes the girl's face. A close-up takes note of snow and tears together there. She leaves us no doubt about her thoughts, saying: "It doesn't matter where his father or mother come from, that should not concern Ushimatsu!"

Like her counterpart in the novel, she tells Ginnosuke of her intention to marry Ushimatsu. Our earlier curiosity about her feelings is satisfied here. And now, once she and Ginnosuke have found Ushimatsu in the woods, we discover, as he does, that she has good reason for her decision to marry the man she loves, even though he is an outcast. When Ushimatsu tries to dissuade her from society's idea of a shocking misalliance, Oshiho protests that Inoko's wife is not from her husband's class. Yes. It turns out that Oshiho has read *Confession.*

Her strength of character is conveyed in visual as well as verbal terms. A close-up emphasizes her lively, determined expression as she says, "Even a woman can stick to what she knows is right if she really wants to!"

This touch of romance working its magic on a very stubborn problem of discrimination yields a related happy outcome when the abbot and his wife are reconciled. When the camera cuts to the temple, Ushimatsu is brought together with those whose feelings toward him remain the same: the abbot and his wife, Inoko's widow, and Tsuchiya. As if to atone for having broken a commandment himself, the abbot has taken Inoko's body in and offers it Buddhist services. In place of Toson's unconvincing rescue by way of Texas, here we see Ushimatsu acquiring a new mentor in the person of Inoko's wife.

For that matter, Ichikawa (or possibly scenarist Wada) transforms Toson's submissive wife into a well-developed, strong-willed character. Ichikawa uses her long conversation with Ushimatsu to offer us some insight into the plight of a woman married to an outsider. This places the *buraku* liberation movement in its historical context. Inoko's wife describes her husband's formative suffering, the lifelong agony of humiliation that comes from being born into a class despised by society. It turns out that in her heart of hearts she regrets his total absorption in the cause of social justice; she wishes he could have been more like an ordinary man and husband. She even dares to doubt that individuals can change the course of history; not even a movement's heroes can do that, she thinks, but only time and its slow changes.

Ichikawa gives this woman quite a long lesson to deliver to Ushimatsu. In essence, she argues that the new constitution of the Meiji Restoration guarantees equality to all citizens. She sees life as a struggle for everyone, regardless of social status. Ushimatsu, she insists, must not blame all his suffering on his lowly origins.

This woman's own sense of independence now compels her to go to Tokyo, where she will work as a kindergarten assistant. Ushimatsu's transformation occurs suddenly, as he announces his intention to accompany her to the capital to follow in her late husband's footsteps.

A cut to the principal's office shows us that hypocrisy and prejudice are still alive and well in that theoretically enlightened place. As in the novel, the principal is adamantly opposed to Ushimatsu's pupils going to see him off.

Again, Ichikawa is not about to follow the novelist's path of least resistance, allowing Ginnosuke to announce his acceptance of a better position in Tokyo. In the film, he is more than a right-thinking man who knows a hopeless cause when he sees one. This Ginnosuke has the courage of his convictions, and some political will as well. He has indeed been offered a far better post in Tokyo. He turns it down. He intends to become "the only educator" in this provincial town dedicated to the proposition that someone has to guard its children against the contamination of prejudice.

Ichikawa also gives Ginnosuke the political clout it takes to force the principal to reverse his position on pupils going to see Ushimatsu off. At the same time, Ichikawa himself seems anxious to deal evenhandedly with this situation. His principal is also portrayed as a victim of social forces in this case, the prejudice characteristic of a closely knit, isolated little community. He confesses that he, too, was once imbued with the ideals of an educator; but alas, a lifetime of accommodating the manners and mores of Iiyama has made him a petty and vindictive opportunist.

This interesting encounter between two such different educators leads to the final sequence. Here we see how different the ending of this film is from the novel. As we have seen, Toson's protagonist leaves Iiyama an exile and quite alone. Even Oshiho's promise to marry him has no real narrative legibility to it, since the novelist gives us no sense of her real feelings.

Ichikawa is, if anything, too solicitous for his young man's future here at the end of the story. Ushimatsu's departure unites him with all his near and dear in this benighted little town. Ginnosuke, Oshiho, Inoko's widow, and his own devoted pupils—all are on hand to offer the exile a support so firm that questions of narrative legibility almost become superfluous.

The final sequence begins with a shot of the snow-covered, deserted banks of the Chikuma River. What better reminder that Iiyama has given this young idealist the cold shoulder? A dissolve yields to a shot of Ushimatsu and Inoko's wife pulling a sled through this desolate winter landscape.

Our sense of this scene as a dismal one soon changes as Ichikawa sets to work conveying a sense of touching solidarity between these two. Here again, Inoko's wife is given ample opportunity to speak for the director's views as they relate to Ushimatsu's decision to live more fully in every sense.

We witness the conversation of these two in a series of reverse-field shots that show us clearly how each responds to what the other says. Ichikawa's anxiety to get his message across makes for a rather repetitious reprise of Ushimatsu's earlier declaration of intent to follow in Inoko's footsteps. The camera shifts dramatically to underscore that determination with a low-angle shot aligning Ushimatsu and Inoko's widow against the wintry sky. The rustling wind merges with Ushimatsu's voice. The camera's ostentatious angle and spatial arrangement

Raizo Ichikawa (l) and Shiho Fujimura (r) in *The Broken Commandment* (1962) directed by Kon Ichikawa. Courtesy of the Kawakita Memorial Film Institute.

unmistakably celebrate the bond forged between these two people by their difficult mission. A close-up shows the woman's tearful gratitude for Ushimatsu's commitment to her late husband and his cause.

A much-needed lighter touch is offered by Ushimatsu's pupils arriving with Ginnosuke. Again, Ichikawa spares no visual sign to indicate a bond no force of prejudice can sunder. Children crowd the screen with their teacher in the center. He breaks away to fetch a parting gift from the sled—a dictionary. The children crowd round to receive it. One of them reciprocates with a packet of boiled eggs. The camera frames the two of them as the child explains that this gift is a present from his mother. Clearly, there are significant exceptions in the mindset even of a community as staunchly conservative as Iiyama.

Nor is the young man allowed to depart sweetheartless. Oshiho appears. She and Ushimatsu meet in a medium shot. The music swells as she removes her hood and looks into his eyes.

The temple gong sounds in the distance, as if to remind Oshiho that she comes bearing gifts of sandals and foot warmers from the caretaker-bellringer, Shota. Oshiho tells Ushimatsu that the poor boy's fate is worse than his own, since he is deaf and an orphan so that no one is likely to give a home. Ushimatsu asks if Oshiho will join him when he gets settled in Tokyo. Of course she will.

Ichikawa risks oversaturating this scene with visual and verbal bonding motifs. Oshiho offers Inoko's wife her hood. Ginnosuke and Ushimatsu shake hands, promising to meet in Tokyo. The scene ends with a long shot of waving wellwishers and departing sled. The sound track offers an appropriately sentimental rendering of the theme music, while the subtitle places Ushimatsu's fate in the larger context of Japanese history: "Ushimatsu left Iiyama in December, 1904, the first year of the Russo-Japanese War."

The film ends with a dissolve to the temple where the orphan Shota is seen striking the gong for all its worth. No viewer could miss the poignant/hopeful valedictory tone there, though just to make sure, the sound he makes merges with the sound track's telling crescendo.

Surely one can say that Ichikawa recasts *The Broken Commandment* as a vehicle suitable for an audience more confident of social change than Toson's had reason to be. If, by some miracle of cinematic rare device, readers of that era could become viewers in our own, what, one wonders, would they think of Toson's women as presented by Ichikawa? What old commandments has the director broken in order to give them such strength of commitment and conviction?

Notes

1. Yoshiyuki Oshikawa, "*Hakai*" (The broken commandment), in *Nihon eiga sakuhin zenshu* (A complete collection of Japanese films) (Tokyo: Kinema Jumpo, 1973), p. 205.
2. For example, see Hiroshi Noma, "*Hakai* ni tsuite" (On *The Broken Commandment*), in *Nihon no sakka: Shimazaki Toson* (Japanese writers: Toson Shimazaki), ed. Nobuo Ooka, et al., vol. 4 (Tokyo: Shogakkan, 1992), pp. 118–19.

3. Nowadays, the correct term would be *hisabetsuburakumin*, literally "undiscriminated people from the *buraku*." Though "eta" is a derogatory term now, I use it here as Toson did.

4. Ken Hirano, "Buraku kaiho undo no nagare" (The progression of the movement toward the improvement of Buraku), in Toson Shimazaki, *Hakai* (The broken commandment) (Tokyo: Shincho, 1954), pp. 395–96.

5. Toson Shimazaki, *Hakai*, p. 6.

6. Ibid., p. 99. The translation is the author's. For a complete English translation of *Hakai*, see *The Broken Commandment*, trans. Kenneth Strong (Tokyo: University of Tokyo Press, 1974).

7. Ibid., p. 126.

8. Ibid., p. 144.

9. Ibid., p. 155.

10. Ibid., p. 169.

11. Ibid., p. 210.

12. Ibid., p. 168.

13. Ibid., p 256.

14. Ibid., p. 303.

15. Ibid., p. 307.

16. Ibid., p. 320.

17. Ibid., p. 334.

18. Ibid., p. 310.

19. Ibid., p. 349.

8

Cuts in Plot and Characters: Higashi's *A River with No Bridge* (1992)

Japan's social outcasts, the *burakumin*, have been studied in numbers of literary works, but very few such works have been adapted as films.[1] The earliest instance on record dates from 1910, a film whose print has been lost. Titled *Hanafubuki* (Scattering cherry blossoms), its story concerns a doomed love affair between an aristocrat and his *burakumin* maid.[2] Perhaps the best-known postwar example is Kon Ichikawa's *Hakai* (The broken commandment, 1962). It adapts a novel of the same title by the Meiji era writer Toson Shimazaki.

The sensitive nature of the *burakumin* issue may be judged by the fact that this class of nonperson has not officially existed in Japan for over a century. A Meiji government edit of 1871 outlawed all discrimination against these people, and with the term of abuse expressive of it. The *burakumin* became the *shinheimin*, or "new commoners." But, of course, as in every such situation, the burden of so many centuries of discrimination dropped away with painful slowness.

In the context of Japanese cinema, this has meant that few films on the subject of the *burakumin* have made it through a complex system of censorship brought about by studio policy and external pressures. A noteworthy influence in this regard has been the Buraku Liberation League (Buraku Kaiho Domei). Founded in 1946, this organization has operated as a kind of censoring and regulating committee whose effect on directors (as we later see) has tended to be restrictive.

Hashi no nai kawa (A river with no bridge), Yoichi Higashi's 1992 film adaptation of Sue Sumii's novel on the *burakumin*, offers a good incentive to reexamine the troubled history of interplay between fiction and film as they share a subject so sensitive, one that is so problematic and painful.

In this instance, the troubled history of novel-to-film adaptation goes back to 1968, when Tadashi Imai decided to make a two-part film using Sumii's work. He soon clashed with the author. Sumii harshly criticized the script. So did the president of the Buraku Liberation League. In the end, Imai was forced to revise his screenplay, with help from the veteran scriptwriter Yoshikata Yoda.

Even so, Imai proved stubbornly faithful to parts of his original. The resulting film bore all the hallmarks of his communist ideology, most notably in highly charged scenes giving melodramatic emphasis to his sympathies with the oppressed. Among the film's critics was the editor of the Buraku League's official newspaper. He accused Imai of deliberately distorting the image and history of the *burakumin*. Speaking on behalf of the oppressed minority, this critic denounced the film itself as "discriminatory."[3]

Twenty years later, Yoichi Higashi came to Sumii's work through an interest in women victimized by society. One such film, *Saado* (Third, 1978) had been voted best picture of the year by the prestigious journal *Kinema jumpo*. Other works in the same vein followed, notably *Za reipu* (The rape, 1982) and *Kashin* (Metamorphosis, 1986). In *A River with No Bridge*, the range of victimization expands to include both men and women suffering as *burakumin*. Higashi had this to say about his creative drive to realize this subject on film:

> After I read Sumii's novel, I felt that I should be the one to adapt it for the screen. It is an interesting work—the first thing to consider with any adaptation. Its appeal comes from the author's keen insight. She understands life in the *hisabetsuburaku*, the segregated area. She has a sharp eye for detail, for the little things that show how those communities really lived. And she portrays her characters with great sympathy. . . .
>
> I never intended to make this film serve some cause of "enlightenment." The novel itself is not cast in that mold. What the novel offers is potential for commercial success—for a film which targets viewers willing to pay to see a good adaptation. As a director, I did not want to pass up such an opportunity.[4]

Higashi's blend of artistic drive and commercial intent yielded a two-hour and twenty-minute film that nonetheless shows clear signs of compromise with the forces of "enlightenment." The script was written by Hidekichi Kim, who had directed his own first film, *Kimi wa hadaka no kami o mita ka?*(Did you see God naked? 1986). Kim was forced to submit to a great deal of input from the Buraku Liberation League. Higashi had no intention of seeing his film savaged as Imai's had been.

Even so, Higashi's epic treatment of *A River with No Bridge* shows that no outside interference got in the way of his thematic constant: victimization. In fact, it could be said that the venue offered by Sumii's novel gives him scope for a different and more ambitious approach.Inevitably, a number of major differences develop out of Higashi's own view of the plight of the *burakumin*, the most noticeable one being Higashi's persistent concern with the issue of primitiveness related to *burakumin*. As one critic has noted, every adaptation inevitably becomes an interpretation of its source.[5] To see how this happens, we must consider Sumii's novel in some detail.

Covering the period from 1909 to 1922, *A River with No Bridge*, a six-volume work, offers a history of the suffering *burakumin* as they awaken to their rights and face a painful struggle. (Volume 7, published after the film was released, carries the story on past 1922). The novel is set in a *buraku*, or segregated village, named Komori, in Nara Prefecture. The episodic narrative treats the *burakumin* of Komori as a collective suffering "character" forced to live as outcasts. Continuity of individual character is offered by Koji, who passes from

Atsuro Watanabe (l) and Saki Takaoka (r) in *A River with No Bridge* (1992) directed by Yoichi Higashi. Courtesy of the Kawakita Memorial Film Institute.

childhood to manhood through all the stages of oppression, awakening, and liberation (as a goal to strive for). Along the way he faces the vagaries of social pressure, achieves solidarity within his own group, pays a price for loving outside the sphere allowed, and knows fulfillment through commitment to the Suiheisha movement. This drama is set in contexts rife with historical detail related to various phases of Japanese political and economic upheaval: the Russo-Japanese War, the execution of the Taisho liberals, World War I, and the Rice Riots, to mention but a few.

The first two volumes span a six-year period when Koji is in elementary school. In Volumes 3 and 4 he is a youth gradually finding identity and purpose through work with the Suiheisha movement. Volumes 5 and 6 show him as a fully committed activist.

The central problem of the novel is this: "How does Koji come to terms with his life as an outcast?" Sumii's narrative strategies are conventional enough. Various formative events in Koji's life illustrate his growth toward liberation through greater awareness. These events are given repeated emphasis through his own or another character's recollection of them. A similar process gives witness to Koji's sufferings as a *burakumin*. The plight of the novel's central "character," the *burakumin*, is developed in contrast and in parallel to Koji's. Sumii is also fond of using information withheld for later disclosure. These piece-meal revelations lend interest to the story line, adding to our sense of Koji's growth; his limited perspective changes as gradually he gains access to events that have shaped his life.

Significantly, Sumii's writing is rich in metaphor used to depict the inner reality and emotions of her characters. Her best comparisons are drawn from nature. This serves to emphasize the ties that bind the *burakumin* of Komori to their tenant-farmer life. Very often, nature is personified in relation to Koji's shifting emotions.

As the story begins, Koji appears as a bright and sensitive child. As such, he is precociously aware of the prejudice that separates the villagers of Komori from those outside. Still, at this stage of his life, his awareness of segregation is more communal than personal. Sumii provides many examples of the Us versus Them that rules in such cases. It is obvious from the outset that children and adults both find their lives defined by the destructive polarities of prejudice. At school, the children of Komori are stigmatized in the most elementary sense: the other children say they stink. The "stink" of the *burakumin* is cruelly historic, deriving from centuries of bondage to trades considered "unclean," for example, butchering and grave digging.

The stinking image of contempt and rejection returns in many guises. When Koji's family takes sweet potatoes to soldiers bivouacked near Komori, it becomes a joke with the privileged "other" children at school. They laugh about soldiers so hungry they have to eat "stinking sweet potatoes." These same privileged schoolmates refuse to share a bucket of water with the children of Komori, saying that water touched by *burakumin* will stink.

Worse yet, the Komori children internalize the prejudice so that the notion of stinking becomes part of their own sense of self, of class distinction. Koji's elder brother, for example, believes that another Komori child stinks, not because he is poor but because he is an *eta* (a vile, polluted person). Here we have one child bestowing on another an odious synonym for the outcast status that rules and ruins both their lives.

One example after another shows the Komori children betrayed by their outcast poverty. Hunger and prejudice come together in a dramatic episode involving a child named Takeshi. Desperately hungry, he attempts to roast soybeans for himself and his baby brother. The beans are a luxury item, kept in reserve for emergencies. Trying to roast them, the boy sets the house on fire. The fire damages other homes before neighbors mobilize to staunch the blaze. The district fire department, like nearby villagers, will not come to the aid of a house in Komori. It is well known that a fire there creates a terrible stench.

Meantime, the child Takeshi is so terrified of his father's anger over the handful of beans than he lies to the police: he says he set the fire on purpose. Here, as elsewhere, Sumii makes use of withheld information. Only several years later, the day before Takeshi commits suicide, does Koji learn the true story. As a child, this incident served to reinforce his sense of collective prejudice against *burakumin*.

Koji's own developing awareness is more deeply touched by another recurring image of contempt for the *burakumin*: the snake. Again, Sumii uses the technique of withheld information to defer our full understanding of a trivial incident with far-reaching consequences for her character. According to prejudice, the body of an *eta* grows cold in the evening, like that of a snake. This notion carries more weight than the commonplace human mistrust of reptiles, snakes especially. In this case, the aversion includes the idea that no human would want to be reincarnated as a creature so fearsome and reviled as a snake.

The connection with Koji's development begins early in the story, at a ceremony mourning Emperor Meiji's death. Koji is quite a small child when, as everyone stands in darkness, the young girl Machie, an "outsider," grips his hand unseen. The fleeting touch will haunt him for years and return to define his relationship to the outside, nonoutcast world, and his own maturing identity. At the outset it is only natural that he, a child of Komori, should wonder at the touch of an outsider, and a girl at that. What did it mean that she grasped his hand? Could it mean that she really liked him? So it is that Koji's earliest years are marked by "forbidden" love for this girl Machie.

The novelist is in no hurry to make sense of this unlikelihood. First we must see Koji develop a sense of *burakumin* life and status through episodes involving the novel's collective "character" of inhabitants of Komori. These episodes clarify how these *burakumin* act out options or nonoptions for adjusting an outcast status. We quickly see that there is little chance for change of place—with all that means for chances of social mobility. The poor villagers of Komori are tied to their hard-scrabble land at lowly trades, making glue and sandals. For young women, marriage is a shift from entrapment to entrapment, from one house in Komori to another—or to some other *buraku*. Marriage to a real "outsider" is an impossible dream. Those born outcasts die outcasts.

There are of course instructive incidents of Komori women who do try for a better life. They all fare badly. One is Natsu, daughter of Koji's next-door neighbor. She merely changes one bad slot for another, working three years a maid in a rich man's house. She is the dutiful daughter sacrificed to family poverty. True, the impossible dream of "outside" marriage takes shape, but her intended drops her the minute he finds out where she comes from.

The outlook for women of Komori remains bleak in the novel until Suiheisha comes to the village toward the end. Even then, an element of sacrifice persists as women elect to stay put in the village, improving conditions by working for the movement. Koji's cousin Nanae does this. When the time comes to marry, her bridegroom is in the hands of the police. She is wed to Suiheisha instead. (In Volume 7, not included in the screenplay, she is seen studying for a nursing degree in order to work in a *buraku* clinic.)

The men of Komori appear to enjoy more options, though the taint of *buraku* follows them, too. Koji's elder brother, Seitaro, for example, leaves to become an apprentice in a rice shop in Osaka. He is promoted to manager and is chosen to be

Saki Takaoka (r) in *A River with No Bridge* (1992) by Yoichi Higashi. Courtesy of the Kawakita Memorial Film Institute.

the husband of the owner's daughter. Still, he cannot bring himself to reveal his past to the prospective bride (who turns out to share his shameful secret).

Hideaki stands at the top of the village heap, being the wealthy heir to the temple in Komori. He attempts to change his outcast status by leaving the village to attend high school. When his classmates discover his origins, he transfers to another school. The agony of deception continues when he falls in love with an outsider, the daughter of his art teacher. However, Hideaki's values right themselves, as he learns from his failure to appear other than what he is. He gives his real self to a worthy cause, taking on a leadership role in Suiheisha.

Sumii's narrative technique requires that Koji make piecemeal sense of all this village history. He is a child when Seitaro and Hideaki leave the village. He learns about their motives as a youth, through a kind of confessional testimony. Seitaro writes Koji a long letter. Hideaki tells his story at a public lecture held in the village temple. In other cases, the child Koji picks up bits of *buraku* history in passing, overhearing his mother and grandmother, for example, discussing Nanae's case.

Koji turns out to be an apt and outrageous pupil, learning from *buraku* history enough to map out a course for his life. He decides to accept his *eta* status as "privileged." He will work for his people by remaining rooted in Komori. Of course, this decision can only come about thanks to the community support offered by the foundation of Suiheisha (1922), whose manifesto declares "The time has come to be proud of our heritage as Eta."

As might be expected, in order to reach this stage, Koji needs mentor figures. Throughout the novel, his uncle Kazuichi and friend Hideaki, by virtue of their education and affluence, serve as such for Koji, who has only a six-year elementary education. They "initiate" him into the outside world by updating him on major current events. They also introduce him to the world of literature. For example, in his childhood, he is given a magazine that contains a short story called "Toge no aki" (Autumn on the mountain pass) dealing with the love of two *burakumin.* This is his first exposure to a world of fiction in which discrimination is just as real as that which Komori residents experience. Other books that serve Koji's awakening to ideals of freedom and equality are Shusui Kotoku's autobiography and Whitman's *Leaves of Grass.*

As we have just seen, Koji grows in response to experience with the division between insider-outsider in society as he knows it. One major causal line derives from Koji's relationship with Machie, the affluent girl from outside. Koji harbors secret yearnings for her as early as elementary school days. His feelings combine the painful polarities of hope and fear. Throughout this novel, their relationship appears as that rare instance of the in-out division bridged, not through interclass marriage, but through understanding. Koji's yearning for this impossible alliance is channeled into social activism. Machie herself learns from the values Koji espouses, and begins to understand what it is to be a *burakumin.* In Volume 6, she is seen planning to go to Tokyo, away from her insular community, with its burden of privileged prejudice.

Another in-out bond results from the friendship that develops between Koji and Toyota in their childhood. The latter, though rich, is held in contempt by other privileged children because he is a bastard. This friendship overcomes the barrier of in-out opposition. Toyota becomes a university-educated reporter and serves as a kind of mentor, helping Koji understand the world and politics.

Though her narrative strategies may be simple, Sumii forcibly waves the central metaphor of the title, the river with no bridge, into the story line. It vividly articulates the in-out and dream-reality oppositions that form the backbone of the narrative. In fact, various images of impurity and confinement earlier stated revolve around this controlling metaphor, which is introduced three times in the novel. On each occasion, it elucidates the way Koji or Fude, his mother, conceives of the "separation" between the two worlds: this world pitted against the world to come, the world of wish fulfillment versus the world of reality, and the *burakumin* community against the world outside. As might be expected, such images take the form of dreams.

The novel opens with a lyrical depiction of Fude's dream. In it, a boy and a girl in love are separated by water—a ditch in a field. A series of metamorphoses follows. The girl becomes Fude, and the boy, whom she has not seen for several years, turns into her late husband, Shukichi. The ditch she prepares to jump becomes a roaring river. Fude runs up and down, hoping to find a bridge. For her, the bridge connects this world with the other world. She rushes to what she takes for a bridge, but it turns out to be a rainbow, connecting earth and sky. The river becomes wider, and on the other side, Shukichi is found walking in the snow.

The lyrical texture suddenly yields to a prosaic account of Fude's actual life of hardship. Why did she dream such a dream? This question is answered later, when the author informs us that Fude's husband died on the battlefield in Siberia during the Russo-Japanese War, leaving her a widow still in her twenties. Koji was only three, and Seitaro, seven. The "snow" in the dream articulates Fude's perception of her husband's death in terms of harsh winter weather, more real to her than a hail of bullets. Moreover, the bitter cold, as the author tells us, is for Fude a symbol of Shukichi's "cold, poor life itself without any luxury like wearing a warm flannel shirt."

In Volume 2, the same image returns to Fude as she ponders her frequent dreams of a roaring river dividing her and her late husband. Now she relates it to the reality of the life she has led: "The suffering she experiences, running along the river to find a bridge, not only exists in her dream but also in her real life. Born a *burakumin* to marry a *burakumin*, she lives the life of a struggling peasant. . . . Her whole life has been spent suffering on this side of the river with no bridge, no boat, no raft. She will never be able to make it to the other side, no matter how hard she may cry, weep and appeal."[6]

More important, later on, when Koji's dream is introduced, its central metaphor externalizes Koji's sense of futility in pursuing his love for Machie. The river is now configured into a strait impossible to cross. Koji envisions himself standing on a cape in the far end of Siberia. From the dismal gray that surrounds the area, Machie's figure, clad in a "freshly vivid purple" kimono, looms, the color itself associated with nobility in the Japanese cultural context. In front of Koji there lies "a crevasse in the dark Bering Strait—too huge a river to cross—without a bridge." His despair is expressed by the purple kimono fading into gray as Machie looks at Koji only for an instant. Koji, still dreaming, weeps. His dream also echoes Fude's sense of chill, as Koji suddenly shivers and wakes up, feeling his shoulders frozen. Here, too, the chilliness is real as it expresses Koji's awareness of "a frozen state" of society. It is an apt metaphor for his *burakumin* status, coupled with other images, such as a chain and a heavy stone.

Later on, Koji repeats the river metaphor, not on a personal level but more inclusively. He ponders his outcast status, which has existed in all periods in Japanese history. He remembers a poem by Yakamochi Otomo, an eighth-century poet: "How White is the frost/On the bridge on a river with herons./The night deepens." Yakamochi, a court noble, read this poem after visiting a lover or on his way to a trysting place. Koji thinks how an outcast like himself had no bridge to cross to see his lover; he lay on the grass, weeping, because even "in that era the distinction between privileged and lowly offered some protection as a social rule or order."[7]

Why does such a class distinction occur? This persistent yet fundamental question is posed by Koji as he matures, and by Komori residents as well. The novelist Sumii offers an answer. She considers the emperor system as the genesis of this class distinction, which she refers to as "the man-made structure of high and low." In fact, the novel is full of questions about the Imperial system, as a number of critics point out. Though this work is basically in the melodramatic mold, it exhibits touches of the social novel as it seriously criticizes the Japanese fanatic worship of the emperor.

While she was still at work on the seventh volume, Sumii had this to say about the way the Japanese responded to Emperor Hirohito's illness and death in the time between August 1988 and January 1989:

> Because there was a class structure created by men, there exists discrimination. Because the Japanese people recognize the emperor's authority, there was such a commotion (as seen in cancellation of many joyous events all over Japan and the media solely devoted to the emperor's condition). The Japanese are not free from the misconception that they must be grateful to the emperor. . . .
>
> I thought that in order to realize human equality, the fundamental principle of life on earth, we need to shake off this illusion of a ruling Imperial system. I did not distinguish clearly enough between natural law and man-made law in my first six volumes. . . .[8]

Significantly, Sumii also offers various questions about the divinity of the sovereign raised by residents of Komori, underprivileged as they are, with a limited sense of perspective. From the outset of the novel, a young Komori girl asks such a question. This happens after the emperor's inspection of the special military drill conducted on Mount Miminashi in Nara, which turned out to be "a burden" for farmers busy with harvest. A peasant from Komori mentions how great the emperor is because he has the power to make a road for the Imperial visit in a short span of time. His daughter immediately contests that the road was not made by the emperor but by farmers recruited for construction, adding that an emperor considered divine does not do such a menial job. But then the daughter innocently goes on to ask if the emperor really is a god.

The issue of the divinity of the emperor keeps returning as various Komori people respond to it in different manners. Later, Koji, still a child, learns about the Shusui Kotoku incident in which Shusui, the founder of the Anarchist Party, and his followers attempted to assassinate the emperor with handmade bombs and were hanged after their treason was discovered. The child then asks this innocent question: "If the emperor is god, why does a bullet kill him?"

Interestingly, Sumii's inclusion of such social-political overtones is counterbalanced by some superbly lyrical descriptions of nature. Nature is seen as a physical and psychological extension of Komori residents whose lives as peasants are deeply rooted in the earth. One of the simplest means Sumii employs to heighten this effect is personification. For example, Koji and Seitaro see Mounts Katsuragi and Kongo "tightening their skins in preparation for the approaching winter." The mountain "vies with" the sky for blueness. Small irrigation ditches, which surround rice paddies, "easily swallow" the endless sky in the water, like the ocean.

Importantly, personified nature is also used to express the major characters' shifting attitudes toward their plight as *burakumin*. For example, Fude, whose childhood dreams and yearnings mercilessly clashed with the reality of her identify as a *burakumin*, steps into "the initial stage of suffering and ordeal." She thinks that "running streams, mist-shrouded mountains, the bright sun, and the waxing and waning moon—all intently looked at her as an *eta* child."[9] She thus "harbored hatred toward nature, rather than appreciating its beauty and being sentimental about it."[10] Her hostility suddenly disappears when one evening she looks at the pale moon. With this experience as a turning point, she begins to appreciate nature's sweetness and beauty.

Koji's great moment of awakening occurs in his youth when his friend Toyota points out that Nui is just like the Yamato plateau. Toyota says that the plateau appears to follow seasonal changes quietly, but it knows everything (about the law of nature and human life with its ups and downs); and so does Koji's grandmother. Without complaint, this old woman, the very incarnation of the earth, has led a life of suffering, always showing a zest for living and making the best of it.

Hints of this Mother Earth's vibrant drive for survival are abundant throughout the novel. For example, Fude notices how hard her mother-in-law's hands are while they are plowing the field together with Koji. Nui's strong hands are an index of silent endurance as they "have kept gripping the sorrow and indignation of discriminated people, and the pain and bitterness of poverty for some seventy years."[11]

In his childhood, Koji unknowingly emulates his grandmother's long-suffering holiness. As Fude recollects, this sensitive boy is compared to the rape-seed flower that silently blooms with its crown "bending downward." But in his maturation process, the drive for life that he shares with Nui is channeled into a publicly significant action. Koji's commitment is to improvement of the *buraku*, while Nui's energy is given to life deeply rooted in the earth.

Transposition to the screen of such a long novel, rich in many intertwined episodes, historical references, and poetic metaphors, offers a great challenge for a filmmaker. First, he must define the nature of his film. Then too, some external matters, especially the existence of the Buraku Liberation League as a censoring group, make this challenge more difficult. Perhaps, an assessment of Higashi's own comments provides a good starting point for approaching *A River with No Bridge* as an adaptation of literature.

> During the long period of shooting this film, I was thinking that I would make it an expression of the most "primitive" world for the Japanese.
>
> The English word "primitive" has so many meanings and nuances, conjuring up such Japanese notions as primordial, ancient, premature, simple, fundamental and the like. The kind of world I wanted to depict as fundamentally Japanese is then best summarized by this all-inclusive English term, "primitive."
>
> With focus on the lives of *burakumin* between the Meiji and the Taisho period, I wanted to portray the "primitive" quality, which runs through all the Japa-

nese or, I should say, I tried to find the most primitive spirit in those "discriminated" people. . . .

The movie, starting with such a premise, can be approached from different
perspectives In one sense, it can be a historical tale and in another a story about
love. As I often told my staff while shooting this film, one can view it as a story
about six women who help a young boy grow. . . .[12]

It seems that the director has described the film's central theme in too simple
terms. All the aspects of the film he has mentioned are indeed subsumed into the
film's main narrative thrust. That much is faithful to the original: Koji's maturation process is helped by the women and is marked by an awakening to love and
an awareness of history in progress. Then, too, in this process, the primitive qualities of the main characters—their close ties with nature and strong drive for survival—are unfolded, often aided by a notable use of the expressive power of the
camera.

Though his approach is rather outdated, given a flood of new theories on
narrative in the contemporary scholarship of cinema, George Bluestone gives an
age-old fundamental, yet useful, venue of approach when we consider the adaptation of a novel for screen: deletion/addition/alteration of narrative events.[13] This
method is all the more appropriate for *A River with No Bridge* because the director's
concern is how to turn the six-volume novel into a 140-minute film.

The principle of deletion/alternation is clearly at work on this film, while the
main narrative thrust of the novel—Koji's awakening and maturing process—is
maintained. Various events that the director retains as essential to the film's thematic progression, in chronological order, include the Komori children's walk to
school in a group, Seitaro and Toyota's fight with bullies, Seitaro's resistance to
his teacher, Takashi's arson, the school mourning services for the late Emperor
Meiji, the tunnel accident, the competition of fire drills between Komori and
Shimana (a privileged village), Takeshi's suicide, Seitaro's success as a manager
of a rice shop, the Rice Riots, the formation of Suiheisha, Koji's imprisonment,
and Nanae's marriage.

Higashi rearranges the chronological order of some important events because
of his concern with "primitiveness." One of the most notable examples is the way
the film begins and ends. Then, too, the film's radical departure from the novel is
Higashi's treatment of Fude, which is a natural outcome of his persistent concern
with women's victimization. Into the main story line, Higashi weaves the subplot
of romance between Koji's mother and a man from another *buraku*, which weighs
considerably in the film's narrative progression.

The most salient feature of the principle of deletion is that the director dispenses with numerous episodes that in the novel have great impact on Koji. Sumii's
indictment of discrimination is extended to a racial level; many episodes illustrate Japanese prejudice against Koreans as a "national" consciousness deeply
rooted in the country's social fabric. The massacre of Koreans during the Kanto
earthquake offers one such example. During this incident, a Komori girl's Ko-

rean husband was killed in her presence. The fact that she was ostracized by her own family because of her marriage to a Korean deepens not only Koji's awareness of inequity but also the truth about social "injustice."

Another racist episode involves a Korean umbrella peddler's visit to Komori. This is used to highlight shared feelings of the two discriminated or subhuman "kinds." Poor Komori laborers, who live on starvation wages, making straw sandals, buy umbrellas from the peddler, whose hand-to-mouth existence is even worse than theirs. The Korean notices the declaration of the Suiheisha on the wall of their workplace: equality of people. This experience, as a turning point in his life, drives him to fight for the liberation of his own race later.

In the latter half of the novel, the child Kumao becomes an important character. His father is serving a prison sentence, charged in connection with the Rice Riots. The boy is sent to Komori to be with his uncle. His relationship with Koji and Seitaro reinforces the important motif of mentor/pupil that runs through the novel, as the brothers help the little boy in his awakening and maturing process. Then, too, Kumao's experience also fortifies the novel's repetition pattern—the *burakumin*'s awareness of carrying a heavy burden considered hereditary—as he suffers from the same humiliation and discrimination at school even a decade after Koji's graduation.

In terms of characterization, as mentioned earlier, Higashi gives Fude a completely new treatment. The novel treats her as the epitome of the enduring widow/ mother/daughter-in-law, who silently surrenders herself to the fate of the oppressed. For that matter, her yearning for her late husband is presented in almost idyllic terms, taking the form of dreams. Her counterpart in the film, however, undergoes transformation as a woman still capable of loving another man.

The plot of romance between Iseda, a man from another *buraku*, and Fude, offers only one instance of this woman's longing to escape from her cramped and outcast life. In the original novel, Iseda comes to Komori simply to give details of an accident in a tunnel under construction. A son of Fude's neighbor, Kane, has been involved in it. The film, on the other hand, lends a lyrical, almost melodramatic texture to a number of scenes in which Iseda and Fude appear. For example, one scene shows Fude showing Iseda the way along a wet road. Fude slips. The lantern goes out. When Iseda strikes a match, his face, taken in close-up, looms out of the darkness, conveying Fude's awareness of his masculine charms.

Later, as Iseda takes a bath, Fude comes in to check the fire in the boiler. When Fude's face is shown in close-up, her face is lit, reflecting the fire. It is one of the rare instances in which the director calls our attention to the sudden momentary surge of suppressed passion as expressed on her face. Mutual attraction between man and woman is then suggested by an age-old familiar metaphor for fleetingness: a firefly. The camera captures one emitting a flickering light and another flying to it. The point-of-view shot from Fude and Iseda's perspective offers the two fireflies twinkling their lights as if in unison.

The climax of their love has its tragic ending on the bridge in the appropriate setting—in a pounding rain. Each carries an umbrella as they approach the camera. Iseda stops and says that since he has a large family to support at home, he cannot come to Komori to marry her. For the first time, Fude rebels against her allotted role and replies that she will go wherever he goes. But her inclination to follow her heart's desire simply remains in the world of wishful thinking. It is Iseda who reminds her that it will be an impossible task for her. The concluding shot shows Fude, alone on the bridge, turning around to face the Komori village. Though she is not facing the camera, her back—not stooped or shaking with sorrow, but straight   says something about Fude's strong character. Undaunted by the suffering caused by her unrequited love, she is ready to face the same daily repetition of what is imposed on an oppressed woman in Komori.

As stated earlier, the novel is rich in nature images, often personified, the central metaphor being a river with no bridge. Higashi dispenses with that and, for that matter, with all the psychological dimensions related to Koji's and Fude's dreams. Given the title of the film, the director seems to count on the audience's ability to take cues about all-inclusive meanings of "separation" and "discrimination."

Transposition of personified nature on the screen creates a problem for the filmmaker because the question involved is one of the basic differences between novelistic and filmic properties. "The coldest season will come very shortly. As if to warn this, the wind from Mount Kongo *whistles its tone* past the mountain valley towards the east." (Italics mine.) The director can convey a life of nature only through visual means, literally presenting a long shot of the entire village with the harvested soil exposed to the coldness. The rest is up to the viewer's capacity to surmise.

Counting on the camera's selectivity, reinforced by the acoustic effect, Higashi succeeds in re-creating the rhythm of nature with life, decay, and rejuvenation, of which man is a part. His intention is evident from the outset. A series of long shots shows the vast stretch of green rice paddies. One gets a closer look at a bunch of rice plants swirling in the morning wind, as if they were pulsing with life. As a group of Komori children enters this uninhabited landscape of bountiful nature, their closeness to the soil—one aspect of their "primitiveness"—is immediately transmitted to us.

In another scene, Koji and Seitaro are shown in a long shot among the growing wildflowers. From what we have seen of their character, of their perseverance amid dire poverty and discrimination, the parallel between the brothers and the flowers is easily made. Then, too, their close affinity with nature is expressed as the camera approaches to show them picking flowers and tasting their sweet nectar.

The Komori residents' adaptability, even to nature's unfriendly aspects, is shown in a remarkable scene of the post-rice harvest season. Wheat having been planted, the villagers must stamp on the furrows to firm the soil. Again, an extremely long shot shows three women in the paddy. Each, wearing boots and wrapping her head with a towel, braces herself. Each looks down at the earth. Without a word, they work, their posture showing the effort it takes to fight the cold weather. Their existence is intimately tied to nature, rejoicing in its blessings and enduring its hardships.

Then, too, the conclusion of the film reinforces our sense of this primitiveness. It is Nanae's wedding day, and for the first time Nui is shown dressed for festivity. Kazuichi, one of her relatives, gives her a lift on a bicycle. As the two ride on a path through the rice paddy ready for harvest, a series of long shots remarkably conveys a sense of them blending with their surroundings. Remembering a number of earlier scenes that showed Nui's adaptability to nature, we feel that she is part and parcel of its cyclical pattern of ups and downs. Ernest Kabur's lyrical music with almost sentimental overtones helps induce this feeling.

Into this almost idyllic texture, however, Higashi slips a disturbing shot that almost breaks down our aroused sense of the rhythmical flow of the natural cycle: a close-up of Fude's face. Suggesting the long years of hardship that this widowed mother and daughter-in-law have undergone, this powerful shot, in a simple yet most effective manner, elicits very complex responses in the audience. Though her face registers shared joy for the happy occasion, it suggests a sense of resignation to her given fate as well. It is as if in this final shot, evocative of the plight of a Komori woman tied to the values of fixity, Higashi condensed the tragedy of all women like Fude. The shot size returns to a long shot, showing Fude busily engaged in cutting rice stocks. A sense of the "primitive" the director has mentioned is also transmitted as we are convinced that Fude, like Nui, is also a part of nature's cycle—like weeds blessed with an exuberant life force, enduring the heat of summer and the coldness of winter.

For the director whose thematic constant has been the plight of the oppressed woman, such a conclusion might be a natural outcome. Nonetheless, this is an entirely new departure from the novel.

The end of the novel's sixth volume brings together the two men victimized by a shared fate: the fate of loving somebody outside the *buraku*. A girl whose sympathy toward the unprivileged has been awakened by the Suiheisha's public speeches, is now in love with Kazuichi. Machie's affection and adoration for Koji is shown developing into "pure" love. The novel has been at pains to show the impossibility or insurmountable difficulty of such a liaison. Kazuichi's love for his girl is such an example. At the end, the author suggests that this romance is doomed to failure. The girl's declining health is only the final blow. Such is not the case with a Koji-Machie alliance. When withheld information on Machie's true feelings is fully revealed at the ending, there is a ray of hope for their relationship.

It is Kazuichi who fills in this narrative gap for Koji. He tells how Machie suffered from her yearning for Koji, trapped as she was in a class hostile to such a forbidden love. But suffering has been an educational process for her. She has learned from the Suiheisha's activities to see how illogical this world is and how important the values of freedom are. During Kazuichi's recount, the reader, like Koji, learns that Machie is ready to test these important lessons by leaving her village with all its association with the values of discrimination and insularity. In order to seek female independence, she will attend a professional school of handicrafts and home economics—one of the few specialized schools open for women at that time. As Kazuichi explains, the only salvation in the insurmountable difficulties that lie in Machie's future is to see that "Koji will grow in the right way." Sumii stresses Koji's determination to stay in his *buraku* and work for its improvement once more, and she concludes the sixth volume with a lyrical affirmation of Koji's roots:

> Katsuragi River was meandering like a sash. The nightly wind blowing from its bottom lands was cold. Koji listened: the water was murmuring. Looking up, he saw stars shining in the cold sky. . . . As if pushing aside the remaining winter, a lantern was seen moving through the distant field. Shining and shedding radiance, it moved toward Shimana and Matsukawa. . . .[14]

Needless to say, a lantern here suggests enlightenment of outsiders like those living in Shimana and Matsukawa—an enlightenment to be made possible through the Suiheisha members' efforts to awaken the masses' consciousness of manmade laws of discrimination. Needless to say, the lantern image also recalls Suiheisha's aim: "Let there be enthusiasm in the world, and light to human beings!"

This resolutely idealistic finale is not to the taste of Director Higashi, who is more eager to emphasize the primitive qualities of Komori residents, especially the women tied to the soil.

Finally, Higashi's *A River with No Bridge* offers some fine examples of the exquisitely pictorial effects that compensate for the lack of psychological depth. The expressive power or selectivity of the camera propels itself here and there, as if to show how the director translates essentially novelistic properties into filmic ones. As mentioned earlier, the novel is replete with similes and metaphors, especially of nature and animals, to describe the plight of *burakumin*. Other than the prime reptile image of a snake, a chicken—a familiar index of the rural community—often appears in Sumii's description of Komori kids. "As usual, their stomachs with only watery rice porridge rumbled when they ran. Koji and others who passed through the gate found themselves gathering at a corner of the school gate like chickens hatched been chased."[15] And again: "When Koji left for school, he took an umbrella with him. . . . He was well prepared, anticipating the rain that afternoon. Most of the Komori kids walked, scooping their necks like wounded chickens."[16]

A collective sense of children discriminated against and bullied is effectively conveyed through this simple bird image. The director translates such similes into the camera's wordless equivalent via selectivity and cross-cutting. A shot of Komori children gathering at a corner of the school yard yields to a shot of their privileged schoolmates joyfully playing baseball in the yard. Then, the camera singles out several kids to scrutinize their emotions in close-up. One Komori child's face is an open book, expressive of envy. When the camera cuts to show a privileged child, we cannot miss the sign of disdain and contempt for his inferiors.

These are examples of the director's fairly successful transfer of novel to cinema. Nevertheless, the film contains some problematic aspects in this regard. As mentioned earlier, Higashi's ideological aims lead him to sacrifice the novel's psychological dimensions.

This is especially obvious in his treatment of Koji's continuous yearning for Machie. As in the novel, it constitutes an important aspect of his growth and development, from childhood onward, becoming a source of suffering and encouragement in his young manhood as well. In both the original and its film version, Koji's first awareness of Machie as the opposite sex happens during the mourning ceremony for the late Emperor Meiji. Machie holds Koji's hand. From this point on, Sumii counts very heavily on nature imagery to convey Koji's increasing, yet forbidden, affection for her.

Koji, sensitive to nature, seeks an objective correlative in an old red plum tree outside the classroom. He gambles on the old tree, thinking that if it blooms, he will get a letter from Machie. Sumii renders Koji's inner thoughts as follows:

> While he was watching an old tree through a classroom window before the winter break, he was urged to bet his future on it. For a moment, he thought it as an act of treachery [against nature] and was caught up in lonesome feelings. But at the same time he realized that this act was a manifestation of his soul's prayers rather than gambling.[17]

Koji's anxiety increases when he realizes that the tree fails to bud, while plums in other villages begin to bloom. Koji is even afraid to mention that "the old tree's life cycle is already over." His psychological shift from hope to total despair is rendered through a deft transition of imagery from lyrical to boldly factual.

> Look at Sakata and Shimada. There are moats around them, and plenty of trees nearby. Even from the distance, they look like decent villages fit for well dressed people. But Komori is a naked village in the middle of a field. . . . It's a poor, dirty village, and no wonder the village people look lowly. . . .[18]

The image of the village exposed to the rough weather is consonant with the subsequent image of a heavy stone—an index of collective awareness of a larger sociocultural environment, the "man-made" fate of being branded as *burakumin*. The authorial voice summarizes the meaning of the stone for Koji, who has already gained enough experiential knowledge of "the stone" even in childhood, but has yet to be exposed to its full meaning:

> For those who are not the least aware that the heavy stone is created by other people, it is inevitable to think that being born *eta* is their fate. Even if a few notice the mechanism of the established caste system, the stone is so heavy and so large that they will be exposed to more danger once they try to get rid of it.[19]

Despite the heavy burden of the stone, Koji harbors his forbidden love for Machie, assuming that she held his hand because she liked him. The revelation of Machie's seeming "true motive" occurs to Sadao, Koji's best friend, not to Koji. The recurrent reptile image, a radical departure from the initial aesthetic image, makes Koji's plight extremely poignant. Sadao learns from Machie's cousin that she held Koji's hand out of curiosity; she wanted to see for herself it was true that Komori people's skin becomes cold, like a snake's. Sadao imagines Koji's response conjuring up the image of a Buddhist guardian, Ashura, expressive of Buddha's anger. The face, like the deity, "looms in space," as he exclaims: "How stupid people are, saying that our skin is like a snake! Only a bastard would think of checking to see!"

Here we see narrative suspense created by information withheld on two levels. Koji, not knowing her curiosity at the time, "engraved Machie's gesture in his record of love." Then, too, both Machie's cousin and Sadao are blind to Machie's "true motive." The adoration and affection for Koji that Machie has had since the mourning ceremony are not fully revealed to Koji until the final climactic moment that closes Volume 6.

In Volume 4, a plum-tree image returns to reinforce this romantic theme. Five years have lapsed since Koji's childish hope for a natural miracle was disappointed. Koji, now in his youth, visits his old school yard after giving a speech in a public hearing: a speech about his bitter experience as a *burakumin* and his belief in the universal law of equality. The old plum tree is gone now, and a new plum tree is bearing pink blossoms. He smiles, wondering if his "hope for good news from Machie has been revived." But his pain again overrides such spontaneous feelings. Ironically, Koji's speech itself has awakened Machie to the reality of prejudice and eventually prompts her to take action. Though Koji is denied access to such information at this stage, the blooming tree suggests a ray of hope for his love for Machie.

Higashi oversimplifies such causal lines by dispensing with nature images— at some cost to the subtle workings of Koji's feelings. Instead, Higashi counts on what the camera can communicate: visual clarity and selectivity. The initial motivating force for romance is rendered through a simple yet effective close-up: one of Koji's and Machie's hands together against the semidarkness of the auditorium.

In the scene of Sadao's discovery of Machie's motive, his mental image of anger is dropped altogether. Instead, we see the *burakumin*'s shared sense of anger at being branded as snakes. This is directly transmitted by the camera's expressive power: Sadao's face, an open book of indignation, is captured in a close-up.

As in the novel, another important scene strengthens the causal line of romance: Nanae accuses Machie of being a bad girl. In the novel, the reason for her accusation is not given, but Sadao's learning account of Machie's motive clues the reader in.

On the contrary, Higashi highlights the sense of confrontation implicit in the novel. Here, Nanae says that Machie held Koji's hand only because she wanted to check the age-old rumor about *burakumin* being snakelike. As elsewhere, close-ups of Koji's face as he hits Nanae serve as the most direct way of rendering his emotional plight.

Thus, in the film, numbers of instances attest to the director's tendency toward simplification, often at some cost to narrative legibility. One might say that Higashi prefers visual legibility. A major episode in the novel fosters the in-out opposition via the Komori children's' walk to school, led by Seitaro. He carries a purple flag with five white lines drawn on it, indicating that the Komori village has the highest absenteeism among the five villages.

In fact, the film opens with a reference to this episode. The opening shot shows green rice paddies. Young rice plants are swirling in the wind, as if they were breathing fresh air and vibrating in accordance with nature's rhythms. Into this almost idyllic scene, suggestive of nature's bounty, comes a procession of children, taken in a long shot. Seitaro is seen carrying a flag. As they approach the camera, the viewer sees five lines on the flag, the meaning of which Higashi conveys through a simple dialogue between two brothers. Koji, referring to two friends who cannot make it to school, complains that the Komori village always ranks lowest in attendance. As the camera takes a closer look at the purple flag, strongly contrasted with the surrounding green, the image has a pictorial vividness, but it fails to function beyond a mere high absenteeism, possibly associated with poverty.

In sum, despite its obvious handicaps, Higashi's film remains a film to be reckoned with. Like Imai, who preceded him, he has faced the difficult challenge offered by the *buraku* and their plight. Regardless of some flaws, as shown in its lack of psychological depth and narrative legibility, the film reflects the director's sincere effort to select what he considers important out of a wealth of episodes, events, and characters that make up a complete web of the original saga.

Notes:

1. The history of *burakumin*, literally translated as people living in designated communities (*buraku*), goes back to the Nara period (710–84). They were then labeled *hinin* (nonhuman) because they were beggars and those penalized for their attempt to escape from corvée service. In the feudal period, the term *hinin* became more inclusive as actors/performers and fabric dyers fell into this category. In this period, too, the synonym *eta* gained currency, adding its meaning of unclean to inhuman. During the Edo period (1600–1868), *eta-hinin* were legally designated outcasts and assigned a place outside the four-class hierarchy (warrior-farmer-artisan-merchant). As outcasts, *eta-hinin* were permitted to live only in the designated community called *buraku*. Hence, the term *burakumin* was also used. They were engaged in unclean jobs ranging from butchering to grave digging. The 1871 edict issued by the Meiji government legally abolished the use of derogatory terms like *eta* and *hinin*. A new class was created and named *shinheimin*, "new commoners."

    For a comprehensive study of *burakumin* as treated in literary works, see Toshihito Umezawa et al., *Bungaku no naka no hisabetsuburaku-zo: senzen-hen* (Images of *buraku* in literature: prewar period) and *Bunraku no naka no hisabetsuburaku-zo:*

sengo-hen (Images of *buraku* in literature: postwar period) (Tokyo: Akashi Shoten, 1982).

2. The following year, Shozo Taguchi turned this scenario into a novel entitled *Tofu monogatari* (The story of the east wind). See *Bungaku no naka no hisabetsuburaku-zo: Senzen-hen*, p. 91.

3. Tetsu Hijikata, "*Hashi no nai kawa* no saieigaka ni attate" (On the second film adaptation: review of *A river with no bridge*), in *Shinario: Hashi no nai kawa* (Scenario: *A river with no bridge*), ed. *Hashi no nai kawa* Production Committee (Tokyo: Kaiho Shuppansha, 1992), p. 205.

4. Tetsujiro Yamakami, "Masshiro ni mite eiga to taiwa shite hoshii" (I want you to give the film an unprejudiced view so you can create your dialogue with it), an interview with the director in *Shinario: Hashi no nai kawa*, pp. 174–75.

5. Stuart Y. McDougal, *Made into Movies: From Literature to Film* (New York: Holt, Rinehart and Winston, 1985), p. 6.

6. Sue Sumii, *Hashi no nai kawa* (A river with no bridge) (Shinchosha, 1981), 2: 233.

7. Ibid. b: 255.

8. Sue Sumii, "Hosoku to jini no chigai ga wakaru eiga ni" (I want the movie to make the audience understand the difference between universal law and man-made law), in *Shinario: Hashi no nai kawa*, pp. 172–73.

9. Sumii, *Hashi no nai kawa* 2: 336.

10. Ibid.

11. Ibid. 6: 157.

12. Yukichi Ohashi, ed., *Hashi no nai kawa* (A river with no bridge) (Tokyo: Toho Shuppan, 1992), p. 5.

13. George Bluestone, *Novel into Film* (Berkeley: University of California Press, 1973).

14. Sumii, *Hashi no nai kawa* 6: 432.

15. Ibid., 1: 307.

16. Ibid., p. 473.

17. Ibid. 2: 297.

18. Ibid., p. 298.

19. Ibid., p. 302.

9

More of a Just-So Story: Shimazu's
The Story of Shunkin (1935)

Okoto to Sasuke (The story of Shunkin) made Shimazu into a controversial figure. In spite of everything said for and against this film, it is a unique achievement. It is in fact a failure, but I would call it "great" poor work rather than a work of poor quality. The director should be admired for taking up such challenging material. He does very well evoking atmosphere in the first half of the film. Instead of attacking his work for being a far cry from Tanizaki's original, we should applaud his courageous attempt to give it a new life on screen. . . .

Shimazu's filmmaking career of many years now has not shown any tendency to limit itself to any one genre. He has in fact ranged widely that way, showing himself to be versatile and adventuresome in a way all his own.[1]

The critic Tadahisa Murakami gave this assessment of Shimazu's film at the time of its release in 1935. As he notes, this was the first screen adaptation of Junichiro Tanizaki's novel *Shunkinsho* (The story of Shunkin), published in 1933.

Shimazu was a well-established director. Along with Heinosuke Gosho, he had made some of the most celebrated early talkies. His *Tonari no Yae-chan* (My neighbor Yae, 1934) and *Arashi no aka no shojo* (A maiden in a storm, 1932) enjoyed success on a par with Gosho's *Madamu to nyobo* (A neighbor's wife and mine, 1932).

Despite his wide-ranging experience of genres, Shimazu was most comfortable with *shomingeki*, the drama of lower middle-class life. That was just as well, since *shomingeki* was the specialty of the Kamata Shochiku Studio where he worked.

But the studio had another reason for giving Shimazu Tanizaki's book to work on. The "pure literature movement" was making its presence felt on the Japanese literary scene, and the cinema industry was beginning to take note. Between 1935 and 1937, studio production schedules reflected a vigorous marketing response to public demand for screen adaptations of "serious" literary works.[2]

Tanizaki had this to say about his book and that trend:

The Shochiku Kamata Studio has decided to adapt *Shunkinsho* for the screen. They have chosen a work very difficult to cinematize. But this indicates their serious effort to turn to pure literature for subject matter rather than to popular fiction. . . .[3]

The first thing to say about Shimazu's *The Story of Shunkin* is that it represents an accommodation to studio market strategy. Though based on a work of belles lettres, the film had to be accessible to the common man. For example, critics had praised Tanizaki's masterful handling of a complex narrative. All the more reason why, thinking of a rather different cinema audience, Shimazu had to dispense with the novel's complicated strategy.

One might say that he did the obvious marketable thing by focusing on the romance between the film's protagonists, the willful, tyrannical blind girl, Okoto (Shunkin is Okoto's professional name as a *koto* teacher) and Sasuke, the humble apprentice enslaved by her. Shochiku gave those roles to Kinuyo Tanaka and Kokichi Takada, stars who practically guaranteed a box office hit. Shimazu would concentrate on making the best of their talents in an atmosphere well known to audiences of *shomingeki* melodrama: the everyday life of the Osaka merchant class.

Tanizaki's novel tells the story of an unusual and tragic romance that begins and ends in that milieu. The story follows its hero, Sasuke, from youthful naive apprenticeship into old age quite literally and ironically benighted. He suffers torments and ecstasies of love, and finally blindness, too, though Tanizaki presents him as a man who, in his way, has survived to see life whole. At the outset, his goal in life is modestly conventional. He becomes an apprentice, hoping some day to have a shop of his own. Yet another, unexpected choice soon presents itself. He becomes, in effect, an apprentice to love. And since his beloved is his master's daughter, that entails continuing servitude on those premises.

The novel shows how Sasuke proves strangely consistent in his response to what appears to be a nonchoice, given the fact of his adoration of a woman absolutely tyrannical.

The Story of Shunkin is representative of modern Japanese literature in two ways. Its unorthodox relationship between a tyrannical female and her willing male victim is a major thematic constant in Tanizaki's work. In *Shisei* (The tattooer, 1910), his story concerns a girl with a monstrous spider tattooed on her back. What better symbol for a victimizing female? The willing male victim in *Fumiko no ashi* (Fumiko's feet, 1910) is an elderly foot fetishist obsessed with being trampled by his young mistress. *The Story of Shunkin* takes its hero along a more tortuous path to self-inflicted blindness, a price he willingly pays to preserve his vision of a domineering blind beloved whose lovely face has been disfigured.

Tanizaki's careful study of Sasuke's progress toward entrapment in Okoto's blind, cruel woman's world makes use of a complex narrative strategy. That is the second "modern" element in his book. His theme is developed with the help of a narrator-researcher seeking to reconcile different sources of evidence, some apparently contradictory.

In Chapter 5 the anonymous narrator-researcher tells us that Sasuke is apprenticed at thirteen. His master's nine-year-old daughter, Shunkin, is blind.

Yet the impressionable country boy adores her instantly. Tanizaki attributes the boy's attraction to a fixation familiar in his work: the beauty of a woman's skin.

> At the present time, the upper classes in Osaka are vying with each other in their haste to remove their residences to the suburbs, and their daughters, enamored of various sports, spend their time basking in the sunshine in the open air. . . . But even today, children who live in the central part of Osaka are generally of delicate build, and their complexions are inclined to be pallid in comparison with the glowing skins of country boys and girls; one may call them ethereal— or unhealthy. . . .
>
> At that time Shunkin's elder sister was twelve, and the younger one six; to the boy fresh from the country, they all had a loveliness which was not to be met with in the provinces. But most of all it was the unearthly beauty of blind Shunkin that so captivated him.[4]

"A flame of adoration" in his heart thus sets the story in motion as Sasuke tries to integrate himself into the blind girl's world. We see this first in Chapter 6, when Sasuke volunteers to be a guiding hand for her. Tanizaki is quick to set in motion his signature theme of man's subjugation to tyrannical woman:

> If she required anything of him she expressed her desire by gestures, by knitting her brows, or by talking to herself in such a way as to convey a hint to him. . . .
>
> Whenever he failed to notice these indirect commands it always put her in a very bad humor, so that Sasuke had to keep constantly on the alert in order not to miss any fleeting expression or gesture; he felt that his care was being tried and tested.[5]

Ironically, Sasuke himself feeds the cruelty and whims of the object of his adoration:

> Such was Shunkin's obstinacy and waywardness. But it was chiefly to Sasuke that she behaved in this way; not to the other apprentices and servants. Her natural temperament, his presence alone. . . . For Sasuke, on his part, it was a labour of love to carry out her capricious commands, and he gave her a willing obedience.[6]

This is no mere youthful infatuation. Having in effect apprenticed himself to this form of servitude, Sasuke's goal in life itself has changed:

> . . . had he not been given the opportunity of ministering to Shunkin, and had not his ardent affection for the girl inspired him to share his life in every possible way, he might well have been set up in business and lived out his life as an apothecary until the end of his life.[7]

The rest of the novel details the various stages of Sasuke's attempt to "share his life." It is structured around the familiar narrative device of elimination of obstacles one by one.

First he tries sharing his beloved's devotion to a musical instrument. Tanizaki devotes five chapters to Sasuke's efforts to learn the samisen, with help from his beloved, who proves to be a harsh disciplinarian indeed. He has turned fourteen. Having purchased a cheap samisen, he smuggles it into his tiny room, where he practices shut up in a closet, lest he be heard by the other apprentices asleep nearby. His practice in darkness, in the dead of night, obviously refers us to the world his beloved lives in, and which he is so anxious to share—and will share quite literally when all is said and done:

> But he never regretted the darkness. With the blind, he realized, it was always thus; and Koisan [the youngest daughter] too played her samisen in this same sightless world. He was overjoyed to find himself sharing her darkened exist-ence. Even after he was allowed to learn openly, it was his habit to close his eyes whenever the instrument was in his hands, and to excuse himself by saying that he must do all things as she did them.
>
> In other words, the boy whose faculties were unimpaired desired to suffer the same hardships as the unhappy blind. . . .
>
> The underlying motive which drove him to blind himself at a later date can be traced back to these feelings he cherished in his boyhood.[8]

The plot takes a new turn when Shunkin discovers his secret. It suits her whim to become his tutor on the samisen. Her father, Yasuzaemon, agrees. This is a refinement on apprenticeship that ought to establish Sasuke in a form of servi-tude that goes beyond apprenticeship. But the way of the world is not that kind:

> Now that he was making use of him to keep his daughter in a good humour, he may have felt a trifle conscience-stricken when he thought of the boy's parents in the country. But with Yasuzaemon, consideration for one apprentice's future career counted for little in comparison with keeping Shunkin amused. Besides, he was well aware that Sasuke asked nothing better than to serve as her compan-ion. . . .[9]

Ironically, Sasuke's attempt to share the blind girl's life exposes him to a new and painful barrier. The difference between privileged and unprivileged was there from the beginning. Now, thanks to what begins as an innocent "playing school" game, Shunkin becomes his teacher, authoritative and tyrannical. He must address her at all times as "teacher." She now calls him, not "Sasuke-don," an affectionate diminutive, but simply "Sasuke." And she commands respect in no uncertain terms.

At the end of Chapter 9, we get a glimpse of the verbal and physical abuse he suffers:

> It was by no means unusual for the young teacher to strike him on the head with a plectrum, and cover him with abuse: "You fool! Why can't you learn it?" until the pupil broken down and sobbed.[10]

For Sasuke, however, sharing his beloved's life requires mastering the in-strument that she plays so extremely well. He interprets Shunkin's cruelty as a sign of her good intentions, especially when he overhears her saying: "Being an apprentice, he cannot receive lessons from a good Kengyo. Taking pity on him because he was trying to learn by himself, unskilled as I am, I have undertaken to instruct him, and am helping him to achieve his ambition."[11]

Sasuke meets Shunkin's abuse with patience and perseverance.

> It is true that Sasuke used to cry; but when he heard her speak like this he realized how deeply indebted to her he was. He cried partly because he could not endure the rigour of the practice, but partly in gratitude for being spurred on by the girl on whom he depended both as a mistress and a teacher.[12]

Sasuke's patience finally pays off. He learns to play well enough to be relieved from his duties as apprentice, becoming instead Shunkin's official companion and fellow student of her teacher.

Things appear to be going well for him:

> It goes without saying that Sasuke himself was delighted, while Yasuzaemon on his part did all in his power to persuade Sasuke's parents in the country to fall in with the arrangement; promising that, having been the cause of the boy's abandoning his original plan of becoming a merchant, he would make himself responsible for his future.[13]

That future is put in doubt by any number of obstacles. The most painful is provided by Shunkin. In Chapter 12, after Sasuke is released from his apprenticeship, her parents propose to arrange a marriage between them. Sasuke is twenty, Shunkin sixteen. The girl declares herself both displeased and adamantly opposed: "I shall never take a husband as long as I live; and Sasuke, of all people, is utterly out of the question."[14]

Yet she is found to be pregnant. Everyone assumes that Sasuke is responsible. Shunkin wastes no time heaping scorn on the very idea, saying that "an apprentice like that" could never be the father of her child.

Even so, when offering private lessons makes it possible for Shunkin to set up house independently of her parents, she moves Sasuke in with her. They may live under one roof, but she remains implacably domineering:

> . . . without any feeling of constraint in the presence of others, he called her "Teacher," and she called him "Sasuke."
> Nothing was more distasteful to her than to be thought of as Sasuke's wife. She expected from him both the courtesy and respect of a servant for his mistress. . . .[15]

One instance after another shows how Sasuke's self-sacrifice is never reciprocated, never allowed to lessen "the social gulf between them." Blind as she is, Shunkin manages to be an exacting tyrant in every detail having to do with the meticulous care she has for her body: "Her nails were kept in exactly the same shape; afterwards, she would feel every finger and toe, and never permitted the slightest variation."[16]

She is similarly obsessive and intolerant in matters of food: ". . . she required many different dishes, and satisfying her desires was such a troublesome problem to Sasuke that it seemed as though her meals were deliberately planned to perplex him."[17]

Three chapters (from 16 on) are devoted to the vexatious minutiae involved in one of Shunkin's most extravagant tastes: the keeping of nightingales and larks. The real cost of her favorite hobby is borne by those whose misfortune it is to live in a household ruled by her whims:

> Sasuke and the servants were compelled to exercise the most rigid economy. Even their daily allowance of rice was subject to restriction, and they did not always get enough to eat.[18]

The economic burden Sasuke must assume becomes heavier with the death of Shunkin's father, which reduces her family stipend.

Ironically, Shunkin will never admit that Sasuke is indispensable to her. The narrator leaves no room for doubt on that question: "Sasuke had been accustomed to look after these matters ever since her childhood, and was thoroughly familiar with her habits; so that he alone was able to manage them satisfactorily."[19]

Sasuke is also, in his way, indispensable to her tyranny. Her sadistic tendencies feed on his long-suffering endurance of them. Nor is he the only one to suffer. Her teaching methods become unreasonably harsh: "At all events, her thrashings finally degenerated into mere displays of willful temper, not untinged with sadism."[20]

There is a kind of poetic justice in the novel's climax on a note of violence: someone steals into Shunkin's house and pours a kettle of scalding water on her face. The identity of her assailant is never disclosed in the novel. But Shunkin is disfigured for life. As if responding to that as yet another challenge to his goal of sharing her life, Sasuke does something really extraordinary: without hesitation, he blinds himself with a sewing needle.

The reader is left to ponder the meaning of this astonishing proof of Sasuke's devotion. Is that in fact what it is: the lover's ultimate act of servitude? The narrator says only this:

> . . . did Shunkin expect this of Sasuke? When she made that tearful appeal to him not long before, was she hinting that, having met with such a calamity, she wished him to become blind?[21]

One thing is clear. Blindness, for Sasuke, is more than a means to an end—his goal of sharing Shunkin's life; it secures her in his possession. Now that he is blind, her beauty can live on in his mind; he is free of the torment of daily exposure to her disfigurement.

> On the morning after the operation, soon after it was done, Shunkin rose; and Sasuke felt his way into the inner room. "Teacher, I have become blind!" he said, bowing before her. "Now, as long as I live, I can never see your face." "Is that true, Sasuke?" she said simply, and for a long time remained lost in thought. Never before, and never afterwards, did Sasuke know such happiness as those few minutes passed in silence.[22]

Chapter 24 concludes with Sasuke's celebration of "sharing":

> As they faced each other in silence, the sixth sense peculiar to the blind sprang to life in him, and he knew that Shunkin's heart was overflowing with the purest gratitude. It was as though, no longer restrained by their relations as teacher and pupil, they were at last clasped in each other's arms with their hearts beating as one. Memories of his boyhood, when he had practiced the samisen in the dark of a closet, crowded into his mind; but the sensation of darkness was different now. . . .
>
> . . . As a sphere of dull light, like the form of Buddha welcoming the souls of the dying, there loomed before his eyes, harmonious and subtle, the white face of the teacher that he had gazed on with adoration until two months ago.[23]

Yet the final two chapters return to the theme of abject servitude. Blindness may unite the lovers, but the bond they share is based on bondage, and the woman is the master here.

Still, ironically, now it is Shunkin who attempts to bridge the social gap by marrying him; and it is Sasuke who refuses. Even though she now bears herself "with an unwonted meekness," he remains a stubborn visionary. Just as blindness ensures that his vision of her beauty remains intact, tyranny guarantees the original character of the woman he has loved all this long while!

> As Sasuke was making use of the real Shunkin in order to evoke the woman of his imagination, he was careful not to put himself in a position of equality. By humbling himself before her more than ever, and ministering to her with all sincerity, he sought to make her forget her trouble as quickly as possible and regain her former self-confidence.[24]

In this way *The Story of Shunkin* ends with an affirmation of Sasuke's devotion to his mistress, long after her death.

Tanizaki's own long-standing devotion to his theme of male subjugation is given a new venue in this book, along with his characteristically careful control of a complex rhetorical stance.[25]

As in many Tanizaki novels, the narrator tells the story, reconstructing the past for the reader. The opening chapter of *The Story of Shunkin* describes the event that prompts the narrator to reconstruct this piece of human history. He happens to see an old woman tending a pair of tombs. His curiosity is aroused. The tombs contain all that remains of Shunkin and Sasuke. He finds himself wanting to search the past, hoping to find them.

Wayne Booth's seminal work on narration, *The Rhetoric of Fiction*, made the reliability of narrators an important issue in the discussion of rhetoric.[26] Throughout *The Story of Shunkin*, the narrator's posture is that of neutral researcher looking for answers to questions whose aim is to resolve the element of mystery that surrounds these two people. His chief resources are the old woman's account of their lives and *The Biography of Shunkin* written by Sasuke himself. He also makes certain assumptions based on a surviving photograph of Shunkin at the age of thirty-seven.

All the information we need is supposedly provided by the I-narrator, whose posture is that of a detached observer of the lives he describes. From the outset, however, we are warned against drifting into easy identification with this narrator. Our initial impression is that there is nothing wrong with his intellectual alertness. But we are prepared to question the validity of his reconstruction and interpretation of past events. This is what the author carefully maps out for us. In Chapter 2, as the narrator identifies Sasuke's biography of Shunkin as his primary tool, and quotes from it: "Shunkin was an exceptionally bright child from the very beginning, and her graceful figure was lovely beyond description."[27]

The narrator immediately questions the validity of this account because Sasuke considers his subject "like a divine existence." The narrator does this repeatedly throughout the novel. He cites Sasuke's biography in order to re-create the past and assess its truth to fact insofar as that is possible to do. Obviously, he is evoking an image of Shunkin that seems most plausible—to him.

When it comes to Sasuke's claims for Shunkin's "exquisite figure and beauty," the narrator has at least some objective evidence: the photograph. It gives her age as thirty-seven. And it does suggest that she was to some extent beautiful. But the narrator is careful to qualify Sasuke's worshipful account: "It is a beautiful face, but there is no trace of a vivid personality, and the general effect it produces is very slight."[28]

What bothers us more is the narrator's deliberate withholding of information. The old woman he mentions in the opening chapter is not reintroduced until Chapter 13. Only then is she identified as one Teru Shigizawa. Only then does he say that she "appears" to have known both Sasuke and Shunkin.

For the first time, we are reminded that she is the second source of information for the narrator's reconstruction. She is in fact an important source of information. Her account clarifies the extent of Sasuke's devotion and emphasizes the price he paid, day in day out, for his devoted care of his blind beloved.

But how do we know the old woman speaks true? We are not told how she happens to know what she claims to know. How, then, are we to assess the truth of the narrator's account of Sasuke and Shunkin, based as it is on such a source?

Chapter 20 again cites Teru on the subject of Shunkin's students. Based on what she says, the narrator plays detective this long after the fact. He thinks a tormented student got revenge by disfiguring Shunkin.

The rhetorical dilemma or confusion deliberately created by the author is resolved only toward the end of the novel, in Chapter 25. For the first time, the narrator convinces us of Teru's reliability. Only then does he let us know that she is the sole surviving member of the household. After Sasuke blinded himself, she was hired as a live-in apprentice to serve as a kind of go-between for the blind couple.

At this stage we feel sure that the narrator's reconstruction of the past is based on two sources, one biased, the other apparently not so. Now it is our turn to do some reconstructive work. We must compare the narrator's views with ours. The novelist calls the narrator's attention, and ours, to some important questions. One has to do with Shunkin's image; another with the reason for Sasuke's blindness.

We have seen how the narrator used the photograph to modify Sasuke's view of his beloved's beauty. Yet what of her selfish cruelty? Fully a third of the book is devoted to the narrator's account of it. What can have caused such a propensity? The narrator offers two explanations. The first is the obvious one: doting parents spoiled their handicapped child. The second is based on a psychological commonplace: this girl was a born sadist. The narrator puts it this way:

> Although it was not uncommon for masters to resort to corporal punishment, there are few or no instances of a woman like Shunkin so far forgetting her sex as to beat and thrash a pupil. For this reason it has been suggested that she may have had a streak of sadism in her character, and enjoyed some kind of abnormal sexual pleasure on the pretext of teaching. . . .[29]

What the narrator does not say here seems equally, and obviously, significant. He says nothing about so much evidence pointing to an equal and opposing (or, say, collaborating) power of masochism in Sasuke. Readers familiar with Tanizaki are sure to sense a significant omission here. After all, this novelist's novels teem with masochistic males whose joy is akin to pain, whose devotion is given to women who torment and tyrannize.

Shunkin is selfish and stingy, too. Sasuke and her servants are stinted of such basics as food, while she indulges herself in every way. No wonder the narrator's image of her grows increasingly negative. And he is not afraid to judge her accordingly, as in these comments on her arrogance:

> If her behaviour had been a little more modest and retiring, her fame would have spread far and wide. It was a great misfortune that she was brought up in a wealthy home, knowing nothing of the hardships of life. At the same time, she had no one but herself to blame when people resented her waywardness and perversity and kept her at arm's length.[30]

Of course, the most compelling question in the book has to do with Sasuke's self-inflicted blindness. The narrator sees two factors coming together: Shunkin's express wish that Sasuke be blind to her misfortune and his consuming passion to share her world.

The alert reader is not so easily satisfied. By this point, it is obvious that Sasuke's blindness is an extreme and ultimate form of possessiveness. As a blind man, he has in view the mind's-eye image he has worshipped for so long. So now he has that. Why, then, does he refuse to marry Shunkin, now that they are, in a way, ideally suited? Would that not add to his feeling of possession?

The answer seems to lie in our sense that the narrator is right to characterize Sasuke's ideal beloved as a female who is not just beautiful but domineering and tyrannical as well. Marriage would set him on equal footing with her. That would mar his mental image, his ecstasy in being possessed by the woman he adores. Because, of course, for Sasuke, that woman must be addressed as Teacher and Master, not Wife and Partner in life.

A number of critics, playing detective, have ventured to suggest that the person responsible for Shunkin's disfigurement is none of the suspects the narrator mentions, but Sasuke himself![31]

Certainly Tanizaki's novel engages us in a complex rhetoric, counting on us to be intellectually alert. A certain degree of detachment is required throughout as we share the narrator's data and compare his findings with ours.

Shimazu's approach is altogether simpler, as it has to be. To begin with, he dispenses with the narrator and all the complex doubts he brings in his train. Shimazu tells it "straight." He orders events as they presumably happened, his aim being to account for the relationship that developed between the beginning of Sasuke's apprenticeship and his blinding. This narrative simplification alters the viewer's point of view.

The omniscient camera dominates throughout. The viewer is not asked to bear the novel reader's burden of assessment and deduction. Here, the viewer is urged to become the camera eye and to accept what it offers as stated truth. Only a certain few crucial scenes offer a species of challenge in point-of-view shots. After Sasuke blinds himself, a series of tilted, blurred objects indicate his altered perspective. Even then, however, we are not asked to identify with him in any complex way.

Yet how *is* one to tell the difference between inside and outside views on the part of the audience? William Cadbury suggests this:

> The basic distinction between the outside and the inside view, then, is whether our attention is directed most strongly towards the singularizing attributes or the universalizing problems of a character.[32]

As in the novel, Sasuke's devotion to the blind Shunkin forms the focal point. The degree of his subordination is so extreme, however, that his experience is not considered an extension of ours as viewers of the film. We also cannot identify with Shunkin's tyranny, which is far more extreme than we would consider acceptable under any circumstances. As viewers, we are detached observers. None of the omniscient camera's manipulations changes that.

The element of separation is further served by Shimazu's choice stars. He cast the beautiful Kinuyo Tanaka opposite the handsome Kokichi Takada, a major heartthrob for female audiences of 1935. Takada guaranteed the element of romance. The audience saw him as an object of fantasy adoration, not someone really like themselves.

Shimazu's version of *The Story of Shunkin* is a romance strong on atmosphere, evoking life among the merchant class of Osaka. Always a master of *shomingeki*, he felt free to introduce elements of slapstick characteristic of films in this genre.

The first two sequences concentrate on details of the given locale. A long shot begins the film. It takes in a merchant wearing a traveling hat. He crosses the camera's studious view of what appears to be an especially imposing shop front.

An equally imposing signboard identifies it as the Mozuya, an old, established drugstore owned by Shunkin's father.

The inside of the shop is equally impressive. We see it as the merchant enters and introduces himself as one Kahei from Koshu Province. The camera cuts to different areas of the shop to show workers at their various tasks. The head clerk is occupied with his ledger. Apprentices are cutting herbs. Long shots convey a sense of spacious premises occupied by a prosperous and confident enterprise.

We find out more about the merchant as he passes along a corridor to emerge in a sunny lot in front of a warehouse. Two apprentices are sorting herbs. One of them tells the other that Sasuke's father has just arrived from the country.

Shimazu offers various clues to the period of his drama. The apprentice Naosuke makes fun of the long beard worn by Sasuke's father. It is too old-fashioned for the fifteenth year of Meiji (1883). Sasuke's father is old-fashioned in other ways as well, as we discover through his conversation with Yasuzaemon, Shunkin's father. Kahei refers to his sense of great indebtedness to Yasuzaemon. He was himself an apprentice at Mozuya; now his son Sasuke is following in his father's footsteps.

Yasuzaemon, however, shows himself to be more abreast of the times, at a time of rapid modernization in Japan. He mentions that his son (Shunkin's elder brother) is away, studying Western medicine in Nagasaki.

Shimazu is in no hurry to introduce his heroine. First he lets us see the measure of luxury she is accustomed to. We hear about her before we see her. Significantly, her blindness is only hinted at. We overhear an apprentice saying that Sasuke considers the word blind taboo. We do not yet know why.

As Kahei speaks with Yasuzaemon, a maid appears, looking for Sasuke. She says that Shunkin insists on being helped by him and no one else. When the camera cuts to Shunkin's room, we see only the maid in the doorway. Only her mistress's voice is heard, haughty and irritable.

The maid's distress suggests that her lot is not a happy one. Yet, when she finds Sasuke one of the apprentices is heard to say that he is lucky, getting to touch "the miss's hand." Another apprentice counters by saying that a fellow's career is over when he becomes a guiding hand.

Finally we see her. At first, only her hand in close-up reaches out to another, that of a boy. The following shot shows her feet slipping into a pair of sandals. The camera dollies up to the long-awaited view of her face.

Tanizaki's narrator must render a detailed description of Shunkin's beauty as he has imagined it. Shimazu lets the camera do the talking. We are free to accept as accurate whatever impression it gives of her face and figure, which of course we know belong to the charming Kinuyo Tanaka.

A long shot takes in Shunkin moving toward a doorway with Sasuke in the foreground (lower right of the screen) waiting on her. This scene turns out to be a point-of-view shot from Kahei, who is seated with Shunkin's parents in a room nearby.

Kinuyo Tanaka in *The Story of Shunkin* (1935) directed by Yasujiro Shimazu. Courtesy of the Kawakita Memorial Film Institute.

This mode of revealing Shunkin's beauty gains in effect from a bystander's comment: Kahei says admiringly that Shunkin has grown so beautiful. His reaction is the usual one, as we see later on, when Shunkin's beauty turns heads as she passes down a street, guided by Sasuke.

Shimazu continues to mount evidence of the effect this girl has on others. We see her mother weeping, worried about her blind daughter's future. Yasuzaemon tells Kahei of his fear that their doting care may made Shunkin self-centered.

The blind girl's selfishness soon becomes a familiar topic of conversation. We see it at work in a sequence showing her leaving her teacher Shunsho's house. The anteroom is filled with other students waiting their turn. Shunkin enters, led by Sasuke. She responds to a general greeting with a silent nod. This sequence is shown in a series of long shots with two brief close-ups that speak for the girl's haughtiness and pride. Bad temper is there too. When she complains of the cold, Sasuke is quick to offer a charcoal brazier. He gets no thanks from his mistress, whose expression is sullen as she warms her hands.

This episode is also included in the novel. There the narrator offers a lengthy description of Shunkin's thankless attitude to her servant Sasuke. The camera says it all quickly. We see how she expects him to anticipate her every wish; and how quick she is to lash out if he is slow to do so.

As in the novel, her haughty cruelty is most vividly portrayed in the lesson she gives Sasuke on the samisen. There the narrator speculates on the reasons behind her heartlessness.

Shimazu wastes no time on conjecture, but goes directly to a visual evocation of the motif of domineering woman and her victim. Interestingly, he gives Shunkin's cruelty a richly lyrical setting. It begins with a shot of Shunkin's parents and her elder sister seated in a room. Their conversation reveals that they have acceded to Shunkin's wish to give Sasuke samisen lessons.

A cut to Shunkin's room shows her in a good mood, in quiet triumph, because she has gotten her way. Yet she quickly assumes the coldly authoritarian manner required by her role as the one Sasuke must call "Teacher." Here, too, as in the novel, she quickly reduces him to tears.

As he sobs, the camera pans slowly out to the garden. Snow is falling silently, covering the branches of trees. It is a kind of stasis, as this symbol of seasonal change expresses supreme indifference to the human drama being played out.

A fade suggests a passage of time. The next scene takes up the same landscape, now thickly blanketed with snow. A cut to Shunkin's room points to a stark contrast between nature's serenity outside and human turmoil within.

Obviously, Sasuke is failing to play well enough again. Shunkin berates him for his stupidity. A close-up shows his face in tears. A medium shot shows her throwing a teacup at him. Another cut shows three maids in the hallway. Their talk confirms our sense that scenes like the one we have witnessed are an everyday event. One of the maids says as much. Another is glad that Sasuke, not her, is their mistress's whipping boy.

The camera closes the sequence with another pause in the deserted garden. This time, the quiet of deep snow is marred by the sound of Shunkin's shrill scolding coming from the house.

Shimazu is generally faithful to the novel's depiction of this tragic love affair; but he adds a good deal of play with shifts in mood. The novel is consistently unsparing in its study of this tragic relationship. The film, however, lightens its melodrama with comic relief in the form of slapstick. This is not surprising in a work allied to the *shomingeki* genre so important to Shochiku Studio marketing in the 1930s.

Our first view of this tendency frames the sequence showing Shunkin's haughty demeanor in the teacher's anteroom. As she and Sasuke made their way there, the camera took note of a man skulking along, obviously spying on them. Later we find out that this fellow is one Shokichi, servant of Ritaro, a good-for-nothing son of a wealthy rice dealer. Ritaro is infatuated with Shunkin, so he has his servant spy on her. The servant reports back to his master in a one-dolly shot that shows them walking down the street. We see what a vainglorious fool Ritaro is. And, knowing as we do that his lady-love is blind, we laugh at all the unconsciously comical references to eyes made by these two conniving rascals. The scene ends with a parody of Shunkin's dependence on Sasuke—here, Shokichi steering his master away from a mess some dog has left.

We next see the two together in the teacher's anteroom. Shunkin has gone in for her lesson. Ritaro makes a fool of himself, expressing in dumb show his desire for just one touch of Shunkin's hand. Shokichi's sly suggestion is that Shunkin is cold to all handsome men. Ritaro agrees, convinced that his voice alone has tipped her off to his good looks.

Shimazu uses this farcical element even in contexts as serious as Shunkin's pregnancy. That subject gets little play in the novel. The film devotes ten scenes to it. There is ample room to explore a variety of reactions on the part of major characters.

First we witness the mother's despair. This sequence begins with a shot of what appears to be a resort spa. Cherry trees are scattering their blossoms everywhere. A cut to an inn shows a maid hanging a quilt out to dry. Shunkin's mother arrives. We do not yet know why she has come here.

A cut to the servants' quarters at the Mozuya household gives the answer. Shunkin is pregnant. One fellow says that Sasuke may soon be a father. Sasuke is shown in close-up, saying that he would never do such an outrageous thing. Indignant, he leaves the room.

A cut to the spa shows Shunkin and her mother, Shige, walking through the countryside. A series of intercut close-ups records their emotions when the question of paternity comes up. The mother is desperate, the daughter obstinate. Shige presses Shunkin for an answer: *is* Sasuke the father of her child? Shunkin's expression is angry and disdainful as she asks how anyone could think her capable of any such relation with a lowly apprentice like Sasuke.

Shimazu gives this moment of high drama a notably lyrical setting. The two women walk along a path in a long shot that frames an idyllic picture of nature's springtime bounty. They pass under cherry trees in bloom. Shunkin says that her baby should be put up for adoption, since she plans to remain single for the rest of the life. A close-up studies her face. The camera pans up to the sky when she mentions hearing the happy song of a lark. A full ninety seconds are given to this shot, with its poignant contrast between young blind mother-to-be and lark arising in cherry blossom time.

Yet even within this sequence a shift in mood returns us to comic relief provided by Shunkin's would-be suitor, Ritaro.

A close-up of Shunkin's mother in tears yields to a long shot of ten palanquins in a procession along the road across the stream. That passing magnificence turns out to be going to a bash Ritaro is throwing for a show-off number of geisha at an inn. The sound of a *koto* in the distance connects him to Shunkin as the comedy of his absurd infatuation is played out in public there.

A cut to another inn shows Shunkin playing a *koto* while her mother looks on sadly. This scene ends with a dissolve expressive of an elegiac mood in sympathy with Shunkin's plight.

This contrast of moods is used throughout the film to move the plot along in a number of events shared with the novel. One instance is the flower-viewing sequence depicting Ritaro's pathetic attempt to seduce Shunkin. Sasuke is shown leading her through a garden. He guides her to a plum tree in blossom. She touches it. The camera cuts to bystanders. Ritaro and Shokichi are there, along with two clowns. One strikes a farcical pose, saying he wishes that he could be a plum tree. The other does something even more ridiculous. He runs up to Shunkin and Sasuke, saying, "I am a plum tree."

The climax of the sequence comes with Shunkin's rejection of Ritaro. Ritaro has managed to invite her into a room at the inn. Annoyed, she throws a sake bottle in the direction of his voice. It hits his forehead, drawing blood. She leaves. Her suitor, farcically dejected, nurses his wound, taking it for a serious injury.

The film's radical departure from the original is especially evident at the end. As so often before, the ruling principle is simplification. Shimazu dispenses entirely with the novelist's complex attempt to explore the psychological dimensions of Sasuke's self-afflicted injury. Instead, he concentrates on a visual presentation of the act. Mirror and needle are convenient enough icons for a state of abject servitude to a domineering woman. Shimazu has made sure to offer close-up familiarity with the hairpin earlier on. Now we see it lying close to the mirror Sasuke looks into. He has sent the maid away. Alone now, he picks up the hairpin and looks into the mirror. It shows him Shunkin's face unmarred by any injury. Clearly, this is the mind's-eye view he wants to be his forever.

The camera cuts to Shunkin's room where the doctor is saying that her bandages will be removed the following day.

A cut to Sasuke's room shows him with blood running down his face. The diegetic sound of Shunkin's *koto* plainly underscores the link now forged between the two. The *koto* plays somewhat out of tune, as if to express their shared emotional turmoil. The last shot in the sequence is a close-up of the mirror reflecting Sasuke's face now. His eyes are closed.

The ending of the film is also simplified yet melodramatically charged. Sasuke's loss of vision is conveyed from his perspective, by a tilting camera passing along blurred room partitions as he feels his way along the corridor. Shunkin herself opens her door. A close-up of Sasuke's face tells us that she knows that something terrible has happened.

The final scene of her room offers our first and last glimpse of their physical intimacy. Sasuke takes the initiative now. Saying that he, too, is blind, he crawls close to her and puts his hands on her wrap. Then he takes her hands and raises them to his eyes. Shunkin embraces him.

All through the film, the long take has been Shimazu's cinematic rubric for thematically crucial scenes. As we have seen, the novelist Tanizaki uses a complex rhetorical strategy to engage us in an intensely intellectual game involving deduction and surmise. In place of that, Shimazu uses the camera's long focus to direct our intense "visual" gaze to significant incidents affecting Shunkin's and Sasuke's lives.

Our first such view occurs when Shunkin's father visits Sasuke's father in the country. It begins with a dolly around the interior of a backroom, the most

Koichi Takada (l) and Kinuyo Tanaka in *The Story of Shunkin* (1935) directed by Yasujiro Shimazu. Courtesy of the Kawakita Memorial Film Institute.

respectable space for receiving a guest. Having framed the two old men in the center foreground, the camera stops to direct our attention to their manners. The way Kahei behaves clearly indicates a rigid master-servant relationship. For almost two minutes, the camera records the progress of their conversation. They are about to make a decision that will affect the rest of Sasuke's life. Yasuzaemon begs Kahei to entrust Sasuke's life to him. Sasuke will become his daughter's companion rather than a merchant, the role initially set out for this dutiful son.

Now, at the end of the film, the camera directs a similar steady gaze for an even longer time—almost two and a half minutes. This sequence celebrates the two lovers' union at last. Here the system of denotation makes use of subtle words and movements.

A medium shot shows them seated against a room partition. This time it is Shunkin who takes the initiative in bridging the social gap. She moves closer to Sasuke. For the first time, she expresses her concern for him, asking if his eyes cause him pain. Their lengthy dialogue is almost redundant, pushing the limits of melodrama. Sasuke draws on the image of the beautiful Shunkin he will keep in his mind's eye and vows eternal love for her. Shunkin responds by saying that they will live together just by themselves forever. The shot ends with their tearful embrace.

Yet there is more. Like the novelist, the director feels compelled to round the matter out. A long take dissolves into a shot of Sasuke outside the house. A subtitle affirms his devotion to Shunkin—for the rest of her life and his. *Koto* music swells to enhance this final melodramatic touch.

In sum, Shimazu's *The Story of Shunkin* offers another interesting case of the transposition onto the screen of a literary work of considerable narrative complexity. Here, that means transforming a novelist's study in tragedy into melodrama, *shomingeki*-style. Shimazu shows how that could be done by an old hand working for a studio whose orders were to give wider audience appeal to this work of "pure literature."

Notes

1. Tadahisa Murakami, *Nihon eiga sakkaron (On Japanese filmmakers)* (Tokyo: Oraisha, 1936), p. 222.
2. Joseph Anderson and Donald Richie. *The Japanese Film: Art and Industry*, expanded ed. (Princeton: Princeton University Press, 1982), pp. 122–25.
3. Quoted by Nobuo Chiba in his *Eiga to Tanizaki* (Tanizaki and cinema) (Tokyo: Seiabo, 1989), p. 208.
4. Junichiro Tanizaki, *Ashikari and The Story of Shunkin*, trans. Roy Humpherson and Hajime Okita (Westport, Conn.: Greenwood Press, 1970), pp. 84–87.
5. Ibid., p. 90.
6. Ibid., p. 91.
7. Ibid., p. 92
8. Ibid., p. 94.
9. Ibid., p. 101.
10. Ibid., p. 102.
11. Ibid., p. 107.
12. Ibid.
13. Ibid., pp. 110–11.
14. Ibid., p. 111.
15. Ibid., p. 117.
16. Ibid., p. 121.
17. Ibid., p. 123.
18. Ibid., p. 136.
19. Ibid., p. 119.
20. Ibid., p. 139.
21. Ibid., p. 156.
22. Ibid.
23. Ibid., pp. 156–57.
24. Ibid., p. 163.
25. For a comprehensive study of Tanizaki's manipulation of the reader's point of view in *The Story of Shunkin*, see Sumie Jones, "How Tanizaki Disarms the Intellectual Reader," *Literature East and West* 18, nos. 2–4 (June–December 1974): 321–29.
26. Wayne Booth, *The Rhetoric of Fiction* (Chicago: University of Chicago Press, 1961), pp. 169–240.
27. Tanizaki, *The Story of Shunkin*, p. 76.
28. Ibid., p. 77.
29. Ibid., p. 105.

30. Ibid., p. 138.
31. For a critical study of comments on Sasuke as a mutilator, see Kohei Hata, *Tanizaki Junichiro* (Junichiro Tanizaki) (Tokyo: Tsukuma Shobo, 1989), pp. 191–232. For a study on this subject done in English, see Ken Ito, *Visions of Desire: Tanizaki's Fictional Worlds* (Stanford: Stanford University Press, 1991), p. 179–80.
32. William Cadbury, "Character and the Mock Heroic in *Barchester Tower*," *Texas Studies in Literature and Language 5* (1963): 569.

10

Differently True: Toyoda's *A Strange Tale from East of the River* (1960)

Kafu Nagai's novel *Bokuto kidan* (A strange tale from east of the river, 1937) is acclaimed for exhibiting "a rambling style not generally encountered in any fiction."[1] It is a story with a carefully designed structure, rich in atmosphere but poor in characterization and narrative event.

Such a literary work seems unlikely to attract the attention of filmmakers, whose strategy relies so much on character and narrative development. Yet two directors have taken up the challenge offered by Kafu's seemingly eventless novel: Shiro Toyoda in 1960 and Kaneto Shindo in 1991.

Toyoda's version shows a filmmaker transforming this seemingly unpromising book into an action-packed film alive with well-developed characters caught up in dramatic events. Before we see how that is done, of course, we must have Kafu's work clearly in view. Donald Keene offers a good starting point for analyzing this peculiar novel:

> *A Strange Tale* is a surpassingly beautiful example of Kafu's style and the most affecting expression of his longing for the vanishing past. This longing now embraced the Meiji period, which he had hated in his youth; the passage of time and the rapid deterioration of manners had enabled him at least to understand what was unique and genuine in that period.[2]

Elsewhere, Keene adds:

> *A Strange Tale* deserves its reputation as one of Kafu's best works, though it defies most of the prescriptions for effective writing. Its success depended on Kafu's ability to evoke the derelict Tamanoi Quarter, where the past lingered on in the battered old houses.[3]

Two questions inevitably come to mind. First, if this work's thematic thrust lies in Kafu's longing for the past, then how does he achieve his desired effect? Second, why does Kafu, as Keene says, defy "most of the prescriptions for effective writing"?

Keene is quite right in his interpretation of the novelist's thematic concern in general. As the novel progresses, however, the novelist's nostalgia for the past prompts him to take action, in an attempt to recapture his youth. This attempt, of course, is filtered through the actions of the persona he has created.

196

Kafu deliberately dispenses with what he knows full well are the basics of "effective" writing: well-developed character, tightly linked causal line, narrative legibility. Yet his very avoidance of those means serves another end: a carefully calculated, elaborate design of heightened self-awareness on the part of his narrator.

The story Kafu tells is simplicity itself. The writer Tadasu Oe *happens* to meet Oyuki, a prostitute from the Tamanoi red-light district (italics mine). After a brief affair, he breaks with her.

That story contains another: the one the writer is struggling to complete. Its protagonist is the retired teacher Jumpei, who elopes with his former maidservant Osumi, now a waitress at a bar. Kafu plays one story off against the other in one of the complex narrative strategies he uses to give his "strange" tale its elaborate design. We see how he contrives to expand his "discourse time" by telling two stories that interact and complement one another.

Steven Carter says this about Kafu's seemingly "loose" style, with all its diversity of narrative modes:

> . . . although one may argue that it is precisely this feature of Kafu's writing that makes it so charming—Kafu's tale is told in a rambling style not generally encountered in fiction. The characters are faintly drawn, and there is more time devoted to descriptions of the Tamanoi streets than to psychological analysis or even dialogue. Add to this the fact that Kafu chose to include a number of other kinds of writing in his work besides the story of Tadasu and Oyuki—a letter from an old geisha friend, quotations from *Dream of the Red Chamber* and Yoda Gakkai's *Twenty-four Views of the Sumida*, an essay on the recent history of the Tamanoi district, a few Haiku by Kafu himself, and even a chapter from another unfinished fiction the narrator is supposedly working on at the moment. . . .[4]

Again, all these stray notes have purposes. They are used to evoke a particular atmosphere as they relate to the cultural-literary milieu of the Meiji era. They are also deftly used to create the author's persona. As we later see, they are details that repay study.

The novel begins with the narrator-persona's resistance to contemporary taste:

> I almost never go to see a moving picture. If vague memories are to be trusted, it was toward the end of the last century that I saw, at a Kanda theater, a moving picture of a San Francisco street scene. I suppose it must have been about then, too, that the expression "moving picture" was invented. Today it has almost been discarded. The expression one has learned first comes most easily, however, and I shall here continue to use the old, discarded one.[5]

Even though Kafu himself died in 1959, the reader of his story may want to think of him as living, the better to savor the wholesome ironies that flow from his creation of a persona so much like himself. In fact, readers in his day would have been quick to see how the speaker in this strange tale is a projection of its famous author.[6]

Kafu takes for granted his reader's familiarity with extraliterary materials, especially those of this author's life.[7] Kafu's dislike of "the moving picture" was well known in his day. So is his abhorrence of the sound of radio, a dislike that figures importantly in his novel's narrative strategy. His affinity with the past is clear from the outset, as we have seen. *Katsudo shashin*, "the moving picture," may be outdated, but he uses it anyway. (The more up-to-date word would have been *eiga*, "the picture of images.")

The novel abounds in author-persona likenesses. A visit to Kafu's favorite secondhand bookstore does more than merely anchor an element of the plot; it insists that we take this author-persona correlation seriously.

Modern literary criticism considers any given literary work to be a self-contained entity whose coherence is internal. Even so, a richer understanding of Kafu's *Strange Tale* demands the inclusion of two works in our analysis. One is Kafu's diary, *Danchotei nichijo* (Dyspepsia house days). It offers insights into the kind of life the novelist was leading at the time he was working on this novel. The other, equally significant, is "Sakugo Zeigen" (An author's humble afterthoughts), a kind of commentary on *A Strange Tale*.

Significantly, the diary records the novel's genesis. *The Asahi* asked him to write a long novel, but Kafu declined, claiming that he "did not have any strength."[8] Nevertheless, nagged by creative drive, he did some research. It took him to Tamanoi, the newly developed red-light district. It was a matter of research and then some, as Kafu himself notes: "My desire for visits to the east of the river was not gone yet. As usual, I went to that house." The entry for 20 September says: "Finally, an idea of the novel with this town as the setting was formulated."[9]

"An Author's Humble Afterthoughts" also offers important clues to Kafu's identification of author and persona. Both are seen recoiling from a spectacle of commonplace vulgarity passing itself off as modernization:

> In the following April willows were planted on the street of Ginza and vermilion-colored lanterns lit among artificial flowers to adorn the pavements. Ginza now looked like the town which appeared in a play performed in the countryside. Looking at those vermilion lanterns and the balustrade of the sukiyaki restaurant at Akasaka painted in the same color, I realized how much the townspeople's taste had deteriorated.[10]

How, then, does Kafu advance the persona's action in reaction (as it were) to modernization? He begins with the "chance encounter" so often used by *gesaku* writers of the Edo period. On a late summer evening the persona takes a walk in the vicinity of Asakusa. There a pimp offers to introduce him to "a good girl."

The persona refuses, saying that he is going to Yoshiwara. The story is set in motion. But first he takes a slight detour, stopping in at the secondhand bookstore near the licensed district.

The persona's bookstore experience seems like a casual accumulation of everyday detail, but it is in fact part and parcel of the narrative discourse Kafu employs. Right from the start, he uses these small eventualities to give convincing concrete detail to his narrative thrust: this strange tale of his persona's nostalgia for the demimonde of Edo culture vanishing so rapidly as Japan transforms itself into such a different-seeming nation.

The persona introduces the old bookseller at length:

> His face, his manner, his speech, his dress—they all had in them something of the Edo lowlands, to me rarer and more to be admired than any old book. Before the earthquake you would come upon one or two such old men, children of plebeian Edo, in the dressing rooms of all the theaters and variety halls.[11]

Equally important is the persona's sales transaction during which references are made to *Hotan Gazette* and the *Kagetsu shinshi*. It serves as a partially revelatory moment of the persona's identify, which has been kept in the dark for some time. The persona readily identifies the editor of the first magazine, Tamenaga Shunko, and even the date of its first issue, which he purchases. Here our impression of the persona's likeness to the author, which Kafu established right from the outset, is simply confirmed. Then, too, the central theme of the persona's recapitulation of the past is clearly expressed in his remarks: "It makes me young again, reading magazines from those days."

Another incident at the bookstore—a coincidence—entails the arrival of the newcomer. He sells an unlined woman's kimono and a singlet. As with the magazine, the persona's purchase of the singlet impels the story forward. His buying spree extends to canned goods and bread. His kerchief proves too small to hold these purchases. He has to spread it out on the grass and rearrange his things.

A policeman's suspicion is aroused. As he investigates, we learn more about our man. Only now do we know his name: Tadasu Oe. Thanks to the policeman, we also learn his address and date of birth.[12]

Sure enough, he is not all that young. He is fifty-seven, well past the prime of youth. We understand more about his attempt to recapture a world now vanishing, transformed before his very eyes.

Two important coded systems are revealed in this incident involving the policeman. We see how much care and thought the persona takes to manipulate facts and withhold information. He uses a difficult kanji to obscure his given name. We see that he is a person of some intellectual sophistication. And though he is single and lives alone, he claims to have a wife and old maidservant. He is clearly afraid that the basic facts of his life will put him under even stronger suspicion.

While the policeman learns little, we learn enough to see how much this man resembles Kafu. The time given to this interrogation is time well spent as far as we are concerned, since it is filled with detail about this increasingly interesting persona.

It may not be surprising that someone interrogated by the police should shield himself with lies and withheld information. But we will see that same pair of narrative strategies form the basis of the persona's relationship with the prostitute Oyuki.

What follows is the process of writing the novel Oe has been working on for some time: *Shisso* (Whereabouts unknown). Structurally, the rest of Kafu's *Strange Tale* unfolds the main story line of Oe's romance with Oyuki interspersed with this embedded story.

The first installment of *Whereabouts Unknown* is introduced immediately after the police interrogation. It concerns the beginnings of a familiar triangular relationship. The hero is Jumpei Taneda, a middle school teacher in his fifties. His marriage to Mitsuko also involves story patterns typical of melodrama. She is impregnated by her wealthy employer and married off to a man who needs money.

Jumpei and Mitsuko pass the rich man's child off as their own and have two more children themselves. Some years elapse. The children are grown and gone. Mitsuko is absorbed in the affairs of a religious sect.

Taneda is shy and reserved, a classic alienated nobody. The day he receives his retirement money, he disappears. He sets out to meet Sumiko, once the family maid. He just happened to meet her on a train earlier. Now she works as a hostess in a bar.

The persona has gotten that far with his story. Where should it go from there? His attempt to complete the plot he has set in motion takes its place alongside the other narrative devices Kafu uses to forward his "own" *Strange Tale*.

> The things that most interest me when I write a novel are the choice and description of background. I have from time to time fallen into the error of emphasizing background at the expense of characterization.
>
> Wishing to use for Taneda's hideout a once-famous place that had quite lost its character in the rebuilding of the city, I thought of Honjo or Fukagawa or the outskirts of Asakusa perhaps, or a back alley in the regions beyond, open countryside until but a few years before.[13]

The persona's link with the past is manifest in his choice of fictional background. His research takes him to the Tamanoi Licensed Quarter, the neighborhood "appropriate for the denouement" he has in mind.

The subsequent portrayal of this district, like a chain of events, echoes his preference for description of background. The alleyways run among hemmed-in shops. Lamps beckon to passers-by. All these objects, as in the novel of manners, elucidate the particular atmosphere reminiscent of the old tradition.

The Tamanoi District becomes not only the setting Oe intends to use for his story but the background for the main story, which features himself as the hero. A chance encounter—the narrative strategy already forwarding plots in both stories being told—awaits him in Tamanoi.

A woman, caught out in a sudden summer thunderstorm, runs to Oe, asking to share his umbrella. This casual courtesy is used to begin the affair that takes the main story to its end, and the embedded story along with it.

By Chapter 3, the persona's description of his first visit to this woman's quarters has passed through several narrational modes. The story's main thrust concerns his growing intimacy with this young woman, whose business and manner he studies with a writer's attention to nuance and detail. This is rendered mostly in terms of their conversations, which are spiced with a certain amount of spying as the persona studies her. There is also an element of authorial witness as the persona gives an account of the licensed district. Both methods appear to interrupt the narrative flow, as in the following exchange:

> Taking her hand and pulling her toward me, I whispered my request in her ear.
> 'I will not!' she glared at me, and gave me a rap on the shoulder. 'Be sensible, won't you!'
> Those who have read the stories of Tamenaga Shunsui will remember how from time to time Shunsui breaks his narrative to apologize for himself or his characters. Thus a girl in love for the first time forgets all demureness and thrusts herself upon the man whom her heart demands, and Shunsui warns the reader that her acts and words in such circumstances are not grounds for calling her a wanton. . . .[14]

Again we feel Nagai's deliberation in such extraliteral reference. The persona's familiarity with Edo culture is evident in his comments on Shunsui Tamenaga (1790-1843), a specialist in *ninjobon*, a genre noted for its amalgamation of popular fiction forms.[15] Those remarks also serve as a correlative to Kafu's nostalgia for the past and thus confirms the author-persona linkage. Furthermore, such seemingly tangential remarks expand an earlier casual event in the secondhand bookstore: his purchase of the magazine edited by Takenaga Shunko, who was a disciple of Shunsui.

Another narrative diversion takes the form of the persona's connoisseur assessment of the beauties he sees for hire:

> There are said to be some seven or eight hundred women in the Tamanoi Quarter, and perhaps one in ten still does her hair in the old style. The rest wear Japanese dress of the sort waitresses affect, or Western dress such as dancers might choose. The fact that the woman who took me in from the rain belonged to the old-style minority made me think the tired old device appropriate. I cannot bring myself to do injury to what happened.[16]

Here Kafu as cultural critic is filtered through the persona. Then, too, the omniscient intervention again takes note of the research on background, which the persona considers the most important aspect of fiction writing.

Also significant is the persona's perception of this woman's linkage with "the old-style minority." It hints at his increasing attraction to the woman he met so casually. What is it that he finds in her? Why does he become emotionally involved? The main story line gradually clarifies these and other questions the reader is anxious to ask.

The pattern that forms the main story line is "the journey." This journey, as we have seen, takes the form of rather perfunctory research. But it is a journey of soul as well. The persona looks into himself and at the past he yearns to recapture, and with it his own lost youth. Needless to say, this woman serves as a mere catalyst of a process that is his alone. Such rejuvenation is short-lived, he knows;

and as he comes closer to finishing the novel he is writing, he gives more thought to the ending most fit to this real and present relationship.

For him, the Tamanoi is a gateway to the "other" world he yearns to know. His initiation into it takes place one early summer evening at the end of Chapter 2. Kafu's text is redolent with notes of changes wrought by landscape and the weather. The persona climbs "through the summer grass to the embarkment." Following a path there, he "descends" to the Tamanoi Licensed Quarter. Lights are now "shining in the windows below the embarkment." A sudden gust of wind sends paper and rubbish fleeting down the street "like ghosts." Lightning flashes. A thunderstorm changes the beautiful evening sky completely. A woman's voice calls out to him.

The guide to this other world he seeks is that woman. His first impression of her "old beauty" is registered through the sensual image of her neck. It sees "a white neck" ducking in under the umbrella he holds.

We have already seen the narrative proceed by way of deception and withheld information. Here they are used to explore this new relationship. The first time they meet, he uses casual conversation to find out more about her. She is a woman hired for pleasure, so naturally he is curious to know where she has worked before.

He also assesses her claims to beauty and charming manners. She appears to be twenty-three or twenty-four. She has good features and a nice complexion. Just as important, she is only a passing fancy, a woman to study and contemplate, not enjoy in the flesh. He does not sleep with her. He is in any case a finicky man. He is conscious of hygiene. He drinks only water that comes directly from the faucet. He never asks her name. At the end of his visit, we learn it from her business card. She is called Oyuki.

From these introductory chapters on, the persona's romance progresses in parallel to the embedded romance between Taneda and Sumiko. Chapter 4 presents a chapter from *Whereabouts Unknown* the persona has completed. The remaining six chapters focus on the persona-Oyuki causal line, though it is often interrupted by views of the manuscript in progress.

Many critics have written about the persona-author relationship in this work. But only a few have paid close attention to the liaison between the main story and the embedded one—an element central to Kafu's narrative strategy. To begin with, the persona's continuing returns to Tamanoi serve as an apt device for advancing these two plot lines. He needs to do research in order to complete his novel, but this research in turn causes his increasing involvement with Oyuki.

Oyuki serves as the persona's catalyst in a number of ways. First, she is the very embodiment of the past, a sort of medium for contact with that other world. Hints of this function abound. For example, the sound of the radio—so disturbing where he lives and writes—is blessedly missing here: ". . . when the women took their places at the windows, radios and phonographs were forbidden. . . ."[17]

The persona finds many reasons to reinforce his notion that Tamanoi and Oyuki put him in touch with the romance of days gone by:

The figure of O-yuki, her hair always in one of the old styles, and the foulness of the canal, and the humming of the mosquitoes—all of these stirred me deeply, and called up visions of a past now dead some thirty or forty years. I must, if it seems at all possible, state my thanks to her who was the agent for these strange, insubstantial visions. More than the actor in the Namboku play, more than the Shinnai singer, Tsuruya somebody or other, who tells of Rancho and his tragic love, O-yuki was the skillful yet inarticulate artist with power to summon the past.[18]

Equally important is the fact that Oyuki makes this sixty-year-old persona feel alive, as if he were reliving the youth he had lost so long before. Chapter 6, which begins with the seasonal metaphor of a buzzing mosquito, revolves around this feeling. He takes heart when Oyuki casually remarks that he looks twenty years younger than his age. She adds that he is more than a stranger to her: he reminds her of her first love. There was a time when she thought she would die if she could not be with that man. The persona puts Oyuki in touch with her dream, and even gives promise of helping her make it real. It was she who took the initiative when they first met. She it is who thinks of putting their casual relationship on a firmer footing. She asks the persona if he can marry her after she pays off her contract.

Kafu invests considerable significance in Oyuki's causal conversation. She responds in easygoing general terms to the persona's questions about her past and how she came to her present line of work. A woman she had known told her about being in business this way. Oyuki adds: "People my age are meant for this sort of thing, or so she said. But you never know what will happen afterward, do you?"

Her steady gaze at this moment makes her questioner uneasy. Lightning has been flickering on the horizon all this while. A sudden sharper flash seems to stir something in Oyuki's memory. This threat of storm connects past and present: the storm they met in and the one they watch together now. She makes the connection obliquely, but clearly enough. He has just said, "It looks like another shower." She says, "I was on my way back from the hairdresser's. It's been three months, . . . *hasn't* it."

On the surface, her comment is simple, matter-of-fact. But he is alive to its deeper meaning, to its connection with her comment on the future: "You never know what will happen afterward, do you?"

The persona experiences a moment of truth:

"It's been three months," and, slightly protracted, "*hasn't* it": the words seemed to carry a vague, broad, appeal, as of calling something up from the very distant past. . . . But the protracted "*hasn't* it" had the ring less of an exclamation than of a device for drawing out an answer. I found even the word "yes" falling back in my throat, and I answered only with my eyes.[19]

Their "three-month" relationship also bridges real and fictional worlds. The persona has been wondering whether his hero and heroine's falling into "the deepest of relationships" is premature, and this deliberation has halted his progress. Now his own experience helps him solve this problem: "her tone and manner as she has spoken of those three months" have convinced him that there is nothing unusual about his original plot.

Thus, when the manuscript is near completion, the persona defines Oyuki as a muse who stirred his declining creative energy:

> O-yuki was the muse who had accidentally called back into a dulled heart shadows of the past. If she had not been drawn to me, or if I had not thought she was, I should without doubt have torn up the manuscript that had long been waiting on my desk. O-yuki was the strange force to make a forgotten old author finish a work, in all probability his last.[20]

Even so, as we have seen, Oe's liaison with Oyuki is doomed to dissolution because it is based on deception and information withheld. He has never revealed his real profession. Oyuki assumes that he is a pornographer, and her proposal that troubles him is based on such an assumption. What is it that keeps him from disclosure while the men who visit her take off "their masks" and leave behind "their pretensions"?

A number of critics have pointed to signs throughout that the persona is a confirmed egocentric and a personality divided against itself. Even though Oyuki just "happened" to function as a catalyst, Oe's motives for cultivating her are purely egoistical:

> I have said that I had many reasons for coming here almost every night. To reconnoiter the ground for my novel *Whereabouts Unknown*. To flee the radio. To avoid Marunouchi and the Ginza and the other busy centers of the city, for which I had a deep dislike. There were other reasons, too, but none that I could tell the woman. I had made O-yuki's house a resting place on my nocturnal walks, and to suit my purposes I had told her lies quite as they came to me.[21]

Importantly, Oe does not try to find out Oyuki's real name or facts about her birth. She herself, he notes, has had "no occasion to reveal them." He prefers to investigate Oyuki's plight by way of a guessing game. He is out to gather material for his work. Yet he is not an egotist immune to self-reproach. He is in fact nagged by guilt for having toyed with her true feelings.

At the same time, Oyuki's proposal precipitates his decision to act on lingering thoughts about their inevitable separation. He may feel remorse, but egotism wins out as he prepares to excuse himself:

> Outside were the masses. The world. Inside was one individual. Between the world and the individual there was harmony. Why should this have been so? Because O-yuki was still young. Because she had not yet lost her feeling for the masses, the world outside. Seated at the window was a lowly O-yuki, while in her heart there lay hidden another O-yuki. And the men who came into the alley had taken off their masks and left behind their pretensions.[22]

Implicit in such embellished language of praise is the harmony between Oyuki and the world outside that is possible only in the confinement of the licensed district. She is in her element because another Oyuki—the respectable woman she wants to become—lies hidden. Taking her out of her element would destroy that harmony. Or so the persona tells himself:

> Under the pressure of circumstances, I had more than once followed the wishes of a woman and brought her into my house and set her at broom and dustpan. . . . When such a woman leaves behind her old surroundings and no longer thinks herself lowly, she soon becomes unmanageable, either the slovenly wife or the fiery wife.[23]

Oe's defensive reflex continues to rule his thoughts as he considers how to terminate his relationship with Oyuki. Will he reveal to her the other side of his double nature? Will he just leave, sparing her a terrible disappointment?

He opts for the latter. At this stage he is inclined to accompany Oyuki on a shopping trip and then have a "farewell cup." But no. Doing that might expose him to a chance meeting with "a reporter or a gentleman of letters and again be assassinated by pen." Trivial as his wavering seems, it has multiple implications. His relationship with Oyuki is confined to the Tamanoi District. There, any harmony between the two is maintained through deception. But the Tamanoi is safe. Outside it is the world of reality where the persona is exposed to danger: his mask could be ripped away. Oyuki could lose her lowly power as muse and catalyst for art.

Furthermore, it is precisely in this fabricated reality built on the dismal reality of an underclass tormented by buzzing mosquitoes that the would-be salesman of pornography and the would-be innocent prostitute enliven the past.

Significantly, his farewell gift is money for a winter kimono. This garment image relates to a larger pattern of seasonal change—an important narrative strategy. Oe happens to meet Oyuki in a flash of lightning in early summer. Their subsequent meetings are filled with references to summer heat and mosquitoes. Mosquitoes speak for Oyuki's status: a geisha reduced to a lowly prostitute. As the persona says, Tamanoi was built on reclaimed land. Mosquitoes bred in its foul ditches. Yet he found a certain old-fashioned charm in the netting used to keep them at bay. Even their vexatious buzz, he feels, is better than the modern-day din of radios.

This doomed relationship reaches its high point in summer and, like nature itself, declines as autumn comes on. The winds of that season, and the harvest moon, replace the sultry heat of evenings and the mosquito's whining drone. Once people are shut up indoors, their radios cease to vex the persona. His awareness of seasonal change underscores his sense of the flux of time to which every human is subject. This traditional idea of passingness, of *mujo*, is all the more poignant for a man "past the border of old age."

Predictably, the egotist in him dwells on that felt reality. He takes refuge in texts to suit. He indites the poem about stormy evening and autumn window from *The Dreams of the Red Chamber.*

Again, we see the embedded novel *Whereabouts Unknown* enriching the narrative mode, in parallel to and in contrast to the *Strange Tale* being told. In both man and woman from different social strata come together through romance. In *Whereabouts Unknown*, however, the couple's relationship is placed in a somewhat different light. Even as Oe's harmonious union with Oyuki thrives on deception and withheld information, the fiction he writes depicts a relationship based on growing intimacy and truth.

Moreover, Taneda and Sumiko's elopement leads to a happy ending. The last segment of the persona's fiction, introduced at the end of Chapter 8, says it all. Just like Oe, Taneda feels that he is rejuvenated by his younger lover. Unlike the persona, however, he can say what he feels: that love has given him something to live for. Sumiko decides to run a stall in Tamanoi to earn a livelihood for them both. Though Taneda may be ostracized by his family and society, he will start a new life with Sumiko as his source of moral strength.

Obviously, the fiction he writes shows how much the persona is willing to indulge himself in wishful thinking. It is something like his eulogy to his fictional character, who has found "something to live for" in the younger woman and is determined to pursue it.

The persona's completion of *Whereabouts Unknown* ought to end his visits to Oyuki. But Kafu suggests Oe's lingering attachment by adding one more final meeting. This time, the inevitability of separation insists.

The rest of the final chapter shows how time does pass, inexorably. Summer passes into autumn. The cheerful, youthful Oyuki falls ill. The familiar metaphor of the radio returns to provide finality to the old persona's brief recapitulation of what has been lost in his life: "That radio, now behind shutters, no longer tormented me as it once had. I managed to keep busy under the lamp in my study."

The persona's narration ought to end there, as does this novel, he claims. That way, the novel could have an "open" text that will suspend the reader's sense of incompleteness. Thus, the reader's power of surmise is challenged when she or he tries to answer this legitimate question: what will be the fate of abandoned Oyuki?

Kafu chooses to overwork the aspect of closure, offering additional narrative legibility to the persona's afterthoughts. Thus, Oe, the Kafu-like novelist, ponders what he should do if he is to give his own "romance" an ending in the old style:

> I would perhaps add a chapter describing how, quite by accident, six months or a year later, I met O-yuki in a wholly unexpected place. She had changed her profession. And if I wished to make the scene yet more effective, I could have the two of us see each other from the windows of passing automobiles or trains, unable to speak, however intense the longing.[24]

Moreover, the persona tries to answer the question that the reader would have legitimately asked in the open text:

> But times have changed. There seemed little likelihood that she would fall ill and die. Nor did it seem likely that, pressed by a sense of duty, she would give herself to a man she did not care for.[25]

The critic Moriyasu Yasufumi observes that what the writer in Kafu's *Strange Tale* tries to hide is more important than what he actually tries to express.[26] Throughout the novel, the persona's action, speech, and even feelings are often colored with deception.

Nevertheless, the ending serves as a rare moment when Kafu and the persona become one and the author-persona's real feelings filter through to express a sense of pathos, of an old age whose course no one can reverse:

> The roofs of the dirty, jammed-in-houses, on and on. O-yuki and I, in the black upstairs window, looking up at lights reflected in a sky heavy before a storm, one damp hand in the other. Suddenly, as we sat talking in conundrums, a flash of lightning, and her profile. The picture is here before my eyes, and will not leave. I lost myself in the sport of love when I was twenty; and now, past the border of old age, to have to tell of this foolishness! The jokes of fate can be cruel.[27]

The very ending of *A Strange Tale from East of the River* once more puts us off balance by offering a poem that suddenly breaks the rhythm of prose narrative. It is tinged with lyrical overtones and embellished with seasonal images: a stricken butterfly fluttering broken wings and a dying stem of amaranth. We are painfully aware of an element of self-conscious artificiality on the part of the persona-author. Is the poem really a rendition of the feelings of the persona who says: "I too am now alone/I have taken leave"? Or is he simply toying with his emotions? The novel ends with this rhetorical ambiguity about the persona's deceptive self and his real self.[28]

Rich as it is in mood and meticulous in narrative technique, Kafu's novel seems far too uneventful to attract a filmmaker working in the studio system of the 1960s. Yet Toyoda took up the challenge of this unpromising work and made it into a colorful and appealing film well calculated to interest the film-going public. His ingenuity lies in the way he completely overhauls the novel's structure and main characters. The result is a melodrama focused on a lowly woman victimized by socioeconomic forces yet capable of exhibiting a gift for challenge and confrontation.

An auteurist approach to Toyoda's films suggests a readily identifiable thematic constant in the struggle of the hero or heroine against adverse circumstances. For example, in *Gan* (The mistress, 1954), Toyoda explored the plight of a woman still held captive by feudal values in the Meiji society then undergoing modern transformation. In *Yukiguni* (The snow country), adapted from Yasunari Kawabata's novel of the same title, Toyoda radically modified the central theme of the original: Shimamura's search for a holistic vision of life. Instead, his film concentrated on the geisha Komako's search for an identity she can live with. It is scarcely surprising to see this director making radical changes in Kafu's novel.

Toyoda's approach to *A Strange Story from East of the River* involves casting the novel's central problem in a completely new light. While the original concerns the persona's attempt to recapture the past through his contact with Oyuki, the film makes shift to focus on the woman. The central problem here has to do with Oyuki's attempt to come to terms with her own life. That problem presents her with two choices: staying in the Tamanoi District or getting out of it. Unlike Kafu's heroine, Oyuki in the film really acts out a nonchoice, since escape from her prostitute's bondage remains in the realm of wishful thinking.

In order to accommodate his thematic concern, Toyoda dispenses with the embedded novel. Sumiko disappears. Taneda is used for the one romantic affair used in place of Kafu's two. Taneda becomes a central character as Oyuki's lover. The writer persona Oe is relegated to the periphery. As in the original, he visits the Tamanoi District in search of material. But he is all about research. He remains uninvolved, a detached observer of the manners and mores of this licensed district. He serves as a commentator and critic of culture, providing background information through his voice-over narration.

This different thematic orientation also improves characterization. The other characters are given much more substantial treatment. Jumpei's conflict of values between social conformity and individual freedom is dynamically explored. His wife, Mitsuko, who is underdeveloped in the original embedded story, has an important part to play in Toyoda's much more complex single-romance plot. Mitsuko vies with Oyuki for her husband's affections. And she wins out in the end.

Furthermore, Toyoda gives Oyuki a sick mother and uncle. Along with the boatman who serves as a go-between, these family members are used to augment the melodramatic effect of the film because they are the root cause of its heroine's suffering.

Such melodrama also demands an ending quite different from that of the original. There, as we have seen, Taneda and Sumiko's elopement ends with the promise of a new life, while the relationship between the persona and Oyuki results in the dissolution expected from the beginning. Toyoda cannot end his film on such a quiet note. His Oyuki is betrayed by her lover and then dies in the flower of youth.

Toyoda does make good use of the intrinsically cinematic qualities of his script. Deep space, wide screen, and panning all serve as an effective means to narrative verve and economy. They also contribute to a deft evocation of the manners and mores of the Tamanoi District, whose character Kafu's persona labors to capture in so many words.

Toyoda's version of the story is notable for the use it makes of the long take. It is introduced at moments of moral crisis in order to invite both our visual and intellectual scrutiny of the given individual's plight.

A number of scenes in the film show how Toyoda brings his characteristic methods to bear on his version of Kafu's work, always with an aim to improve on the dramatic element in the text.

The opening two sequences offer good examples of this. They do more than establish the historical and geographic milieux of the film: they cue us into one of its controlling metaphors and the narrator's functions. During the credits, a series of prints offers views, first of an unspoiled Sumida River, then of life and manners in the red-light district. At the same time, the non-diegetic sounds on the sound track combine samisen and Western music in support of our sense of changes rapidly taking place along this river.

Our general impression of both milieux is particularized when static pictures suddenly yield to actual river scenery. A small steamer confirms the motif of change suggested on the sound track. A subtitle gives the year as 1946. The following six shots particularize the locale described by the narrator in voice-over. An initial long shot shows him crossing the river as he names his destination: east of the river Sumida. The rest of the shots take cues from his narration as he enters the Tamanoi Licensed Quarter. Pictures do the work of many words given to description in Kafu's novel. The film's narrator speaks his piece in just a few lines:

> What had been the front and rear of the Quarter were quite reversed in recent years. Rows of shops are cluttered on the center street. Prostitutes live in alleys off the street.[29]

Brief as it is, this description serves the director's motif of change. He also counts heavily on the camera's expressive power to convey lots of information in a very few shots. As the narrator enters one of the alleys, the camera pans down to show a ditch.

The last shot of this opening sequence shows the narrator in the tavern: the conversation between the owner and his wife satisfies our curiosity about the narrator's identity: he is the novelist who frequents the quarter seeking material for his books. Toward the end of the shot, the sound track tells us it is raining. A customer looks outside and comments on the downpour.

The narrator's stroll is brief but richly suggestive. The ditch so much in evidence at the outset here will serve as a recurring metaphor. When Jumpei visits Oyuki, he is frequently seen walking along it. At one point, women are seen fanning themselves in the narrow alley that separates the ditch from their quarters. We cannot fail to feel the point of this visual reference: this foul drainage was once a beautiful small canal. Its present condition says much about the shadowy existence of the women who work in this lowest form of licensed quarters. The proprietor of one brothel refers to the ditch as a breeding ground for mosquitoes. Kafu's persona finds reason to consider this pest in a sense poetic. To him, veils of mosquito netting are reminiscent of a longed-for past now vanishing. The uncompromising reality of Toyoda's ditch divests it of any such connotations. The mosquito here is a tormenting bloodsucker—a fit enough image for life in an environment that speaks so clearly of the dismal economic realities as they are known to women like Oyuki.

Toyoda's introduction of the narrator is also significantly different. He starts out as a kind of cultural critic of the red-light district. This makes his profession all the more appropriate for the dramatic role we see him play. As his knowledge increases through frequent "research" trips, so does ours. He returns four times in the role of voice-over narrator, very much like an investigative reporter answering the need of his audience for fuller background detail.

His function that way grows in importance with each appearance. Our second view of him in that role is in the tavern again. He is discussing the pricing structure of the district—how much a customer should pay for various types of services. Jumpei walks in and overhears, just after his first meeting with Oyuki. He has escorted her back to her quarters in the rain. The narrator, all unknowing, is instructing a novice in the ways and means of the Tamanoi. In fact, he puts Jumpei on the road to his first adventure there. Emboldened by what he has heard, and by some sake, Jumpei returns to Oyuki's quarters.

The narrator appears a third time after a scene depicting the plight of Oyuki's sick mother. Four long shots record his stroll down some alleyways of the Tamanoi, giving us a view of an area left derelict, even as other parts of the quarter attempt to modernize. As in the opening sequence, a sound-track mix of samisen and Western music reinforces our visual impressions of a changing, intermingling world. Here the voice-over narration uses Kafu's words for what seems an almost redundant reinforcement of a mood of obvious nostalgia for the vanishing past:

> It seemed to be a rule of the Quarter from four in the afternoon, when the women took their places at the windows, radios and phonographs were forbidden, and it was also against rules to play the samisen. . . . When one strolls in the back

Hiroshi Akutagawa (l) and Fujiko Yamamoto (r) in *A Strange Tale from East of the River* (1960) directed by Shiro Toyoda

alleys, one feels the dreariness associated with the unfashionable, out-of-the way quarter. The figures of women with old-types coiffure, the foul ditch and humming mosquitoes—all of these call up visions of the past with a touch of loneliness. . . .[30]

The narrator's fourth appearance is limited to voice-over. This happens after Oyuki leaves to see a dentist. We see her tiny little room with its wind chime in the window. The chime hangs motionless. This shot speaks clearly of the sultry heat Oyuki must endure in her cramped little space. Jumpei comes in. The camera gradually closes in on him, while the non-diegetic music merges with the narrator's comment: "Outside are the masses. The world. Inside was one individual. Between the world and the individual there was harmony. Why should this have been so?"[31] Why does the scenarist quote these lines from Kafu? In the original, the narrator answers the question for the reader by describing Oyuki's good traits: her youth and feelings for her customers. The film's novelist cum narrator leaves us to answer this question ourselves: what brings Jumpei and Oyuki, the outsider and the insider, together?

From the structural point of view, however, the scene is rather problematic. Throughout the novel, there is no indication that the narrator has come to know Jumpei and Oyuki. Why does his narration suddenly accompany this interior scene to which he has no access? Here we sense self-conscious artistry on the part of the omniscient director. He brings narrator and Jumpei together when each is unaware of the other's actions. The viewer is expected to make the connection by applying the narrator's generalization to Jumpei's and Oyuki's particular experience.

The same rhetorical stance is imposed on us in the following shot, which shows Jumpei outside Oyuki's house. He squats out front, fanning himself. The ditch is seen in the center of the screen. A woman appears screen left. Jumpei casually tells her how hot it is. Toyoda's hallmark deep space registers another customer in the back alley, far in the background. This single shot confirms the degree of Jumpei's involvement with Oyuki: he is very much at home in this sordid world.

The narrator's voice-over offers more commentary, using Kafu's words: "The men who came into the alley had taken off their masks and left behind their pretensions." We, as viewers, judge the truth of his remarks on the basis of what we know about Jumpei's relationship with Oyuki. Like Kafu's couple, they are presented in an ironic context. Earlier events have emphasized Jumpei's growing intimacy with Oyuki. He has discarded the social mask associated with his academic profession—thanks to his experience of Oyuki's genuine affection, a thing so unexpected in a woman in her profession.

As in the novel, their growing intimacy leads Oyuki to suggest getting married. Toyoda deftly conveys the logic of that idea in the single shot of Jumpei at ease in the Tamanoi. Unfortunately, this confident romance is compromised by an element of deception. Jumpei, like Kafu's persona, has no intention of revealing his real identity to Oyuki.

Hiroshi Akutagawa (l) and Fujiko Yamamoto (r) in *A Strange Tale from East of the River* (1960) directed by Shiro Toyoda. Courtesy of the Kawakita Memorial Film Institute.

While Kafu's heroine assumes that her lover is some kind of pornographer, her counterpart in the film has a vague idea of Jumpei's status. She believes that he is from the respectable class, but never asks. All that matters is that she thinks him "a reliable person." Even so, at this point it is already suggested that this relationship must inevitably founder on the man's deceit.

The narrator's presence continues to reinforce that inevitability. The following single shot shows the narrator's favorite spot: the tavern. He sits at the counter in the foreground. A man seated between them puts Oyuki in the background. That man moves screen right, leaving an obviously significant space between the narrator and Oyuki.

We see that they are not acquainted. The space between them confirms the narrator in his role as detached observer whose job it is to draw the women out in order to learn about their experiences. His voice-over narration quotes Kafu again: "Once a woman leaves her old profession, with a man's help, and begins to think herself no longer lowly, she will change into a slovenly or a fiery wife beyond control. . . . It is cruel for me to let her know it. . . ."

Even as we hear this, we see Oyuki smile. The irony is there, speaking to us. All we have to do is apply the narrator's comments to the particulars of Oyuki's life. We know that her happy face expresses the pleasure she feels at having entered this tavern, not to treat herself to a drink, but to order shaved ice for Jumpei. Like a loving, caring wife, she enjoys the very idea of surprising her man with his favorite summertime treat. We see that, even as the narrator gives us reason to know that this very joy will turn out to belong to a world of wishful thinking on Oyuki's part. The narrator comments again on the fate of women in the final sequence, analyzed below.

Toyoda's narrator guides us from stage to stage in this chance encounter summer romance ending in early autumn—much the same as in Kafu's *Strange Tale*. Yet Kafu's uneventful ending changes in the film to outright melodrama. The Jumpei-Oyuki romance borrows complications from the Jumpei-Sumiko liaison of the novel. Toyoda adds a troubled relationship between Oyuki and her mother and uncle. And, finally, Oyuki lies dying in the hospital.

After the film's opening voice-over, several events map out Toyoda's narrative strategy: Oyuki's chance encounter with Jumpei and their first love affair are followed by the boatman Otokichi's visit with Oyuki. Then the camera cross-cuts to Jumpei on his way home; another cross-cut shows his wife, Mitsuko, there. A series of descriptive shots shows the life of the married couple in detail. Cross-cutting takes us back to events on the street in the Tamanoi District and in Oyuki's house.

Each time the Tamanoi scene elucidates Oyuki's deeper involvement with Jumpei, cross-cutting takes us home with him or elsewhere. This way, we learn much more about Jumpei's attraction to Oyuki—and about his neglected wife and her spirited attempt to win her husband back. His indecisive deceitfulness also becomes more familiar as he vacillates, torn by commitments to both women.

By varying the scene this way, Toyoda enlarges our sense of the forces arrayed against a woman like Oyuki. We know more about her predicament, especially the element of betrayal, than she does. That knowledge intensifies our sense of Oyuki's victimization. Toyoda makes sure that we are spared none of the cruel ironies involved.

His depiction of events at Oyuki's house hints persistently at her coming misfortunes. This narrative pattern shows how Toyoda's stylistic hallmark—the long take and deep focus—are superbly incorporated into the context of this film.

Take, for example, his handling of Jumpei's return to Oyuki's house the day they met. We last saw Jumpei in the tavern, a novice in the Tamanoi. Now he comes to the ditch outside Oyuki's house. Another prostitute is catching mudfish in the overflow caused by the same downpour that brought Jumpei and Oyuki together.

This deft cross-reference of narrative is enriched by a suggestion his Japanese audience can be counted on to catch: mudfish having clear associations with polluted waterways and very poor fare for the table. The woman's catch is all of a piece with the miserable surroundings surveyed as the film began.

The camera cuts to Jumpei and Oyuki inside her door. Oyuki closes the door within the same shot. The following long take offers two spaces for cinematic action. At first, Oyuki and Jumpei are shown in a long shot with the doorway in the background. They enter the room in the foreground, then move to sit on opposite sides of a charcoal brazier.

The camera's long gaze records the progress of their intimacy. Oyuki begins to eat a quick dinner. Jumpei moves closer, clearly growing passionate. The camera closes in on them as the sound track adds a lyrical touch.

Oyuki's casual reference to his smelling of sake speaks for his inexperience. Only a drink could give him the courage to approach a woman of the Tamanoi. Even now, he is stymied, gazing abashed at Oyuki. Yet she knows what to do. Oyuki stands up and moves in the foreground to get tea. The camera studies the progress of their mutual interest in the next few shots. All are in medium close-up, in reverse-field setup. The rest of the sequence takes us to Oyuki's room upstairs where Jumpei succumbs to her charms.

That sequence is followed by a three-shot scene of a visit to Oyuki by a boatman. He is sent by her uncle to get money for her mother's hospitalization. Brief it may be, the scene clearly shows Oyuki victimized by poverty. We know by this point that she has come down in the world, having begun as a geisha at Utsunomiya. Now we see how even within the family she is a victim of male exploitation. Her uncle, rather than helping his own sister, counts on Oyuki to pay for all her mother's medical costs.

The last shot shows Oyuki moving screen right, closer to the boatman in order to give him money. Both of them are centered in a wide-screen space that calls attention to Oyuki's impoverished surroundings. The dingy, sparsely fur-

Fujiko Yamamoto (l) and Masao Oda (r) in *A Strange Tale from East of the River* (1960) directed by Shiro Yoyoda. Courtesy of the Kawakita Memorial Film Institute.

nished downstairs room says all about the plight of the woman who must capitalize on her physical charms. Will Taneda, her new customer, be able to rescue her?

Toyoda does not keep us in suspense for long. Three long shots follow Jumpei as he crosses a bridge, walks along the river, and turns down a footpath as the street lamps are being lit for the night.

We assume that he is going home after his visit to Oyuki. The next long take confirms that assumption by introducing us to a surprising new aspect of this man's family life. First we see Jumpei's wife, Mitsuko, in the entryway of their house with another man. He is Endo, the Takuma family's butler.

Toyoda's characteristic deep-space view offers us a glimpse of the living room in the foreground. We see the house of an ordinary middle-class family. They are nothing like well-off. Husband and wife enter the living room and seat themselves. Their conversation tells us much that we are eager to know. Much of Kafu's original is here. Sumiko was a maid in the Takuma household until she got pregnant by the head of the family. The Takumas did the respectable thing: married the girl off to the serving man-student Jumpei, also a member of the household. Sumiko's child, Minoru, is passed off as Jumpei's son, though the Takuma family gives the couple a generous monthly allowance for his maintenance. We also learn that Jumpei has a habit of getting home late and that Sumiko is a fanatic member of a new religious sect.

The rest of the sequence confirms the unhappy impression we have of this marriage. Jumpei waylays Endo in the doorway. Having seen Jumpei making his way home from the Tamanoi so short a time ago, we now see him acting the part of pater familias. A close-up studies his look of anguished embarrassment, having to deal with the butler of a family whose financial power touches his small life so directly. He is, after all, just a teacher in a night school; his salary does not go far toward making ends meet.

Our sense of rift between husband and wife is confirmed when Mitsuko leaves and closes the door. A cut to another room shows her frantically beating a prayer drum near her sleeping child.

Oyuki knows none of this. It is we who see how Jumpei's troubled domestic life and chronic need of money bode ill for the lowly prostitute who has been so kind to him. In due course we see how Jumpei's very desperation leads him to seek solace in Oyuki's company—and to lead her that much more astray in her hope of marriage and rescue from the sordid trade to which she is enslaved.

The cinematic pattern of cross-cuts between Oyuki's quarters and another location is powerfully demonstrated in the middle of the film. Consider the sequence that immediately follows the fourth tavern scene, where Oyuki is shown in the narrator's presence. First we see a shot of the proprietor of Oyuki's house sitting downstairs with Jumpei. Oyuki returns from the dentist. A tooth must be extracted to prevent septicemia. Suddenly the sound track features a sinister variation on the lyrical music used for her trysts with Jumpei. We sense the change but do not yet know its meaning.

Several shots later, another long take is introduced. It lasts two minutes and forty seconds. Again, deep focus defines two areas of cinematic action. Jumpei is in the background near a tiny sink. Oyuki is in the foreground at a tiny dining table. She tells him to bring a tea kettle so they can eat together. Jumpei acts like a husband, not a customer.

The long-shot duration corresponds to Jumpei's changed situation; he is that settled-in here. Oyuki wears a housewifely apron. They smile across the table at one another. She dishes him his favorite food. This is when Oyuki announces her intention to open an *oden* (hotch potch) store. She is counting on him to help her. Again, they look like husband and wife, not customer and prostitute.

The sinister music plays again, however. It offers a poignant contrast with the happy mood created by Jumpei's concern. He says she really must have her tooth extracted as soon as possible because septicemia can sometimes cause death.

Then casually he asks why they no longer hear the *koto* being played next door. Just as matter of factly, Oyuki replies that the prostitute Omachi, who played it, has died. Oyuki's toothache and Omachi's death appear to be equally inconsequential in their lives; yet both come to have far greater significance in the film's overall narrative pattern. Jumpei's warning will come true; and Oyuki's fate will be like Omachi's. (Earlier the tubercular Omachi is shown playing the small *koto* and singing a song about a woman yearning for her lover. The woman in the song has been deserted by her lover, as Oyuki will be.) They are briefly sad for Omachi's sake and then quickly happy together again.

The lovers' happy mood is sustained in the following scene with Oyuki and the boatman. She cheerfully tells him of her plans to begin a new life with her lover. The sound track continues to echo that hope.

But a cross-cut takes us to a scene destined to have dire consequences for Oyuki's dream of happiness. We see Jumpei and Mitsuko in the respectable living room of his colleague Yamana. This scene consists of one long take that lasts a little more then two minutes. The camera draws back as Yamana denounces Jumpei as a philanderer. Yamana's wife leaves so that our attention is focused fully on Jumpei and Mitsuko as they confront this threat to the respectability of their family. The scene ends with Mitsuko's declaration that she will win her husband back from this other woman. As she says, she has the bond of matrimony on her side.

The following scene shows Mitsuko acting on her decision. Given what we have seen of the couple's unhappy wedded life, we expect a measure of confrontational behavior. On the contrary, Mitsuko is seen trying to beat the prostitute at her own game, by reviving her husband's appreciation of her charms.

This scene consists of several shots, two of them long takes rather weighty in effect. In the first, Mitsuko offers Jumpei money, the child's monthly allowance from the Takuma family. She wants him to give it to Oyuki as heart balm. Mitsuko also renounces her commitment to the religious sect her husband hates so much.

Jumpei, shown facing her, moves to sit in a chair. Mitsuko moves toward him. The camera closes in as Mitsuko asks how she is different from Oyuki in . . . Her voice tails off, so Jumpei can pretend not to have caught her drift. His emotional reaction is hinted at, however, by music suddenly introduced on the sound track. Its low register and tremulous character speak for his agitated uncertainty. He gets up and leaves when she asks what that woman does for him. Mitsuko's smiling face closes this shot.

An immediate second long take shows Jumpei in the background, in the kitchen. He enters the living room in the foreground to join his wife. She closes the room partition all the way so that they are aligned against it.

The camera studies her attempt to seduce her husband. The ambiguous expression she hinted at in the previous take is clarified now, as she plays the coquette, gazing into his eyes and asking if she has really lost what he used to like.

Her success is conveyed by his motion falling on her, leaving only the room partition to dominate the screen. The lyrical sound track removes any lingering doubt about Mitsuko's conversion from religious fanatic to seductress. In the next scene, narrative legibility is served by Mitsuko herself speaking proudly of marital harmony restored.

Kafu's novel ends with a dissolve. Oe and Oyuki part company. The question of the effect of this on Oyuki's fate is simply left to the narrator's conjuncture. Toyoda deals with the end of the affair in much greater detail. He is not afraid to use melodrama in service of his theme.

Oyuki's fortunes begin to decline the moment her lover succumbs to his wife. Toyoda takes us directly from that scene to the funeral of Oyuki's mother. Already her suffering is burdened with additional ironies. She arrives thinking to visit a sick mother and finds her already in a coffin, being taken away on her uncle's boat. She is accused of having neglected her mother. Only at this moment does she learn that her friend, the boatman, has taken the money she sent and spent it on licensed-quarter pleasures.

Oyuki's loss of faith in men is reinforced by her last meeting with Jumpei. Now a sense of change is visible everywhere. A new maid is working busily. A new girl accosts a customer. The camera studies Oyuki's sudden transformation. She is drunk. For the first time, she upbraids him for being away so long. Sinister music anticipates the inevitable outcome. Oyuki comes to the foreground. Her face in close-up hardens in anger as she speaks of her loss of faith in everyone. The scene ends with a shot of her collapsing on the stairway.

What will happen to Oyuki after this incident? How will Jumpei fare after their final meeting? Again, this director wastes no time satisfying our curiosity. He cross-cuts between Jumpei's house and the hospital, where Oyuki lies dying.

The household scene contains only one long take of three minutes and seven seconds. Jumpei's restlessness is conveyed quite literally. He shifts in his chair, clearly jittery. Mitsuko draws the curtains against an air raid. We sense a correspondence between the dimmed light and his obvious depression. As Mitsuko comes near, he moves away. He goes to the bookcase. He paces the room. Finally he closes the room partition and confronts her.

The camera pans left to show them standing. Jumpei sits down and asks his wife to be seated, too. For the first time, he speaks his mind: he wants to beg forgiveness, both from her and from Oyuki. He has toyed with both their feelings. The nature of Mitsuko's reaction is left to conjecture when she leaves without a word, closing the door behind her.

The ensuing hospital scene is charged with melodrama. It takes up the motifs of betrayal, desertion, and death itself. It is shot in one long take lasting five minutes. As in the previous scene, an air raid is used to enlarge the context of gloom and doom. Even the room Oyuki dies in must be darkened by forces far beyond her power to change.

Again, deep space is used to draw our attention, not only the condition of the room, but the commotion in it. Nurses scurry down the corridor in the background. Two beds occupy the space screen right. Oyuki's bed in the foreground is attended by a nurse and the boatman. It is of course a public ward, the kind of hospital space the poor die in. Sinister music and blackout-curtained darkness set the tone for Oyuki's final contact with those who betrayed her.

The camera closes in on Oyuki and her uncle. He accuses "that man" for having failed to visit her. Here, through Oyuki's own admission, we are keenly reminded that the relationship built on deception has had a damaging effect on her life: she has never asked Jumpei's name, profession, or address; and he has never volunteered that information.

Our knowledge of Jumpei's yearning to ask forgiveness gives Oyuki's words a cruelly ironic twist. The camera moves screen right to single her out in close-up. The quietly sinister music persists. We see her one last smile and hear her say that she will work harder if she lives.

The camera cuts once more to Jumpei's house. Mitsuko is seen adjusting the curtain to make sure no light is leaking out. Jumpei ignores her request for help. She grows angry. The shadow of discord falls across the domestic harmony restored in the previous scene. Jumpei steps out into the garden. Sweet music steals in—the same music used to accompany his happy time with Oyuki. Clearly, Jumpei will be haunted by a sense of loss for the rest of his life. Less clear is the nature of his future relations with his wife. That is left to conjecture.

The final sequence features the narrator, whose knowledge of the manners and mores of the licensed district helps provide convincing closure to this melodrama. Yet that effect seems damaged by a sudden challenge to our assumptions about that knowledge.

The sequence opens with a shot of Oyuki in bed, tears streaming down her face, while the narrator says in voice-over that he has heard a rumor that Oyuki is dying. We have been given no reason to believe that he knows Oyuki, so naturally we are left wondering about the progress of his research. As it is, we must accept his closing remarks as proof of a link between him and the woman whose plight he commiserates. Sorrowful music announces her death as two freeze frames show us her face.

The narrator is seen walking along the street near the ditch. This image, used so often now, has a feel of coming full circle. The ditch remains a ditch, just as the Tamanoi remains the Tamanoi. The women who work there come and go; but the system that enslaves them never seems to change, not with any amount of modernization. The narrator's walk along the ditch echoes the view and viewpoint of the opening sequence. That sadness is here, more poignant now that we know Oyuki's story.

Taking the narrator's point of view, the camera pans to the women's faces in the windows. It pans from face to face. Each one solicits the passer-by. Here, for the first time, the narrator goes beyond mere data collecting. He tries to read these faces, to tell us what they express:

> These faces in the shadows, though looking despondent, lacked sadness. Is it because they have outgrown the sadness of their fate, having realized that there is nothing they can do about it? . . .

This lateral pan with no cut underscores the truth of the narrator's comments with admirable economy. Oyuki's tragedy is shared by all these women. It's as simple as that, and as sad. But do we, the viewers of this film, feel free to grow away from the sadness of this awful truth? The pan yields to a long shot of the narrator walking away from the camera as he continues on his stroll. Deep focus shows only a few customers in the background.

Brief as it is, the shot clearly offers another twist of irony: air raids make for slow business in the Tamanoi. The camera pans to the faces of the women once more. One thickly powdered face after another invites us to ponder the nature of this fate.

Unlike the novel, Toyoda's *A Strange Story from East of the River* has a closed text. The novelist's research is now complete. He has gained valuable information on the case history of one Oyuki. He is more educated now. He is more sympathetic, more human, more than merely a novelist on the lookout to satisfy a novelist's curiosity. His final voice-over narration is well calculated to end such a melodramatic film, but it is also, in effect, a personal, elegiac tribute to Oyuki: "Never before has the Tamanoi District moved me so deeply as tonight."

Critic Tadao Sato offers this interesting comment on a weakness in this film: "The prostitute and the guest, played by Fujiko Yamamoto and Hiroshi Akutagawa respectively, appear to be elegant dolls. They are in stark contrast with the narrator who is much more deeply rooted in realism."[32]

As in so many Toyoda films, *A Strange Story from East of the River* depicts a woman's search for the identity she can live with. He has made good use of a difficult source, changing Kafu's novel to suit his thematic purposes. Like Kafu's novelist, and like his own narrator, Toyoda turns a studious gaze on a difficult reality: the manners and mores of a lowly pleasure district. In his case, of course, it is a filmic gaze, intelligent and compassionate.

Notes

1. Steven D. Carter, "What's So Strange about *A Strange Tale*? Kafu's Narrative Persona in *Bokuto Kidan*," *Journal of the Association of Teachers of Japanese* 22, no. 2 (1988): 152.

2. Donald Keene, *Dawn to the West: Japanese Literature of the Modern Era*, vol. 1 (New York: Holt, Rinehart and Winston, 1984), p. 433.
3. Ibid, p. 434.
4. Carter, "What's So Strange," p. 153.
5. Edward Seidensticker, *Kafu the Scribbler: The Life and Writings of Nagai Kafu*, 1879–1959 (Stanford: Stanford University Press, 1965), p. 278. Copyright © by Stanford University Press. All the translations quoted here are Seidensticker's.
6. For a comprehensive study of Kafu's creation of the persona, see Carter, "What's So Strange."
7. For a biographical study of this novel, see Koichi Isoda, *Nagai Kafu* (Kafu Nagai) (Tokyo: Kodansha, 1979), pp. 224–51; and Saburo Kawamoto, *Kafu to Tokyo: Danchotei nichijo shichu* (Kafu and Tokyo: Personal thoughts about *Dyspepsia House Days*) (Tokyo: Toshi Shuppan, 1996), pp. 396–433.
8. Kafu Nagai, *Daichotei nichijo* (Dyspepsia house days), vol. 23 of *Kafu zenshu* (A complete collection of Kafu's works) (Tokyo: Iwanami, 1993), p. 457.
9. Quoted by Amao Takemori in "Kaisetsu" (Commentary); Kafu Nagai, *Bokuto kidan* (A strange tale from east of the river) (Tokyo: Iwanami, 1947), p. 176.
10. Kafu Nagai, "Bokuto kidan zeigen" (Afterthoughts on *A Strange Tale from East of the River*), in Kafu, *Bokuto kidan*, p. 151.
11. Seidensticker, *Kafu the Scribbler*, pp. 279–80.
12. Carter writes that this name came from one of Nagai's own relatives. See Carter, "What's So Strange," p. 153.
13. Seidensticker, *Kafu the Scribbler*, p. 286.
14. Ibid., pp. 291–92.
15. For a concise discussion of Shunsui Tamenaga's contributions to popular literature in the Edo period, see Edward Pulchar, *Japanese Literature: A Historical Outline* (Tucson: University of Arizona Press, 1973), pp. 166–68.
16. Seidensticker, *Kafu the Scribbler*, p. 292.
17. Ibid., p. 302.
18. Ibid., pp. 303–4.
19. Ibid., p. 309.
20. Ibid., pp. 321–22.
21. Ibid., pp. 309–10.
22. Ibid., p. 321.
23. Ibid.
24. Ibid., pp. 326–27.
25. Ibid., p. 327.
26. Moriyasu Masafumi: *Nagai Kafu: Hikage no bungaku* (Kafu Nagai: literature on shadowy existence) (Tokyo: Kokusho Kankokai, 1981), p. 256.
27. Seidensticker, *Kofu the Scribbler*, pp. 327–28.
28. For an analysis of Kafu's use of irony at the end of the novel, see Carter, "What's So Strange," pp. 164–65.
29. The first line is Seidensticker's translation because the scenarist Toshio Yasumi borrows Kafu's line. The rest is my translation.
30. Seidensticker, *Kofu the Scribbler*, p. 309.
31. Ibid., p. 321.
32. Tadao Sato, *Nihon eiga no kyoshotachi* (The master directors of Japanese cinema) (Tokyo: Gakuyoshobo, 1979), p. 218.

11

Living the Postwar Life: Naruse's
Older Brother, Younger Sister (1953)

Saisei Muro's "Ani Imoto" (Older brother, younger sister) was given the prestigious Literary Confab Club Award the year after it was published in 1934. In retrospect, it is easy to see how this story spoke to the zeitgeist of a Japan caught up in its version of worldwide depression and social upheaval.

Muro's characters are undeniably low class, though honest and good in their hard-pressed way. Not that their virtues are the least bit glamorized. Muro deals directly with the rough-and-tough exterior of these down-and-outers. Their language and manners, as we later see, can be shockingly crude. Yet the story also reveals some complex psychological realities masked by hard facts of life. Muro shows, for example, how hard it can be for such people to deal directly with such tricky emotions as family love and loyalty.

Japanese cinema had fixed its attention on family relations from its earliest days. Muro's story offered a new venue and approach: contemporary low-life family drama vividly portrayed. Sotoji Kimura adapted the work for the screen in 1936, seventeen years after which Mikio Naruse expressed his admiration for that film and the original story by making a version of his own.[1]

Audie Bock sees Naruse's *Older Brother, Younger Sister* as "one of the few instances in which a remake has done better critically than the original."[2] It is an interesting claim, though it needs to be qualified somewhat.

Although the original short story is, in fact, rather plotless, it does put forward a concise, rather concentrated study of lower-class family relationships enlivened by the novelist's deft movement in and out of each character's innermost thoughts and feelings. Though he often appears to ignore the psychological dimensions of the original, Naruse succeeds remarkably well in approaching the novelist's thematic focus from a new perspective.

To begin with, the film counts heavily on the principle of addition and expansion in character, settings, and narrative events. This is especially noteworthy, given the limitations of the short story genre used by Muro. Naruse also aims for historical immediacy by moving from prewar to postwar Japan. Thus the film illustrates conflicts of values in a social context often referred to as a "community in transition." The resulting contrast between characters is particularly notable where the two sisters in the story are concerned.

The original story shows what Muro offered Naruse in the way of material suitable for shifting forward in this way. "Older Brother, Younger Sister" marked a turning point in Muro's career as a writer. It showed him abandoning a lyrical style in favor of something very like its opposite. The labels used by critics for this latter style are telling in themselves. Many call it *shiseiki-mono*, freely translated as "a piece on streetwise devils." Similarly, another label, *chimata no bungaku*, could be rendered simply "street lit."

Both labels point to Muro's choice of low-life settings and subject matter depicted unsparingly, but not despairingly. Unlike many "naturalistic" writers, Muro sees men and women not so much foredoomed by circumstance as rising to its challenges. His characters exhibit a kind of desperate energy that argues for survival, come what may. Their very roughness derives from a wild, instinctive response to life that Muro clearly admires, finding in it a "genuinely human quality."[3]

In "Older Brother, Younger Sister," Muro's archetypal patriarch, Akaza, is the boss of a river construction crew. The portrayal of his character and his attitude to wife and children easily take precedence over plot and action in this story. Muro gives us a definitive glimpse of Akaza's down-to-earth character in the opening sentence of his tale: "Akaza 'lived' naked on the bank of the river throughout the year."

That notion expands as we learn of Akaza's work and fame as a craftsman in charge of shaping the channel of the river. Every barrage built under his supervision has to be done just so. Crew members guilty of the slightest negligence are dismissed on the spot. Akaza himself is a rough-hewn equivalent of a river god, and no one is more at home in the water than he is. No one can fish as well as he does, wielding a bamboo spear, and he is even said to swim "like a fish."

Whereas Akaza is seen in the rough, as a man of all seasons outdoors, his wife, Riki, is a creature of indoor life, a gentle woman loved by all the river crew, who call her "Mother Buddha."

Yet there is nothing pious or prosaic in Muro's depiction of this couple. Scraps of their conversation show them speaking plainly of everyday things. Akaza asks if their elder daughter, Mon, has come home yet. "Nope," says Riki. Well then, has Inosuke, their only son, gone to work? Mother Buddha Riki offers no excuse for the ne'er-do-well son. All he's done so far that day, she says, is goof off and sleep.

The narrational rhythm achieves a careful balance as Muro proceeds to expand on our knowledge of this family's life. Evidence quickly accumulates in confirmation of the couple's brief exchange. Sure enough, two of their three offspring are headed for disaster.

Inosuke is a good-for-nothing wastrel and womanizer, gifted as he is as a gravestone engraver. Mon is the black sheep. While working as a temple maidservant, she met a student who got her pregnant. That mistake has led to others: a string of casual affairs and moves from job to job. She appears to have settled for life as it is known to a loose-living waitress and barmaid.

At first glance, the family's troubles appear to be resolved by a characteristic underclass expedient: lowering expectations to match abandoned hopes. Conflict seems an accepted part of the daily routine. Each member of the family seems almost indifferent to the trouble the family is in. Yet things are not what they seem. Under the surface, these common people are deeply disturbed.

A stranger arrives to bring matters out in the open. He is Obata, the student who fathered Mon's stillborn child. He comes from a very different social sphere, yet Muro uses him to get below the surface of low-life experience. Thanks to this callow, rather pathetic fellow, Muro helps us see what he calls "the genuine human quality" of the love-hate instincts at work in Akaza's family.

The old man's reaction to Obata is a mixture of feelings past and present. The young man's coming revives the pain Akaza felt during his daughter's disgraceful pregnancy and sorrowful delivery of a child born dead. Now the old man must witness Obata's obvious relief to learn of that outcome—convenient as it is, given the social differences and all. Akaza is forced to know the child's father for what he is: an apparently sincere, weak-willed young man who nevertheless knows something about the ways of the world.

The novelist deliberately avoids direct discourse in describing Akaza's recollections. In fact, Muro gives the old man's past experience a feeling of immediacy by using a kind of interior monologue. Thus, when he recalls a scene between his disgraced daughter and her layabout brother, we find it given in this form:

> Ino stood over the quilt bed where Mon was lying. He looked like someone getting ready to handle filth. Look what happened when she flirted with her beau, the sniveling slut. Look at that fat belly. Better get rid of the thing before it pops out a dog or bird or whatever the hell it is. Who wants to listen to her brat howling all night anyway? Bastard brat of that bastard greenhorn student. Ino yelled on and on. . . . [4]

Muro does not spare the unpleasant details when he gives us Akaza's memories of that time of sibling rivalry. As before, the father remembers one of Ino's rages in interior monologue:

> How could an ugly duckling like you have the gall to flirt with any man alive? Makes me puke to think about it. At least your bastard loverboy is ten times smarter than you. Took what he wanted then dumped you for damn sure. He knew what a useless slut you are. . . . Now everybody will despise you as your belly swells on up and you pop out a bastard. . . . Better take your bastard brat and get out of town. Go to Tokyo. End up in a wallow like the fat sow you are![5]

Akaza remembers his daughter talking up for herself in the very same vein. She tells her brother he's a fine one to talk. "You're loose as a goose yourself, aren't you? How many women have you knocked up—then made them wipe your precious ass? . . . Why do you always have to treat me like a dirty puppy?"

The mother, of course, does try to come between her raging children. The echo of her goodness in this family is the younger daughter, San; however, Muro makes little use of her. Ino does hold her up to Mon as a model daughter and sister: one who works as a maid and keeps her virtue, too; one who never comes home without bringing the family a little gift or two. Furious, foul-mouthed, and un-ideal as he himself is, Ino clearly admires San's dutiful character.

Akaza's recollection of domestic discord quickly impinges on the present, though with an unexpected result. His original intention was to take Obata out to the river and there (as he thinks of it) "beat the hell out of this bastard as a price a young man has to pay for making a mess of his daughter's life." As it turns out, Akaza finds himself pitying Obata, thinking of him as a bumbling youth, a snot-nosed shaveling, not a suave Don Juan. Instead of bruising his daughter's seducer, the old man finds himself giving him a lick or two of plain-speaking good advice.

Muro conveys this psychological shift through Akaza's fatherly warning: "Mister Obata, you better think twice before you get another woman in this kind of trouble. You got off easy this time, that's all. Don't do it again." Simple as they are, his words convey a fund of genuine human kindness underneath this workingman's rough exterior.

His wife's reaction to her husband's change of heart fosters a subtle bond between her and the timid young man who has wronged her daughter. Riki's first reaction is relief that Akaza did not punish Obata after all. She, too, remembers the past for our benefit. We learn that she herself used to be a target for Akaza's abusive belief that "a beating works ten times better than talking."

Riki yearns to speak to Obata before he leaves, but the situation is so awkward. The young man senses her goodwill, and some simple facts of nature do the rest: they speak about the flowers Riki is growing.

The old couple's conciliatory attitude is in marked contrast to Ino's. His intentions toward Obata give this quiet story one of its few dramatic highlights. Again, Muro draws on animal imagery to convey a sense of low-life behavior. Hearing that Obata is walking toward the station, Ino follows, his face a mask of "animal" rage. Obata feels that the man following behind is getting ready to "jump" him; he feels hunted, trapped.

Again, we get a sense of Ino's state of being through interior monologue. This time, we learn of a brother's unexpressed love for a sister in disgrace. Suddenly it surfaces as Ino gives memory words: "I used to let her cuddle up to me when she was just a kid . . . I know everything about her, even that secret scar. . . ."[6]

As he thinks about his reasons for wanting to beat up the father of his sister's child, we discover Ino's secret:

> When she came home pregnant with your brat, I treated her like shit, like a dirty bitch. . . . I did it so mother would take up for Mon, so she wouldn't be thrown out of the house and told to get lost.[7]

Again, the notion of giving Obata a beating yields to a strain of basic humanity somehow ingrained in this rough-and-tough family. Ino begins by slapping the defenseless Obata's face and pushing him to the ground. Then, the same as his father, he relents in the face of Obata's obviously sincere remorse and acceptance of all the blame for what happened. Feeling somewhat ashamed of himself, Ino tells the young man where to find the bus stop.

Still, the climax of Muro's story adds a final confrontation between brother and sister. Mon is furious when she hears that Ino has hit the father of her child. She calls him every name she can think of. Again, their shouting match is a shocking display of basic emotions stripped of any pretense of civilized behavior. We learn still more about the life Mon has led since her disgrace. Riki registers our sense of the situation. Shocked by the violence of Mon's language, "she was terrified to think what kind of life her daughter must have been leading in the city."

Worse is to come. Brother and sister attack one another physically. Animal imagery abounds as Muro describes their grapplings. Mon rakes Ino's face with her nails, "leaving three scratches, each dripping blood as red as silverberries." For his part, he knocks her flat every time she returns to the attack. Finally, having shouted herself hoarse, Mon tells Ino over and over again to go ahead and kill her. She is so furiously fought out, her voice, Muro says, sounds like "the croaking of a frog."

Yet even now, furious and degraded as she is, Mon surprises us with what amounts to a declaration of love as it is known in this embattled family. After the fight, she says: "I came home because I wanted to see you, Mother. I also wanted to see my brother, even though he is such a despicable person."

The end of Muro's tale reaffirms the close connection between Akaza's lowly status in life and his work close to nature. It is as if his bond with the river transcends the petty discords of his domestic life. He is seen naked aboard one of seven barges laden with stones. He is a leader of men and commander of one of nature's most elemental forces. Nature in his view is personified: "The river water looks despondent and sorrowful when its force is checked with stones. But the water, momentarily held in check, flows into any outlet violently, as if angry." Muro's last tribute to this hard-working man's zest for living is refreshingly concise: "Akaza ordered his men to fill the outlet with stones. At that moment his rough-hewn body stood like a monument to the work of all aboard the ship, the very hair on his chest bristling with all that energy."[8]

As we have seen, Muro's work focuses the reader's attention on the rawly human aspects of life among the lowly in the author's own day. He may deal in the main with the common man, yet his work speaks to the sociocultural milieu of the Taisho period.

Naruse brings Muro's tale forward in time, to the so-called postwar period of the 1950s, when the film was being made. At the same time, he somewhat elevates the social status of the characters. Riki is no longer just the obedient peacemaker housewife of a riverboat ruffian. She owns and runs a tiny eatery on the banks of the river. Mon's sister, San, now works in a factory in a nearby town. These changes smooth away some of the low-life vulgarity so much a part of Muro's characters. In fact, the critic Heiichi Sugiyama considers Naruse's family *shomin*, common people belonging to the lower middle class:

Suppressing their vulgarity, itself a charming character trait, Naruse focuses on their life as common folk—the subject he feels most at home with. Father, mother, brother and sisters are all treated with as much nostalgia as if they were his own neighbors. Then too, he avoids delving into their lives, as if he were respecting the privacy of neighbors. For these reasons, his film is lighthearted and lacks the tenacious intensity which runs through the original.[9]

Given this somewhat different historical setting and social status, Naruse's screen version focuses on a rather different central problem as well: how each family member copes with a society in the throes of transformation.

Thus San's character, left unexplored in Muro's story, is fully developed in the film. She is still the model decent and dutiful daughter. But now she is set in conflict with an elder sister destroyed by big-city values—those of postwar Tokyo. This shift is not surprising. Naruse had dealt with women's struggle in such earlier works as *Meshi* (Repast, 1951), *Okasan* (Mother, 1952), and *Inazuma* (Lightning, 1952). Instead of focusing on life and family troubles presented mostly through Akaza's recollections, the film dramatizes the effect on family life of two sisters locked in conflict.

Similarly, Muro's original makes the most of a quality intrinsic to literature: the psychological rendition of Akaza's mind as seen through his character. Naruse drops that complex narrational device, letting filmic qualities do its work. Action and speech give cues to thought and feeling here. Naruse also challenges Ozu's hallmark narrational device of uninhabited landscape charged with emotional overtones. Instead, Naruse's camera cuts to the river repeatedly, using it as a controlling metaphor he counts on for access to the major characters' inner feelings.

The film's larger frame of reference brings with it a larger spatial dimensions as well. The novelist may content himself with Akaza's immediate surroundings: house, river, and nearby tavern. A director addressing problems of an entire community in transition must be more inclusive. The Akaza family drama plays out by turns in their home and in Riki's eatery. Naruse's stage encompasses the nearby rural community, too: the crowded downtown area near the railroad station, a pachinko parlor, and other shops. We also see life in relation to the noodle factory owned by San's boyfriend Taichi's family. It is found near a bus stop in front of the station.

Naruse wastes no time presenting aspects of a changing society that will pose a challenge to Akaza's family. The opening shot captures the smooth flow of the river in high summer, as if to suggest an aspect of nature unblemished by so much surrounding change. A long shot follows, altering that initial impression. A train is seen crossing the bridge in the distance, though we have yet to see a single soul anywhere along the vast stretch of riverbank.

Then we meet Akaza and his crew, and directly, verbal evidence of change. When Akaza passes near, the older men digging gravel stop work and bow deeply to their boss. The younger men make no such show of respect. Yoshizo, who refers to Akaza as "the boss," talks about their early, hardy days together. Then the men used to jump bodily into the river, laying stones by hand on the bottom. As Akaza continues to inspect the construction site, Yoshizo reminds the young crew members that their boss is a grand old man of the river, a man who overawed crews of seventy men in the good old days. The young men scoff at Kizo's reverent attitude; they liken it to boring old anecdotes in praise of Jirocho, the famous Yakuza boss.

During this opening sequence, a point-of-view shot takes in the river as Akaza sees it flowing smoothly along, echoed by music on the sound track. Clearly, the old man, too, is yearning for the past.

The camera's gaze shifts to the shallows. We see how the river there flows over a concrete bed. Even this body of water, which at first glance we took for pristine, beyond mere human change, has been transformed by encroaching modernization. The camera takes note of change in Akaza, too. He is wrinkled and paunchy, the spit and image of his own profession in decline.

A cut to Riki's eatery on the riverbank tells of a community in transition, too. The building itself is new, but it is little more than a shack. A sign offering shaved ice speaks of catering to visitors from the city, used to this modern luxury. Riki herself is wearing Western clothes, not the kimono of Muro's traditional housewife. Her shirt and loud-patterned skirt are obviously hand-me-downs from her daughters.

Naruse's film teems with visual clues pointing to a rapidly changing society. Young hikers and family picnickers appear again and again on the banks of the river, exhibiting all the signs of the times. Mon in her kimono contrasts with views of San in Western dress and high heels—in one instance, walking down a gravel path through the rural landscape.

At the same time, Naruse's camera is wonderfully adept at paying homage to the age-old customs and manners the Akaza family preserves in the face of so much change. An ancient well with its traditional wooden bucket is an apt metaphor for old Japan. The well remains central to the daily life of the family. Akaza washes there after work. Ino fetches up a small melon cooling in the well and devours it on the spot. Many a Japanese viewer will feel the power of that detail, speaking as it does to childhood memories of melon crisp and well water cold. Even Mon, corrupted as she is by city life, declares that no drink can compare to water from the family well.

Ino is shown wearing his rubber *tabi*-like sneakers (*jikatabi*) common among skilled laborers. Along with a cigarette carried over an ear, they speak of his share in that status at least, Ino being an excellent engraver on stone. His mother also appreciates traditional footwear, such as the *geta* with bamboo soles that San brings her as a souvenir from town. Riki beams with pleasure, saying she has always wanted a pair.

Naruse presents many such contrasting images of old and new as he pursues a narrative contrasting related lines of causality. Both have to do with the daughters coming to terms with their very different lives. We see each coming home and coping with family and community. Mon represents the changeable attitude to values ruled by expediency. San embodies a more time-honored ethos of honesty and moral integrity.

Our first view of the life that Mon has been living in the city comes by indirection, through a kind of trial-by-hometown-gossip. San stops by her boy-friend Taichi's factory on her way home, only to be coolly received by members of his family. As she passes by, she cannot help overhearing Taichi's adoptive mother declaring that this girl's sister, Mon, leads the kind of life that reflects badly on her family's respectability. She goes on to say that San's expenses at nursing school are paid by Mon with money inveigled from various men. Worse yet, we ourselves already know that Mon has been dismissed from her job as a housemaid.

Other evidence of loose living accumulates before we meet Mon herself. San stops by her mother's eatery and mentions something that Taichi's adoptive mother said earlier, namely, that San would be like her sister and take advantage of men. Riki unconsciously confirms the gossip's opinion of her citified daughter, proudly showing San the hand-me-down skirt Mon has given her. The gaudy skirt is defi-nitely not something a really respectable woman would wear.

Another preview of Mon's bad behavior comes in a scene that the filmscript adds to the original story. Ino is seen with his girl friend, busily working one of the machines in the pachinko parlor. His father walks in and tells him to come outside. There, Akaza slaps his son, calling him a loafer. Ino claims that all he was doing was getting out of the house while Mon was there. Akaza's attack on his wayward son is plainly related to his wayward daughter. The scene is brief, but richly suggestive of the stress put on a little town like this by pressures of rapid modernization. The pachinko parlor itself suggests a value judgment on the postwar demand for cheap entertainment.

When Mon appears, she quickly confirms her bad reputation. Worse is to follow as Naruse pursues a larger theme: social ostracism. It begins close to home. San and Riki find Mon packing up to leave when she has just arrived. Already, her brother has succeeded in driving her out.

The subsequent fight between brother and sister retains the offensive lan-guage of the original story. But Naruse adds another element: a modern type of woman actively engaged in mediation. For this, he uses San, making a very real character of Muro's faceless cipher. San defends Mon as her benefactor, the one who has made nursing school possible for her. She also makes a hard-headed, practical suggestion: abortion would ease Mon's immediate problem.

Muro makes very good use of some very plain-speaking dialogue when his characters come in conflict. Naruse counts on the camera's expressive power to get much the same effect. He uses a mixture of shots to study those involved in scenes of domestic violence. We see characters framed together and singled out. Thus, when Mon adamantly refuses to consider having an abortion, a close-up studies her face in tears. She is the very picture of anguish, of rejected lover and daughter and sister. A series of reverse-field shots identifies the emotions of the others present suggested by their demeanor. Ino is unmistakably furious. San and Riki register unhappy helplessness.

Reisaburo Yamamoto (l) and Masayuki Mori (r) in *Older Brother, Younger Sister* (1953) directed by Mikio Naruse. Courtesy of Daici Co. Ltd.

Naruse's version of this conflict between siblings is richer than the novelist's, thanks to the deep bond he creates between the sisters. When Mon does flee the house, the camera cuts to her outside. She is out of frame as Riki and San run to catch up. Music on the sound track intensifies to match San's desperate call to her sister.

The camera cuts suddenly back inside the house. Ino is seen in a medium shot, lounging sullenly on the floor. This glimpse confirms the impression we have had all along, that of a heartless man who cannot tolerate his sister's moral laxity, even while his own behavior is clearly the male equivalent of hers. Naruse, like Muro, has much to gain from repeated reinforcement of our negative view of Ino. He is, in effect, setting us up for the climactic scene. There, as in the short story, we see the deep and abiding love for his sister that Ino takes such care to conceal behind this malevolent facade.

The camera takes us back outdoors. A magnificent long shot captures San's desperation as she runs along the riverbank. Her cry pierces the lonely, looming darkness of the scene, which reduces her to a tiny figure. A series of intercuts shows Mon in flight with San in pursuit. The scene ends with a shot of Mon in tears, squatting by the river. Its flow drowns out the sound of her tears.

The next scene uses the river to restore a sense of balance, referring the flow of its water to the constant passing of time, a metaphor familiar in Japanese literature and film. Here the current moves quietly along, rippling in a late spring breeze. Hikers from the city are seen walking easily along the bank.

Obata's visit in the film, as in the novel, leads to the climactic scene between brother and sister. Naruse follows Muro closely here, though he does modify circumstances somewhat. In place of a *mise en scène* confined to the Akaza house and yard, the film takes place in four locations: family house, Akaza's workplace, Riki's shop, and the country town. This more expansive approach allows the director to highlight changing attitudes toward this outside cause of family discord.

Obata's arrival is preceded by a scene that refers us to the deep bond that exists between mother and daughter. Riki is preparing *oden* (hotch potch) dishes in her shop when San comes in. The girl's devotion to her parents is mentioned in connection with Riki's gratitude for the pan she is using at that moment—bought with money San has given her. The story line is advanced through their mention of Mon. Neither of them has heard from her since the New Year holidays.

Enter Obata himself. He is an awkward youth in an awkward situation. A series of conventional cross-cuts registers the first impressions these three characters have of one another. At first, Riki mistakes Obata for a customer. The camera has scrutinized his timid manner and stammering speech. When it becomes plain who, and what, the young man is, Riki's manner changes abruptly; her hospitable smile becomes a mask of apprehension. When Obata comes out and asks about Mon, Riki's face clearly speaks for the chilly reception this young man will have from her. Another shot confirms this as we see Riki guiding Obata to the family home with every sign of stinting hospitality.

At the house, we see the tension building. As San makes the fire, Obata asks if she is Mon's younger sister. Her back is turned to him, a clear enough sign of her dislike, as is her one curt reply: "Yes." We see how timid the young man is from the way he looks at her back.

Riki, meantime, has run to the river to fetch her husband home. A series of close-ups reveals another dimension of the trouble brewing. Even as Riki warns him not to use violence, we see how furious the old man is.

Again, Naruse follows Muro's dialogue fairly closely in the ensuing confrontation. Again, however, Muro's insightful depiction of Akaza's inner state in words is given vivid visual representation by the camera. Naruse uses a combination of close-ups and medium shots emphasized from time to time by reverse-field setups.

Thus, we have Obata's stammering apology met by Akaza's monosyllabic responses. The old man's indignation shows in the way he smokes his long pipe. A cinematic variation is used to ease the building tension here. Naruse cuts to a little girl bringing a plate of sweets in to Obata. The girl says they come from San. Brief as this interruption is, it speaks for an important change of heart as San thinks about the man who has wronged her sister.

Naruse's use of deep space allows for great economy in his depiction of this tense encounter between parents and newcomer. We see it first as Akaza's anger is met by Obata's boyish naiveté. The young man explains that he could not come to apologize sooner because his parents never let him out of their sight. As he explains, Obata occupies the foreground with Akaza. Riki sits calmly in the middle ground, witnessing this moment of high emotion. In the background, we see the outmoded kitchen stove, itself an icon speaking of the difficult question of status for families like Akaza's, liable as they are to lose ground in a rapidly modernizing Japan.

The filmscript gives Akaza much the same parting warning to the shamefaced young man: "Mr. Obata, you had better stop fooling around, getting women into trouble. You've been spared embarrassment this time. . . ."

In place of Muro's detailed description of the angry father's sudden mellowing, however, Naruse lets the camera explain that change. After Akaza speaks, we see how close to tears he is as he hurries out of the house. The camera keeps its distance, showing him next in a long shot, striding along the river shore. Still, we have clues enough to his emotional state. His hands are thrust deep in his sash, as if helping brace him against defeat. Naruse puts him in the upper left corner of the screen in order to let the river dominate the space. The current runs smoothly along, as if to suggest that this hard-working old man's continuity and source of comfort is this river he has shaped and tended all his life. Inevitable, too, is the age-old time and the river association with flow and change transcending the petty fixes people get themselves into.

Meantime, Obata and Riki are reconciled in much the same way we have seen in Muro's story. Their growing intimacy also leads to a pair of confrontations.

Obata's encounter with Ino is like the original, heavy with abusive language. Here, too, Ino's verbal violence reveals to us the depths of his love for his sister, even in disgrace, especially in disgrace.

Naruse works more changes in the fight that follows between brother and sister. He works on the principle of expansion/addition. Before the climactic struggle, we are shown a series of scenes set in different places: a bus stop near the noodle factory, the riverbank, Riki's eatery. All serve to reinforce our sense of Mon's status as a fallen woman; all add to the drama of the upcoming confrontation.

When Mon gets off the bus, we see her snap open a gaudy parasol, hardly the gesture and artifact of a demure unmarried woman. Her kimono is equally inappropriate. It, too, is gaudy. The collar is of an open-slack design favored by women whose business it is to advertise their charms. The camera notes expressions of shock and curiosity on the faces of such bystanders as Taichi and his adoptive mother.

Mon continues along the riverbank, her dress and manner eliciting whistles from young laborers. One of them imitates the easygoing motion of her hips. Mon smiles, casting a come-hitherish look their way, then passes on.

Inside Riki's eatery, Mon takes her ease. She rolls up her kimono sleeves and even hitches up her skirt. No woman concerned with matters of respectability would adopt such an attitude. Worse yet, Mon's ostentatious vulgarity draws attention to her swollen figure, and therefore to the obvious fact that she is not in a respectable condition.

Even so, Naruse takes pains to emphasize a sense of solidarity among the women in Akaza's family. This prepares a poignant contrast to the upcoming conflict between sister and brother.

Mon and San meet up as each is heading for home. They greet each other cheerfully and enter the house side by side. Riki greets them with a smile. Mon produces gifts she has brought from the city: three rolls of *yukata* material and a dress. Her mother and sister are overjoyed. Unfortunately, Mon's very generosity works like a boast apt to draw attention to the kind of life she leads in the city. Thus the happiness of the moment shades over into anxiety as Riki mentions Obata's visit.

Ino comes in, and things change quickly for the worse. He spurns the gift his sister offers him. The fight he has with Mon is faithful to Muro's text when it comes to abusive language. An important departure from the story is Naruse's use of San as a pivotal character seeking to mediate this quarrel. The richness (as it were) of verbal exchange is joined by the camera's expressive power. Both give narrative legibility to the characters' felt feelings. Thus, we see the shift from surprise to indignation on Mon's face when Ino boasts of having drubbed her former loverboy. Mon is virtually speechless with fury, her voice taking on a strident, squeaking tone as the camera surveys her angry disarray. The blowzy collar of her vulgar kimono has slipped down, uncovering her from nape to shoulder line. She has the air of a low-life streetwise woman getting more dangerous by the moment.

When brother and sister come to blows, the camera behaves like a spectator angling for a clear view of a street fight. The variety of shots used ranges from close-ups to reverse-field setups. Mon is thrown out of the house onto the ground, but struggles to her feet and rushes back to push Ino up against a chest. San, meantime, comes in and out of view, sometimes aligned with Mon as she struggles to calm her sister. Finally, San's screaming helps end the fight.

Naruse balances the climactic fight with a memorable final shot outdoors. Ino is seen walking along the riverbank in dazzling sunlight. The camera shows us his face in tears. This single shot epitomizes the cruel paradox of this sad story: the brother really does love his fallen sister and is keenly sympathetic to her plight. The pity is that Mon knows nothing of his feeling.

Naruse's approach to plotting this tale has more to do with the sisters' completely different approaches to the challenge of life in a rapidly changing society. Their opposing value systems are most clearly juxtaposed when Naruse contrasts the Mon-Obata liaison with the San-Taichi friendship. The sisters share a common difficulty: both must leave the security of home to seek work in a city fraught with danger for young women, and both end up rejected by the men they have chosen to love. Mon falls prey to her boy friend's egotism and is ruined. San

Yoshiko Kuga, Kumeko Urabe, Masayuki Mori and Machiko Kyo (clockwise) in *Older Brother, Younger Sister* (1953) directed by Mikio Naruse. Courtesy of Daici Co. Ltd.

manages to avoid her sister's fate, thanks to her sense of such traditional values as filial piety and female chastity. Yet Mon's disaster costs her sister dear, ruining her hopes of marriage to Taichi. His adoptive family refuses to ally itself with a family whose daughter has brought such shame to it.

So it happens that San's moral conflict comes after Obata's visit. Taichi is being forced to accept a bride of his family's choosing. He decides to elope with San, who reluctantly agrees. Ironically, the lovers' flight by bus and train brings them into contact with, of all people, Obata.

As we have seen, San's initially harsh attitude toward the unfortunate young man changed before he left. Strong as her convictions are, San is a peacemaker, too. Now her feelings for her sister's lover grow even more forgiving as she sees how much of a mere boy he really is. Her glimpse of him on the bus is shown in a point-of-view shot. San sees him eating the sweet bean jam cakes she herself arranged for him to have. There is even a touch of humor here as we see how the cakes were in fact smashed flat when Ino threw Obata to the ground. Later, San will speak directly of her feelings for Obata at this moment, describing it to her mother.

Once San and Obata recognize one another on the bus, she avoids looking his way again. Clearly, he reminds her of her sister's downfall; and here she is, herself having to think it possible that she is making a similar mistake.

By the time the bus delivers the fugitive lovers to the train station, San has made up her mind. Her conflict resolves itself into a matter of principle entirely consistent with her image as model daughter and sister. She has the strength of character it takes to round on Taichi and accuse him of lacking courage. She insists that if he really does love her, he will resist marrying against his will. He can do it by dissolving the adoptive parent-son relationship.

Here, a telling likeness between Obata and Taichi clearly reveals itself. Both are sons of respectable families headed by domineering parents. Neither young man really has a mind of his own. So it is San who ends this relationship. The departing train literally carries out the final separation. San is aboard, duty-bound; Taichi is left standing on the platform.

This scene concludes with a shot of San pressing her face against the window of the train. She is in tears. Yet what effect, really, will this breakup have on her? We know that she is headed back to the city and her work; but will she be able to overcome this suffering, this humiliation? Naruse leaves us in suspense until the end of the film, until after the climactic confrontation between Ino and Mon.

The screenplay makes poignant use of the principle of addition. First, Naruse introduces a sequence centered on the lantern festival. This traditional public celebration is shown being observed by the little community, surrounded as it is by newly sprawling suburbia. Again, the river is used to set the scene. This time, the smoothness of its flow is emphasized by the countless lanterns floating along. A cut to the riverbank shows a crowd of merrymakers moving along sedately, their demeanor suggesting an affinity with the river, a kind of mannerly natural character unspoiled as yet by the "progress" encroaching all around.

San and her mother are seen setting their lanterns afloat. A point-of-view shot shows that San has caught sight of Taichi. He is not alone. We have seen the woman with him somewhere before: busily working in the noodle factory. This is how we know that she must be Taichi's new bride. Naturally, we want to see San's reaction. She and Riki pass by the couple. Yet the sequence closes with Taichi's reaction, not San's. He is clearly surprised to see her. What she feels on seeing him is not ours to know—not yet. Naruse saves the resolution of that causal line in San's moral conflict for later.

The film ends with a deft affirmation of family solidarity, come what may. Everything we see and hear suggests that mother and daughters have renewed their loving bond. San's face beams with happiness in close-up as she waves to her mother in the distance (out of frame). We see that San has managed to survive the suffering caused by Taichi's weakness in the face of his family's small-minded righteousness. Mon, too, looks happy as she leaves with her sister. We have a sense that somehow all may yet be well with her. A long shot of Riki (seen from her daughters' perspective) shows her standing at the gate, waving her children out of sight.

Only now does Naruse enlarge on Akaza's deeply felt affection for his daughters. He has shown no sign of it in their presence. Now we see him silently serv-

Yoshiko Kuga (l) and Machiko Kyo (r) in *Older Brother, Younger Sister* (1953) directed by Mikio Naruse. Courtesy of Daiei Co. Ltd.

ing shaved ice to a customer. He turns abruptly to go outside. He stands in front of the shop, looking intently off screen right.

The subsequent long shot clarifies his view. Mon and San are seen walking along a country path, unaware of their father's silent leave-taking. Mon asks if they are going to walk all the way to the next bus stop. San replies in a series of bemused ellipses. "But . . . for some time . . . I have to work harder." Her meaning lies in those pauses, suggesting much in so few words. We find ourselves filling in what Naruse omits so deftly. After all, this is the theme he has labored on throughout the film. San wants to leave slowly, enjoy a leisurely good-bye to a country landscape still intact, despite all the change of postwar modernization. Her desire is all the more intense because she knows that visits home will be rarer now that she has lost Taichi. Her final remark points to a determination to make it on her own in the city. It echoes something she said to her sister earlier, namely, that marriage is not her goal in life; no, she will give that energy to work and study in order to become a professional woman.

Naruse shares Muro's reliance on the narrative device of withheld information. Here it returns with fatalistic circularity. Mon says that she, for her part, will come home to see her brother, even though she considers him utterly despicable. Here Naruse obviously seeks to enrich the context of her remark. The sound track plays cheerful music in tune with the happy look on Mon's face as she speaks.

Here, as in Muro's story, we see the peculiar irony: brother and sister can express their genuine affection only in shows of violent hatred.

Visually and poetically, the last two shots of the film enrich the bond between these sisters, different as the values are by which they lead their lives. Mon opens her gaudy parasol for the two of them to share. The sound track still plays cheerfully on as they vanish in the distance, each ready for the life she has chosen to lead in the distant city. Then the camera pauses, taking note of the long country lane. It offers gravel underfoot. It, like the idyllic country landscape all around, may well give way to the forces of change that will swallow up the world these people love.

Notes

I am grateful to *Asian Cinema* for permitting me to reprint my article, which appeared in vol. 8, no. 1 (Spring 1996).

1. Audie Bock, *Naruse: A Master of the Japanese Cinema* (Chicago: Art Institute of Chicago, 1984), p. 22.
2. Ibid.
3. Kiyoto Fukuda and Hiroshi Honda, *Muro Saisei: Hito to sakuhin* (Saisei Muro: the man and his works) (Tokyo: Shimizu Shoin, 1988), p. 169.
4. Saisei Muro, "Ani Imoto" (Older brother, younger sister), in *Gendai bungaku taikei* (A collection of Japanese literary works), vol. 30 (Tokyo: Tsukuma Shobo, 1966), pp. 185–86. For an English translation, see Ivan Morris, ed., "Brother, Sister" in *Modern Short Stories* (Tokyo: Tuttle, 1964), pp. 144–61.
5. Ibid.
6. Ibid., p. 189.
7. Ibid.
8. Ibid., p. 194.
9. Heiichi Sugayama, *Eizo gengo to eiga sakka* (Film language and filmmakers) (Tokyo: Kugei Shuppan, 1988), p. 167.

12

The Pain of Emancipation: Shinoda's *Maihime* (1989)

Soseki Natsume and Ogai Mori are considered the two most important figures on the Meiji literary scene. Both took part in the Japanese quest for knowledge of the West. For them, this meant study in Europe followed by a return to Japan to face the crisis of reintegration characteristic of so many Meiji intellectuals. Soseki and Ogai faced a dilemma posed by bringing home a somewhat altered ego: an emancipated one, aware of new freedoms and self-assertions bound to pit someone Japanese against many of his country's most deeply ingrained customs and beliefs.

As might be expected, their works offered filmmakers ample ground to explore. In Ogai's case, the earliest film adaptation of his work was *Abe ichizoku* (The Abe clan), Hisatora Kumagai's 1938 film based on the historical novel of the same title. Postwar adaptations included *Gan* (The wild geese, 1953, a.k.a. The Mistress), Shiro Toyoda's adaptation of the novel of the same title.[1] Kenji Mizoguchi's also brilliantly transposed *Sansho Dayu* (The Sansho bailiff) onto the screen in 1954, which brought him the San Marco Silver Lion award at the Venice Film Festival.

Most recently, Masahiro Shinoda made his film version of "Maihime" (The dancing girl), released abroad as *Die Tänzerin* or *The Dancing Girl* (1989). It was a joint venture between Japan's Herald Ace and Germany's Manfred Durniok Produktion. Why did he return to Ogai's world just then? Thirty-five years had elapsed since Mizoguchi's work. I think there are several reasons why this happened in the late 1980s.

First, this work can be considered a natural outcome of Shinoda's lifelong conviction that the individual's relationship with society is essentially one of victim and victimizer. As early as 1969, Shinoda's *Shokei no shima* (Punishment island) probed deep into the damaging effects of the Imperial system on individuals. In that film, a former military police official exploits juvenile delinquents on a remote island. Among his victims is a boy whose family the official had killed in the line of duty. Shinoda treats a similar theme in *Setouchi shonen yakyudan* (MacArthur's children, 1984). This time, his venue shifts to the plight of young children who must grow up in the aftermath of World War II. The director's concern for moral dilemmas is also evident in his adaptations of Monzaemon Chikamatsu's domestic plays, *Shinju ten no amijima* (Double suicide, 1969) and *Yari no Gonza* (Gonza: the spearman, 1986). Both unfold the tragedy of a man and woman caught up in the basic incompatibility between *giri* (social obligation) and *ninjo* (personal needs) in an oppressive feudal society.

Ogai's "The Dancing Girl" fits in well with Shinoda's creative drive. Its story deals with the dilemma of an intellectual in the grip of irreconcilable demands: those of individual freedom and its antithesis in the moral absolutes of Japanese society in the Meiji era.

The original story is largely autobiographical. It is based on the young army doctor Ogai's romantic involvement with a German girl during his four-year stay in Berlin (1884–88). The relationship ended when he was ordered home to Japan, never to visit Europe again. Because of its celebration of love between youths of different ethnic and social backgrounds, many critics credit "The Dancing Girl" with introducing Romanticism to Japanese literature.[2] Along with Shimei Futabatei's *Ukigumo* (The drifting cloud), it is considered a touchstone of modernity in Japanese literature for another reason as well: its poignant depiction of a Meiji bureaucrat's awakening to the demands of "ego"—the same that must inevitably collapse under pressure from society.[3]

A second reason for Shinoda's interest in Ogai's romantic tale "The Dancing Girl" lies in the true-life correlation between the writer's youthful experience and his later creative work. Put another way, one might say that this twentieth-century film director could not fail to take an interest in a nineteenth-century novelist's very real confrontation with the crushingly rigid traditional values of Meiji society—all the more, since Ogai, as a man of his time, was forced to project the inner conflict between freedom and bondage into this work.

Here is Shinoda's own account.

His [Ogai's] last will and testament mainly concerns matters like his refusal of the Buddhist name customarily given to the deceased. He also repudiates all tribute of honor and praise bestowed on him by the Imperial administration and the army. In angry terms he claims that, facing death, he will not allow those external factors to determine a life he considers his own. . .

When I started this film *Die Tänzerin* three years ago (following the suggestions made by a West German, M. Dornick) I had this last will and testament in mind. . . . Ogai's repudiation of the privileged status that was his—thanks to his ties with the Imperial household agency and the army—I take to be a literal manifestation of his attempt to escape from the nation itself. How else to explain a hatred so powerful that it saw honor as a blemish on his life. . . . In my opinion, the turning point in Ogai's career which led him to compose such a testament is described in "The Dancing Girl." That is what prompted me to adapt it for the screen.[4]

As Shinoda himself acknowledges, suppression of freedom in love was one of the most devastating effects that feudal Japan had on individual lives:

Nowadays, "liebe" is a commonplace word for love in the Japanese vocabulary. In Ogai's time it was not easy to love a person freely as a human being. Nation and family were of paramount importance for a man. In the Edo period, pursuit of eros often led lovers to death. The sexual urge was feared as an evil which blemished respectability. . . .

Bound as he was by such a cultural climate, Ogai found its burden too great; hence his failure to sustain the love he experienced in Berlin at the end of the nineteenth century. After all, he did leave Elice and return to Japan. . . . Yet bitter remorse led him to write first 'The Dancing Girl' and then, such a final testament.[5]

Thus Shinoda's *Die Tänzerin* is the director's own interpretation of the traumatic experience of Ogai, the Meiji intellectual, who acted out the choice, or nonchoice, between conformity to the nation and fidelity to his own heart.

Finally, *Die Tänzerin* may be seen as offering this director yet another opportunity to give form to thoughts he himself had struggled with since Japan's defeat in World War II: how the Imperial system came to have such a deep and abiding effect on the lives of individual Japanese, most notably his own. On that connection, Shinoda had this to say:

I was willing to sacrifice my life for the emperor. Ever since then I have wondered about the root of my patriotism. It is still an enigma to me. How can such absolutism take hold in any individual? Why did this moral imperative persist in Japan as a social phenomenon?[6]

For the filmmaker anxious to explore all these aspects, the original work presents a difficulty: it is a short story. Shinoda must expand it, and so he does. He is fairly faithful to the given story line. Most of his collaborative energy is spent on character delineation and on enriching certain events. He also develops a complementary romance running parallel to that of the hero and his dancing girl.

In order to see how Shinoda achieves his desired effects, we first must turn to Ogai's work itself. The story line is very simple, following the familiar formula of a conservative youth's rebellion against social standards and the resulting conflict. The protagonist is a young government official, Toyotaro Ota, who is sent to Germany to study law. Ogai describes the various stages of awakening the youth experiences, the focal point being his involvement with Elice, a revue girl.

This element of romance gives the age-old classical theme of *giri/ninjo* (social obligations/personal feelings) a refreshingly new context. Ogai's work shows how Meiji literature responded quickly to Western influences. For the Japanese, the modern quality of "The Dancing Girl" lay in two areas. Unlike the samurai or the commoner hero in feudal Bunraku and Kabuki plays, its modern counterpart is a new type of hero: a young intellectual of mid-Meiji Japan. The new government policy of strengthening the nation through Western technology had reached its apex; a new class of Japanese intellectual was looking for ways to move with this mainstream of modernization. Accordingly, the classical notion of *ninjo* is extended to a modern level defined as the awakening of one's ego. Then, too, the protagonist's "awakening" does not take place on his home ground but in Germany, a country whose legal system the new Japan was seeking to emulate. A high point of this aim was the promulgation in 1889 of the Imperial Constitution.

Ogai fortifies this familiar polarity of freedom/constraint and individualism/collectivism through some equally familiar contradictions furnished by a conventional romance plot. (Naturally, Japanese readers of the time would find a great deal of innovative melodrama in this *mésalliance* between a Japanese man and a foreign woman, and lovers from incompatible social strata, too.) The strain of his love with a mere music-hall girl is intensified by Toyotaro's ties to the Japanese government. His own father being dead, Imperial patronage becomes more than just a metaphor for father figure, demanding absolute loyalty from him.

Ogai tells his story, not in the order of actual events, but as events unfold in the mind of his hero thinking back on his experience. This leads to considerable rearrangement and a more compelling narrative, since the "real" story is one of self-enlightenment leading to moral conflict and its resolution. Toyotaro is a hero who has grown wise through suffering. He knows only too well where the absolute power of national values and identity can lead. Having come to view the outcome as tragic, he views his traumatic years in Berlin in a rueful and repentant spirit. Through him, Ogai shows us the present impinging on the past as Toyotaro's feelings of guilt and remorse filter through his memories of the past, in some ways modifying them as well.

The story begins with a famous evocation of the atmosphere that puts the persona/Toyotaro in a contemplative mood:

> Coals have already been loaded. It is so quiet around a desk in a middle-class cabin. The bright lamp does injustice to this serenity. My friends who were seen each night here for a card game are now staying at a hotel. I am the only one left on board.[7]

Toyotaro's progress toward maturity is then suggested as he thinks back to the young man he was just five years previously. Then he was at the same place, Saigon, en route to Europe. His view is notably self-critical. For the young bureaucrat whose constant desire for travel abroad had been granted, everything seemed new and edifying. His accounts of his travels, published in various newspapers, had been widely acclaimed. Yet that impetuous, fame-seeking traveler had yielded to his present self: still in his youth, yet sadly measured now; a young man who exhibits the *nil admirari* attitude developed in Berlin. Thus the autobiography set to unfold becomes a record of his progress toward a feeling that rules him now, the feeling that "what was right yesterday is wrong today."

The exposition is then given in the light of Toyotaro's own life in Germany. His first exposure to the West is rendered in elementary terms: his "visual" responses to manners so different from what he knows. The earlier prosaic description of his opportunistic goals at the outset of his journey now yields to a poignant contrast as Ogai offers some remarkably metaphorical passages describing

this youth's first perceptions of Europe. A group of nuns passes by. Square-shoul-
dered officers in colorful uniforms stride along, chests thrown out. Girls appear
dressed in the latest fashions from Paris. Carriages run smoothly back and forth
along the asphalt road.

This lyrical vision soon gives way to an introspective mood as Toyotaro reflects on his inner life, which is ruled by convention, by the strict social mores of
his native land. This reflection sets the stage for the narrator's first sensations of
inner conflict.

Ogai refers us to Toyotaro's life at home, a life defined by commitment to the
behavior expected of a paragon of dutiful filial piety. He has been very strictly
brought up. Since his father's death, he has followed his "mother's instructions"
and has achieved academic distinction. He has never failed to rank at the top of
his class in the department of law at the university. His travel abroad is designed
to further his success. In fact, this young man is motivated by the kind of goal that
goes well with an opportunistic frame of mind. It is up to him to achieve fame and
recoup the family fortunes.

Toyotaro remains steadfast, pursuing that goal for his first three years abroad.
Then comes awakening, a newly formative stage taking its cues from elements of
self-doubt prompted by his exposure to the West. He begins to question the
values of conformity. His thoughts move along these lines:

> . . . I lived, abiding by my father's will. I followed my mother's teaching and
> never let others' praise of me affect my study although they called me a gifted
> child. The director of my department was happy to have such a good assistant.
> His encouragement also pleased me—another incentive for harder work. I had
> no idea what I was: a mere functionary, a mechanical person. Now that I am
> twenty years old, the freedom which I have experienced at this university, has
> made me uneasy. Ego, so long suppressed deep in my heart, has now surfaced,
> ready to launch an attack on my past self.[8]

This self-critical spirit soon breeds rebellion in the young man. First, he
refuses to play "roles": the letter-perfect son his mother wants him to be; the
"incarnation of the law" his boss wants him to become. His reports to the director
testify to this rebelliousness. Boldly, young Toyotaro states his conviction that
once one acquires the "spirit of law," one is no longer bound to the petty details of
the legal system. Accordingly, he starts cutting law school classes in order to
pursue his interest in historical literature. This challenge to the values of his group
brings alienation. His relationship with other Japanese students in Germany was
less than friendly at the outset. He was too much of a paragon to get along easily.
Now he sets himself up to become a pariah. Classmates envious of his success
and prestige are only too glad to report his dereliction of duty.

"The Dancing Girl" builds its tale on repeated instances of Toyotaro's re-
examination and rejection of his country's traditional values. He is especially
hard on the drive to persevere, to define success in conventional terms. He subjects himself to increasingly harsh self-criticism. Those around him have always

seen Toyotaro as an ascetic: someone too dedicated, too steadfastly high-minded to yield to the vulgar distractions of student life—to bars and billiard parlors, for example. Now the exalted young man sees his abstemiousness as mere cowardice and self-deception. It is a kind of self-fulfilling critique. As his story unfolds, Toyotaro sees himself revealed as a kind of insipid hero. A "cowardice" (his own word) becomes his characteristic moral flaw. He sees his own cowardice working with conventional outside forces to bring his love affair to its sorry and commonplace end.

Ironically, Toyotaro's romantic entanglement marks the high point of his experience of freedom. This episode occupies the middle part of Ogai's tale. The pattern of behavior is entirely familiar. It begins when a privileged youth makes contact with the seamy side of life; there he finds true love in the person of a poor but pure and innocent and strikingly beautiful girl. Her obvious qualities attract him; but this cautious, inexperienced youth is bound to her by the element of paradox, for this girl is untarnished by all the sordid world around her.

Of course Elice's plight is desperate, and in quite a practical sense. She needs money to pay for her father's funeral. So what is a high-minded youth to do but give her his watch to pawn? And where should such sympathy lead but to love—and love but to fatal liaison? Still, progress that way is not easy, as Ogai makes plain. His attraction to Elice weighs heavily on Toyotaro's sense of duty: "The girl who came to my lodging to express her thanks was like a splendid flower blooming outside the window of the room where I sat pondering the thoughts of Schopenhauer and Schiller."[9]

Heady as these new sensations of freedom are, Toyotaro still struggles to reconcile the old value system with the new. Even as he struggles to exercise this parlous duality, the values of his homeland close in, forcing Toyotaro to choose between individual freedom and traditional conformity. This comes about through his countrymen in Germany; his fellow students are entirely comfortable with the values Toyotaro has come to see as insular, close-minded, and conformist to an intolerable degree. His colleagues report his friendship with Elice to his supervisor. Judged by the standards of Meiji Japan, any such relationship can only be seen as a matter of fleshly lust. Toyotaro's supervisor already sees his academic career abroad in an unfavorable light. This revue-girl business is the perfect excuse to cancel the young rebel's appointment.

Another blow quickly follows. A relative writes from Japan to inform Toyotaro of his mother's death. Ogai does not give the reader a view of the mother's last letter, but Toyotaro's reaction clearly suggests the awful truth: his mother committed suicide, driven to it by the shame of her son's disgrace overseas. Tragic as it is, his mother's death cuts the irksome family bond. In an ironic sense, Toyotaro has achieved a measure of freedom from nation and family. Yet what is he to do?

A financial crisis had brought Toyotaro and Elice together; now the money question, along with injured pride, plays a decisive role. A dismissed bureaucrat abroad has one remaining "perk": the Japanese government will pay his passage home. Accepting that would be tantamount to tracing disgrace back to its source. The alternative is scarcely less threatening: to remain in Germany as an impoverished foreigner. Predictably, Toyotaro's platonic relationship with Elice blossoms in these newly dire circumstances. The narrator describes the change this way: "My love for Elice grew stronger, and finally we became inseparable."[10] Toyotaro sees the available choices in these terms: "If I return to Japan now, without my degree, and in disgrace, I'll never get anywhere. If I stay here, how can I pay my tuition?"[11]

Help arrives from an unexpected quarter: his friend, Kenkichi Aizawa, secretary to Count Amagata. Aizawa persuades a newspaper editor to use Toyotaro as an overseas correspondent stationed in Berlin. Toyotaro's new job exposes him to the perils of individual freedom in a different context. Writing about politics and art is his only tie with the homeland whose values he has repudiated. Ironically, in the long run this assignment returns him to the very values of opportunism and conformity Toyotaro has tried to escape.

The change from affluent student to struggling employee also reinforces the overall motif of quest. Poverty forces him to move in with Elice's family. There he lives a working-class life at the low end of the pay scale. His articles are written on a stone table in a public place mobbed by "young loafers, poor old folks living by lending their tiny savings, and merchants taking a break." Toyotaro's hopes of academic advancement are frustrated by the poverty which, in its way, educates him in another kind of humanistic sense. Looking back on it, the narrator sees the young man learning about life and people in a broader sense, thanks to the vast amounts of reading a journalist/foreign correspondent must do to stay on top of his job.

The story takes a very different turn when a letter arrives from his friend Aizawa. This time, opportunity brings with it a chance of personal and ideological about-face. Aizawa urges the journalist-in-exile to solicit an interview with Count Amagata, then in Berlin.

Ogai describes Toyotaro as a character unable to shake off a penchant for restoring his "honor." Protesting that he has long given up any hope of rising in the political world, Toyotaro does the expedient thing. He promises Aizawa that he will sever relations with Elice temporarily.

That done, Toyotaro is free to join the count's entourage on a visit to Russia. That distance works to make the heart grow fonder—and moral conflict correspondingly more cruel. Letters from Elice, now pregnant, confirm Toyotaro in his desire to be with her and to embrace the values of a "poor yet pleasant life." Unfortunately, Count Amagata asserts what might be considered a prior claim. Impressed with Toyotaro's knowledge and gift for languages, he offers to take him back to Japan. Clearly, an appointment is in the offing.

The narrator sees two forces at work in the inevitable break with Elice. The first is Toyotaro's utter inability to shake off external influences. Looking back on it, the narrator holds the basic insecurity of life abroad responsible for this weakness: "It occurred to me that if I refused the count's offer, I would lose my home country, and with it the chance to restore my honor. I would vanish, swallowed up in the ocean of this vast city."[12]

The other factor the narrator sees responsible for Toyotaro's apparent change of heart is illness—a narrative convenience Ogai puts in the way of direct confrontation between his protagonist and his love.[13] The same illness also invites outside intervention. Aizawa, finding Toyotaro in serious condition, makes the final decision for him. He forwards Toyotaro's acceptance of the count's offer of a trip to Japan. Toyotaro's earlier commitment had been by way of a courteous gesture enforced by the count's presence. Thanks to Aizawa, that gesture became a fait accompli.

Toyotaro's conflict of interest vis-à-vis Germany and Elice resolves itself in a commonplace of romantic tragedy. Elice goes mad. What can her Japanese lover do but revert to the very values of conformity and opportunism he has been seeking to escape?

Ogai treats his protagonist's wishy-washy character as a kind of theme in his story. We are not surprised by the young man's reluctance to confront Elice with his decision to leave her—literally. He could scarcely export such a *mésalliance* to Japan. That would end all hope of a career. In the Meiji era, as in feudal Japan, the profession of dancer/entertainer was held in very low esteem. Marriage to such a woman, not to mention a foreigner, would amount to social suicide, disgracing Toyotaro once and for all.[14]

Thus Elice's lapse into madness is more than a rather obvious narrative convenience. It prevents Toyotaro from doing something entirely mad from the point of view of Meiji respectability. It is interesting that while the young man's earlier period of awakening was marked by harsh self-criticism, he is now blind to the fact that his chief moral flaw, insipidity, is the motivating force for this tragedy. Instead of holding himself accountable, he blames his good friend, the very paragon of traditional Japan. "This benefactor," he says, "killed me spiritually." This accusation surfaces again at the story's end: "Kenichi Aizawa is the kind of good friend you can scarcely find. Even so, hatred for him still lurks in a corner of my heart."[15]

In adapting a short story for the screen, the first thing any filmmaker must face is the need to expand the narrative. Shinoda maintains the basic formula of conflict in values. But he attempts to reshape the various stages of Toyotaro's life by giving each one more narrative legibility, creating a subplot and even reshaping the protagonist himself somewhat. Then, too, some minor characters, even those who serve as part and parcel of the background, are given much more substantial treatment. All these changes contribute to his exploration of the victim/victimizer theme Shinoda pursues so relentlessly.

His counterpart of the novel's protagonist is not a government official who studies law at the university but an army surgeon who is sent to study hygiene under the famous Koff. This way, Shinoda's Toyotaro becomes more akin to Ogai himself, who in his own life traveled to Germany in such a capacity. Needless to say, Shinoda's recasting had a lot to do with his attempt to render his own interpretation of the moral dilemma the novelist experienced as a Meiji intellectual. Thus he hopes to bridge the gap between Ogai's promising career and the last will and testament in which he offers such a bitter indictment of his nation. (Shinoda cast teen heartthrob singer Hiromi Go as Toyotaro. He worked with this notable soft-touch actor in a film for television and in *Gonza: The Spearman* (1985) and liked his acting style.) Moreover, Shinoda adds a few major incidents in order to pursue another thematic vein: the notion of the Imperial system in an individual life that has haunted him ever since Japan's defeat in the war.

Like the novel, the film begins with first-person narration. Toyotaro, aboard the ship on his way back from Germany, reports on his present situation. Significantly, the opening sequence poses the question Toyotaro himself has already established as the main theme. Waiting for Count Amagata and his secretary Aizawa, Toyotaro continues his narration on the sound track: "They changed my fate. How did I find myself aboard this ship?"

What unfolds after this is his recollection of his experience in Germany, through which Toyotaro tries to grope for the answer for his haunting question. Significantly, Toyotaro's narration in the opening sequence is rendered in German, not in his own language. This deft touch is Shinoda's way of impressing us with Toyotaro's gift for languages. The director stresses this point a number of times, most notably in the pivotal scene in which the count finds himself relying on Toyotaro's interpreting skills on a tour through Europe. Then, too, it is precisely this talent, coupled with his experiential knowledge, that serves as a crucial factor in the young man's shift in values.

Ogai's description of Saigon in the opening paragraph is concise and minimal: it is no more than the locale Toyotaro passes through on his way home and the place where his recollection takes place. Shinoda puts more stress on locale. Counting on the camera's expressive power, he makes sure of various symbolic and aesthetic values. The panoramic vision of the African desert—not the port of Saigon—taken from Toyotaro's perspective is in fact overwhelming. Stylistically, this vast terrestrial stretch is superbly balanced with the ocean that pervades the final sequence. Then, too, since a film critic is always eager to dig into symbolism, the film might literally associate the desert as an apt metaphor for Toyotaro's emotional state: a sense of emptiness caused by the fatal clash of ego in confrontation with the absolute standards of morality.

In the original, the linear progression of Toyotaro's awakening process is often interrupted by earlier events, namely, recollections of his earlier life in Japan. Shinoda follows a much more strictly straightforward chronology of major events. Thus, events at home before Toyotaro's departure are given at the outset. Other than that, his mother's attempt to kill herself is rendered through a crosscut as an event concurrent with Toyotaro's dismissal from his government position. These events create a vivid image of traditional absolutes of family and national life as influences on the young man's formation.

We see how the family reacts to Toyotaro's appointment to a position with the army. His mother, a samurai's daughter, is presented as the very paragon of respectability and loyalty. She holds a going-away party for her son. She is attired in a ceremonial kimono correct in every detail, with equally appropriate coiffure. She places Toyotaro's appointment letter on a Shinto altar, and in the presence of guests, seated with all due ceremony, she instructs all assembled to face in the direction of the Imperial palace as an expression of their gratitude to the ruler. A close-up of her face firmly registers her patriotism as she says: "Great Imperial Japan under the emperor!" The ensuing shot shows the Imperial palace with a moat around it. Loud and clear, as mentioned above, this is Shinoda's way of exploring thoughts he himself has struggled with since Japan's defeat in World War II: feudal notions of Imperialism.

The going-away party closes with Toyotaro's night out in the red-light district, a detail added to Ogai's story. The scene is reminiscent of the prowlings of Gonza, a revelation of the other side of the respectable retainer hero, in *Gonza: The Spearman.* Of course, Toyotaro's adventure is not undertaken on his own initiative. It is his friends who consider a brothel visit a necessary preparation for a "chaste" youth about to leave on an educational tour to Europe. Here, too, Shinoda has deftly managed to bring in another aspect of the feudal remnants in modern Japan: the double standard governing notions of chastity in men and women. Shinoda also fortifies these feudal remnants with another level of worship, again absent in the original. Toyotaro's preparation for the trip abroad ends with his and his mother's visit to a Shinto shrine. The camera studies them piously praying for safe passage in front of the altar.

With these feudal values firmly rooted in Toyotaro's life, the film then explores two story lines: Toyotaro's enlightenment and his ensuing moral dilemma with its devastating outcome. Conventional narrative devices—contrast and parallelism—advance these story lines.

Importantly, the events abroad unfolded on the screen are those recalled in Toyotaro's mind. However, his narration on the sound track during the previous scenes simply disappears. Initially, the subtitle says *Berlin, 1884,* as Toyotaro's journey begins. What happens thereafter constitutes a lineal rendition of various stages of Toyotaro's past experience. By eliminating the narrator's comments altogether, each event is given a sense of greater immediacy. Shinoda counts on the camera's potential to explore many stages of Toyotaro's awakening. His world is initially defined by stuffy classrooms with microscopes, a splendid reception room at the Japanese embassy, a count's villa, and a respectable boardinghouse. The camera surveys the fashionably dressed people behaving respectfully, as if to suggest a rigidly regulated life. The camera's restricted movement quite literally emphasizes a sense of confinement as Toyotaro's felt reality. In fact, his landlady says that she prefers Japanese boarders because they behave so respectfully.

This privileged yet insular world of the upper classes offers a pointed contrast to Elice's world of tenement housing clustered around central courtyards open to all the sordid commonplaces of life among the lowly. The narrow confinement of the building itself becomes an index of poor yet hard-working people

Hiromi Go in *Die Tänzerin* (1989) directed by Masahiro Shinoda. Courtesy of the Kawakita Memorial Film Institute.

oppressed by their burden of "poverty." The contrast is absolutely stark, and for that matter it quite legibly transmits the cost Toyotaro will have to pay for choosing life as a "free" individual, as opposed to being a comfortable cog in the Imperial system.

This contrast in characters comes much more to the fore in the film, thanks to Shinoda's creation of new personages. Set against the lone hero Toyotaro are two rather schematic worldlings, one a colleague, Takashi Tanimura, the other a military attaché to the embassy, Tazusaburo Fukushima. In order to bolster a sense of Toyotaro's individualism, Ogai describes a powerful faction of students who are not favorably disposed to his aloofness. But they simply remain nothing but a group of characters. Shinoda individualizes the faction through his portrayal of Tanimura. He is the very antithesis of Toyotaro—a worldly student on his own, not at all bothered by having to borrow money from others for his pursuit of pleasure. His values are associated with sycophancy, insularity, and envy. Fukushima represents the value system of the military: absolute conformity to discipline. He tries to control the private lives of students by using his authority, his informant being Tanimura.

They join forces to bring about Toyotaro's loss of his appointment, thereby setting the stage for his first moral conflict: having to choose between leaving Germany or staying with Elice. Both the original and the film version share the dramatic function of Count Amagata as a kind of savior/benefactor. Ogai's portrayal of this character is minimized by virtue of the genre: a short story. He is in stark contrast with Toyotaro's boss, a government official characterized by inflexibility and conformity. Ogai presents him this way: "At first the count spoke nothing but business. Later, he began to ask for my opinions about what was going on at home. Often we laughed together when he described the mistakes his people had made during the trip. . . ."[16]

Shinoda gives the count much more narrative/visual legibility. Needless to say, Toyotaro's initial impression of this political figure is rendered through the camera's expressive power. The count's well-dressed, middle-aged figure is seen in an impressive pose amid the equally imposing furnishings of the luxurious hotel. Then, too, Shinoda labors on the process of Toyotaro's gaining trust from the count, an the event that will eventually guarantee his future in Japan. For example, Shinoda expands Ogai's narrative events by giving thorough treatment to the scene in which the count is impressed by Toyotaro's translation of German newspapers and the travel sequence in which Toyotaro demonstrates his excellent command of French. His new creation is the banquet sequence to finalize the prestige Toyotaro has earned. Here, all those assembled characters—Toyotaro's enemies, best friend, and benefactor—are brought together. The people whose envy and prejudice had been so detrimental to Toyotaro's career earlier are now reminded of his success. A close-up shows Fukushima bowing to the count's party, clearly registering his awareness of this reversal of fortunes.

Many other characters are also given more than a novelist's finishing touch to those who simply fade into the background. In the original, Elice's mother is not fully developed. Ogai presents her as the very index of poverty, as Toyotaro's first impression of her appearance attests: "The lady who opened the door was an old woman with half white hair. She was not bad looking but her wrinkles showed suffering from poverty, so did her old wool/cotton clothes and worn out shoes."[17] Other than that, her sense of propriety, still unblemished by circumstances, is given only cursory treatment. She apologizes to Toyotaro for shutting the door in his face the first time he came.

In the film, she represents not only the lowest class but the values associated with that class: self-imposed class distinction and greed. Toyotaro's initial impression of her is rendered through the camera's scrutiny of her features. This time, we see a middle-aged woman, not soiled, but in clean, respectable clothes. Her cautious response to a foreign intruder is shown in her act of shutting the door on Toyotaro, as in the story. Then she also apologizes for her impoliteness.

As Elice's relationship with Toyotaro develops, Shinoda pays more attention to the liaison between the Oriental youth and the German widow. We see Toyotaro bringing a bouquet of flowers, and her joyous response in close-up. She says she has never been given flowers before. The poverty represented by her class is most strongly demonstrated toward the end when she accepts money from Aizawa for taking care of Elice's baby. Ogai objectifies this event in one line: "Aizawa gave Elice's mother funds sufficient for their livelihood."[18] Shinoda makes more of the poor woman's life. After she is given money, the camera scrutinizes her response.

She counts it, then sighs and says, "It is a lot of money. The poor just have to sacrifice their self-respect for such."

The principle of expansion/addition is most strongly at work in Toyotaro's relationship with Elice, the focal point of his awakening process. Their initial meeting is presented in the same format: a chance meeting. Toyotaro, seeing Elice crying, asks why. She explains that the family does not have money to pay for her father's funeral. Ironically, money—an index of the modern value newly acquired by the Japanese in the Meiji Westernization—is what brings man and woman together.

The degree of Toyotaro's growing intimacy is presented in a number of memorable scenes. For example, Ogai economizes on Elice's visit by using romantic metaphors, like a flower adorning the window of Toyotaro's room. Shinoda makes it concrete. Intercutting between Elice and Toyotaro in his room clearly shows their mutual awareness. Elice's face registers genuine gratitude for her benefactor as she kisses his hand. Toyotaro fairly beams. Then, too, the landlady, a paragon of propriety, is given more than her share. This respectable middle-aged woman—the same who earlier commented on her preference for Japanese tenants because of their decency—eavesdrops outside her lodger's room.

In Ogai's novel, the entire story is told from Toyotaro's perspective. Interestingly, Shinoda's creation of those German characters, including the landlady, helps the viewer form an image of this elite Japanese from inside and outside. In other words, we pit Toyotaro's self-image against what foreigners say about and see in

Lisa Wolf (l) and Hiromi Go in *Die Tänzerin* (1989) directed by Masahiro Shinoda. Courtesy of the Kawakita Memorial Film Institute.

him. This German lady's xenophobia is well concealed behind a facade of polite behavior; yet we learn that Toyotaro disappoints her. When he explains to the inquisitive landlady that Elice came to settle a debt, she misunderstands the entire situation and thinks that he has been sponging off the poor girl.

Elsewhere, the old German shoemaker, Elice's neighbor, is given the role of silent commentator on the progress of the liaison. Whenever Toyotaro passes by, the camera pauses on the old man's face; it is enigmatic, showing no indication of his approval or disapproval of their relationship. Only in the final sequence does he express resentment against Toyotaro, who by that time has deserted Elice.

Toyotaro's taste of freedom is given a remarkably memorable visual celebration in a rendezvous sequence added to the original. Here, the entire texture of the scene teems with evidence of stylistic finesse, thanks to veteran cinematographer Kazuo Miyagawa's mastery of his art. He capitalizes on the intrinsically filmic quality of the episode. Lyrical music accompanies the lovers on their walk. They meet on a bridge, walk through a park, and ride a boat on a lake. The outdoor setting itself is a welcome relief from spaces defined by walls and windows. The lovers' very freedom of movement through the landscape (like the distance they cover) corresponds to the sense of freedom Toyotaro is experiencing. The viewer is struck by the camera's remarkable fluidity, in stark contrast to the restrained camera motion used for scenes depicting Toyotaro's boardinghouse or classroom. Long shots predominate in the rendezvous sequence, subsuming the lovers into the natural surroundings.

In order to expand on the Toyotaro-Elice romance, Shinoda creates a parallel subplot. It involves German lovers similarly mismatched. A baron's daughter, Louise, engaged to an army lieutenant, is in love with Michael, an artist active in a socialist cause. This episode is drawn from another Ogai story, "Fumizukai" (A courier). Unlike the original, the film emphasizes differences in political philosophy, not class distinctions per se, as the force separating the lovers. By letting Toyotaro play the role of the messenger, Shinoda reinforces the central theme of his learning process by adding a political dimension. Acquaintance with Michael's group shows him a parallel between his country's and this advanced nation's system: the absolute authority of government used to crush dissent.

The rest of Toyotaro's moral conflict faithfully follows the original in a lineal order. Structured around a well-patterned causality, these events include Toyotaro's ostracization from the Japanese community; his appointment as a correspondent, thanks to Aizawa's assistance; his lodging at Elice's apartment; Elice's pregnancy; and his encounter with Count Amagata, which brings him face to face with his final moral decision.

As may be expected, each narrative unit is given more substantial treatment. All are well orchestrated, guaranteeing our visual perception of the material/social sacrifice caused by Toyotaro's decision making. Toyotaro, well-attired, was earlier seen "moving" in higher circles. At one point, wearing an officer's uniform, he appeared in the company of German officers watching a drill. Once he is "free," his movements are shown to be quite literally restricted. Two sordid locations define his environment as a working correspondent: the drab coffeehouse and Elice's shabby room. The camera surveys the tiny bedroom with its dirty, oppressive walls. Toyotaro himself looks seedy: sprouting a beard, no longer dressed in a suit.

Toyotaro's eventual shift in values in favor of opportunism is already visually prepared for in a number of sequences that occur after Toyotaro is summoned by the count. Toyotaro is now back in the best clothes Elice has prepared for such an occasion. A series of long shots keeps registering the gorgeous hotel room, whose luxurious furnishings seem almost to absorb him. Toyotaro's manners confirm that impression. He clearly has it in him to be a paragon of propriety, the very mirror of those values of conformity and uniformity that he will inevitably return to in the end. When he returns home from a tour of Europe, he is again seen getting out of a carriage in his best clothes. The driver follows, carrying his luggage. The camera powerfully captures a sense of discord as his figure contrasts with the drab setting: the familiar squalid courtyard with its walls—an apt metaphor for this level of society. In the most elementary visual sense, the camera tells us that this Oriental youth does not fit in here.

As might be expected, Shinoda labors over the resolution of Toyotaro's moral conflict: the dissolution of romance. But a fuller treatment of this narrative line is endowed with the director's different interpretations of Elice's plight and

Lisa Wolf (l) and Hiromi Go in *Die Tänzerin* (1989) directed by Masahiro Shinoda. Courtesy of the Kawakita Memorial Film Institute.

Toyotaro's trip back home. In the original, Ogai gives considerable weight to the internal turmoil Toyotaro experiences after he impulsively accepts the count's offer to take him back to Japan. Toyotaro's recollection starts with a fairly prosaic assessment of the effect that his impulsive decision has on him: "I know I'm a bright fellow, and articulate, yet how can I possibly explain my situation to Elice? My confusion seems inexplicable."[19] Then Ogai delineates Toyotaro's wandering at night in a vividly pictorial manner. Objects as he perceives them are rendered in a rapid, rhythmical succession. His hat and overcoat are covered with an inch of snow. The horse carriage railway is also covered with snow, while gas lamps flicker, as if "lonely."

Shinoda easily transposes the essentially filmic quality of Ogai's description onto the screen. A series of shots takes in the places he wanders through, giving each a great deal of visual legibility. Quite literally, the camera takes note of Toyotaro's constant movement, often through a reverse-field setup. The only drawback in Shinoda's transposition is his lack of access to Toyotaro's thoughts. Toyotaro in the original recalls "the absolutely unforgivable guilt," the only feeling that overwhelmed him at the time. At best, Shinoda gives us clues to Toyotaro's state of mind through the camera's scrutiny of his face and behavior.

Though novel and film share the disastrous effect of separation on Elice, they put it in different lights. While Toyotaro is sick in bed, Ogai's heroine learns of her lover's forthcoming departure from Aizawa. She becomes paranoid and is committed to a hospital. "Her rational faculty is completely gone, reduced to that of an infant."[20] After his recovery, Toyotaro is often seen crying, holding the insane Elice in his arms.

Fate is also unkind to Shinoda's heroine, but in a different way. Elice miscarries. The sense of desertion is portrayed more poignantly because Toyotaro, accompanied by Aizawa, is urged to depart without saying farewell to her.[21] This heroine is spared madness, but not the consequences of courage—the agony of having the strength to chase after Toyotaro's departing carriage.

Each stage of her suffering is put in the limelight and rendered from multiple points of view. Because of the absence of first-person narration, these sequences strike us as being, not Toyotaro's recollection of past experience, but a realization of past events as he now understand them. Yet he is barred from certain events that the omniscient camera supplies for the viewer. Our picture of Elice's plight is the whole one—thanks to witnessing what neighbors say and see, and the departing lover too, and what the camera's objective eye takes into account.

Elice's miscarriage occurs right after Aizawa tells her of Toyotaro's decision to leave Germany. As they talk, a series of cross-cuts offers a close view of each character's face. Aizawa's emotion is well under control, as if to suggest that he is but a messenger, not a guilty schemer forcing Toyotaro into betraying his love. While Aizawa speaks, Elice's face is an open book. She rejects the money he offers. Finally, she says what her face has said already: "Toyo has been deceiving me. He has been lying all these years!" The scene concludes with a shot of Elice falling down a flight of stairs.

The sequence of the lovers' separation brings the element of ethnic confrontation to the fore, a motif Shinoda develops in a very personal way. He opens with a shot of Aizawa and Toyotaro hurrying across the drab courtyard. The camera takes note of a sense of discord: their figures clad in expensive fur coats simply do not fit in here. Two women appear and approach them. A cut to a window shows Elice's mother silently watching the commotion below. Two more residents, a young girl and the shoemaker, also approach the two Japanese. Aizawa and Toyotaro are silent, but traditional solemn *koto* music suddenly invades the sound track; we sense again that these two men are very much out of place. The four residents encircle the two Japanese. The woman shouts in Toyotaro's face, accusing him of betraying Elice's love. The camera cuts to a close-in view of the shoemaker. Until now he has been an almost silent observer of the lovers' life. For the first time, he expresses his xenophobia: "Didn't I say all along that this is what you get, falling in love with foreigners?" A cut shows Elice's mother closing the window.

All these responses simply echo a number of earlier scenes that showed these inhabitants apparently indifferent as Toyotaro passed in and out of their little world. This repetitive device, though trivial, says something about Toyotaro's life as it would have been, had he opted to trade his homeland and its values for this place and its ethos. A sense of alienation, of nonacceptance, would be his doom, though family solidarity might have held out against it to some degree.

The effects of leave-taking on both Toyotaro and Elice are then offered through Shinoda's deft use of cross-cuts and point-of-view shots. Toyotaro and Aizawa step out into the morning light from the dark courtyard. Perfunctory as it is, this transition succeeds in conveying a sense of Toyotaro's leaving behind a shadowland life with all the dingy associations of poverty, anonymity, and fruitless struggle. The two men board the carriage, which speeds off through the deserted streets of Berlin. Needless to say, this echoes the beginning of the film: streets crowded with well-dressed people and adorned with impressive monuments serving as symbols of the spirit of the West that Toyotaro was so eager to make his own. Now those same streets, captured in this different light, poignantly remind us of the result of Toyotaro's acting out in that spirit: he is betrayed by the very values of freedom.

A cut to the interior of the carriage shows Aizawa preventing Toyotaro from leaping out. Another cut shows Elice standing in the square. She has just returned from the hospital. A high-angle shot registers each party's location. From that point on, the camera records each stage of Elice's attempt to chase after the running carriage. She comes out to the road. A shot of the empty road yields to a shot of Elice running toward the camera, calling her lover's name. A long shot shows Elice in the background, the road dominating the foreground. Finally, she loses strength and falls. Thanks to the camera, the distance separating the lovers widens before our eyes with sad finality. A cut to the interior of the carriage shows Toyotaro peeping through the back window. Though the shots of Elice's pursuit are objective, not taken from Toyotaro's point of view, the insertion of this interior shot gives them that immediacy anyway. It is as if Shinoda means to suggest that Toyotaro's imagination can propel him back her way, to witness her suffering. Another shot offers a closer view of Toyotaro's face in tears, seen through the window of the carriage. A point-of-view shot shows the statue of Victory. Birds are seen flying over it, as if to suggest the impossible dream of freedom for Toyotaro. The shot dissolves to mark a different temporal mode.

As mentioned earlier, Ogai's work ends with Toyotaro's emotional response to separation: guilt mixed with resentment toward his best friend, Aizawa. The film expands the narrative line, giving substantial treatment to Toyotaro's course of action on his way back to Japan. The final scene picks up what was presented in the opening sequence: Toyotaro is still in the cabin, this time reading a letter. This closes one subplot line: his mother's suicide attempt in an earlier sequence. Unlike the mother of the novel, this one has survived. The letter happens to be from the mother. She is now anxiously awaiting her son's return. We are offered a close-up of his face as a clue to his emotional quandary after he finishes reading it.

The camera then follows Toyotaro crossing a room on the ship as someone shouts that Mount Fuji is now in view. He reaches the deck, where the camera cross-cuts between mountain and passengers. Then the camera zooms in on Mount Fuji. Shinoda's focus on this image seems rich in implications. We get a clear sense of the powerful emotion evoked by that lofty eminence, especially for these wayfarers in the Meiji era, so long abroad, so glad to be coming home. There is, too, a sense of the Mount Fuji revered since ancient times, the mountain of everlasting life, of Shinto's worshipful approach to nature. Shinoda's message is especially well taken because this image echoes that of the emperor and of Shinto worship as shown at the outset of the film. In a rather elementary way, Shinoda articulates the unwavering sense of nationalism deeply rooted in people in the Meiji era, whatever form it took. Coupled with close-ups of Count Amagata looking sternly at Toyotaro, the mountain image simply affirms the young man's necessary coming to terms with the values of the tradition he comes from. Tradition has won the battle for the soul of this young Meiji intellectual; the world of freedom/ego retreats into the realm of wishful thinking.

On the whole, Shinoda has worked hard to expand the frame of reference of Ogai's romantic tale, giving narrative legibility to important events. Here we have a director offering a very personal interpretation of a novelist's very real moral dilemma, a dilemma experienced by Ogai in real life as a Meiji government official. This film shows Shinoda discovering a new venue of approach for his lifelong concern with feudal remnants—the Imperial system especially—as they affect and mold individual lives, even in our own time.

Notes

I am grateful to *Post Script* for permitting me to reprint my article, which appeared in vol. 15, no. 3 (Summer 1996).

1. For a critical study of Toyoda's *The Mistress*, see David Desser, "*The Mistress:* The Economy of Sexuality," *Post Script* 11, no. 1 (Fall, 1991): 20–27.
2. Donald Keene, ed. *Modern Japanese Literature* (New York: Greenwood, 1963), p. 23.
3. Tadaharu Kageyama, *Ogai bungaku nyumon* (Introduction to Ogai's literature) (Tokyo: Furukawa Shoten, 1980), p. 19.
4. Masahiro Shinoda, "*Maihime* e no watakushi no messeji" (My message for *Die Tänzerin*), in the film pamphlet *Maihime* (Tokyo: Herald Ace, 1989), p. 5.
5. Ibid.
6. Quoted by Midori Yajima in "*Yari no Gonza*" (On *Gonza: the Spearman*), *Kinema jumpo*, no. 927 (January 1986): 52.
7. Ogai Mori, "Maihime" (The dancing girl), in *Maihime: Utakata no ki* (The dancing girl: a transient life) (Tokyo: Shincho, 1964), p. 74. The English translation is mine. For the complete English translation of this work, see Richard Bowring, trans. "The Dancing Girl," in *Mori Ogai: Youth and Other Stories*, ed. Thomas Rimer (Honolulu: University of Hawaii Press, 1994).
8. Ogai, "Maihime," p. 77.
9. Ibid., p. 83.
10. Ibid., p. 85.
11. Ibid.
12. Ibid., p. 96.
13. Since the publication of this novel, many critics have pointed out Ogai's deliberate avoidance of Toyotaro's final decision. For example, see Yukiko Miyoshi, *Ogai to Soseki: Meiji no etos* (Ogai and Soseki: ethos in the Meiji era) (Tokyo: Rikitomi Shobo,1983), p. 32. For an intensive analysis of Ogai's treatment of the hero, see Fumitake Seita, *Ogai bungei no kenkyu* (A study of Ogai's literature) (Tokyo: Yuseido, 199), pp. 278–310.
14. Kageyama, *Ogai bungaku nyumon*, p. 18.
15. Ogai, "Maihime," p. 80.
16. Ibid., p. 81.
17. Ibid.
18. Ibid., pp. 98–99.
19. Ibid., p. 98.
20. Ibid.
21. One critic observes that the film's hero is portrayed as much more egoistic because of his way of leave-taking, while Toyotaro's desertion of Elice may be justifiable due to her insanity. See Yukichi Shinada, "*Maihime*: Komyo ni saigen sareta jukyuseikimatsu no moeru koi "(*Die Tänzerin*: passionate love at the end of the nineteenth century exquisitely re-created), *Kinema jumpo*, no. 1012 (June 1989): 53.

13

Back to the Mirror of the Past:
Morita's *Sorekara* (1985)

At first glance, it seems an odd combination. On the one hand, we have the dazzling Meiji novelist and intellectual Natsume Soseki (1867–1916); on the other, the versatile post–modern director Yoshimitsu Morita (b. 1950). Yet the film of 1985 and the novel of 1907 come together in an adaptation that makes *Sorekara* a fascinating study in the process of transference from linguistic to visual medium. Soseki's achievements in literature have long been familiar to readers and critics.[1] Now we have an opportunity to see a filmmaker calling on the cogent "visual" properties of cinema, taking full advantage of the camera's expressive power, of effective diegetic and nondiegetic sounds and of carefully composed setting.[2]

> Though the young director is not really on familiar ground with the Meiji period, all this helps him to capture its ambiance in a uniquely refreshing way. No wonder the prestigious journal *Kinema jumpo* voted *Sorekara* Best Film of the Year, and Morita Best Director.

Asked what inspired him to put the Soseki novel on screen, this postmodernist emphasized its contemporaneity:

> Daisuke Nagai (the hero in the novel) considers working solely for bread as beneath his dignity, and claims that a man's privilege is experience of luxury. He also thinks that a civilized man ought to cultivate any type of beauty, pursuing his own taste and hobby as the goal of life. Nowadays this type of man is emerging in Japan, I think.[3]

Morita has added that in his portrayal of Daisuke, raised in bourgeois society, he continued to work out the theme of "a stranger" he had earlier explored in the 1983 work *Kazoku gemu* (The family game).[4]

As might be expected, Morita modifies the narrative of the original to accommodate this thematic thrust. The critic George Bluestone has suggested a commonsensical way to deal with these kinds of changes: we should consider additions, deletions, and alterations for a film script.[5] Such variants here shed some light on Morita's transformation of the novel he endows with such salient "postmodern" overtones in his film. Then, too, Morita's stylistic experiment undoubtedly serves as a contributing factor.

256

Soseki's novel *Sorekara* (And then) explores the central problem of the protagonist Daisuke Nagai's coming to terms with late Meiji society. Edwin McClellan has observed of that period, just after the Russo-Japanese War: "Japan has now attained her goal of world recognition as a modern power, and the struggle for recognition has now been replaced by the struggle for survival. Industrial expansion resulting from the war has introduced a new kind of insecurity, and thus selfishness and cruelty, into Japanese society."[6] Put another way, one might ask what price Japan had to pay for its modernization. Then one might begin to see the sharp inconsistency studied by Soseki through his protagonist's struggle with opportunistic materialism pitted against moral authenticity. His main character, Daisuke, puts the case this way:

> Look at Japan. She is the kind of country that cannot survive unless she borrows money from the West. In spite of this, she tries to play the role of a first-class power; she tries to force her way into the company of first-class powers. . . . Because of the pressure of competition with the West, the Japanese have no time to relax and think and do something worthwhile. . . . They think of nothing except themselves and their immediate needs. Look all over Japan, and you won't find one secure inch that is bright with hope. It is dark everywhere. . . .[7]

Thus Daisuke represents the moral dilemma of a Meiji intellectual caught between conflicting value systems. He is forced to adapt to a changing world either by continuing to depend on paternal authority or by striking out in some new direction of independence. At the outset, thirty-year-old Daisuke has no intention of earning independence by the sweat of his brow. He considers that beneath the dignity of someone belonging to a "superior class of people possessed of hours unspoiled by work." He sees no indignity in living off his father's bounty. After all, Daisuke thinks that he is independent, living in his own house with maid and servant, all paid for by his father, Seigo.

This state of complacent impasse is changed as the narrative gains momentum, thanks to external pressure for him to marry. If he resists the girl of his family's choosing, he risks losing his comfortable independence, which matrimony could in fact increase in a material sense. At the same time, a reunion with his former classmate Hiraoka puts him in touch with his former sweetheart, Michiyo, now Hiraoka's wife.

Thus Daisuke is suddenly caught up in a web of conflicting choices—conformity/dependence and rebellion/independence—and odious comparisons. The route to financial independence on his own involves moving counter to his self-image by following an elder brother into the business world.

Even worse is Daisuke's determination to steal his sometime sweetheart away from her husband. In the Meiji world of strict conventions and acute awareness of respectability, this is a radical departure, an act of rebellion with serious consequences.

Even so, Daisuke decides to risk the ultimate societal catastrophe: ostracism by his family. He tells himself nevertheless that another, more universal law must rule a man like him: fidelity to his inner self. By no longer lying to himself about his feelings for Michiyo, and by taking action accordingly, he thinks he has found new purpose and meaning in his life. There is more than rash decision here; there is rescue in a risk he sees as saving himself "from his effete existence."

The novel moves slowly to bring Daisuke to his actual decision to confess his love to Michiyo. That takes place in Chapter 14, fourth from the last in the book.

> If he had not felt that his attitude toward Michiyo had been pushed to the brink, Daisuke would undoubtedly have adopted this course with his father. But now, regardless of his father's countenance, Daisuke would have to cast the die in his hand. Whether the face turned out to be inconvenient to Hiraoka or disagreeable to his father, as long as he was going to cast the die, he had no choice but to obey the laws of heaven. . . . Daisuke decided in his heart that the final authority rested with him. . . .[8]

His progress in self-knowledge is correspondingly gradual. Until that climactic moment, Soseki relies on rhetorical tension by pitting Daisuke's perception of his own image against our view of it. For example, this protagonist imagines that by not participating in the world of material struggle he is leading a more meaningful life. We see it the other way around entirely.

The evidence is there from the beginning. At the novel opens, we meet with some deft touches of metaphor signaling the progress of a self-centered man. Daisuke puts hand on heart—to check his pulse rate. He has seen a red camellia lying on the floor. This flush of exquisite anxiety in response to beauty passes without harm to his organism. The critic Doi diagnoses Daisuke's case as cultivated hypochondria, "the penalty one pays for being endowed with a fine mind and keen senses, a disadvantage attendant on a good education."[9]

Daisuke then studies himself fondly in the mirror. Combing his hair, he thinks how he does not mind in the least being thought a dandy. This narcissism leads to doubts about the Confucian values of his father. We begin to understand that Daisuke is alienated, not just from the patriarch, but also from the rest of the family. Possibly closest to him is a sister-in-law, Umeko, who has served as a sort of surrogate mother.

Daisuke sees himself as a man free to follow the natural inclination of his spirit and therefore more capable of serious work. This is, of course, the classical aesthete definition of labor as of consequence only when it is free of economic necessity. Thus the privileged individual must be free to live for beauty unspoiled by questions of everyday necessity. Daisuke seeks to follow that star. Then we wonder why he is significantly lacking in vitality. Soseki attributes this to his hero's ennui.

The climax of the novel picks up speed with a number of narrational units contributing to a well-patterned causality. Daisuke invites Michiyo to his house and confesses his love. He confronts his father and refuses to marry the girl his family has chosen for him. He tells his friend Hiraoka that he means to have his wife.

Yet a significant narrative omission is Daisuke's neglecting to tell his father about Michiyo. That news comes in a letter from Hiraoka to the father. Causal chains are thus all linked, the outcome being Daisuke's loss of family ties and alienation from his friend. He is correspondingly strengthened in his conviction that he is following a higher law of nature by hearkening to his inner voice.

Soseki's protagonist seems to be following a principle that the novelist explores more concretely in late novels like *Kokoro* (1914) and *Meian* (Light and darkness, 1917). This is the concept of *sokuten kyoshi* (conform to heaven and forsake ego). Echoing ancient Chinese philosophy, "Heaven" refers to absolute and ideal infinity transcending the human world. It follows that Heaven's law, or Nature, asserts its primacy over any man-made law. According to Soseki, man must live in accordance with this higher law, forsaking his smaller existence in order to achieve a holistic vision of life. Soseki seems to consider that a man's decision to be true to himself, even by going against accepted societal norms, is in fact following heaven's way, the way of ego negation. Thus, he offers this advice as a way of understanding life's dilemma as it troubles those who have strong egos.[10]

This philosophical idea must be understood in connection with a calligraphic rendition of the text "Sincerity Is Heaven's Way" hanging framed in Seigo's room. Daisuke always hated this reminder, considering it "not the way of the world."

Since Soseki does not explain the reason behind Daisuke's abhorrence, we must surmise it. Yet surely the psychology of the novel's protagonist is readily understood. Daisuke sees himself as having broken a universal law by deceiving himself. Acting on a specious "generosity," he helped Hiraoka marry Michiyo, denying himself the expression of his own true feelings. Now he sees this (grace of hindsight) as hypocrisy, linking his life with those who live falsely for the sake of conventional respectability. Thus, after being torn between becoming "a child of Nature" or "a man of will," he decides to choose the first. To seek fulfillment in his sincere love for Michiyo is, for Daisuke, following the dictates of Heaven, not committing adultery. Thus, seeking to right hypocrisy in himself, and to act responsibly toward Michiyo, Daisuke obeys Heaven's higher law in a most this-worldly way: by going out into the real world to look for work.

The color red dominates the novel's texture throughout as an objective correlative to Daisuke's uneasiness. In Chapter 5, for example, he ponders a Western painter's choice of red for rooms meant to stimulate intellectual encounter. Daisuke himself feels uncomfortable every time he sees a vermilion *torii* gate of a Shinto shrine. His letterbox has a red lid. Thus, together with these, the red camellia metaphor from the opening of the book returns for our final view of Daisuke acting on his decision:

> Suddenly, a red mailbox caught his eye. The red color immediately leaped into Daisuke's head and began to spin around and around. An umbrella shop sign had four red umbrellas hanging one on top of the other. The color of these umbrellas also leaped into Daisuke's head and whirled around. At an intersection

someone was selling bright red balloons. As the streetcar sharply turned the corner, the balloons followed and leaped into Daisuke's head. A red car carrying parcel post passed close by the streetcar in the opposite direction, and its color was also sucked into Daisuke's head. . . . Finally, the whole world turned red. And with Daisuke's head at the center, it began to spin around and around, breathing tongues of fire. Daisuke decided to go on riding until his head was completely burnt away.[11]

The novel's ending is open to interpretation. Soseki does not tell us what is to become of Daisuke and Michiyo. Will he in fact see her again? Will he find work? Doi dismisses endpoint meanings of this kind by saying that Daisuke is in fact on the verge of lapsing into psychosis.[12]

I would suggest that Daisuke's symptoms are symbolic of a confrontation with the threat of a real world looming near, imposing its terms on him. The fiery red of the commercial billboard, for very real reasons, will wither the red camellia of aesthetic sensibility, as the dandy effete rides everyman's public transportation into the depths of the city. Significant, too, is the fact that he rides alone. Will he muster the courage to fight by himself? Is the motion of journey meant to suggest a decision to let fate run its course? The reader is left to decide.

Morita takes on Soseki's thematic concern with the individual's conflict with Meiji society. As a filmmaker, however, he must solve problems of transfer from one medium to the other in his pursuit of the moral dilemma dramatized by the novelist. This he does chiefly by shifting narrative focus, rearranging sequences of cause and effect, and most importantly, by taking full advantage of the formal potential of cinema.

The focus of the novel on Daisuke's shifting awareness of Michiyo and his rekindling love means that his point of view predominates. Hers, in fact, scarcely comes into it. For example, Soseki's first depiction of Michiyo's presence takes place in the scene of her reunion with Daisuke. Soseki labors on his hero's impression of her physical traits pitted against his memory of them:

Hiraoka's wife had rather dark hair for a fair-complexioned woman. Her face was oval with clearly shaped brows. . . . . Her complexion had noticeably lost its luster since their return to Tokyo. . . .

Michiyo's eyelids had two beautiful lines, one above the other, making a distinct fold. Her eyes were on the long and narrow side, but whenever she fixed her gaze, they somehow became extremely large. . . . He had often observed this eye movement of hers in the days before she was married and he still remembered it well. Whenever he tried to picture her face in his mind, those black eyes, blurred as if they were misty, rose immediately, even before the outline of her face was complete. . . .[13]

Toward the end of her visit, Michiyo asks Daisuke for a loan. Soseki elaborates on Michiyo's reason for this request, but bars us from inquiry into her inner feelings. Instead, we are given Daisuke's perception of how Michiyo might have felt: "'You could not lend us some money?' Michiyo's words were as guileless as a child's, but her cheeks were nonetheless red. Daisuke found Hiraoka's situation painful indeed, that he should have to force this woman to undergo so humiliating an experience."[14]

Morita adds this missing dimension by conveying a refreshing mutuality of awareness. Michiyo's subtle feelings for Daisuke are first presented in a scene at the inn, where his name is mentioned by her husband, Hiraoka. He announces that he has asked Daisuke to help him find a job. Michiyo says only that Daisuke will do his best, and she continues her needlework with her head lowered. Up to this moment we have been given only the scantiest information about these three. We know that Hiraoka and Daisuke were classmates, that Michiyo has lost her baby, and that she has been wondering if Daisuke is married yet.

This shot of Michiyo sewing offers the viewer a clue to her inner feelings, carefully concealed though they may be. Her first encounter with Daisuke thus confirms our suspicion of a mutual awareness that goes beyond the feelings of "just friends" reunited.

As Daisuke mounts the stairs of the Japanese inn, his posture suggests obvious tension. Subsequent shots confirm this impression. Michiyo's face, caught in close-up, looms out of the darkness of the ill-lit room. She stares at Daisuke, her pallor yielding to an unmistakable flush. The cinematic composition makes use of deep space to show that Daisuke is not near Michiyo. Instead, it registers quite clearly his sense of her reaction to his presence. This aspect is confirmed once more as Hiraoka and Daisuke leave. Deep space is deftly used again to show Michiyo in the background at the end of the corridor, leaning forward to see them off.

In the novel, Daisuke reminisces about the past, so we learn that he had been in love with Michiyo but had yielded to his friend Hiraoka. These memories of having done the noble thing also serve to reinforce Daisuke's awakening attachment to Michiyo.

George Bluestone claims that "the rendition of mental states—memory, dream, imagination—cannot be as adequately represented by film as by language" because "conceptual imaging has no existence in space."[15] I suspect that many viewers will find Morita's use of the camera's expressive power equal to the novelist's evocation of perceptual images. This is done through shot variation, filmic texture, and nondiegetic sounds. Taken together, these render information in a pictorial manner entirely adequate to the purpose and indeed more concisely than the text.

This may be clearly seen in two flashbacks. The first occurs just after the inn sequence mentioned above. Michiyo and Daisuke meet on an overpass and walk down the stairwell. The entire scene is done through a simple yet effective mode of representation. The nondiegetic sound of piano music adds what lyrical touch there is. The texture is controlled by the color blue. Yet cultural icons hinting at mutual awareness are an umbrella, a rich, culturally controlled metaphor suggesting of *ai ai gasa*, understood as lovers sharing this shelter from a drizzling rain. As they approach the camera, we notice Michiyo's hairstyle—the "gingko leaf" worn by maidens. It seems in striking contrast to the more ordinary housewife's coiffure she wore before.

More important, this scene introduces the controlling metaphor for Michiyo: the lily in her hand. For Daisuke, this simple white flower embodies his beloved's attributes—her feminine purity mixed with a sense of aloofness. Unlike other flowers of the field (the violet, for example), the lily is a noble bloom, though lacking warmth and liveliness. Filmmaker and novelist seem to agree that Michiyo should be invested with a sense of unattainability, since she and Daisuke are ill-fated lovers. One might add, however, that Morita introduces this icon so persistently, in ways so visually perceptive throughout the film, that this essentially Western flower adds a uniquely modern touch not found in Soseki.

The scene ends with a freeze frame of the two in close-up. This gives us a telling impression of things as seen from Daisuke's point of view. Previously, his line of sight was directed into Michiyo's sparkling eyes. Now his own are averted, as if he fears seeing his feelings for her reciprocated.

A second flashback sequence confirms the feelings of mutual attraction merely hinted at in the first. The same piano music returns, as does the color blue dominating the filmic texture. Michiyo, her elder brother, Hiraoka, and Daisuke are strolling in Ueno Park. Again, Morita does much with little, showing us the lovers looking at or away from each other. Michiyo is paired with Hiraoka, Daisuke with her brother. She steals a glance at Daisuke while talking with Hiraoka. Feeling her eyes on him, Daisuke is unable to meet her glance.

Toward the end of this sequence, Morita makes deft use of deep space to suggest this rivalry in love. Daisuke has purchased a pearl ring for Michiyo, and Hiraoka a watch for her. Hiraoka is closest to the camera, with Daisuke midway, and Michiyo near the door, holding an open parasol. The tension among the three is readily apparent.

The two major departures from the original narrative involve Daisuke's visits to the red-light district, which is given brief mention in the novel, and the climax of the final sequence.

Daisuke's forays into the pleasure quarter are first presented as acts of rebellion against patriarchal authority. In fact, his pursuit of passion follows on events like the chamber concert, where he has been forced to meet a prospective bride. More significantly, his licentiousness is seen as a manifestation of sublimated passion for Michiyo. Evidence of this is presented in a number of ways. We first see him flirting with two geisha after he confesses to his sister-in-law that he has a love of his own. The scene cuts to Michiyo scrubbing her husband's back with a wet cloth. Her slim white arms create a strange, erotic atmosphere.

Throughout the film, Daisuke fondles and savors lilies, clearly as projections of Michiyo's physical charms, especially her fair skin. At one point he pretends not to like lilies any more. She reminds him that he used to be fond of their fragrance. A brief flashback shows Daisuke sniffing a lily glazed with rain. This detail was carefully omitted in the first flashback scene, but now returns to fill in the narrational gap.

In the novel, an expensive bottle of perfume purchased by Daisuke has nothing to do with Michiyo. In the film it is used to evoke her presence. The brand, in

Miwako Fujitani (l) and Yusaku Matsuda (r) in *Sorekara* (1985) directed by Yoshimitsu Morita. Courtesy of the Kawakita Memorial Film Institute.

fact, is "White Lily." Daisuke sprinkles it on his bed and around the room. Later on, his brother visits and notices the fragrance. By this time, we understand that Michiyo haunts Daisuke's life through such means. Even as he bought the perfume in the first place, the camera's observant glance took note of a lamp hanging from the ceiling, blinking on and off. The ominous shadow it casts on the bottle suggests Daisuke's fear of involvement with his friend's wife.

Morita also arranges narrative events to bring Daisuke into more open conflict with Meiji society at a climactic moment. As mentioned before, the novel's ending comes in a single causal line. Hiraoka writes to Daisuke's father, who sends the elder brother to announce the family's decision to disown him.

The film reverses the flow of conflict, pitting a more decisive rebel against the family. Before leaving for his father's house, Daisuke is shown engaged in calligraphy. The aphorism "Sincerity Is Heaven's Law" was first introduced as part of the *mise-en-scène* early in the film as father and son sipped tea. Now each Chinese ideogram appears in close-up as Daisuke writes. A new meaning emerges for the text as Daisuke's mind yields to its deeper meaning by accepting responsibility for his true feelings and declaring his love for Michiyo.

As he copies the aphorism, he adds three more ideograms to say "Sincerity Is Not the Way of the World." (Its implication is "Sincerity Will Not Be Ruled by Human Law.") Daisuke's conflict clarifies and complicates the given text. He sees how a higher law transcends the social laws created by man. At the same time, he cannot help but see a basic incompatibility between an honest, spiritually satisfying life and a materially rewarding one. Clearly, he must choose between a difficult moral authenticity and a more convenient conformity to social rules. Needless to say, and in spite of the time elapsed between novel and film, novelist and filmmaker agree in assigning the cause of this dichotomy to Japan's rapid Westernization, with its value put on utilitarianism and opportunism.

Daisuke's confrontation with his family is given a notable amount of visual disarray. This is far removed from the formally structured symmetrical alignment of hostilities we saw in the earlier scene of father and son sipping tea (as in an Ozu film). Here, father slaps son and brother grapples with him. Chairs collide and overturn. A deep focus shows Umeko weeping in the background.

The ending of the film is much more open than the book. Symbolic clues provided there by various icons are conspicuously absent here. We see nothing of Daisuke's intent to find a job. Instead, there is only a final shot of him walking toward the camera, wearing a white hat. In contrast to the otherworldly atmosphere presented in the recollection scenes, the earthly color now predominates, suggesting Daisuke's hope of settling in with everyday reality. (Most of Daisuke's recollections have been rendered in this realm of blue.) What Daisuke's inner feelings are, we can only guess. The hat casts a shadow over his face. All we know is that he is not looking at the moon, as in the earlier scene, where the moon suggests his affinity for Heaven's law. What happens next is any viewer's guess.

Morita's narrative additions and deletions free him to make the most of cinema's formal properties. A notable example is his frequent use of the long take for dramatic scenes. Daisuke's proposal to Michiyo, for example, is given a 7-minute 50-second medium shot of the couple. The camera is fixed at eye level as the two sit with a bouquet of white lilies between them.

This single take is sustained by a wealth of information. The dialogue articulates the lovers' view of a solution to their moral dilemma. Their remembrance of past events is triggered by the lilies, whose metaphorical value has long been clear to us. The emotional overtones are provided by a mixture of nondiegetic and diegetic sounds. Soft violin music prevails up to the point when Daisuke prepares to confess that he needs her for his future life, which is why he sent for her.

Suddenly, the music stops. A violent rainstorm beats against the windowpanes, as if in sympathy with the emotional turmoil inside. Music replaces rain then, as Michiyo tells how she married Hiraoka four years before in order to punish herself because Daisuke had not revealed his true feelings. The scene ends with Michiyo saying that they must prepare themselves. The rain returns with distant thunder.

What little movement there is of the couple's bodies and eyes also reflects their gradual reconciliation. All this while, the two move only once: Michiyo, still seated, slides a bit closer to the lilies as they talk. The only other motions are her wiping away tears and both of them inclining their heads. As Daisuke finishes his confession, their heads are tilted almost symmetrically. Toward the end of this take, when Michiyo's decision is made, their eyes meet for the first time.

Yusaku Matsuda in *Sorekara* (1985) directed by Yoshimitsu Morita. Courtesy of the Kawakita Memorial Film Institute.

Morita deftly centers the lilies within the frame so that their whiteness cannot escape our attention. This creates a subtly erotic texture calling up rich associations with earlier images of whiteness: Michiyo's foot slipping into a *tabi*, her pale hand with Daisuke's gift of a pearl ring; and, most tellingly, her throat bared as she drinks a bottle of soda in Daisuke's presence. (Western readers might draw a Freudian implication about Michiyo's suppressed sexuality in view of the fact that Daisuke drinks soda, pouring it in a glass. But her bare throat creates a much stronger impression, I think, than the bottle itself).

The scene of Daisuke's final confrontation with Hiraoka is given two long takes, the first lasting three minutes, the second a trifle longer. Here Morita relies more on character and camera movement and deep space.

The first take begins with action shown on three planes. In the background, the live-in servant, Kadono, is cleaning a room. The middle ground consists of a courtyard where Daisuke is sweeping up leaves. Hiraoka enters the foreground, a corridor adjacent to the drawing room. Kadono closes a door, which blocks him from our sight. The door now serves as a backdrop for the garden. The camera moves left to frame Hiraoka and Daisuke in the center. They sit together in the corridor. A cicada chirps—a sure sign of summer heat. The physical movements of the two men express their nervous anxiety as the moment of actual clash draws near. Finally, toward the end of the second take, Daisuke grapples with Hiraoka.

Another unique stylistic experiment is found earlier in a parody of Ozu's use of intermediate spaces. This occurs when Daisuke visits his father. Daisuke is near the gate of the father's house. Suddenly the son's back dominates the screen. (For this shot, Morita lets the actor Yusaku Matsuda ride a swinglike wagon, raising his figure gradually from below.) The next shot (91 seconds) makes use of deep space in two planes. Down below in the garden, we see the tiny figure of Daisuke. The second-floor drawing room of the house forms the foreground, where Daisuke's niece is playing a violin. A director like Ozu would have cut to the intermediate spaces (gate or corridor, for example) that Daisuke must pass before reaching this room. Not Morita. His shot transfers Daisuke directly to the room, which he enters, moving toward the girl. (Matsuda had only one minute to run up the stairs when this shot was taken!)

Morita is especially deft with deep space. This is masterfully done to point up the contrast between the affluent Nagai and impoverished Hiraoka households. In the former, the drawing room has a wide glass door. When Daisuke comes to visit, he sits on an expensive chair near a piano while the camera takes note of goings-on outdoors: well-dressed children, for example, playing with a pedigreed dog. Cherry trees are in blossom, too, while indoors the family moves freely around the room as if enjoying the privileges of spaciousness.

The same deep space intensifies a sense of narrow confinement in the Hiraoka house. Michiyo is seen hanging clothes in her tiny yard in the foreground. In the background, Daisuke's head appears in a bamboo door. The small distance between them speaks for the want of luxury here. We cannot help remembering Hiraoka's comment that only a lucky strike on the stock market would bring a decent house within his reach. The sense of a cluttered inner-city neighborhood is also much in evidence. A vendor's voice is heard, and somewhere a baby is crying.

The thirty-five-year-old Morita obviously enjoys none of his illustrious predecessors' direct contact with survivors of the Meiji era. (Of all his cast and staff, only Chishu Ryu, playing Daisuke's father, had that advantage.[16]) Yet the director makes brilliant use of cinematic means to re-create a feeling of those times. This is especially noticeable in the evidence of eclecticism in that cultural climate. Morita's view of Daisuke's house takes in deep space on at least two planes: the corridor with its *tatami* mats and sliding glass doors of semitransparent panes, and a courtyard with palm trees.

Elsewhere, as in the Nagai household, a counterpoint of eclectic images is used: glass windows and cherry trees set in Western plots of grass; a huge piano and assortment of brandy snifters; and moving in and around these Western artifacts, the kimono-clad Umeko with a Japanese coiffure. Elsewhere, as a trolley moves away from the camera, a temple is seen to the right, and to the left is a Western building.

In contrast to the array of noise so important to his 1983 film *The Family Game*, Morita calls on few sources of this characteristically present-day pollutant. His diegetic evocations of the Meiji era seem appropriately subdued. A creaking trolley car or a trilling cicada suffice for one scene. (The disproportionate volume given to the chewing of father and son in one scene is used to give a comical dimension to the incommunicativeness of the two).

As the art par excellence of visual perception, the film offers its director a much freer hand with color images. We have seen how red dominates in the texture of the novel, most often in order to express states of emotional crisis or anxiety in Daisuke. This color takes on somewhat different connotations as a controlling metaphor in the film. Naturally, Daisuke's incursions into the world of geisha are viewed in red. But Michiyo also displays a red kimono made for her stillborn baby. Later we see her using the same cloth to scrub her husband's back.

More significantly, Morita's ingenuity manifests itself in a magnificent single take of the trolley. Daisuke is seated closest to the camera. As the car moves, the passengers are all seen lighting firecrackers. The collective sense of these images points to a passion for artificiality in a world in which sincerity and honesty are being destroyed on every side. The red of these Meiji fireworks may be seen contrasting with the bluish moon Daisuke gazes up at from the trolley. Clearly, this is a sign of a closeness to nature, or the universal law of Nature Daisuke wants to follow by committing himself to life with Michiyo.

Sorekara is a fascinating instance of a brilliant young director controlling and refashioning raw material provided by his equally brilliant predecessor a world away in time, yet close enough in his richly psychological novel. Morita also offers glimpses of still more wide-reaching possibilities in the cinematic mode of representation.

Notes

1. Western readers unfamiliar with Soseki's philosophical/intellectual growth and literary achievements may want to consult the following works: Jun Eto, "Natsume Soseki: A Japanese Meiji Intellectual," *American Scholar* 34 (1965): 603–19; McClellan Edwin, *Two Japanese Novelists: Soseki and Toson* (Chicago: University of Chicago Press, 1969); Makoto Ueda, "Natsume Soseki," in *Modern Japanese Writers* (Stanford: Stanford University Press, 1976), pp. 1–25.
2. A number of Soseki novels have been made into films. The earliest adaptation is Kenji Mizoguchi's *Gubijinso* (Poppy, 1935), based on the novel of the same title. More recent ones include *Kokoro* (The heart, 1955) and *Wagahai wa neko de aru* (I am a cat, 1975), both directed by Kon Ichikawa; and three versions of *Botchan*, two by Shochiku Co. (1958 and 1966) and one by Toho Co. (1953).
3. Hideo Nagabe, "*Sorekara*: Autosaida no unmei" (*Sorekara*: the fate of an outsider), *Kinema jumpo*, no. 823 (October 1985): 61.
4. Ibid.
5. George Bluestone, *Novel into Film* (Berkeley: University of California Press, 1957), p. 21.
6. McClellan, *Two Japanese Novelists*, p. 34.
7. Ibid, p. 37.
8. Soseki Natsume, *And Then*, trans. Norma Moore Field (Baton Rouge and London: Louisiana State University Press, 1978), pp. 188–89. Copyright ©by Nonma Moore Field.

9. Takeo Doi, *The Psychological World of Natsume Soseki* (Soseki no Shinriteki Sekai), trans. William Tyler (London and Cambridge: Harvard University Press, 1976), p. 42.

10. In his late years, Soseki had this to say about *sokuten kyoshi*: "Lately I have entered a certain state which I would call *sokuten kyoshi*, although others might label it differently. It is something like this: to forsake the small self which I usually regard as myself, and to leave it to the dictates of a larger and universal self, so to speak. But I cannot describe it fully in words. And in this state all assertions, all ideals, and all isms, however grandiose, begin to look trivial, whereas those things which ordinarily seem insignificant find a place for their own existence. From this angle one can view with impartiality, discriminating nothing. *Light and Darkness* I am writing in this attitude. . . ." Quoted by Beongcheon Yu, in *Natusme Soseki* (New York: Twayne, 1969), p. 155. The translation is Yu's.

   For more comprehensive study of *sokuten kyoshi* as revealed in Soseki's major works, see Yoshie Okazaki, *Soseki to sokuten kyoshi* (Soseki and the idea of sokuten kyoshi) (Tokyo: Hobutsukan, 1978).

11. Soseki, *And Then*, p. 257.

12. Takeo Doi, *Psychological World of Soseki*, p. 52.

13. Soseki, *And Then*, p. 43–44.

14. Ibid., p. 47.

15. Bluestone, *Novel into Film*, p. 48.

16. Hideo Nagebe, "*Sorekara*," p. 61.

14

Stylistic Experiment: Teshigahara's
The Face of Another (1966)

In Japan, as elsewhere in the world, questions of identity loomed large in the 1960s. A great number of novelists and film directors responded in various ways. For example, such young *nouvelle vague* filmmakers as Masahiro Shinoda and Nagisa Oshima defined the identity crisis of rebellious youth in terms of sex and violence. In contrast, Hiroshi Teshigahara, working closely with the novelist Kobo Abe, explored existential themes arising out of contemporary man's quest for identity.

Teshigahara's first feature-length work, *Otoshiana* (The pitfall, 1962) was an avant-garde adaptation of a television script by Abe. Three other faithful renditions of the writer's novels followed: *Suna no onna* (The woman in the dunes, 1964), *Tanin no kao* (The face of another, 1966), and *Moetsukita chizu* (The ruined map, 1968).[1]

In *The Woman in the Dunes*, Teshigahara, like Abe, allegorically pursues the struggle between the threat of society and contemporary man's effort to preserve his intrinsic human nature. Trapped in a pit in the dunes, the protagonist thinks only of escape at first. Yet he finally accepts this limited and precarious existence as a fit expression of contemporary man's real plight. The protagonist in *The Face of Another* does the opposite. He seeks to change the terms of the given predicament.

Abe's *The Face of Another* and Teshigahara's film version share the psychological story line that concerns a scientist whose face has been destroyed in an industrial explosion. Disfigured and alienated, he decides to regain contact with society by assuming a new, entirely artificial identity. His instrument is a prosthesis: a mask made to conceal his loss. He does more than hide behind this device, however; he embarks on an aggressive masquerade, making the mask his "real" face, living in terms of its "reality." A handicapped person's test of strength, therefore, becomes a contest between conflicting identities.

Despite this shared narrative, both works differ significantly in their approaches to this existential theme. The novel uses first-person narrative in the form of the protagonist's confession recorded in three notebooks. Toward the end, this main narrative thrust interacts with two others: a wife's letter, and the

269

story of the film as told by the protagonist. His notebooks teem with abstract, sometimes verbose, questions and statements about human existence in contemporary society.

To some degree, Teshigahara tries to maintain Abe's hallmark tendency to abstract philosophizing, but he dispenses altogether with the confessional mode. The wife's letter becomes a face-to-face confrontation between husband and wife. From its midpoint on, Teshigahara's narrative of the protagonist's search for a new self is locked in dynamic counterpoint with another, quite convoluted plot contributed by the film. Together, they advance the action of the film. There are also significant changes in characterization. Teshigahara adds a plastic surgeon, creator of the protagonist's mask. He fulfills a number of dramatic functions, most notably that of the person most influential in his patient's final action, as we later see.

More important, by transposing the essentially prosaic novel's overcharged, heavily philosophical overtones, Teshigahara relies heavily on a rich array of "filmic qualities," especially avant-garde stylistic conventions. Many of these prove to be as challenging as the film's "argument." In order to see how the director transforms the original into a work noted for its refreshingly experimental stylistic manipulations, we need to examine Abe's original.

The protagonist is presented as anonymous throughout the novel. Significantly, in Abe's works, a name, like a registration card, serves as contemporary man's mechanical identity. This victim of industrial expansion—explosion may be the better word—is nameless and faceless. He belongs anywhere and nowhere, really. (From this point on, I refer to him as the man, the protagonist, or the narrator.)

The protagonist's confession begins with a description of his hideaway. Here, too, we find familiar Abe images—the walls and darkness indicative of the doomed condition of contemporary man. At the outset, Abe makes use of withheld information, which helps create a mounting tension in his novel. The narrator speaks: "At last you have come, threading your way through the endless passages of the maze. With the map you got from him, you have finally found your way to my hideaway. . . ."[2]

Second-person address is used consistently in this passage. We are put on alert; but several pages pass before we realize that the narrator is keeping us deliberately in the dark. How could we know that he is addressing this note to his wife? And why is he in hiding? Abe leaves us guessing.

The introduction to the narrator's notebooks is filled with ambiguous statements, which are clarified in due course, as the plot unfolds. Here, at the outset, all we know is that this entire volume is being written so that someone will know why the writer's "masked play" has failed. The writer asks: "Have I lost to him or has he lost to me? Either way, my masked play is over. I have murdered him. . . . I shall confess everything, entirely."[3] Later, the narrator reconfirms that intention: "To make the end of my masked play more real, I have decided to go on waiting, while you look through the deposition."[4]

Thus the body of the text represents the narrator's own attempt to clarify his abortive search for a new identity. He aims to recall events in chronological order, with frequent detours into the past. For example, he tries to justify, assess, or even impose a certain philosophical structure on matters he confesses to. As might be expected, his reflections return with a nagging persistence to Abe's central thematic concern throughout his career. It can be phrased as a question: how is a contemporary man to come to terms with the self and society? *The Face of Another* approaches this query by attempting to clarify "the idea of a collective unit." Abe himself puts it this way:

> The twentieth century theme I have in mind—it may be called *my* theme—is the destruction of togetherness, of neighborliness, the idea of a collective unit. To put it another way, let me ask you: How do we know who our neighbors really are? How do we pierce so many layers of concealment?[5]

The Face of Another plots two choices: adopt a mask and live its life, or show the world a human face and take the consequences. In the protagonist's confession, major narrative events map out his shift from the second choice to the first. As we have seen, his opening account of his hideaway is rich in images of walls and darkness. A "leech-like mass" creeps across his bandaged face. The reason for such seclusion becomes clear as his confession goes on. An explosion of liquid oxygen has disfigured him horribly. The worst humiliation of living with this "real" face involves the way it alienates him from his wife.

Dr. K, a specialist in artificial organs, claims that faces are "a roadway" between man and his fellows. Thus the disfigured man's assumption of the mask is his attempt to "restore the roadway" and thereby overcome his "basic humiliation." Recalling his meeting with Dr. K, the narrator poses some of the same thought-provoking questions that haunt all of Abe's heroes. Does an identity card fully identify the man it represents? Don't we actually cling too much to our identity cards? Business cards, drivers' licenses, and registration cards: are these mechanical creations of a civilized society not used to define a person's "real" identity? Nevertheless, the narrator must acknowledge "the face" as the basic form of identification even in this society doomed to a technological dissociation of sensibility. He puts the question this way: "What would it be like if a man's face were as expressionless as an egg, with no eyes, or nose, or mouth?"

With his meeting with Dr. K as a turning point, the narrator decides to make a mask and "to be reborn in another face." His desperate search for escape from alienation is variously described. He says: "I was seized with an impulse to rip off my bandages in earnest and to jump into the midst of this landscape that seemed like pasted bits of paper. But without a face, it was impossible for me to take a single step away from my bondage."[6]

Elsewhere, he says: "If I could cover my face with an imitation completely indistinguishable from the real thing, however fake the landscape might be, it couldn't make me an outcast."[7]

Nevertheless, a subtle dilemma between adapting a mask and keeping his disfigured face is expressed through the narrator's self-doubt. On the one hand, he is inclined to argue that "facial expression is an adequate communicating roadway"; on the other hand, he is convinced that the opposite is the case: "I am more concerned about intercourse between human beings narrowed down and stereotyped by too much dependence on a habit of faces."[8]

Once the dilemma is solved, the protagonist acts on his decision. The main narrative events involve his "purchase" of a "face" from a stranger (i.e., borrowing features from a mold), making the mask that will become his social identity, and donning the mask and discovering the consequences of his masquerade.

This motif of the borrowed face is particularly suited to serve Abe's persistent concern with the idea of "a collective unity." The narrator's decision not to use a replica of his own face translates quite literally into a search for a new identity. So it happens that by killing the masked identity, he also literally kills "the other" he has become.

Abe's story line studies the radical transformation of his anonymous hero after he dons the mask. We see him allow the mask to dominate his real face, as his newly gained sense of self acts out his fantasy, freed from the yoke of reason. Early in his transformation he foresees what will happen to him:

> I had begun to feel an intolerable desolation brought on by the widening gulf between the mask and myself. Perhaps I was already anticipating the catastrophe that was to come. The mask, as its name implied, would forever be my false face; and although my true nature could never be controlled by such a thing, once it had seen you it would fly off somewhere far beyond my control, and I could watch it go in helpless blank amazement.[9]

Again and again, the narrator claims that his new self's original intention was to escape from a hell of loneliness—"a solitary cell" with no "roadway" out. He tries mingling in a crowded bar. His first sensation is one of a mass of faces serving as a roadway for all these people: "Faces, faces, faces, faces. . . . I rubbed my eyes . . . and scowled, peering through noise and cigarette smoke at the innumerable faces packing the place."[10]

The narrator's notebook then records a significant change in his or the mask's personality: he becomes more arrogant and defiant. This is the beginning of the taste of freedom from social constraints that he experiences living behind his mask.

Once he has tasted freedom, the masked man grows bolder, a "shameless" rogue following his every inclination. Looking in a mirror, he is convinced that the plastic he sees is "a far more living face" and that the mask has already become "just as real" as the real thing.

Despite this transformation, Abe uses his narrator to pose important questions about contemporary mankind: "Does the mask express contemporary man's true inner self, or does it remain a merely fabricated identity? Which way does freedom lie?' Such questions are directed not just to the reader but to the protagonist himself, who inevitably is brought to face them at the end of his journey of transformation.

In the course of the narrator's relentless pursuit of freedom, the mask leads him into erotic adventures. He reasons that "the perverse expenditure of freedom is actually the satisfaction of sexual desire." He touches a girl on a crowded train and gets away with it.

Yet, ironically, the high point of the masked man's quest for freedom takes him full circle in the erotic sense: he goes to great lengths to seduce his own wife, hoping that way to restore the "roadway" between them. Early in the process, his precious anonymity is threatened. The apartment manager's retarded daughter knows that the bandaged man and the masked man, who have leased two different apartments, are one and the same. The girl whispers to him: "Let's play secrets." The narrator is shocked by the girl's instinctive penetration of his disguise:

> "Play secrets?" What did she mean? Yet surely there was nothing to worry about. A girl with her disadvantages could never understand such involved tactics. It would be easy to put it down to a restricted field of vision—a dog with a re-stricted field of vision compensates by a keener sense of smell. In the first place, the very fact that I had to be so worried seemed to prove that my self-confidence had again begun to waver.[11]

The narrator's last notebook records in minute detail the progress of his in-volvement with his wife. Significantly, their physical union results in a rift between masked and true selves. The "poison of jealousy" creeps from the one to the other! The mask, however, tries to reassure the real, the suffering, man behind it:

> Even though I did wear a mask on my face, my body was the same as before. . . . Suddenly the mask and I became one, and there was no "other one" to be jealous of. If it was I myself who was touching you, then it was I, too, who was being touched by you; and there was no need to falter.[12]
>
> Even so, there is a struggle. It results in a victory of self over mask:
>
> My betrayed love had been drawn into a corner and changed to hatred; my desire to rebuild the roadway had been frustrated, turned into a desire for re-venge. Since I had come this far and had made quite sure of your infidelity, even though it had not been my motive to do so, the result was that my actions had fallen into step with the mask's.[13]

The protagonist's revenge takes the form of this act we are witnessing—his showing the notebooks to his wife. A sense of his defeat is also recapitulated with reference to the retarded girl with the Yo-Yo:

> I suppose she was able to see through me precisely because she was retarded, just as my mask would not fool a dog. An uninhibited intuition is often far more keen than the analytical eyes of an adult.[14]

Thus, at the end of the novel Abe reinforces the protagonist's abortive effort to "establish the roadway" through a more complex narrative mode and irony. His wife's letter interacts with his final gray notebook. Then the narrator's record of actual events is spiced with his lyrical delineation of events in a film he once saw: *One Side of Love.*

The wife's cursory letter serves an irony carefully prepared for the conclusion of the narrator's masquerade. Like the girl with the Yo-Yo, she has known all about his masked play. Ever since his injury, she argues, there has been a lack of communication between them—a basic misunderstanding, the very stuff of contemporary man's doomed condition. There lies the source of this tragedy. She lays it out plainly enough:

> You went from one misunderstanding to the next. . . . You wrote that I rejected you, but that's not true. Didn't you reject yourself all by yourself? I felt that I could understand your wanting to. In view of the accident and all I had more than half resigned myself to sharing your suffering.[15]

As might be expected, the narrator's reaction to his wife's letter is a poignant recognition of his defeat in the masquerade of the mask: "My mask, which I had expected to be a shield of steel, was broken more easily than glass. . . ."[16]

What will be the outcome of this recognition? Can he restore the "roadway" with his wife as the unmasked man? Or must he continue the masquerade? The answers to these questions are withheld. The narrator continues searching for a philosophical raison d'être for the mask. At one point he decides that the mask is "the expression of a poignant aspiration to get beyond man in an effort to consort with the gods."[17] He then rejects the idea as horrible, a freak of imagination.

The otherwise abstract quality of this confessional mode is enlivened by the narrator's sudden recollection of that film he has seen—the one titled *One Side of Love.* This intrusion prolongs the feeling of suspense; we are anxious to know what the narrator will do. Yet this episode's strikingly lyrical texture puts us in contact with an alternative method of coming to terms with self and society.

Like the narrator, the film's heroine is disfigured with keloid ridges and distorted features. She is a survivor of Nagasaki. She takes refuge from a hostile world in volunteer work, "acts of charity," in a mental institution for old soldiers. The roadway between her and the men is only "a feeling of sympathy," since no words pass between them. Quite a different roadway is established between her and an elder brother in their small suburban house. The film elaborates on a picture of familial love threatened from outside, by uncertain tomorrows amid the hustle and bustle of an impersonal world. Abe gives this atmosphere of anxiety a rich array of metaphors: "deep sea of exhaust gases," "numberless construction sites;" and "garbage bins groaning with their loads." The narrator views all these as signs of a "prodigal waste of life."

This wretchedly mechanized society offers the poor deformed girl an archetypal avenue of escape: a trip to the seaside. She is in fact a castaway in an even more desperate sense: brother and sister cement their bond through incest. Abe's narrator recalls how the film treated that moment of truth: "She brought her lips closer and closer to her brother's, her breath coming in gasps."[18]

The narrator sees an element of the poetic in the film's treatment of this terrible act, which he interprets as a search for freedom from social restraint. He describes it as "the desperate destruction of a taboo" beginning with a "mad, incomplete fusion between the two discordant hammers of anger and desire."

Of course, the poor girl, deformed as she is, cannot "face down" such a menacing society. She can only escape into death. The narrator describes it from the brother's perspective, which adds an almost apocalyptic touch: "At last he [the brother] saw the girl, like a white bird, running with little steps toward the black, heaving sea. Again and again the white bird was thrown back by the waves until at last it rode upon them, appearing and disappearing as it swam toward the open sea."[19]

The conclusion of the novel begins with the masked man's refusal to take that way out, much as he admires the girl: "She tried splendidly to break down an especially difficult sexual taboo, and even death, since she chose it herself, was far better than doing nothing."[20] He sees no such escape for himself. All he can do is continue the masquerade.

This time, however, his search for a new identity takes another turn. He decides to test the waters of freedom by endowing the mask with a more extreme power of choice. He reasons that this new "free" self will partake of the wild, the animal. He is ready now to kill his wife, who has penetrated his disguise: "Since you have seen through it already, the mask will concentrate on its lawlessness, unweakened and unblinded by jealousy. You have dug your own grave."[21]

The novel's ending is left "open." Abe leaves us in the dark about the fate of this individual who has failed to find his "roadway." We do not know whether he actually shoots his wife or simply drops his pistol. We are given only a sense of the utter hopelessness of the man who created his own mask only to be destroyed by it:

> Suddenly I heard the sharp clicking of a woman's heels. Only the mask remained.
> I had vanished. Quickly, without thinking, I concealed myself in a nearby lane,
> releasing the safety catch of my pistol. . . . The footsteps are coming closer. So
> nothing will ever be written down again. Perhaps the act of writing is necessary
> only when nothing happens.[22]

As we have seen, the narrator's confession is replete with abstract philosophizing and reasoning about the issues that haunt contemporary man. Teshigahara retains this abstract quality, though he modifies it considerably. To begin with, his film does not take the form of a single person's confession. He also spares his protagonist the fate of anonymity.

The main body of the film concerns the objective narrative about Okuyama's search for a new identity. The elements of reasoning and philosophizing emerge in conversation between Okuyama and his doctor. This exposes us to a more complex narrative rhetoric because we must pit Okuyama's shifting views of his own existence against the doctor's view of his own creation. Then too, like Abe, Teshigahara makes no attempt to answer the questions they raise.

The film's arrangement of the narrative varies accordingly. Instead of a permutation of chronological events, we have a linear progression based on a well-patterned causality. Another significant departure from the original lies in Teshigahara's characterization. Doctor and nurse (the filmmaker's creation) are given much more substantial treatment. The doctor is directly involved in Okuyama's physical and psychological transformation. Moreover, from the outset the keloid-scarred girl is pitted poignantly against Okuyama as she shows the other way of confronting a hostile society.

The film begins with the doctor's speech. Pointing to the plastic hands and limbs floating in a tank, he speaks to the camera: "Do you understand what they are? They are replicas of a human body." The camera studies the finger he picks up, as he says: "This is not a finger. This is nothing but inferiority shaped like a finger." The doctor throws the finger back into the tank, adding that he is more like a psychologist because he has not treated a patient's damaged finger but instead cured his inferiority complex.

Brief as it is, this opening scene is significant in several ways. The doctor's speech is charged with an abstract quality, already setting the heavy texture of the film. Then, too, we have to wonder who the doctor's speech is meant for. The way he talks, facing the camera, creates the impression that we are patients in his office. But we also get the impression that maybe he is talking to a patient outside the screen frame. This rhetorical ambiguity, coupled with the doctor's philosophical reasoning, prevents us from drifting into an obvious and easy emotional involvement. Instead, from the beginning, the film establishes intellectual detachment as its basic rhetorical stance.

The opening sequence also previews a variety of stylistic effects the film will rely on heavily. Here, as the doctor speaks, the camera examines in detail various modes of human anatomy. Teshigahara insists on the theme of dissection, both visually and verbally. Like some ideal psychologist gifted with intellectual clarity and open-mindedness, the viewer is invited to examine and analyze the existential problems facing contemporary man.

This sequence with its tally of dissected human parts also introduces another aspect of modern-day identity crisis: the question of alienation. After the doctor speaks, ears and hands and a bandaged face fill the screen. They suggest that man is no more than an assemblage of biological yet lifeless parts. A shot of a face on a registration card yields to another of many such faces. These are the labeled and sorted faces of a social identity. A shot of such faces crowding a busy street suggests humanity in close contact but not in touch in any genuine sense. *Homo sapiens* has become *homo incommunicado*.

This opening glimpse of the elaborate stylistic manipulation and the rhetoric of the film to follow free Teshigahara to make the best use of these elements in order to pursue the central theme.

Okuyama's search for a new identity does share important narrative events with the original. Among them are Okuyama's rental of an apartment unit, the assumption of the mask, his encounter with the retarded girl with a Yo-Yo, and the masked man's rental of another unit. All those factors culminate in the masked man's seduction of his own wife. But Okuyama's role playing results in an outcome entirely different from the one Abe's hero experiences.

Teshigahara also presents a different venue for the disfigured man's identity crisis. The doctor makes the mask for Okuyama so that the relationship—between creator and created—complicates the issue of the masked man's alienation. That motif of alienation is also extended to the doctor's wife (another Teshigahara's creation) and is much more forcibly enacted through the episode of the keloid-scarred girl filmed within the film, as we later see.

The first thing that strikes us is the stylistic experiment that Teshigahara uses to advance the story line. Among the avant-garde stylistic conventions used is eerie electronic music (composed by Toru Takemitsu) set against the hard-driving Western music used to open and close the film. An uneasy, hand-held camera movement is used to subvert the customary steadiness of tracking shots; and surrealistic highlights occur in scenes of moral crisis. Even the decor of the doctor's office speaks for this sense of a world whose meaning extends beyond the limits of comfortable discourse. A strange mixture of artificial body parts ornaments the room, along with authentic clay sculptures executed by the noted architect Arata Isozaki.

These elaborate manipulations force us into distancing ourselves from the outset, precluding easy identification with any individual character. In the novel,

Mikijiro Hira (l) and Tatsuya Nakadai (r) in *The Face of Another* (1966) directed by Hiroshi Teshigahara. Courtesy of the Kawakita Memorial Film Institute.

the protagonist's sense of alienation is rendered through abstract, almost verbose statements about human existence in contemporary society. Although Abe introduces such familiar images as walls, bandages, sunglasses, mirrors, and metals, their metaphoric influence is lost in the author's rather heavy-handed shuffling of philosophical notions. For example, the narrator's impression of Dr. K's room at the High Molecular Chemistry Institute is rendered as follows: "The light filtering through the blinds lay in white, milk-like pools. On the table by the window a variety of unusual instruments, like hypodermic equipment, was menacingly laid out; beside the table stood a cabinet for medical charts and a swivel chair with arms; opposite was a waist-high dressing cubicle on rollers and a single-paneled screen with a metal frame. . . ."[23]

Needless to say, these images are meant to point up a sense of technical alienation of human sensibility in a contemporary society. But this section is tucked rather conspicuously into unmetaphorical surroundings as Abe describes Okuyama's visit to Dr. K's office and his subsequent conversation with the doctor. This seems to be why the novelist's metaphors fail to evoke much in the way of contemporary man's sense of quandary.

Teshigahara, in contrast, knows how to let "filmic" qualities create a vivid and immediate sense of the doomed condition of a man of our time. The viewer's sense of alienation is ably reinforced by Toru Takemitsu's eerie music. Okuyama's face in X-ray illustrates his remarks on the suffering of a man who, like himself, has become quite literally faceless in a crowd.

The theme of verbal and physical isolation is also shown in the earlier scenes in Okuyama's home, a place worlds removed from the *locus classicus* of communication and togetherness. While he sits, his wife moves around. A table clearly interposes a barrier between them; it is one the wife welcomes, since she shuns his very touch. He describes himself as buried alive.

Teshigahara gives this loveless, dehumanizing isolation a number of deft, symbolic touches. Frequent cuts to the wires and syringes of the plastic surgeon's craft speak in close-up of clinical efficiency. If is as if warm human relations were taking cues from the cold metallic clink of the doctor's office. Then, too, Teshigahara tends to pose individual characters, especially the doctor and patient, against pitilessly barren backgrounds. Time and again, he lets blank white walls speak of an empty, impersonal world.

Images of windows, keyholes, and eyeglasses recur obsessively, suggesting that alienation offers only a one-way view. Contemporary man is shown peering out of his isolation, afraid of being seen for the empty, damaged entity he is. Okuyama's face is mummied in bandages; a narrow slit allows him to see out, through others cannot look into his eyes.

Unlike the novel, the film extends this motif of alienation to the doctor's wife, who is perceived as a threat to the nurse, apparently his mistress.

This stock situation seems overdone in various scenes Teshigahara devotes to stylistic experiment. In one instance, a patient is shown seated on a huge sculpture in the shape of an ear. This avant-garde construction hangs suspended in space, while the tiny figures of doctor and nurse walk underneath. The doctor issues a mechanical order, telling the nurse to administer an injection. The nurse complains that the doctor's wife is spying on them. Sure enough, a dark female figure is seen crossing the screen behind them. The audience readily understands this image as an apt metaphor for the loss of a familial bond, yet another element of dehumanization in modern society.

The nurse throws open the door. Behind it, we see only a wavy, hairlike material floating in the air. In lieu of a clear significance, we sense an eerie discomfort. Later, a similarly troubling discontinuity follows a shot of the doctor's wife in a kimono, seated on a sofa, knitting. The sofa appears to tilt backward in space to meet a background high-rise leaning perilously near, as if about to fall. The outcome is uncertain, a baffling disruption of visual continuity, though certainly we understand that some reference is being made, again, to a rift in family relations.

Abe's *The Face of Another*, like his later novel, *Hako otoko* (The box man), studies the dissociated aspects of human relationships in terms of seeing and being seen. Teshigahara uses the filmic qualities of his medium to render this motif more forcibly. This is especially noticeable with regard to Okuyama's hideout. Repeatedly, the camera's candid glance comes to rest on the keyhole of the apartment where he dons his mask. We come to understand how his anxiety focuses on the mentally retarded child of the building superintendent. Okuyama is convinced that this little girl, more than anyone, sees through his masquerade. Significantly enough, his mask incorporates sunglasses in its design. It is another indication that alienation puts on an ersatz human face, only to develop a defensive, morbid fear of being really seen.

Apart than its final sequence, the film's greatest departure from the novel comes in its parallel structure. As we have seen, Abe's protagonist dwells on the film about the girl from Nagasaki only toward the end of the novel. It offers an alternative way (also abortive) of searching for a new identity, but only after Okuyama's masquerade has failed.

Teshigahara makes use of that remembered film from the outset. Using cross-cuts, he advances two narrative lines at once, both exploring the central problem of a contemporary man's coming to terms with self and society. One narrative line pursues Okuyama's choice of action: adopt a mask and live its life. The second is devoted to a nameless girl's action in the interpolated film: show the world a truly human face and take the consequences. The scarred girl is played by Miki Irie, a tall, exotically beautiful Japanese-Russian fashion model. An introductory close-up shows her in right profile, a study in beauty that astonishes us. But our view is blinkered, as if the camera eye were peering out from a narrow opening.

The likeness to Okuyama's restricted field of vision is of course inescapable. The shot is troubling, too, because the transition from the earlier hospital scene is so abrupt. We are thrust into perceptual dismay: we cannot be sure whether we are watching real events or events within the film. This rhetorical confusion is sustained throughout, though viewers familiar with the original may assume that events unfolding belong to the interpolated film. In the subsequent shot, some young men are shown passing by and whistling appreciatively, giving the camera its cue to look the young woman up and down. Then two freeze frames taken in close-up register the men's shock and horror. They call her a monster. Only then do we see her hideously disfigured left profile.

Teshigahara gives his victim of Nagasaki a different refuge from the hostile world. She has a menial job in a lunatic asylum. Yet even there, cruelty pursues her in the form of a lustful former soldier, unlike the case of her counterpart in the novel.

Our first view of the girl yields to a cross-cut showing Okuyama in the process of transformation. The man who puts his trust in a mask succeeds well enough at first. As the assistant nurse at the operation observes, his artificial face is handsome enough to make a good impression. Once on, the mask becomes an inner self unbounded by social and moral constraints. Donning it, Okuyama enjoys a paradoxical freedom that wipes away name, profession, family, and troublesome ties such as official registration. The mask becomes him—only too well.

We follow Okuyama's pursuit of freedom. Like the novel's protagonist, he rents a small apartment to serve as a base of operations for this new life of anonymity. Teshigahara, however, gives his actions much more narrative legibility, thanks to the camera's candid eye, which seems to share in his newfound sense of freedom. Previously, its restricted movements corresponded to the rather sedate life lived by the disfigured introvert. Then the camera was satisfied to take note of Okuyama doing things like sitting in a chair, lost in self-pity as his wife moves around him. Now the camera's observant eye picks up and registers a flow of versatile energy coming from the man behind the mask.

In the film, Okuyama's night out at a bar follows the novel closely, but with a twist: he is accompanied by the doctor. Abe's doctor raises questions about contemporary man's plight throughout the story. Teshigahara shows him doing that here, too. The bar scene also uses the camera to focus our attention on Okuyama's affirmation of freedom. It pans freely, representing his point of view— nothing here of its previous stolid focus on the passive, disfigured alien. The doctor observes that his patient is drunk on the mask and nothing else. Yet various clues point to an element of sham in this life of unbridled license. A singer breaks off in mid-song as the camera pans the noisy crowd. A montage shows individual faces, picking out now this, now that obviously alienated individual. The bar is packed. At first glance it looks like a good enough place to meet and make contact, if only temporarily. Yet not even alcohol can sustain the illusion. The doctor says that these revelers are seeking relief from the "masked life." According to him, they want to get drunk in order to forget who they are, but the proof is always there, like an identification card. Teshigahara has already suggested that Okuyama is a victim of the same illusion.

Yet his story continues, studied in cross-cut views of his mounting obsession with the newfound freedom created by his mask. The doctor notes that Okuyama's

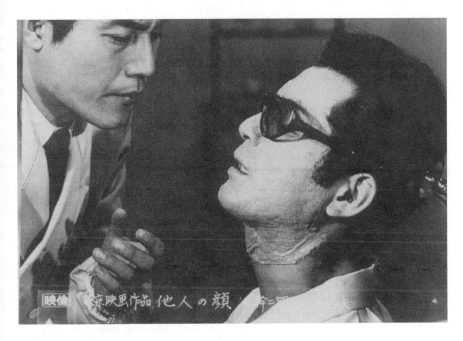

Mikijiro Hira (l) and Tatsuya Nakadai (r) in *The Face of Another* (1966) directed by Hiroshi Teshigahara. Courtesy of the Kawakita Memorial Film Institute.

clothes speak for a new self-confidence "You have never worn such loud things," he says. Even so, we sense that Okuyama, like the crowd in the bar, continues to be a victim of illusion.

The turning point comes when he decides to practice the seducer's art on his own wife, in his secret hideaway. Teshigahara analyzes this foray into a new area of freedom and identity through a deft narrative ploy. In contrast to the original, scenes of Okuyama's tryst with his wife are again carefully intercut with similar ones of a rendezvous between the scar-faced girl and her elder brother. The thematic parallels provided by these parodies of romantic love in present-day society are enriched by a complex matrix of spatial contrast and character conflict.

The narrative segment opens with a scene showing Okuyama incognito, picking his wife up in the crowd. He follows her through the jostling commuters in a situation that may well stand as the epitome of modern high-tech civilization. Suddenly the pair are seen against the bare background of the subway station wall. They are alone, like castaways and sole survivors of a cold, impersonal world. Eerie electronic music on the sound track reinforces the likeness.

The camera cuts to a beach where the scar-faced girl and her brother are having a picnic. The scene is alive with life. Water laps the shore in a reassuring rhythm echoed by the music on the sound track. The water here comes as a welcome change from its echo in an earlier image in the clinic, where an artificial limb was shown floating in a tank. An extreme long shot of the girl and her brother emphasizes their harmony with the landscape.

Teshigahara now intercuts shots from the beach scene with those detailing Okuyama's progress in seducing his wife. The two enter a coffee shop, where Okuyama takes advantage of the narrow space to crowd their legs together. We sense an ironic contrast between the lively conveniences of city life and the little space available to enjoy them. We also see that Okuyama's little game of "footsie" will get him nowhere worth going. That point is subtly underscored by the music. The same light Western music so fit and right for the scene on the beach is heard there from the stereo at the coffee shop. Okuyama finds it distracting and annoying—an unwelcome intrusion into his shabby artifice of romance.

On the beach, meanwhile, the rhythm of life picks up. A light breeze (recurrent metaphor associated with her) stirs the girl's hair. Her brother reaches for her hand. His touch is simple, natural, nothing like the sly seducer's hand in the coffee shop, where a man in a mask seeks to manipulate the hapless woman who happens to be his wife.

Yet their familiar love is threatened from without. We recall the earlier scene of the beach where rifle shots were heard. The marksmen could be part of Japan's Self-Defense Forces engaged in military drills. As the shots ring out, the political dimensions of this imagery invite comparison with the bombing of Nagasaki, which made this poor girl the victim she is.

The scene shifts back to Okuyama, to his apartment hideaway and a room in an inn. Ironically, each location turns out to be a point of departure, not a cozy love nest where honeymooners get their start. Okuyama thinks he has succeeded in seducing his own wife. Having slept with her, wearing his marvelously plastic, handsomely deceptive mask, has been an act of revenge, not love. Yet that unworthy aim backfires. He has fallen in love with deception. Blank walls on every side clearly suggest as much, reinforcing the purely mechanical nature of this union.

Teshigahara has previously emphasized the couple's apartness. Here, his camera lingers in a medium shot, as if to celebrate an achievement of togetherness. We are not fooled, of course. And soon enough the wife speaks for our sense of this consummate deception now (as it were) consummated. She says that the apartment has an unlived-in feeling; there is no sense of man or woman either. The camera, meanwhile, takes note of the narrow confines of the place, which suggests by details like a curtain obscuring our view of the couple's embrace, the want of proper moral dimension.

A cruel counterpoint to this idea of impossible love is offered subsequently when Teshigahara cross-cuts to the scar-faced girl and her brother. The camera's eye appears to bear witness to their genuine love. The composition offered is symmetrical, a shot of the girl lying on a futon mat yielding to an identical shot of the boy lying on another. A third shot places the two mats horizontally across the screen. The brother kisses the scarred side of his sister's face. Here there is life, not artifice; sincerity, not a cynical mask.

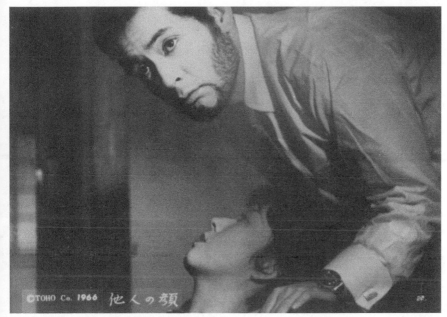

Machiko Kyo (l) and Tatsuya Nakadai (r) in *The Face of Another* (1966) directed by Hiroshi Teshigahara. Courtesy of the Kawakita Memorial Film Institute.

Moreover, toward the end of this scene, the heads of brother and sister are aligned in the same way husband and wife were earlier and will be again when that scene returns. This visual parallel again reinforces the contrast between real and unreal love.

Nevertheless, the young couple are doomed as well, their love being incestuous. The motif of role playing here takes the form of brother assuming the manner of lover at the moment of consummation. Having attempted to assume the roles of father, brother, and now lover as well, he inevitably fails. The strain of incest is too much. The scene ends in a close-up freeze frame of the girl's scarred face. This familiar shot is in deliberate contrast to the earlier ones of the protagonist's bandaged face, then his masked one. The effect here is to offer a cruelly exact documentation of this young woman's living agony. The sinister electronic music returns as if to signal the inevitable outcome.

Ironies multiply as the camera cuts to Okuyama's apartment. The wife turns out to have known the identity of the man behind the mask since their first meeting on the street. This exposure of the withheld information adds to the mounting sense of irony. In the novel, it comes in the wife's diary. The film offers direct confrontation between husband and wife. Here the wife believes that only a game of seducer and seduced can bridge the gap between man and wife. Her counterpart in the novel takes the opposite view, considering her husband's ploy no way to build a "roadway" between them. The novelist's view of this irony is rather one-sided. Though he concentrates on Okuyama's decision to follow through with his scheme of revenge by shooting his wife, he leaves the outcome ambiguous.

Teshigahara, in contrast, gives the couple's course of action much more narrative legibility. During this final confrontation, he returns to the motif of mechanical lovelessness in contemporary society. The wife says that true love strips off all masks, but she does not sound convincing. We see clearly that she speaks for a world of mere wishful thinking. We sense a reality, a finality in the way she closes the door behind her, leaving her husband to his hideaway, his seducer's lair, his artificial reality. Her own path will take her out into the faceless anonymity of a world not nearly as human as it pretends to be.

Any doubts we may have about the bleakness of Teshigahara's vision are dispelled in the scene that follows. A series of point-of-view shots witnesses the disappearance of the scar-faced girl drowning herself in the ocean—a fit enough metaphor for escape into oblivion. We see her brother standing near a window of the inn, weeping. The next surrealistic shot delivers a shock: the screen flashes white, then the young man's body is seen (in my view) as a vulture chained to the window. The sudden balancing light of this odd transformation inevitably echoes the bomb blast at Nagasaki--especially since the girl has remarked that another war could begin tomorrow. This powerful image cannot fail to suggest a political metaphor connecting Teshigahara's grim tale of dehumanization with possibly the century's most potent image of anxiety: nuclear Armageddon.[24]

The somewhat abstract, and in some respects baffling, final sequence follows as a poignant counterpoint to the outcome of this girl's alienation. Here, Teshigahara clearly agrees with Abe in seeing contemporary man's pursuit of freedom as doomed to fail. The perfect artifice of the mask becomes a destructive force, the instrument of alienation's self-defeating freedom. Thus, Okuyama shows himself increasingly blind to the value of every social constraint. He loses control and attempts to rape a woman on the street.

Teshigahara has relentlessly pursued the question of man's freedom throughout this film. At first he would appear to have freed himself from social constraints by living behind his handsome mask. But his precious anonymity has been threatened from without. First, his wife has refused to play by his rules, resenting her role of adulteress in his masquerade. Then a child has penetrated his disguise. The building superintendent's daughter persistently reminds Okuyama of his promise to buy her a new Yo-Yo. None of his disguises has fooled this innocent. A shot of her peeking through the door as he prepares his mask is an apt metaphor for a world of threats to his fictitious reality. Worse yet, the child has turned out to be more than just a little snoop. Her penetration of his disguise is humiliatingly personal: she knows him by his smell.

It follows that the plastic surgeon, too, has come to be perceived as a threat. He knows the man behind the mask. He can create other masks for other men seeking this new freedom.

The illusory nature of this freedom has long been in question anyway. Various mirror images have seen to that. The camera has taken note of Okuyama studying himself—his masked self—locked up safe inside his hideaway. It has watched him angle for the truth, which is to say practice the most deceiving expression, in a mirror. The mask is undeniably marvelous, versatile, expressive. It smiles and grimaces at the mirror with virtuoso ease.

The trouble is, the mirror can only reflect the "real" mask, not the real self. As mask and masquerade take on more verisimilitude, Okuyama finds himself more of a prisoner of unreal reality. Having fabricated an identity, he loses contact with himself. Having become entirely reflective in the mirror-image sense, he has no capacity for reflection in the moral sense. Having vanished as a person, he survives as image only.

The final sequence picks up all these suggestions of thwarted freedom for use in an outcome as devastating as the novel's, though in a different way. After Okuyama is released by the police, the doctor escorts him through the crowded street at night. Suggestions of *homo incommunicado* return as the two men walk toward the camera and away from it in silence. Okuyama thinks he sees masked faces coming at him from every direction. Seeing enemies on every hand, he stammers the words "isolation" and "mask." Some, he says, can be taken off, others cannot. He faces his companion. Even as the doctor tells him that he is free, Okuyama stabs him. Is this revenge on the creator of the destructive mask? Can the plastic surgeon's death free the masked man from the curse of anonymity?

The Face of Another ends with a close-up of Okuyama's masked face. He touches it as we have seen him do so many times. Yet his hands are strangers to this image he presents to the world, this factitious identity that guarantees his illusory freedom. We sense a failure to familiarize himself even with this mask he wears.

A freeze frame follows. Again, the alienating tones of electronic music return with fatalistic circularity. Teshigahara seems to charge this final shot with challenging possibilities expressed as questions. What will Okuyama do? Return to the unmasked world? Continue his masquerade? Vacillate between the two? Just like the novelist, the director typically offers no clear answer regarding his hero's fate. Instead, he leaves us holding the mask, Teshigahara's richly reinforced image of contemporary mankind's fragmented life of isolation and alienation.

Notes

1. For Teshigahara's screen adaptations of Abe's novels, see David Desser, "*The Ruined Map*," in *Eros Plus Massacre: An Introduction to the Japanese New Wave Cinema* (Bloomington: Indiana University Press, 1988), pp. 76-81; and Keiko McDonald, "Sand, Man and Symbols: Teshigahara's *The Woman in the Dunes*," in *Cinema East: A Critical Study of Major Japanese Films* (London and East Brunswick, N.J.: Fairleigh Dickinson University Press, 1983), pp. 36–50.
2. Kobo Abe, *The Face of Another*, trans. Dale Sanders (Tokyo and Rutland, Vt.: Tuttle, 1967), p. 3. Copyright © by Charles E. Tuttle.
3. Ibid.
4. Ibid., p. 4.

5. Quoted by Tadamasa Sato, "*Tanin no kao*" (on The face of another), *Kokubungaku kaishaku to kansho*(Interpretation and appreciation of Japanese literature), no. 182 (January, 1971) 105.
6. Sanders, *The Face of Another*, p. 29.
7. Ibid.
8. Ibid., p. 31.
9. Ibid., p. 142.
10. Ibid., p. 151.
11. Ibid., p. 117.
12. Ibid., p. 168.
13. Ibid., p. 189.
14. Ibid., p. 208.
15. Ibid., pp. 222–23.
16. Ibid., p. 227.
17. Ibid., p. 228.
18. Ibid., p. 235.
19. Ibid.
20. Ibid., p. 237.
21. Ibid.
22. Ibid.
23. Ibid., p. 21.
24. A bird symbolizes a god in a number of Japanese avant-garde plays; this final take, therefore, is likely an expression of apocalypse.

15

Rehearsing Death: Takabayashi's
The Temple of the Golden Pavilion (1976)

Yukio Mishima published *Kinkakuji* (The temple of the golden pavilion) in 1956. In 1970 he led the abortive coup d'état that ended with his highly dramatic ritual suicide. Yoichi Takabayashi's screen adaptation of the novel appeared six years later.

Takabayashi was not the first director to be drawn to the cinematic potential in this studiously psychological novel. Kon Ichikawa took it up almost immediately. His *Enjo* (Conflagration, 1956) put Mishima's novel on the screen, with a number of significant differences. Ichikawa allowed himself considerable latitude, especially in the beginning and at the end. His opening sequence anticipates the outcome, showing the arsonist/protagonist on the way to prison under police escort. Counting heavily on flashbacks, Ichikawa then takes us back to the protagonist's world of inner experience. The closing sequence, like the opening, is his own invention. It shows the protagonist taking a suicide leap off a moving train.

Takabayashi's version, as we later see, follows Mishima much more closely. But why should this director take up this novel? He explained it this way:

> Having passed forty, I find myself more and more preoccupied with my own death. Each day I feel that something is coming to an end. Now that I have completed *The Temple of the Golden Pavilion*, this feeling seems especially acute. . . .
>
> When I directed *Gaki zoshi* (The story of Gaki) and *Hika* (Elegy) it seemed like I was making my own last will and testament.
>
> Wasn't *The Temple of the Golden Pavilion* the inevitable consequence of those? If so, the film may have been a manifestation of some latent wish of my own lying hidden since the moment of Yukio Mishima's death.[1]

Clearly, Takabayashi is working on two levels in this film. Like the novelist, he is exploring the image of a man imprisoned in himself, out of tune with the world outside, forced to seek liberation through the destruction of beauty. On that level he shares the novel's thematic orientation. On another level, he is guided by his own preoccupation with death, with what amounts to his interpretation of the novelist's very real death.

Takabayashi creates his own symbolic method on both levels. His innovations modify the novel's narrative focus—the protagonist's relationship with the golden pavilion—and result in a new approach to the film's ending.

This film also offers interesting insights into its maker's deployment of qualities intrinsic to cinema: fluidity in spatial and temporal shifts. It shows us how this filmmaker goes about transferring an essentially confessional narrative mode from the novel onto the screen.

The novel's central problem concerns the difficulty its protagonist Mizoguchi has in coming to terms with the external world and, ultimately, with himself. In the course of his struggle he is confronted by various expressions of two choices open to him: attempt to communicate with the outer world on its own terms, or give up and retreat into a world inside himself. Rejected by society, Mizoguchi opts for the second. The novel charts the course of his regression, using as a reference point his shifting relationship with the temple of the golden pavilion.

The mode of representation is confessional. Mizoguchi speaks of his experience from early childhood into youth. He is still young when the climax of his estrangement takes the form of setting fire to the golden pavilion.

Mizoguchi's experience is rendered mostly in straight chronological sequence, with time out now and then for thinking about a past event. Many critics consider stylistic excellence this novel's strongest feature. Mishima's achievement that way owes much to a perilous balancing act as he accommodates the protagonist's limited vision and expressive ability to the highly embellished language of the narrative.[2] The story may be told by the hapless Mizoguchi, but in his voice we hear the voice of the novelist as well, speaking a language unmistakably his own.

The motif of alienation is established from the outset as Mizoguchi's recalls his boyhood sense of being a social outcast. This was a boy who stammered. He was frail and homely. His family was poor. All the ingredients of alienation were his from the beginning:

> I had a weak constitution and was always being defeated by the other boys in running or on the exercise bar. Besides, I had suffered since my birth from a stutter, and this made me still more retiring in my manner. . . .
> My stuttering, I need hardly say, placed an obstacle between me and the outside world. . . . Most people, thanks to their easy command of words, can keep this door between the inner world and the outer world wide open. . . . but for me this has been quite impossible.[3]

He is a boy apparently born to fall prey to some fixation. And that, quite literally, is what we see happening as he tells his story. He is haunted by images of fixity in various forms. We see it in a formative episode involving Uiko, a pretty girl in the neighborhood. The boy lies in wait for her:

> Then I felt that I had been turned into stone. My will, my desire—everything had become stone. The outer world had lost contact with my inner world, and had once again come to surround me and to assume a positive existence.[4]

Uiko's scornfully cold attitude, especially her look at his mouth, "the ill-formed little hole," makes him keenly aware of his failure to reach the outside world. The notion of being turned to stone conveys his feelings of cold, hard exclusion from the warmly human world outside himself.

That image is coupled with one of a warm human hand in a way that turns out to be paradoxically and cruelly alienating, too. While his father is still alive, the boy happens to see his mother having sex with her lover. His father intervenes:

> All of a sudden my open eyes were covered by something large and warm, and I could see nothing. I understood at once. Father had stretched his hands out from behind to cut off my vision. . . .
> Incomparably large hands. Hands that had been put round me from behind, blotting out in one second the sight of that hell which I had seen. Hands from another world. . . . Those hands instantaneously cut off the terrifying world with which I was confronted and had buried it in darkness.[5]

Earlier, in Chapter 1, another hand image offers even darker suggestions. On this occasion, the father takes the boy for his first visit to the golden pavilion. Together they admire this beautiful medieval creation. Yet, just then, the boy imagines that his father's hand has turned into that of a skeleton. That trick of childish imagination turns out to seem like a telling premonition of his protector's death. In retrospect, the cost of that loss was ironically emphasized by the role his father's hands played in attempting to shield the boy from his later, very real insight into the "hell" of his mother's sin.

And because fixation of this kind plays by the rules of its own awful logic, his father's protective hand also becomes a fixture of his sick imagination. Having seen what he has seen, he fails to mature as a creature of flesh and blood and human frailty. Thanks to his mother's sin and his father's shielding hands, Mizoguchi has learned to associate the world of the flesh with evil.

Ironically too, it is the father who endows the boy's with the focus of relationship that will "place" him so fatefully in the dread in-between world of his isolation. The novel's first sentence speaks of it: "Ever since my childhood, Father had often spoken to me about the Golden Temple."[6]

Even before he actually sees it, the boy forms his own image of the temple his father speaks of with such reverence. This image may be an illusion, yet it represents a world of wish fulfillment—the very antithesis of the one the deprived, alienated boy finds himself living in: "My attachment to the golden pavilion was entirely rooted in my ugliness."[7] In his mind he associates the golden pavilion with unattainable or unknown beauty:

> So when I saw small, dew-drenched summer flowers that seemed to emit a blue light, they seemed to me as beautiful as the Golden Pavilion. Finally it came about that even when I saw a beautiful face, the simile would spring into my mind: lovely as the Golden Pavilion.[8]

Having been to Kyoto with his father, the boy no longer pursues the illusory temple; it has become real. "Gradually the Golden Temple came to exist more deeply and more solidly within me."[9]

The boy is too caught up in his estrangement to know what most people know about this building. Wonderful as it is, most of us know that this artifact of eternity is anything but perfect. It has its elements of discord, of complexity, contradiction, and paradox. Its beauty brings together contradictions as basic to everyday human existence as light and darkness, pure and impure, good and evil.

But the boy Mizoguchi lives in a dream world of dark isolation, and from the perspective of that darkness the temple shines with the only light he sees. Of course, he thinks he sees the building aright:

> The Golden Temple had been built as a symbol of the dark ages. Therefore it was necessary for the Golden Temple of my dreams to have darkness bearing down on it from all sides. In this darkness, the beautiful, slender pillars of the building rested quietly and steadily, emitting a faint light from inside. Whatever words people might speak to the Golden Temple, it must continue to stand there silently, displaying its delicate structure to the eyes of the world and enduring the darkness that surrounded it.[10]

His father's death robs the boy of the only protection he has known. So he looks to the temple. It becomes his all-in-all. Another dimension of Mizoguchi's inner world begins to unfold. From the second chapter on, Mishima shows how, once the outer world is shattered, the boy finds his world of wish fulfillment in the temple.

The novel takes place during World War II. During an air raid, we find the boy's bond with this beauty most tellingly expressed by his wish to perish with the temple, should it be hit.

The pavilion survives unscathed. That fact itself alters the perilous balance between Mizoguchi and this object of his adoration. In Chapter 3, Mishima takes pains to describe Mizoguchi's feelings when he returns from the army and sees the temple still standing:

> To describe the situation properly, I would say that I was standing on one side and the Golden Temple on the other. And from the moment that I set eyes to the temple that day I could feel that "our" relationship had already undergone a change.[11]

By escaping destruction, the temple becomes the very symbol of the eternity that "descended from heaven, sticking to our cheeks, our hands, our stomachs, and finally burying us."[12]

Elsewhere, that conviction is expressed in language clearly beyond the reach of this untutored acolyte:

> What ornamental objects could one put on such shelves? Nothing would fit their measurements but something like a fantastically large incense burner, or an absolutely colossal nihility. But the Golden Temple had lost such things; it had suddenly washed away its essence and now displayed a strangely empty form. The most peculiar thing was that of all the various times when the Golden Temple had shown me its beauty, this time was the most beautiful of all. Never had the temple displayed so hard a beauty—a beauty that transcended the entire world of reality, a beauty that bore no relation to any form of evanescence.[13]

Mishima continues to reinforce Mizoguchi's sense of this rift between the impermanent and the transitory, a rift that ends by altering his outlook on the external world:

> "The bond between the Golden Temple and myself had been cut," I thought. "Now my vision that the Golden Temple and I were living in the same world has broken down. Now I shall return to my previous condition, but it will be even more helpless than before. A condition in which I exist on one side and beauty on the other. A condition that will never improve so long as this world endures." [14]

The external world Mizoguchi faces in the aftermath of the war is filled with signs of decay and vulgarization as a new, enforced democracy takes hold. For him, Japan's defeat is not a liberation, but "a return to the unchanging, eternal Buddhist doctrine," which makes him see his daily life in an entirely new light. The Superior he once considered a replacement for his deceased father now seems far removed from that ideal mentor/father image. Changes in the outside world are mirrored even in the sacred precincts of the temple.

Mizoguchi's judgment on these changes is couched in terms that obviously speak for the novel's covert narrator, Mishima himself: "But now Occupation troops arrived, and soon the licentious customs of the mundane world began to flourish about the Golden Temple." [15]

When his bond with the temple is severed, Mizoguchi is forced to come to terms with the external world. The logic of his response is fearsomely uncompromising:

> "This," I thought, "is the mundane world. Now that the war has ended, people are being driven about under that light of evil thoughts. Innumerable couples are gazing at each other under the light. . . . Please let the evil that is in my heart increase and multiply indefinitely, so that it may correspond in every particular with that vast light before my eyes!" [16]

Mizoguchi sets out to oppose evil in a number of ways. He begins by rebelling against the temple Superior and all that he is supposed to stand for. One snowy day a GI visits the temple with his Japanese girl friend. She turns out to be pregnant. Mizoguchi is a witness to their quarrel. The GI pushes his girl friend to the ground. Here, in this Buddhist temple, he decides to force this dimwit Japanese bystander to step on this Japanese slut.

A world of outcast insight is condensed into this brief experience of sadistic pleasure. It does more than introduce Mizoguchi to the joys of destroying beauty. It connects with a formative wound in him: ". . . this girl partook of a fresh defiant beauty that somehow seemed to come into being as a reaction to my memory of Uiko." [17] Uiko's look of distant cold contempt had turned him to stone. He needed to free himself from that feeling of fixity, of killing cold exclusion. This professional woman and Uiko have that distant look in common. No wonder Mizoguchi is surprised by the "faithful resilience" of the prostitute's flesh under his feet.

Another, larger context is served by this revelation. The American GI and his Japanese concubine typify the vulgar secular culture that Mishima sees as destroying traditions the Japanese have long been proud to call their own.

Now that he is committed to a principled pursuit of evil, Mizoguchi follows that act of perverse obedience with a course of calculated defiance of his father figure, the temple Superior.

The Superior, as we later see, is in fact a man of flesh as well as spirit. Mizoguchi considers him a "nonentity." He sees this father figure as two-faced, as a hypocrite. For Mizoguchi, the dignified manner and ostensible devotion to Buddha are merely camouflage for a priest whose soft pink flesh speaks for a lifetime of sensual indulgence on the sly.

More important, Mizoguchi's conflict between good and evil is symbolically rendered through his newly established relationship with the temple. Once he recognizes it as the very antithesis of himself, he projects his alter ego into it, as Arthur Kimball rightly observes.[18] That done, he can hope to control this artifact of eternity, using it to bring the external world to him, to negotiate on his own terms. Having attained this megalomaniac confidence, he reckons he has "squeezed the universe into one ball," causing the whole outside world to flow into him.

But his grasp of power is not really that complete. The temple itself stands in the way of certain aspects of the young man's will to evil. This is most evident in his sexual encounters with women. That old childhood wound has never healed. That memory of his father's hands is a continual incentive to associate carnal knowledge with sin. Since the golden temple is, in effect, his father now, it acts to suppress his libido.

We see this first when Mizoguchi goes out with a friend and two girls. The friend is his experienced, scapegrace colleague at the temple, Kashiwagi. Mizoguchi's advances to one of the girls are cut short by a vision of the temple:

Then the Golden Temple appeared before me. A delicate structure, gloomy and full of dignity. It was this structure which now stood between me and life. . . .
The Golden Temple which sometimes seemed to be so utterly indifferent to me and to tower into the air outside myself, had now completely engulfed me and had allowed me to be situated within its structure.[19]

Like Uiko, this girl treated him with contempt. The image of rigidity returns. Mizoguchi simply cannot move.

Some chapters later, Mizoguchi's troubled libido is presented again through his relationship with the pavilion. Kashiwagi's discarded lover, a teacher of flower arranging, offers her breast to Mizoguchi. He had seen her offer her breast like this to an army officer three years before. Once again, a vision of the temple comes between him and carnal satisfaction: "The Golden Temple once more appeared before me. Or rather I should say that the breast was transformed into the Golden Pavilion."[20]

He dwells on the resemblance there. The outside of the breast is radiant with fleshly loveliness; but inside all is darkness. Here, as in the golden pavilion, there is this unsettling contradiction: radiant light and loveliness at odds with the heavy luxuriant darkness inside. Like the temple, the breast should be inviolate. Again, Mizoguchi feels turned to stone by the woman's "cold, scornful look."

Later, watching some bees at work, he thinks he has found a way to define his transfer of alter ego to the temple:

> Then, just as I left the bee's eyes and returned to my own eyes, it occurred to me that my eyes which had been gazing at this scene were exactly in the position of the eyes of the Golden Pavilion. . . .
> In the same way that I had reverted from the bee's eyes to my own eyes, so at those instants when life approached me I abandoned my own eyes and made the eyes of the Golden Temple into mine. And it was precisely at such moments that the temple would introduce itself between me and life.[21]

The contradictory aspect of Mizoguchi's personality is reflected in his friendship with two other temple acolytes. Tsurukawa is Mizoguchi's opposite in every respect. He comes from a wealthy family. He is easygoing and self-confident, a natural communicator. Even his Tokyo accent is a privileged one. Tsurukawa is handsome and good-natured, too. As early as Chapter 2, Mizoguchi's sense of his friend's attractiveness is expressed in terms of light:

> His arm was bent round his head and I noticed that though the outside was fairly sunburned, the inner part was so white that one could see the veins through the skin.[22]

Elsewhere, Mizoguchi contrasts himself with this friend:

> I was the negative of the picture; he was the positive. How often had I not been amazed to see how my dark, turbid feelings could become clear and radiant by being filtered through Tsurukawa's heart.[23]

They had become friends during the war. Yet, after Japan's defeat, this human bond could not take the place of the temple Mizoguchi had lost touch with during his time in service. His nature being what it is, he turns away from the outward-tending human connection to the inner world of his identification with the pavilion.

He is even urged in that direction by Tsurukawa's premature death. His friend has been a link, however weak, between Mizoguchi and the external world. (Ironically, the name Tsurukawa means Crane River. The crane is a bird signifying longevity in Japan.)

Here, the implicit narrator Mishima uses Mizoguchi's recollection of Tsurukawa's untimely death to speak for his own aesthetic bias. The novelist's sense of beauty is instinct with the pathos of early death. For Mishima, it speaks for the frailty of human beauty, and for the severe ideals of purity he identifies with samurai ethos. Again, the beauty of the style here betrays the presence of a novelist speaking a language far beyond the capacity of his stammering acolyte:

> The fact that Tsurukawa had not died of illness fitted in perfectly with this image. It was simple that he, whose life had been so incomparably pure a structure, should suffer the pure death of an accident.[24]

Kashiwagi is more like what Mizoguchi might have become, had he been more eager to take vengeance on the world that rejected him. Like the stuttering Mizoguchi, Kashiwagi is handicapped: his ugliness is compounded by ungainliness, crippled as he is by a club foot. He also comes from an impoverished family background. Unlike Mizoguchi, however, he knows how to "transform baseness into courage." Kashiwagi is quite prepared to make the world deal with him on his own terms. Mishima makes him into a kind of devil figure, as when, for example, he succeeds in persuading a beautiful girl to kiss his deformed foot.

Kashiwagi is also linked in an interesting way with Mizoguchi's father's hands—protective hands so ironically and unwittingly destructive a force in the poor boy's life. Here, Mizoguchi finds himself admiring Kashiwagi's hands at work arranging flowers:

> The movement of Kashiwagi's hands could only be described as magnificent. One small decision followed another and the effect of contrast and symmetry converged with infallible artistry.[25]

Kashiwagi's ability to take charge of relations between himself and the world is slyly suggested by his arrangement. Making use of traditional principles of this Japanese art, his skill represents a symbolic disposition of heaven, earth, and man. Yet, as Mizoguchi notes, here the hands of the artist speak for a demonic power of control this cripple brings to bear on the world around.

Kashiwagi's demonic tendency is most strongly suggested by the way he conquers women and discards them. Guided by this Mephistophelian figure, Mizoguchi's apprenticeship to evil begins with the most basic pursuit of carnal knowledge. Yet, as we have seen, the pavilion thwarts his libido:

> Why does the Golden Temple try to protect me? Why does it separate me from life without my asking it? Of course it may be that the temple is saving me from falling into hell. But by so doing, the Golden Temple is making me even more evil than those people who actually do fall into hell, it is making me into "the man who knows more about hell than anyone."[26]

How can Mizoguchi get free of this unwanted interference? He must quell his conflict at its source—his alter ego projected into it, and thus the pavilion itself. This is obvious in the Koan introduced twice in the novel:

> When ye meet the Buddha, kill the Buddha! When ye meet your ancestor, kill your ancestor—only thus will ye attain deliverance. Only thus will ye escape the trammels of material things and become free.[27]

Nonetheless, before Mizoguchi realizes that elimination of one's attachment or obsession is the way of freedom, he must undergo several preparatory stages. His rebellion against the authoritative Superior is expressive of his endeavor to free himself from bondage to the surrogate father and, furthermore, from religion itself.

Mizoguchi spies on his Superior. He shadows the older man who has an assignation with a girl. Mizoguchi acts the part of conscience, adding a picture of the girl to the newspaper he delivers to the Superior's room. He wants this holy man to face up to his basic animality.

Mizoguchi's obsessive nature leads him to cherish an "obstinate desire" to elicit a look of outright hatred from the Superior.

Having achieved his aim of alienation from the father/mentor figure, Mizoguchi now needs to lapse into a kind of prenatal existence. His return to his birthplace signifies this:

> Yes, this was really the coast of the Sea of Japan! Here was the source of all my unhappiness, of all my gloomy thoughts, the origin of all my ugliness and all my strength. . . .
> Now I was confronting the waves and the rough north wind. There was no beautiful spring afternoon here, no well-mown lawn. Yet this desolate nature before me was well-mown lawn. . . . Here I could be self-sufficient. Here I was not threatened by anything.[28]

This return brings with it a sudden insight. The young man who has been so often turned to stone now feels "struck by light." Here at the end of Chapter 7 he realizes that he must destroy the source of his troubled psyche. "I must set fire to the Golden Temple."

The second stage of his liberation demands a return to his mother's womb. This is made possible through his first successful sexual encounter. It is with a prostitute. Why does the pavilion not block his libido now? Because, at long last, he has banished Uiko's baleful image. Her image had combined in his mind with both the other women he had failed with. Uiko's face glimpsed in the moonlight had become the embodiment of all beauty, and that beauty required rejection of the world. Her look of contempt had cut him, had turned him to stone. Then the pavilion reinforced that sense of isolation. Once the temple became his alter ego, its image burned in his mind like a flame, a constant warning not to violate ideal beauty. The temple, like Uiko, turned him to stone.

At the brothel, the situation is different. Uiko no longer haunts him: "It seemed as if Uiko had gone outside of this world of ours to have a bath or something simple of this sort."[29]

As in his earlier contretemps with the flower-arranging teacher, the breast image returns, but with different associations. Mizoguchi's earliest sense of this image was connected with that memory of his mother's adultery. Still a child, he is denied access to the breast her lover fondles. Later, as an acolyte, Mizoguchi sees another breast serve as a sign of separation. This time it is a military officer taking leave of his paramour:

> . . . the woman suddenly loosened the collar of her kimono. . . . Then I saw her white breasts. I held my breath. The woman took one of her full breasts in her own hands. The officer held out the dark, deep colored teacup, white colored and knelt before her. The woman rubbed her breast with both hands. . . . The Man held the cup to his mouth and drank every drop of that mysterious tea.[30]

After the war, Mizoguchi, the distant observer of that prenatal ceremony, is offered that same breast. But it is milkless now. At first, it strikes him as being nothing "but flesh, nothing but a material object." Then a quiet miracle takes place. That breast somehow "regains its connection with the whole" and metamorphoses into "immortal substance related to eternity." Breast and golden pavilion come together to prevent Mizoguchi from retreating into infancy:

> In my mind's eye, I could see the Golden Temple and the woman's breast coming and going one after the other. I was overcome with an impotent sense of joy.[31]

At the brothel, however, Mizoguchi still sees the prostitute Mariko's breasts for what they are: human flesh on which "a fly happens to settle." He also observes that they will never "undergo any strange process as being transformed to the Golden Pavilion." A parallel reference is to eye imagery. Free from Uiko's coldly scornful look, he now sees in Mariko's eyes the act of looking—a proof that he does exist:

> The law of distance that regulated my world had been destroyed. . . . A stranger had fearlessly impinged on my existence. The heat of a stranger's body and the cheap perfume on its skin combined to inundate me by slow degrees until I was completely immersed in it all. For the first time I saw that someone else's world could melt away like this.[32]

Having achieved this sense of return to prenatal existence, Mizoguchi is ready to attempt a breakthrough—liberation from the yoke of his alter ego, from the pavilion itself. He imagines what the destruction of the temple will bring him:

> The rusty key that opened the door between the outer world and my inner world would turn smoothly in its lock. My world would be ventilated as the breeze blew freely between it and the outer world.[33]

After Mizoguchi decides to set fire to the pavilion, his personality shows more positive qualities. Earlier, Mizoguchi's attitude toward the Superior is painfully negative. To his surprise, Mizoguchi now develops a kind of compassion for the Superior: "I even forgot my hatred for the Superior! I had become free—free of mother, free of my companions, free of everything."[34]

He also watches this man he considered a venerable hypocrite bowing low in devotion: "Although I was trying to reject it with all my strength, the fact was I was on the verge of succumbing to affection for him."[35]

He seems on the verge of coming to life. But any tendency to mellow is turned aside by Mizoguchi's hatred of deception in this father figure: "But the thought that he had adopted this posture for my special benefit turned everything into reverse and made my heart even harder than it had been before silence."[36]

Mizoguchi is even sent a worthier father figure. But too late, too near the end of the tale Mishima has to tell. But this monk, Father Genkai, offers interesting contrasts. He has many of the qualities the Superior ought to possess and does not, most notably simplicity. That quality is completely alien to the Superior, and is beautifully present in Father Genkai. This monk also has the moral strength that Mizoguchi's biological father never possessed.

But Father Genkai has, if anything, too much inner power. He was the only person who might have saved Mizoguchi from himself; yet Father Genkai was too strong. Father Genkai's view of Mizoguchi's moral dilemma is reflected in his observation on fundamental human nature: "It's not always so easy. But if you start acting in a different way, people soon come to accept that as being normal for you. They're very forgetful, you see."[37]

In the end, Mizoguchi repudiates this good monk's fatherly influence. That seals his fate. He must proceed. Images of fire proliferate in the last two chapters of the novel. Mizoguchi sees a sign at the entrance to the kitchen: "A-Ta-ko, holy sign—beware of Fire." Later he renders his own interpretation of the sign:

> In my mind I could see the pale form of the captive fire that was imprisoned by this amuletic sign. Something that had once been gay hovered now behind this sign, wan and debilitated. I wonder whether I shall be believed when I say that during these days the vision of fire inspired me with nothing less than carnal lust. . . .
>
> Yet was it not natural that, when my will to live depended entirely on fire, my lust, too, should have turned in that direction? My desire molded the supple figure of the fire; and the flames, conscious that they were being seen by me through the shining black pillar, adorned themselves gracefully for the occasion. They were fragile things—the hands, the limbs, the chest of that fire.[38]

This is a clever and ironic trope on the ancient image of the fires of lust. Mizoguchi's lust is satisfied in the brothel scene where flesh and spirit may be seen meeting in a vision of light and fire. Then, when finally he sees fire engulfing the golden temple, what he sees are the flames of a purgation. They are flames of creation, too. Out of this destruction of his externalized ego there emerges a new order of life for him.

Two earlier incidents anticipate that process of beauty destroyed in an act of creation. In one instance he gets sadistic pleasure from treading on the belly of the Uiko-like prostitute. In the other, he deliberately scratches the scabbard of a sword belonging to a young naval cadet.

Mizoguchi's preparation for arson is very well structured. In this we see already how the new life he is seeking demands a new order, almost, one might say, a heightened liveliness.Even fire grows livelier in his hands as he sets about destroying the temple: "The flames sprang up, puffing out the screen of the mosquito net. I felt as if everything around me had suddenly become alive."[39]

That image of enlivening flame takes on another form at the end of the novel:

> Then I noticed the pack of cigarettes in my other pocket. I took one out and started smoking. I felt like a man who settles down for a smoke after finishing a job of work. I wanted to live.[40]

Many critics think this last paragraph speaks for Mizoguchi's perception of an inner world "which is ventilated with breeze."[41] Yet this ending serves an ironic purpose in Mishima's narrative strategy. It emerges from the perspective of the author, whose presence has made itself felt throughout, especially in Mizoguchi's pronouncements on beauty. The kind of life that awaits him is far removed from a life free from bondage.

Asked by the critic Hideo Kobayashi why he did not kill his hero in the end, Mishima had this to say:

> If a man wants to live, only a "prison" is open to him. This is what I wanted to suggest at the end. Jean Genet's plays concern those who are imprisoned. To live one's life for forty or fifty years means a life of imprisonment.[42]

Mizoguchi naively imagines himself entering a new existence free from the yoke of his "alter ego;" but of course his crime will lead to a life of imprisonment both physically and mentally.

Takabayashi's film follows Mishima's narrative fairly closely. It retains most of the major events in the following order: Mizoguchi's boyhood before his father's death (including his experience with Uiko), his life as an acolyte, his friendship with Tsurukawa and Kashiwagi, his journey to his birthplace; and his final act of arson.

Nevertheless, the film does restrict material from two areas of the novel. The first is Mizoguchi's relationship with the pavilion, which is simplified con-

Katsuhiko Yokomitsu (l), Mariko Kaga (c) and Saburo Shinoda (r) in *The Temple of the Golden Pavilion*(1976) directed by Yoichi Takabayashi. Courtesy of the Kawakita Memorital Film Institute.

Yuki Mizuhara (l), Katsuhiko Yokomitsu (c) and Saburo Shinoda (r) in *The Temple of the Golden Pavilion* (1976) directed by Yoichi Takabayashi. Courtesy of the Kawakita Memorital Film Institute.

siderably. Gone is Mishima's elaborate exploration of his hero's ambivalence, couched in language beyond the capacity of this unsophisticated youth. Takabayashi merely emphasizes the abstract, insubstantial quality of the golden pavilion as perceived by its troubled admirer. Mizoguchi's vision of the pavilion is suggested mostly through corresponding imagery, such as reflection shimmering uncertainly in the water.

Take Mizoguchi's first experience of the beauty of the pavilion. That visit of father and son to Kyoto is presented in a flashback sequence as Mizoguchi walks the beach at his birthplace. When he whispers Uiko's name, his face expressive of his effort to recollect the past, a dissolve into the sea translates into an image more obscure. A bubblelike substance appears against the brightly shining background. We know that it is the pavilion only through the father's voice-over narration: "The beauty of the pavilion is everlasting. Nothing is more beautiful than this." The next shot shows the surface of the pond reflecting the pavilion with its phoenix at the top.

The next time we see it, Mizoguchi is making advances to a girl at a picnic. Again the white, bubblelike substance prefigures the pavilion's reflection in the water. It introduces shots that show Mizoguchi's failure to consummate with the girl. His failure with the flower arranger is similarly introduced.

The second area of reduction goes even further. Takabayashi omits the novelist's study of Mizoguchi's ambivalent relationship with the Superior. He foregoes even cinematically promising episodes like the acolyte following the pious monk into the red-light district—and the young man's subsequent attempt to shame his Superior by reminding him of that amorous escapade. It is not surprising, then, to find the truly fatherly figure of Father Genkai left out of the film as well.

Omitting the surrogate father theme allows Takabayashi to put more emphasis on Mizoguchi's retreat into his inner world. In doing that, he makes the most of two interrelated plot lines derived from the novel: Mizoguchi's abortive obsession with Uiko, and his ambivalent relationship with the pavilion.

Those two lines are intensified by focusing on Mizoguchi's contemplation of death, a focus that itself increases our sense of the director's guiding hand throughout this film.

In fact, Takabayashi shows himself to be even more attentive to death than Mishima. Of course, his film was made after the novelist's spectacular suicide gave that issue more weight. The director even manages to insert a scene depicting a soldier's self-immolation toward the end of the war.

Takabayashi's own imagination supplied the trumpet image he uses as another controlling metaphor for Mizoguchi's inner experience.

All these departures from the novel inevitably raise the basic question of the director's mode of representation. How does Takabayashi transfer onto the screen the subjective world of a character whose experience is rendered in the confessional mode?

As might be expected, he makes good use of essentially cinematic properties such as flashbacks and variations in visual texture and acoustics. Mizoguchi's voice-over narration of past events is used repeatedly. It is our guide in a series of shifts back and forth through time and space; it is our introduction to the context in which important events take place. Sometimes an object this narrator sees evokes a memory; when this happens, the film can use the cinematic punctuation of the dissolve to transport us back accordingly. This serves especially well in scenes depicting the suffering that women cause Mizoguchi. One woman's face easily overlaps in his mind (and hence on screen) with the face of Uiko, whose look of scornful contempt was the *fons et origo* of this aspect of his lifelong alienation.

This facility of cinema allows Takabayashi to add flashback recollections of other characters as well. He does this with Kashiwagi and the Superior. These flashback sequences are easily identifiable, most being rendered in monochromatic tones.

One of the Superior's licentious fantasies is a notable exception. It involves the same prostitute Mizoguchi is forced to humiliate by treading on her stomach. The Superior's fantasy is presented twice. In both instances, her bright red overcoat stands out in sharp contrast to the otherwise subdued background, as if to highlight the holy man's suppressed licentiousness. The second time he entertains this vision, there is even less doubt about his interest in resisting temptation.

He rubs his legs as he imagines the woman's belly exposed, her flesh all the whiter for the red of her coat.

Several sequences at the outset of the film show how Takabayashi's approach to its subject is akin to Mishima's, yet significantly different. The novel's opening words, for example, are direct and matter of fact:

> Ever since my childhood, Father had often spoken to me about the Golden Temple.
>   My birthplace was a lonely cape that projects into the Sea of Japan northeast of Maizuru. . . .[43]

The film is similarly spare, relying on acoustic elements charged with hints suggesting the kind of life its protagonist will lead. As the credits roll, we hear the sound of the bamboo clappers that regulate a Zen priest's life. They merge with intermittent sounds from a temple gong. We also hear the sharp metallic sound of a bucket, suggestive of the acolyte's daily routine of cleaning and pumping water from a well. All these sounds are finally subsumed in the whistle and squeak of a moving train.

The camera's motion now gives us to understand that the natural landscape is being viewed from inside the train. A shift to the inside of the train shows us Mizoguchi. He is reading the *omikuji* (fortune), which tells him that ill fortune awaits him in the northwest. Simple as this device is, it does pique our curiosity. Where is this man going? What "ill fortune" can befall him there?

The train pulls into a station. Mizoguchi goes into the bathroom there and studies his face in a mirror. He tries to speak. A close-up of his face reveals his affliction: though he moves only his lips, we can see that he stutters. Takabayashi uses these few means to lead us into his hero's world of isolated alienation.

Mizoguchi is next seen taking a stroll in the countryside of Nishimaizuru, his birthplace. He sits on the riverbank. When he stands, the ripples of the river dissolve into waves of the sea.

Though his voice-over narration is taken from the novel, here it clarifies the *omikuji* message. The young man says it himself: "Ill Fortune. Omikuji No. 14. This sea is the source of all my ill luck and dark thoughts. It is also the source of my ugliness. . . ." Sinister electronic music echoes that sentiment.

A close-up of Mizoguchi's foot on the beach yields to a medium shot of him picking a half-buried trumpet out of the sand. He tries to sound a note, but the trumpet is broken. The camera closes in to show his face in close-up.

A series of cues offers us a first glimpse of this young man's subjective world. His eyes take on a dreamy look as he murmurs the name Uiko. Something like a pavilion comes into view, glittering in the sunlight. It is out of focus, like something imperfectly visible to the mind's eye. That vaguely perceived pavilion leads into the film's first flashback sequence—the boy's first visit to the golden pavilion, preceded by his father's death.

These early sequences condense a lot of material. Takabayashi's addition of the mute trumpet augments our sense of this young stammerer's sense of being at

odds with the world around. Later, this metaphor returns, taking on more meaning. The second time it appears, Mizoguchi and Tsurukawa are seen devouring
their wartime ration of rather unappetizing hard crackers. A student corps is marching by. The camera singles out a young soldier about Mizoguchi's age. He is
blowing a trumpet loudly. The camera also seems to draw our attention to the
beautiful vermilion color of this shining instrument. It is a far cry from the broken, drab instrument Mizoguchi found on the beach.

The trumpet calling these student soldiers to war is an obvious symbol of
youthful passion consummated in patriotism. The stammering acolyte watching
the parade go by has no share in this realm of passion.[44]

In a third instance, the military metaphor speaks uncompromisingly of defeat and death and is placed in the context of death. A sequence showing the
death of a truck driver yields abruptly to a single shot of an army officer in the act
of *seppuku*. He is shown in bright sunlight facing the camera. No proudly gleaming vermilion trumpet here; just masses of blood and spilling intestine. The sound
track plays the emperor's broadcast declaration that the war has ended.

This brief but unsparing evocation of an important moment in Showa history
is reminiscent of the soldier's self-immolation in *Yukoku* (The rite of love and
death, 1964). Mishima himself directed that film, so it is easy to see Takabayashi
here offering his own interpretation of the novelist's suicide.

Mishima went to his death clad in the military uniform of his ultranationalis-
tic Shield Society. The time separating these two film depictions does nothing to
diminish our sense of the fate these soldiers share, led as they are by patriotism to
kill themselves.

Takabayashi gives his depiction an elegiac note, closing the sequence with a
shot of the Imperial crest. Its sixteen-petaled chrysanthemum, given a forefront
magnitude, fills the screen.

That shot yields to one of the beach where Mizoguchi was seen at the beginning. This time he stands motionless, holding the ruined trumpet. The ocean is
rough. We are troubled by this geographic shift. At this point, we think of
Mizoguchi as based in Kyoto. Is this shift to the beach at his birthplace supposed
to be real or imaginary? No clear cinematic clue is given. We surmise that
Takabayashi is offering Mizoguchi's imaginary vision. Nonetheless, the point is
well taken. The director uses the mute trumpet to link the fates of the young
officer and the student whose stammer disqualifies him for military service. Both
are victims of the times they live in; but Mizoguchi, while still alive, suffers a
kind of living death, being cut off from the world around him.

But the director is not finished with the ruined trumpet. He uses it now for an
ironic twist. The next shot returns Mizoguchi from one visionary level of reality
to another. Standing on the beach, he closes his eyes and listens to a roaring
trumpet sound in the waves. The color fades into monochrome.

First we see two close-ups of a strapping soldier sounding a loud trumpet
call. A long shot shows him telling the student corps around him that he has
shown them how a trumpet should be blown. He hands the trumpet to Mizoguchi,

ordering him to blow it. Mizoguchi cannot answer, much less comply. Another student explains that he is a stutterer. Mizoguchi is, ironically and mutely, testifying to his own unfitness to serve his country. He will serve out the war as a weakling temple acolyte. The following shot, though brief, drives the point of the trumpet metaphor home. It shows the officer in charge telling his cadets that they should die shouting "Long live the Emperor!"

One more trumpet reference reinforces this aspect of Him versus Them. Mizoguchi is left alone on the beach where he finds the trumpet the officer has blown. Along with it are the officer's belongings. The scabbard of his sword glitters in the sun. Like Mishima's hero, he tries to mar the scabbard with a knife. This shot, however, is more effective than the corresponding passage in the novel. Takabayashi uses the trumpet to prepare us for Mizoguchi's destruction of the beauty of the golden pavilion. He tries to blow the officer's trumpet, but it is stubbornly mute. As he looks at it, its luster simply disappears, as if to finalize his doomed awareness of separation from the world around.

Takabayashi's use of flashback throughout shows how that device gives cinema one of its most versatile (not to mention characteristic) qualities. Here, the fluid interchange between present and past gives us much freer access to Mizoguchi's troubled inner world of recollection and imagination.

Takabayashi also uses flashback to recombine elements from the novel in a striking presentation of three key events in Mizoguchi's life. In the film, they come in this order: the boy's humiliating encounter with Uiko; her death, which he witnesses; and an especially painful recollection of his mother's adultery. Takabayashi brings these events into a closer relationship than Mishima does. As a result, we see Mizoguchi acquiring classic oedipal feelings toward women whom he comes to desire and yet fears as sources of rejection, humiliation, and betrayal.

The two events connected with Uiko are condensed into one long flashback sequence. It is introduced with great economy. Mizoguchi is seen watching a troupe of soldiers marching to a trumpet tune. The trumpet is that stand-out color, vermilion, whose significance we have seen, with a resonant trumpet filmed in vermilion. Its sound here seems especially resonant.

Mizoguchi catches sight of a woman yonder. He calls out "Uiko" as a close-up of her face fades into the flashback village setting, given a monochromatic texture. An initial long shot shows Uiko riding a bicycle. She is stopped by Mizoguchi. A series of medium and close-up shots presents their confrontation. Mizoguchi's speech impediment is painfully noticeable. This is the only place in the film that has this degree of emphasis. A close-up of the boy's mouth shows how foolish and disgusting the motions of its stammer would appear to the girl. He is in fact speechless, unable to utter a single intelligible word. A super blowup of Uiko's face shows the look of withering scorn she gives him. It is a look that well might scar an unsettled young imagination for life.

This scene establishes Uiko as a powerful presence in Mizoguchi's memory. She becomes a sort of icon for his ambivalent feelings about women, his love/ hate relationship with them.

Another recollection follows immediately. It, too, works with the motif of humiliation. Uiko watches Mizoguchi's mother slapping him. Again she wears a scornful smile. That scene ends with a close-up of his furious face and voice-over expression of his feelings: "Die, Uiko. You will die with my curse!"

Uiko does die. And while her death is presented as a recollected event in both novel and film, the film makes more of Mizoguchi's subjective awareness of this event. Takabayashi draws our attention to the psychological consequences of the young man's belief that his curse has done its work. The sequence is dominated by point-of-view shots that study these events through Mizoguchi's eyes.

First a series of long shots shows Uiko surrounded by military police and neighbors in front of what appears to be her house in the village. The camera singles out Mizoguchi among the spectators at the police interrogation. Then it closes in on Uiko, as if to share Mizoguchi's view of her as an object of love and hate. He tells us in voice-over exactly what he is thinking: "I have never seen a face so expressive of rejection. It is very beautiful and seems to reject everything in this world." That face defines his fixation as later he imagines ways to cope with feelings increasingly out of control.

This sequence continues the voyeur theme as Uiko goes to meet her lover. He is an army deserter. As she begins to climb the stairs leading to his hideout in the temple, Mizoguchi is seen among those who have shadowed her. A series of long shots shows her at the top of the stairs, silhouetted against the door with her lover. We see it all through Mizoguchi's eyes; the view has that voyeuristic flavor. The final two shots are close-ups of Mizoguchi leaning over Uiko. She has been shot by her lover. Her face, reflecting the moonlight, looms out of the darkness.

Suddenly we hear the temple gong. It signals a break in Mizoguchi's reverie. So does the textual change to a color screen. Again we see the woman whose face triggered Mizoguchi's memory of Uiko.

Takabayashi continues to make use of these conventional transitions from one level of reality to another. When Mizoguchi's mother visits him at the temple, a close-up of her face is presented from his line of sight. A voice-over speaks for the motif of woman's betrayal: "I have not forgiven her, this traitor!" The diegetic sound of bamboo clappers signals the presence of this memory. The color fades into a view of the entangled legs of the adulterous pair.

The rest of the scene is taken in close-up. Intercuts between mother and son reinforce a sense of immediacy of experience. Mizoguchi is, in fact, right next to his mother, who is inside a mosquito net. A medium shot of the adulterous couple shows us his mind's-eye memory of that childhood glimpse of her bare breast. This images echoes the previous tea-ceremony scene in which Mizoguchi saw the mistress of an army officer milk her breast into his cup.

Here in the temple now, the director follows the novel in calling to mind the father's protective hand covering the child Mizoguchi's eyes. Here, that remembered hand is shown in close-up. The father in voice-over warns his son not to look into hell. Takabayashi, however, ends this scene with a metamorphosis. The father's hand dissolves into a carved hand in close-up. It belongs to the statue of Yoshimitsu enshrined in the pavilion.

This flashback sequence contains two elements crucial to the director's rather different approach to Mizoguchi's later relationships with women. The statue's hand, not his father's, is the recurring image used in scenes depicting his sexual encounters. Together with the abstract image of the pavilion, it blocks his libido.

More significantly, Takabayashi treats Mizoguchi's sexual behavior as an attempt to return to a prenatal state, to his mother's womb. The breast image is the controlling one in this view of Mizoguchi's thwarted sexuality.

This happens, for example, in a scene depicting one of Mizoguchi's sexual fantasies. The temple is shown during a thunderstorm. Again, monochrome is used to signal a state of visionary introspection. Clearly, Mizoguchi is reliving his experience of Uiko's death. That scene repeats itself now. He sees Uiko lying dead at the bottom of the temple stairs. A series of close-ups details his fantasy now. He sucks her breast. Milk begins to drop from his mouth. A long shot repeats Uiko's lover's suicide. He shoots himself at the top of the stairs. The earlier flashback view of Uiko's dead face returns. Only now, reflections of lightning, not moonlight, play over it. Her face is different, too; it is no longer beautiful but somehow formless, impersonal, even hideous.

Takabayashi uses this image of oedipal contradiction to epitomize Mizoguchi's sexual failure with the girl at the picnic and the teacher of flower arranging. In each instance, Takabayashi deploys the camera's mobile gaze to study the woman's breast as a lascivious fantasist voyeur might do. For example, the camera switches from one close-up angle to another as it records Mizoguchi's act of kissing and sucking the teacher's breast. The breast image intercuts with three images associated with the pavilion: the rippling configuration of the pavilion reflected with water, the statue's hand, and the phoenix at the apex of the building. Eerie electronic music underscores his impotence.

Takabayashi's treatment of Mizoguchi's relationship with the pavilion is less successful. The temple is not richly endowed enough as a symbolic image. The film does not quite convince us that it becomes a central and powerful focus of delusion in Mizoguchi's imagination. He dispenses completely with an aspect that Mishima labored hard to establish: its ambivalent value as a focus of, and challenge to, Mizoguchi's shifting awareness of it as an artifice of eternity.

In the film, the pavilion does not get beyond its basic and obvious signification as the very antithesis of Mizoguchi's world: the essence of heavenly beauty and eternity. Like Mishima's hero, he himself says: "The pavilion is eternity, and will remain forever even after I perish." Its quality is almost transcendent, something he cannot visualize. That is why Takabayashi searches for ways to visualize its abstract, insubstantial form whenever it interferes with Mizoguchi's attempts to consummate with a woman. Like his priest father's hands and those of the statue of Yoshimitsu, the temple becomes a blinding force, as Mizoguchi associates sex with sacrilege. Initially, the protective father told him not to look into hell. Thus the father's and the religious icon's hands join forces to exert a greater power on Mizoguchi's adolescent life: warning against a cardinal sin for Buddhists.

As in the novel, Mizoguchi's final trip home and his act of arson are the two major narrative events. But they are significantly modified by the director's interest in the subjective realms of reality: Mizoguchi's dream and imagination. As might be expected, acoustic effects are carefully deployed as an essential part of a discursive structure.

One such instance occurs at the inn at his birthplace, where Mizoguchi takes shelter. The camera cuts from outside to inside, where Mizoguchi is asleep. A voice-over narration steals in to say: "You should kill your Superior rather than burning such a replica." The replica is a souvenir miniature of the pavilion Mizoguchi has been seen toying with. The next shot explains the origin of the alarming suggestion just made. It is a close-up of Uiko's face wearing the scornful expression that has had such a baleful effect on his life. The following two shots show Mizoguchi, in this dream, acting on Uiko's command. He picks up a long rope, which occupies the foreground of the screen. Nondiegetic organ music swells, giving an effect of momentum to his decisive elimination of the father figure. Mizoguchi sneaks behind the Superior and strangles him.

The rest of the dream sequence develops this projection of Mizoguchi's inner struggle. Uiko and Mizoguchi are shown seated in a first-floor corridor of the pavilion. He tells her that murdering the Superior has not helped him get free of a world that makes him feel so powerless. She urges him to burn the pavilion— with her in it. The familiar sound of bamboo clappers returns to signal a moment of decision. Yet Mizoguchi cannot light the match.

That failure is intensified by the motif of betrayal that Takabayashi uses so often to dramatize conflict. Here, Uiko scornfully calls him a betrayer. Mizoguchi throws the word back at her. The sound of a pistol shot recalls the earlier flashback showing Uiko shot by her lover, the army deserter who thought she had betrayed his whereabouts. This dream sequence ends with two shots of Mizoguchi back at the inn. The first shows him still asleep. In the second he sits motionless by a window. As the wind blows outside, the scene dissolves.

Before the climactic arson sequence, Takabayashi lingers one more time in the world of Mizoguchi's remembered youth. After a policeman escorts him back to the temple, his mother confronts and slaps him. A close-up of the mother's face, seen from his perspective, switches suddenly to the nocturnal scene that shows his imaginary vision. The motif of killing a betrayer once more returns, as if to suggest that such an act can explain Mizoguchi's final, decisive attempt at liberation. The opening two medium shots recapitulate the earlier scene of the mother's adultery and Mizoguchi's lifelong obsession with her betrayal. The next shot replays that traumatic event, this time with Mizoguchi as a witness closer to the act. His head is in the background behind the mother's body, which occupies the foreground. Weeping, he averts his eyes. Then a close-up captures the mother's face in ecstasy, the object of his gaze. That sight causes him to act. In the following medium shot, he picks up a butcher's knife and attacks, calling her a betrayer. That flashback ends abruptly with a cut to Mizoguchi and his mother standing at the entrance to the temple.

Thus the final climactic sequence resolves Mizoguchi's struggle as the director sees it. Takabayashi's somewhat different narrative focus explains the film's radical departure from the novel. Mishima's hero tries to escape from the bondage of the alter ego that he has projected onto the pavilion. In the film, he sets the temple on fire in order to destroy a larger world—a world that has excluded him:

> The powerless world which engulfs me. My youth and the life I saw have been powerless. In order to escape from the darkness of the fabricated reality which governs this world, I must burn the world devoid of light. In order to destroy the ineffective order deeply rooted within me, I must resort to this personal coup-d'état of mine. . . .

In this conclusion Takabayashi brings together the major perpetuating metaphor and narrative motif, counting heavily on the camera's expressive power.

Two shots serve as a prelude to the final conflagration. The first shows Mizoguchi in his room, examining a knife whose significance has yet to be made clear. The Superior's order to leave the temple is still ringing in his ears. The authoritative voice on the sound track confirms Mizoguchi's sense of rejection and ostracism. He takes up his father's mortuary tablet—his last link with the protective father whose hands have been symbolically transferred to the statue's hands. A second shot of the clock tells us it is one in the morning.

The camera cuts to the ground floor of the temple. Mizoguchi is there. He strikes a match and moves into the foreground, to the small replica of the pavilion. His face is reflected in the glass. A close-up shows the statue of Yoshimitsu looming out of the darkness nearby.

From this point on, Takabayashi makes the best use of the film's intrinsic properties: selectivity, visual transparency, and free movement in space. The omniscient camera begins by letting us "see" each stage of the arsonist's preparations as if we were on the scene. (Takabayashi used a full-size replica for this scene.)

Mizoguchi begins with a painstaking act of sacrilege. Two long shots in reverse setup establish his relationship with the statue in its setting. Then a series of close-ups allows us to scrutinize his behavior and emotions. The saint's face is made to loom large, as if to emphasize Yoshimitsu's role as a witness—the role given him in Mizoguchi's fantasy. He think himself obliged to shut the "eyes of the witness who has been dead for over six hundred years." A blowup of the statue's face shows what he means. He has used the knife to gouge out one eye. He continues to hack away at the wood. The sound of his knife imparts a sense of urgency to the scene, yet two close-ups of Mizoguchi's face show no great emotion, only tension.

When he finishes, darkness fills the screen. The eerie electronic music used for other tense scenes returns. We feel the tension of anticipation it builds. It accompanied the mounting anxiety felt by Mizoguchi in both his failed attempts at intercourse. Now it returns like a mournful memory burdened with anger and nervous resentment. Here the music anticipates Mizoguchi's attempt to break the spell of the other womanlike betrayer in his life: the golden pavilion.

Suddenly the screen fills with light. But not the light of fire. Not yet. Takabayashi is in no hurry. He wants to show us the arsonist studying things of beauty and significance he will destroy. First, the temple murals bathed in light. Then, Mizoguchi's face reflecting light in surrounding darkness. Then, singled out for emphasis, the mortuary tablet in front of the statue.

A series of medium shots shows Mizoguchi facing the statue. We hear his lengthy prayer asking this holy saint to destroy the nation. The compositional flow of these shots is momentarily broken by a close-up of the statue's hand with the "prayer" mudra. This final hand image calls to mind all the others—all the complex imagery of conflict and pain, of protection and suppression, at work in the life and mind of this young man going mad.

Mizoguchi's mental state is suggested with great economy here. After his prayer, he listens. Silence and darkness. Clearly, the saint has not responded to his plea. He says one word: "Useless!" Then he strikes a match. Still, this is a match for light, not fire. This small light surveys things belonging to him, things he will destroy. His father's mortuary tablet stands out. What better (and more ironic) index of his mad desire to break "free"?

But Takabayashi makes dramatic use of another image, as it were, for setting the temple ablaze. This one is not shown, but is in our minds, ready to leap out at the mention of a name: Uiko.

We have just seen Mizoguchi's face reflecting light in darkness, an apt reference back to Uiko's face lying dead in moonlight. She seemed beautiful to him then; later, remembered, she seemed hideous. In Mizoguchi's tormented imagination her face is the very image of rejection and defiance. Like the temple itself, her beauty turns away from this world in defiance of its claims. Mizoguchi saw that fanatic courage in Uiko's face when she was under arrest. That was the face that returned to haunt him in his vision, the face that dared him to have the courage to set fire to the temple.

So now we know in a flash why Mizoguchi cries out "Uiko!" and, without hesitation, acts. As he strikes another match, the camera pans down to show straw catching fire. In the next shot, Mizoguchi is off-center in the background while flames spread in the foreground. A diegetic sound similar to firecrackers augments the desired effect. His father's mortuary tablet bursts into flame.

Here, Takabayashi inserts his own interpretation of Mizoguchi's oedipal attachment. The breast image so familiar in the film is given its final and most resolutely Freudian expression. As the father's mortuary tablet burns, Mizoguchi in his mind reenacts his mother's adultery. But this time, her lover is himself. The sound track introduces lyrical piano music as if to celebrate this union.

Saburo Shinoda in *The Temple of the Golden Pavilion* (1976) directed by Yoichi Takabayashi. Courtesy of the Kawakita Memorial Film Institute.

While Mizoguchi's soliloquy continues to account for what he considers his single-handed coup d'état, the camera studies the destruction of the statue in an interesting way. The same shot size registers a likeness between it and Mizoguchi, whose immobile face speaks for his mad fixation on events at hand.

Cross-cuts between Mizoguchi and the statue are interspersed with cuts to the outside of the building, now aflame. Mizoguchi's face in close-up wears an ecstatic smile, in stark contrast to the statue's hollow face with eyes gouged out. A cut back outside pans up to show the phoenix atop the pavilion. The bird that haunted his failed sexual encounters now glimmers with reflections of fire. Mizoguchi is next seen climbing the stairs to the second floor. The camera surveys the ceiling with its painted scenery—soon to go up in flames.

The tense electronic music returns, to be joined by Mizoguchi's *sutra* chant, broken by coughing, as fire crackles all round. Echoing its first use during the opening credits, this music acquires a final ironic significance, joining the ancient chant sung by a youth whose life was dedicated to a religion he sees as having failed him. His break with it is complete as he watches the replica of the pavilion catch fire. He and his father marveled at it on their first visit. It stands for a smaller universe inside the larger one. Now both go up in flames. Mizoguchi escapes the building to hide in a nearby bamboo grove. The only sound now is fire and the approaching fire engine.

Subsequent shots of the burning pavilion are rather confusing in terms of point of view. Are we supposed to sense the camera's omnipresence? Or do these shots represent a projection of Mizoguchi's acute awareness of the last moments of this artifice of eternity destroyed by him?

Views of the phoenix suggest that Mizoguchi's awareness is depicted here. We see the phoenix still intact at the apex of the golden pavilion wrapped in consuming flames. We see it reflected in the water of the pond. At one point, the camera closes in, as if to vouch for Mizoguchi's consciousness of its integrity.

The camera then cuts to Mizoguchi in hiding. Like Mishima's madman, he is smoking a cigarette. Then, accompanied by the manic electronic music, the camera cuts one last time to the phoenix, still rising above the smoke and turmoil of the fire. We see it first at the bottom of the screen. Quickly the camera pans up, giving the bird the lift of flight, an impression helped by a camera angle focused on its outspread wings.

Again, how are we to account for this? Surely it is all of a piece with Mizoguchi's vision. The departing phoenix, the bird of rebirth, seems to suggest the indestructibility of the spirit of the pavilion, hence the futility of all he has done

The ending of the film confirms that tragic vision, using images familiar to us now. A close-up of Mizoguchi's face shows him calling out Uiko's name. A blaze of red fades into a vast stretch of beach. An organ plays softly. A lateral pan surveys the beach, then stops to single out something half buried in the sand. A close-up shows it to be the trumpet. No human being is in sight. The film closes with an organ swell and rough waves breaking on the desolate beach.

Clearly, Takabayashi's elegiac ending speaks for the likeness he finds in Mishima and his novel's hero. There is the same fixation on youth and trauma and loss; the same frustrated quest for a purity of a spirit that proves so elusive, so little appreciated by the world. Mishima's suicide being the self-made military affair that it was, Takabayashi's introduction of the trumpet image seems especially pointed and suitably apt. Mizoguchi cannot sound the trumpet. And what was Mishima's suicide but a trumpet call for patriotism out of tune with the times? And would the national moral revival he envisioned not require the training and discipline traditionally found in religious and military contexts?

Takabayashi's *The Temple of the Golden Pavilion* is an interesting case of a director meeting the challenge of a difficult novel partly by viewing it in boldly cinematic terms; partly, too, by understanding its relation to the novelist's personal tragedy.

Notes

1. Yoichi Takabayashi, "*Kinkakuji:* Seisaku-goki (The temple of the golden pavilion: afterthoughts), in *Ato Shiata* 122 (1976): 16–17. He expresses the same view in his book *Ano toi hi no eiga e no tabi* (Journey into cinema in the distant past) (Tokyo: Kinema Jumpo, 1988), pp. 217–18.

2. Among them is critic Mitsuo Nakamura. See Mitsuo Nakamura, "Kaisetsu" (Commentary), in Yukio Mishima, *Kinkakuji* (The temple of the golden pavilion) (Tokyo: Shinchosha, 1960), p. 265.
3. Yukio Mishima, *The Temple of the Golden Pavilion*, trans. Ivan Morris (Berkeley: Berkeley Corp., 1959), p. 23. Copyright © by Random House.
4. Ibid., p. 29.
5. Ibid., pp. 75–76.
6. Ibid., p. 21.
7. Ibid., p. 56.
8. Ibid., p. 39.
9. Ibid., p. 47.
10. Ibid., p. 38
11. Ibid., p. 83.
12. Ibid.
13. Ibid., p. 84.
14. Ibid., p. 91.
15. Ibid., pp. 90–91.
16. Ibid., p. 91.
17. Ibid., p. 95.
18. For a psychological approach to this novel, see Arthur G. Kimball, *Crisis in Identity and Contemporary Japanese Novels* (Tokyo: Tuttle, 1973), pp. 65–93.
19. Mishima, *The Temple of the Golden Pavilion*, pp. 173–74.
20. Ibid., p.173.
21. Ibid., pp. 180–81.
22. Ibid., p. 57
23. Ibid., p. 77.
24. Ibid., pp. 148–49.
25. Ibid., p. 25.
26. Ibid., p. 174.
27. Ibid., pp. 164, 281.
28. Ibid., p. 212.
30. Ibid., p. 70.
31. Ibid., p. 173.
32. Ibid., pp. 250–51.
33. Ibid., p. 271.
34. Ibid., p. 224.
35. Ibid., p. 259.
36. Ibid., pp. 259–60.
37. Ibid., p. 269.
38. Ibid., p. 243.
39. Ibid., p. 272.
40. Ibid., p. 285.
41. For example, see Kiyoshi Asai, Masaru Sato, et al, ed., *Kenkyu shiryo gendai nihon bungaku* (Reference: modern Japanese literature) (Tokyo: Meiji Shoin, 1980), 2: 184.
42. Quoted by Junji Saito, *Mishima Yukio to sono shuhen* (Yukio Mishima: his art, works and other writers) (Tokyo: Kyoiku Shuppan Center, 1980), p. 110. For a Nietzchean approach to Mizoguchi's arson, see Roy Starrs, *Sex, Violence, and Nihilism in the World of Yukio Mishima* (Honolulu: University of Hawaii Press, 1994), pp. 44–45.
43. Mishima, *The Temple of the Golden Pavilion*, p. 21.
44. Koichi Isoda, "Anyu to shite no senchu-sengo: Eiga *Kinkakuji* no kozo" (A symbol of the war and postwar periods: the structure of *The Temple of the Golden Pavilion*), in *Ato Shiata* 122 (1976): 12–13.

Conclusion

Scholars are used to catching up with yesterday's news. That is our job. We sort through the past, doing our best to set the record "straight," getting things "right," after the manner of hindsight.

Of course, we do not succeed. If we are definitive at all, it is only for a time. And that is exciting, too. The new facts and connections and interpretations are always out there, waiting.

All the more reason to welcome any sudden wealth of really new connections. I hope the reader will see how that is the subject of this book; how I have attempted to catch up with the fact that Japanese literature and cinema "discovered" each other right from the start. Among my hopes for this book is that it will encourage more scholars to enjoy the pursuit of book/film history past and present.

Scholars of two kinds are in fact tapping this wealth already. Those whose business is literature are turning their attention to film, and those whose business is film are looking to literature. Needless to say, not all these scholars are academics, some are critics of books or films or both. Some are just readers and viewers on to a good thing. I hope I have interested them all.

Best of all, from the "scholarly" point of view, is the fact that so much remains to be done in the way of exploring insights and relationships between Japanese cinema and literature. This is especially true for those whose work appears in English.

This book is comprehensive only in the sense of offering an overview of a vast and complex terrain still awaiting further exploration. That being so, let me end with a bow to just a few authors, works, and trends I have left out for want of space.

Anyone who ventures even just a little way into the rich legacy of Japanese literature on film will see how it offers material for whole lifetimes of work. Let me mention a few examples. A book could easily be written on the film industry's use of the so-called *katei shosetsu* genre of Meiji era novels about domestic life.

I have barely touched on the pure literature movement of the 1930s. There is far more to the fascinating tale it has to tell, especially in connection with a revival of its ideals in the 1950s. That decade is well known as a golden decade for Japanese cinema, so any amount of work could be done on *bungei-eiga* then.

Studies of the Japanese film industry in general could deal in statistics that might well cause writers in other cultures to despair. Leaving aside the scripting of works by authors long dead, we find totals like these for those alive in the era of cinema. Kan Kikuchi is far and away the most often adapted: ninety-nine times. Junichiro Tanizaki and Yasunari Kawabata trail with forty and thirty-two times, respectively. Yukio Mishima has been adapted twenty-four times. Clearly, there is ample scope for more studies such as Nobuo Chiba's *Eiga to Tanizaki* (Film and Tanizaki).

Contemporary film theory has grown wonderfully elaborate, dealing in critical issues arising out of distinctions as finely honed as those between narrative, narration, and narratology. It is hard not to imagine theorists trampling one another in a general rush to test their methods on Japanese literature becoming cinema.

My own commitment is to a more open-ended form of engagement. Coming from the Oriental tradition and working in America, I am always looking for ways to enlarge the Western audience for my native country's rich cinematic heritage. I do this by helping viewers "read" pictures arising out of a culture so different from theirs.

Now that I have shown, however sketchily, how Japanese literature has entered into creative partnerships with cinema, I will turn to another task in a similar vein. This will be the first book-length study of Hiroshi Shimizu, a forgotten veteran director whose best work drew on literature depicting the fate of children.

Selected Bibliography

Abe, Kobo. *The Face of Another*, trans. Dale Sanders. Tokyo and Rutland, Vt.: Tuttle, 1967.

Anderson, Joseph L., and Donald Richie. *The Japanese Film: Art and Industry*. Expanded ed. Princeton: Princeton University Press, 1982.

Bluestone, George. *Novel into Film*. Berkeley: University of California Press, 1957.

Bock, Audie. *Japanese Film Directors*. Tokyo: Kodansha International, 1976.

———. *Naruse: A Master of the Japanese Cinema*. Chicago: Art Institute of Chicago, 1984.

Branigan, Edward. *Narrative Comprehension and Film*. New York: Routledge, 1992.

Carroll, Noël. *Mystifying Movies: Fads and Fallacies in Contemporary Film Theory*. New York: Columbia University Press, 1988.

Carter, Steven D. "What's So Strange about *A Strange Tale*? Kafu's Narrative Persona in *Bokuto Kidan*." *Journal of the Association of the Teachers of Japanese* 22, no. 2 (1988): 151–68.

Chatman, Seymour. *Coming to Terms: The Rhetoric of Narrative in Fiction and Film*. Ithaca, N.Y., and London: Cornell University Press, 1990.

———. *Story and Discourse: Narrative Structure in Fiction and Film*. Ithaca, N.Y., and London: Cornell University Press, 1978.

Chiba, Nobuo. *Eiga to Tanizaki* (Film and Tanizaki). Tokyo: Seiabo, 1989.

Chiba, Nobuo, et al. *Sekai no eiga sakka: Nihon eigashi* (Film directors of the world: the history of Japanese cinema), vol. 31. Tokyo: Kinema Jumpo, 1976.

Desser, David. *Eros Plus Massacre: An Introduction to the Japanese New Wave Cinema*. Bloomington and Indianapolis: Indiana University Press, 1988.

Doi, Takeo. *The Psychological World of Natsume Soseki*, trans. William J. Tyler. Cambridge: Harvard University Press, 1976.

Dunlop, Lane. *The Paper Door and Other Stories: Shiga Naoya*. San Francisco: North Point Press, 1987.

Endo, Shusaku. *The Sea and Poison*, trans. Michael Gallagher. New York: New Directions, 1992.

Eto, Jun. "Natsume Sokeki: A Japanese Meiji Intellectual." *American Scholar* 34 (1965): 603–19.

Fukuda, Kiyoto, and Hiroshi Honda. *Muro Saise: Hito to sakuhin* (Saisei Muro: the man and his works). Tokyo: Shimizu Shoin, 1988.

Hayashi, Fumiko. *The Floating Clouds*, trans. Yoshiyuki Koitabashi and Martin C. Colcott. Tokyo: Hara Shobo, 1965.

Hijitaka, Tetsu. "*Hashi no nai kawa* no saieigaka ni attate" (On the second film adaptation of *A River with No Bridge*). In *Shinario: Hashi no nai kawa* (Scenario: a river with no bridge), ed. *Hashi no Nai Kawa* Production Committee, pp. 205–6. Tokyo: Kaiho Suppansha, 1992.

Iizima, Koichi. *Nagai Kafu-ron* (On Kafu Nagai). Tokyo: Chuo Koron, 1982.

Imamura, Taihei. *Eiga geijutsu no keishiki* (Form of cinematic art). In *Imamura Taihei ega hyoron* (A collection of Taihei Imamura's film criticism), vol. 1. Tokyo: Yumani Shobo, 1991.

————. *Eiga geijutsu no seikaku* (Characteristics of cinematic art). In *Imamura Taihei eiga hyoron* (A collection of Taihei Imamura's film criticism), vol. 2. Tokyo: Yumani Shobo, 1991.

————. *Eiga to bunka* (Film and culture). In *Imamura Taihei eiga hyoron* (A collection of Taihei Imamura's film criticism), vol. 3. Tokyo: Yumani Shobo, 1991.

————. *Nihon eiga no honshitsu* (The essence of Japanese cinema). In *Imamura Taihei eiga hyoron* (A collection of Taihei Imamura's film criticism), vol. 10. Tokyo: Yumani Shobo, 1991.

Isoda, Koichi. "Anyu to shite no senchu sengo: eiga *Kinkakuji* no kozo" (A symbol of the war and postwar periods: the structure of the film *The Temple of the Golden Pavilion*). *Aato Shiata* 122 (1976): 11–13.

Ito, Ken K. *Visions of Desire: Tanizaki's Fictional Worlds*. Stanford: Stanford University Press, 1991.

Ito, Sei, et al., eds. *Shiga Naoya-shu* (A collection of Shiga's works). *Nihon kindai bungaku taikei* (A collection of modern Japanese literary works), vol. 31, pp. 52–509, 518–37. Tokyo: Kadokawa Shoten, 1971.

Ito, Sei, Katusichiro Kamei, et al., eds. *Ito Sachio Nagatsuka Takashi-shu* (A collection of Sachio Ito and Takashi Nagatsuka's works). In *Nihon gendai bungaku zenshu* (A complete collection of modern Japanese literary works), vol. 26, pp. 228–49, 284–427. Tokyo: Kodansha, 1961.

Iwasaki, Akira, et al. *Eiga no rekishi* (History of cinema). In *Eigaron koza* (Lecture on film theory), vol. 2. Tokyo: Godo Shuppan, 1977

Jones, Sumie. "How Tanizaki Disarms the Intellectual Reader." *Literature East and West*, nos. 18, 2–4 (March 1974): 321–29.

Kawabata, Yasunari. *The Izu Dancer*, trans. Edward Seidensticker. Tokyo: Hara Shobo, 1964.

Keene, Donald. *Dawn to the West: Japanese Literature in the Modern Era*. 2 vols. New York: Holt, Rinehart and Winston, 1984.

Kermode, Frank. *The Sense of an Ending*. New York. Oxford University Press, 1967.

Klinger, Barbara. *Melodrama and Meaning: History, Culture, and the Films of Douglas Sirk*. Bloomington and Indianapolis: Indiana University Press, 1994.

Lippet, Noriko, and Kyoko Irie Selden, trans. *Japanese Women Writers: Twentieth Century Short Fiction*. Armonk, N.Y.: M.E. Sharpe, 1991.

McClellan, Edwin. *Two Japanese Novelists: Soseki and Toson*. Chicago: University of Chicago Press, 1969.

McDonald, Keiko. *Cinema East: A Critical Study of Major Japanese Films*. London, Toronto, and East Brunswick, N.J.: Fairleigh Dickinson University Press, 1983.

————. *Mizoguchi*. Boston: Twayne, 1984.

McDougal, Stuart Y. *Made into Movies: From Literature to Film*. New York: Holt, Rinehart and Winston, 1985.

Makino, Mamoru. *Nihon eiga shoki shiryo shusei: katsudo shashin zasshi* (A collection of reference materials on the early period of Japanese cinema: film magazines), vols. 2, 3, 6, and 7. Tokyo: Sanichi Shobo, 1990.

Matsumoto, Kenichi. "Meiji to wa nan de atta ka" (What did the Meiji period mean?). *Kokubungaku* (Japanese literature) 24, no. 6 (May 1979): 72–78.

Mishima, Yukio. *The Temple of the Golden Pavilion*, trans. Ivan Morris. New York: Berkley Publishing Corp., 1959.

Monaco, James. *How to Read a Film*. New York: Oxford University Press, 1977.

Morris, Ivan, ed. *Modern Short Stories*. Tokyo: Tuttle, 1964.

Muro, Saisei-shu, in *Gendai bungaku taikei* (A collection of modern Japanese literary works), vol. 30. Tokyo: Tsukuma Shobo, 1966.

Nakamura, Shinichiro, Tanaka Kunio, et al., eds. *Kishida Kunio zenshu* (A complete collection of Kunio Kishida's works), vol. 13. Tokyo: Iwanami Shoten, 1991.

Ooka, Shohei. *Fires on the Plain*, trans. Ivan Morris. New York: Knopf, 1957.

Moriyasu, Masafumi. *Nagai Kafu: Hikage no bungaku* (Kafu Nagai: literature on shadowy existence). Tokyo: Kokusho Kankokai, 1981.

Muramatsu, Takeshi. *Mishima Yukio no sekai* (The world of Yukio Mishima). Tokyo: Shinchosha, 1990.

Nagabe. Hideo. "*Sorekara:* Autosaida no Unmei" (*Sorekara:* the fate of an outsider). *Kinema Jumpo*, no. 812 (October 1985): 61-62.

Nakamura, Mituso. "*Kinkakuji* ni tsuite" (On *The Temple of the Golden Pavilion*). In *Bungei dokuhon: Mishima Yukio* (Book on literature: Yukio Mishima), pp. 28–35. Tokyo: Kawade Shobo, 1975.

Nanbu, Kyoichiro, and Tadao Sato. *Nihon eiga hyakusen* (One hundred selections of Japanese cinema). Tokyo: Tabata Shoten, 1973.

Natsume, Soseki. *And Then*, trans. Norma Moore Field. Baton Rouge and London: Lousiana State University Press, 1978.

Neupert, Richard. *The End: Narration and Closure in the Cinema.* Detroit: Wayne State University Press, 1995.

Nihon Eiga-Television Producers Association and Iwanami Hall, eds., *Eiga de miru nihon bungakushi* (The history of Japanese cinema seen through cinema). Tokyo: Iwanami Hall, 1979.

Ohashi, Yukichi, ed. *Hashi no nai kawa* (A river with no bridge). Tokyo: Toho Shuppan, 1992.

Okazaki, Yoshie. *Soseki to sokuten kyoshi* (Soseki and the idea of *sokuten kyoshi*). Tokyo: Hobutsukan, 1978.

Ozaki Koyo, Izumi Kyoka-shu (A collection of Koyo Ozaki and Kyoka Izumi's works). In *Nihon gendai bungaku taikei* (A complete collection of modern Japanese literary works), vol. 2, pp. 211–313. Tokyo: Chikuma Shobo, 1965.

Richie, Donald. *Japanese Cinema: Film Style and National Character.* Garden City, N.Y.: Anchor, 1971.

———, ed. *Rashomon.* New Brunswick, N.J.: Rutgers University Press, 1990.

Rimer, Thomas, ed. *Ogai: Youth and Other Stories.* Honolulu: University of Hawaii Press, 1994.

Rimer, Thomas, and Keiko McDonald. *Teaching Guide on Japanese Literature on Film.* New York: Japan Society, 1989.

Saito, Junji. *Mishima Yukio to sono shuhen* (Yukio Mishima: his art, works, and other writers). Tokyo: Kyoiku Shuppan Center, 1980.

Sato, Hideaki, ed. *Mishima Yukio: bi to erosu no ronri* (Yukio Mishima: logic of beauty and eros). In *Nihon bungaku kenkyu shiro shinshu* (A new collection of reference materials on Japanese literature). Tokyo: Yuseido, 1991.

Sato, Tadao. *Kinoshita Keisuke no eiga* (The films of Keisuke Kinoshita). Tokyo: Kaga Shoten, 1984.

———. *Mizoguchi Kenji no sekai* (The world of Kenji Mizoguchi). Tokyo: Chikuma Shobo, 1982.

———. *Nihon eiga no kyoshotachi* (Master filmmakers of Japan). Tokyo: Gakuyo Shobo, 1979.

———. *Nihon eigashi* (The history of Japanese cinema). 4 vols. Tokyo: Iwanami, 1995.

Sato, Tadao, et al. *Musei eiga no kansei* (Consummation of silent films). In *Koza Nihon eiga* (Lecture on Japanese cinema), vol. 2. Tokyo: Iwanami Shoten, 1986.

———. *Nihon eiga no tanjo* (The birth of Japanese cinema). In *Koza Nihon eiga* (Lecture on Japanese cinema), vol. 1. Tokyo: Iwanami Shoten, 1985

———. *Toki no jidai* (The period of sound pictures). In *Koza Nihon eiga* (Lecture on Japanese cinema), vol. 3. Tokyo: Iwanami Shoten, 1986.

Seidensticker, Edward. *Kafu and the Scribbler: The Life and Writing of Nagai* Kafu, *1879–1959.* Stanford: Stanford University Press, 1965.

Shiga, Naoya. *Dark Night Passing*, trans. William Sibley. Chicago: University of Chicago Press, 1979.

Shimazaki, Toson. *The Broken Commandment*, trans. Kenneth Strong. Tokyo: University of Tokyo Press, 1974.

Sitney, P. Adams. *The Avant-Garde Film: A Reader of Theory and Criticism*. New York: New York University Press, 1978.

Starrs, Roy. *Deadly Dialectics: Sex, Violence and Nihilism in the World of Yukio Mishima.* Honolulu: University of Hawaii Press, 1994.

Sugiyama, Heiichi. *Eizo gengo to eiga sakka* (Film image and filmmakers). Tokyo: Kugei Shuppan, 1988.

Sumii, Sue. *Hashi no nai kawa* (A river with no bridge). 7 vols. Tokyo: Shinchosha, 1981–94.

Takabayashi, Yoichi. *Ano toi hi no eiga e no tabi* (Journey into cinema in the distant past). Tokyo: Kinema Jumpo, 1988.

——. "*Kinkakuji:* Seisaku-goki" (On *The Temple of the Golden Pavilion:* afterthoughts). *Ato Shiata* 122 (1976): 16–17.

Takizawa, Haijime. "*Sansho Dayu*" (Sansho the Bailiff). *Eiga hyoron* 11 (May 1954): 69.

Tanaka, Junichiro. *Nihon eiga hattatsushi* (History of the development of Japanese cinema). 5 vols. Tokyo: Chuo Koron, 1976.

Tokutomi Roka, Kinoshita Naoe, Iwano Homei-shu (A collection of Roka Tokutomi, Naoe Kinoshita and Homei Iwano's works). In *Gendai bungaku taikei* (A complete collection of modern Japanese literary works), vol. 5. Tokyo: Chikuma Shobo, 1966.

Tsuruta, Kinya. *Kindai bungaku ni okeru mukogawa* (The other side in modern Japanese literature). Tokyo: Meiji Shoin, 1986.

Tsuzuki, Masaaki. *Nihon eiga no ogon jidai* (The golden age of Japanese cinema). Tokyo: Shogakkan, 1995.

Ueda, Makoto. *Modern Japanese Writers.* Stanford: Stanford University Press, 1976.

Umezawa, Toshihito, et al., eds. *Bungaku no naka no hisabetsuburaku-zo: senzen-hen* (Images of Buraku in literature: prewar period). Tokyo: Akashi Shoten, 1982.

——. *Bungaku no naka no hisabetsuburaku-zo: sengo-hen* (Images of Buraku in literature: postwar period). Tokyo: Akashi Shoten, 1982.

Watanabe, Kazutomi. *Kishida Kunio-ron* (On Kunio Kishida). Tokyo: Iwanami Shoten, 1982.

Yamada, Kazuo, ed. *Eiga no rekishi: cigaron koza* (The history of cinema: on film theory), vol. 2. Tokyo, 1977.

Yamamoto, Kikuo. *Nihon eiga ni okeru gaikoku eiga no eikyo: hikaku eigashi kenkyu* (The influence of foreign films on Japanese cinema: A comparative study of film history). Tokyo: Waseda Daigaku, 1983.

Yoshimura, Hideo. *Kinoshita Keisuke no Sekai* (The world of Keisuke Kinoshita). Tokyo: Cine Front, 1985.

Yu, Beongcheon. *Natsume Soseki.* New York: Twayne, 1969.

Index

About the Author

Keiko McDonald is a professor of Japanese literature and cinema at the University of Pittsburgh. Her books include *Cinema East: A Critical Study of Major Japanese Films* (1983), *Mizoguchi* (1984), and *Japanese Classical Theater in Films* (1994). She has also coedited *Nara Encounters* (1997) with Thomas Rimer and is currently working on a book on the filmmaker Hiroshi Shimizu.